OLD ENGLISH AND
ITS CLOSEST RELATIVES

OLD ENGLISH
AND
ITS CLOSEST RELATIVES

A Survey of the Earliest
Germanic Languages

Orrin W. Robinson

Stanford University Press • Stanford, California

Stanford University Press
Stanford, California
© 1992 by the Board of Trustees of the
Leland Stanford Junior University
Printed in the United States of America
Original printing 1992
Last figure below indicates year of this printing:

02   01   00   99   98   97

Library of Congress Cataloging-in-Publication Data

Robinson, Orrin W., 1947–
    Old English and its closest relatives : a survey of the earliest Germanic Languages /
Orrin W. Robinson.
        p.   cm.
    Includes bibliographical references and index.
    ISBN 0-8047-1454-1 (cl.) : ISBN 0-8047-2221-8 (pb.)
        1. English language—Old English, ca. 450–1100—History.
2. English language—Old English, ca. 450–1100—Grammar, Comparative—Germanic.
3. Germanic languages—Grammar, Comparative—English (Old)   4. Germanic
languages—History.   I. Title.
PE124.R63   1992
435—dc20   90-24700
                                                                 CIP
                                                                 rev.

⊗ This book is printed on acid-free paper.

PREFACE

A number of years ago, I began teaching a class at Stanford entitled "Introduction to the Germanic Languages." Since it was intended to fulfill one of the university's distribution requirements, I did my best to aim it at interested students who did not necessarily have a background either in German or in linguistics. And although I am a linguist rather than a historian or a student of literature, I felt that a survey that treated only the Germanic *languages* without giving some feeling for who spoke them and what, if anything, was written in them would be a poor and dry sort of class. I thus resolved to treat these areas also, and to find a text that would aid me in doing so.

I was more than a little surprised to find that no book existed that was even remotely like what I was looking for. Surveys of all the Germanic languages are rare enough. Surveys that include substantial historical and literary information are nonexistent. And even books on individual Germanic languages that presuppose little or no knowledge of German or linguistics are hard to find. The upshot is, I decided to write the book I was looking for.

This volume is the result. Perhaps not surprisingly, it is a book I expect practically everyone to find some fault in. Students of the individual languages and literatures I treat may feel that I have missed some important points in their own areas. Historians and historical anthropologists are likely to feel the same way. The nonspecialist reader, on the other hand, may well find parts of the book overly technical or overly compact.

Obviously, my hope is that everyone will also find in this book a great deal that is new, interesting, and useful. For the individual languages, literatures, and histories, though often studied as separate subjects, did not exist in isolation. They were and are part of a larger unity, and I hope that this book gives some picture of that unity.

At every point along the way, I have received tremendous help and support from other people. My friend and colleague Ted Andersson read each chapter, each section, as it came along, and the book owes a lot to his comments, even the picky stylistic ones. The students who used earlier drafts of the book in the above-mentioned class were also extremely helpful in making it more readable, and sometimes more correct; I am especially grateful to Keith Denning, Bob Pahre, and Henry Smith in this respect. My editor, Paul Psoinos, was a star. I doubt that anyone will ever read, really read, the book as thoroughly as he. Finally, my wife, Brigid, was immensely supportive during the long years it took this book actually to appear. I trust hers will not be long behind.

It hardly needs to be said that I would like to blame the above people for any defects remaining in the book. Unfortunately, I can't.

O.W.R.

CONTENTS

ABBREVIATIONS

The following abbreviations are used in the text of this book, and in the Glossaries accompanying the Readings for each chapter.

1, 2, 3	first, second, and third persons	nom.	nominative
acc.	accusative	OE	Old English
adj.	adjective	OF	Old Frisian
adv.	adverb	OHG	Old High German
art.	article	OLF	Old Low Franconian
C	any consonant	ON	Old Norse
comp.	comparative	OS	Old Saxon
conj.	conjunction	part.	participle
dat.	dative	pass.	passive
dem.	demonstrative	pers.	personal
E.	English	PGmc.	Proto-Germanic
fem.	feminine	pl.	plural
gen.	genitive	poss.	possessive
Gmc.	Germanic	pres.	present
Goth.	Gothic	pret.	preterite
IE	Indo-European	pro.	pronoun
ind.	indicative	refl.	reflexive
inf.	infinitive	rel.	relative
imp.	imperative	sg.	singular
inst.	instrumental	subj.	subjunctive
interr.	interrogative	uninfl.	uninflected
masc.	masculine	V	any vowel
ModE	Modern English	v.	verb
neut.	neuter	voc.	vocative

OLD ENGLISH AND
ITS CLOSEST RELATIVES

1

THE GERMANIC LANGUAGE FAMILY

English and German

On the face of it, the educated speaker of English would have little reason to think of English and German as variant forms of the same language. There are enormous differences between the two systems of communication, involving pronunciation, vocabulary, and grammar, and monolingual speakers of the two systems cannot understand each other at all. This fact, and other considerations of national identity, separate history, and the like, are indeed what lead us to characterize the two as separate languages.

It is also true, however, that there are startling points of similarity between the two languages on all levels. Thus in the lexicon, or vocabulary, one can see some very close matches between words in the two languages. The list below will illustrate the point:

Mann	man	grün	green
Maus	mouse	haben	have
singen	sing	Vater	father
Gast	guest		

As the following list illustrates, there are also many words that correspond a little less obviously, either because the sounds in the two languages are farther apart, or because the words don't mean exactly the same thing in both languages:

Pfeffer	pepper	Hund 'dog'	hound
Herz	heart	Knecht 'servant'	knight
liegen	lie	Weib 'woman'	wife
lachen	laugh	Zeit 'time'	tide (notice "even*tide*")

We may also note numerous grammatical correspondences between German and English. For example, we can see a definite relationship between the ways that English and German distinguish the comparative and superlative forms of adjectives:

dick	thick
dicker	thicker
(am) dickst(en)	thickest

It is interesting to note that not only the regular pattern, but also the irregularities, correspond surprisingly well:

gut	good
besser	better
(am) best(en)	best

The verb system, too, shows many examples of grammatical correspondence. In the following examples we see, first, that German and English have highly similar ways of forming the past tense of regular verbs:

lachen–lachte	laugh–laughed
hassen–hasste	hate–hated
lieben–liebte	love–loved

Again, they also have similar deviant items:

denken–dachte	think–thought
bringen–brachte	bring–brought

In the examples below we note that both English and German have a peculiar class of verbs that do not take the usual ending to show the past tense, but instead show a change in vowels:

singen–sang–gesungen	sing–sang–sung
geben–gab–gegeben	give–gave–given
fallen–fiel–gefallen	fall–fell–fallen

I could cite many other examples of grammatical and lexical correspondences between English and German, but perhaps these lists will suffice to show that even Modern English and German have many points in common. If we go back in history to the earliest texts available in the two languages, the similarities are even more pronounced, the differences far smaller. The question then arises: How do we account for these similarities? What possible explanations could we devise that would make sense of this widespread correspondence between the two languages? There are actually only two reasonable hypotheses.

The first hypothesis is that the two languages have, at some time in the past, borrowed very heavily from one another (or that both of them have borrowed heavily from some third language). We certainly know that this is a possible type of language interaction. In fact, we can point to other instances of it in the history of English.

One prime example of extensive borrowing is found in the past and present relationship between English and French. Ever since the Norman invasion of England in 1066, the English language has over the centuries borrowed massive numbers of words from French. A small sample is given here:

crown	country	people	baron	color	war
peace	officer	judge	court	crime	marry
religion	altar	virtue	beef	pork	joy

Now in this particular case, we know that the words in question were borrowed from French into English, because we have numerous records from English that predate the borrowings, and we can actually follow the borrowing process over several centuries in the documents.

There are several characteristics of the relationship between English and French that set it apart from the relationship between English and German. Most important, perhaps, is the fact that although English borrowed quite freely from the *vocabulary* of French, it did not in general borrow its grammatical patterns. Thus French has had little impact on the way English speakers form plurals, past tenses, and so forth, nor has French left any lasting impression on English sentence formation, word order, or the like. Note, for example, that the French pattern of adjective after noun, found in the borrowings "court-martial" and "governor general," is still felt as strange in English. When we pluralize, we tend to act as if these borrowings were single words, as in "court-martials," "governor generals," rather than phrases, as they are in French. If we followed the French pattern, we would typically say "courts-martial" and "governors general," which, though technically correct according to the grammar books, sound un-English.

It seems, in fact, that the influence of French on English can be characterized as relatively superficial, and far removed from the central core of the language.

The correspondences between English and German, by contrast, are fundamental, encompassing not only vocabulary but all features of language. Anyone attempting to claim that the similarities between the two languages are all due to borrowing must be prepared to explain how the process could have gone so far and so deep.

Even in the vocabulary alone, one can see differences between the correspondences of English and French on the one hand, and English and German on the other. Whereas the corresponding words in English and German are usually everyday words, of the sort that ordinary people use all the time, the words English has borrowed from French show a peculiar pattern: almost all of them deal with government, affairs of state, criminal justice, official functions, religion, fashion, high cuisine, and other aspects of the upper-class culture that the Norman conquest most affected. They do not, in general, deal with the pedestrian concerns of the common people.

If we reject borrowing as the explanation of the relationship between English and German, there is only one hypothesis left to us. Given that language changes in an inevitable, ongoing process, which we can observe occurring around us all the time, we may speculate that, at some time in the distant past, the ancestors of English and German were merely dialects of *the same language*, and that their present differences result from changes that affected one group of speakers without affecting the other. Or, to put it another way, English and German represent two divergent developments of some originally unified language.

The changes that could have brought about such a divergence are of several well-attested kinds. One obvious factor, already mentioned, is *borrowing*. One group of speakers can diverge in language from another group of speakers when the one, but not the other, borrows a new word from some outside source.

Another, more decisive type of change, known as *sound change*, involves a modification in the articulation of the distinctive sounds of the language. There is an interesting example from contemporary American English, whose speakers frequently confuse such words as "bitter" and "latter" with words like "bidder" and "ladder," all of them (and in addition words like "hitter," "fatter," "fitting," "later") containing a *d*-like medial consonant. Now there is evidence that all the words written with a *t* were at one time pronounced with a genuine *t* sound. First, of course, we still write them with the letter *t*. Second, many of the words involved have a pronounced *t* sound when one leaves off the endings: thus "hi[t]," "fa[t]," "fi[t]," "la[t]e" (where square brackets indicate a phonetic transcription). Third, we can find many English dialects where the change hasn't taken place, especially in Britain. Finally, many of us actually still pronounce the [t] in careful speech ("I said *bitter*, not *bidder*!").

Nevertheless, the normal pronunciation of these words in American English is with a sound something like a [d]. This is one of the features that sets off American from British English, and, as such, illustrates how a sound change can cause a divergence between two varieties of a single language.

Changes may also occur on the other levels of language. Comparing the oldest written stages of English with the modern language, for example, we note that whereas in Old English the ending -s was just one of several productive patterns for forming the plurals of nouns, in Modern English it is the *only* productive one, having pushed out all its rivals. Note below the diverse plural types available for different words in Old English (the letter þ is equivalent to modern *th*):

wulf	'wolf'	wulfas	'wolves'
giest	'guest'	gieste	'guests'
sunu	'son'	suna	'sons'
scip	'ship'	scipu	'ships'
tunge	'tongue'	tungan	'tongues'
brōþur	'brother'	brōþur	'brothers'

All of them now of course take the regular -s plural.

Changes may also take place in word order. In Old English, the type of relative clause exemplified below was very common:

> þā men þe hē beaftan him lǣfde ǣr
> 'the men whom he behind him left earlier'

Note that in the older example the verb *lǣfde* 'left' in the relative clause comes near the end of its clause (as a verb would in Modern German). Such a sentence is no longer acceptable English. The required position of the verb has shifted to immediately after the subject pronoun "he" so that the phrase now would read: "the men whom he left behind him earlier."

Finally, changes in meaning may also take place. A good example of this is the history of the word "bead" in English. It used to mean 'prayer', but shifted to its present meaning because of the practice of keeping track of one's prayers on what we now call the "beads of a rosary."

Our hypothesis, then, is that German and English can be traced back to a common ancestor language. Or, to say the same thing in another way, German and English are *genetically related*. It is the task of that field of linguistics known as *comparative linguistics* or *comparative philology* to demonstrate the existence of a genetic relationship between languages and to explore its details. In what follows I will discuss some of the main procedures and assumptions of this field, and show how it may help us to determine what we can call the English family tree.

The Comparative Method

In general, two languages are said to be genetically related if they are divergent continuations of the same earlier language. The known or hypothesized language that serves as a common ancestor is called a *proto-language*, or sometimes, to use kinship terminology, a *parent language*, in which case the divergent continuations are frequently referred to as *daughter languages*. A parent language and its daughters constitute a *language family*.

Sometimes the proto-language is an actually attested language, with surviving texts and a demonstrable temporal and spatial existence. A case in point is the family of Romance languages, including French, Spanish, Portuguese, Italian, Rumanian, and others, whose common ancestor appears to be a variant of Latin. Linguists can be pretty confident about the origins and relationships of these languages. In most cases, however, we aren't so lucky. Both German and English can be traced back only so far, and then we run out of texts. In such situations, the job of the linguist is to come up with a *reconstruction* of the parent language, that is, a hypothesis about the specific form of the proto-language that could most reasonably have changed into the documented daughter languages. How successful we are in reconstructing such a hypothetical language defines how likely it is that the real languages we are working with are in fact related.

Now how does one go about doing this type of reconstruction? In the classical procedure, and to a great extent still, the first prerequisite is that one have languages with a large number of words similar in both sound and meaning, as we do in English and German. The words in question are referred to as *cognates*, and the first thing to do is to set up lists of cognate words (or cognate grammatical elements, like verb endings). We have already done something like this above for English and German, and I do it again below. But in this case I have gone back as far as I can in the histories of both languages, since the farther back one goes the more similar they are. I have also added Old Norse and Gothic, two other related languages that are represented in old texts.

OE	OHG	ON	Goth.	ModE
fæder	fater	faðir	fadar	father
fōt	fuoz	fótr	fôtus	foot
þrīe	drî	þrír	þreis	three
þū	dû	þú	þu	thou
cūðe	konda	kunna	kunþa	could
ōðer	andar	annarr	anþar	other

If one looks carefully, one sees that there is something interesting in this list of cognates, beyond the fact that it *is* a list of cognates: the similarities and differences between the various words in the various languages show certain regularities.

Let us start by taking the words for 'father' and 'foot', and look at the first sounds of each word in all of the languages. We can see that in each case the sound is *f*, and we can draw up a chart of correspondences involving just this sound, as shown below:

OE	OHG	ON	Goth.
f-	f-	f-	f-

If we looked at a larger number of words in these four languages, we would find that this correspondence continues to hold. We are now in a position to determine the sound in the proto-language that could most easily have resulted in the sounds actually found, in this case absurdly obvious: *f-. We have no need to assume any change in any of the languages to get from the proto-language to the individual languages. Notice, however, the asterisk before the *f* in the reconstruction. This is meant to indicate that what follows is in fact a reconstruction, and not an actually documented sound. This is standard procedure when carrying out a comparative analysis, even in cases as clear as this one. The asterisk is frequently left off, however, in more general handbooks dealing with developments in the individual languages. I follow the latter practice in this book, unless I want to emphasize the reconstructed character of the sound in question.

A slightly more complex situation is presented by the words for 'three' and 'thou' in the chart. Instead of unanimity, we find here that Old High German has *d* in both words, where the other languages have þ, representing the sound found in modern English "ba**th**":

OE	OHG	ON	Goth.
þ-	d-	þ-	þ-

Again the correspondence holds true for many words besides the two given.

Other things being equal, in a case like this the linguist is inclined to let the majority rule. It is simpler to assume that one language made a change from þ to *d* than that three made a change from *d* to þ. We reconstruct for Proto-Germanic, in both words, the sound *þ.

There is, however, a more complicated case involving þ on our list, namely in the words for 'could' and 'other'. Notice that where we find the sequence *u* + *n* + þ or *a* + *n* + þ in Gothic, we find *ond* and *and* in Old High German, *ūð* and *ōð* in Old English (a long *u* or *o* followed by the sound [ð] as in English "bathe"). We further see *unn* and *ann* in Old Norse (a short vowel followed by a double *n*). If we use the symbol V to mean a short vowel, and V̂ to mean a long one, while abstracting from differences in vowel quality, we can write this correspondence as follows:

OE	OHG	ON	Goth.
-V̂ð	-Vnd	-Vnn	-Vnþ

What do we do in a case like this, where again the same correspondence can be found in a number of words? First we must ask which, if any, of the actually attested forms would best serve as a *proto-form*; that is, from which form can the others be most easily derived? In this particular instance, notice that if we posited either the Old English or the Old Norse forms as original, we would have to assume a great number of strange changes in all the other dialects. Thus if Old English V̂ð were chosen as basic, we would have to assume a shortening of the vowel in all the other dialects; the insertion of an *n* before *ð* in Gothic and Old High German, along with a change of *ð* to *d* in Old High German and to *þ* in Gothic; and the total replacement of *ð* by double *n* in Old Norse. Most of these changes are phonetically inexplicable, and in fact have no parallels in other languages of the world. Similarly, if we chose the Old Norse form as primary, a different set of equally unmotivated changes would have to be assumed for the other dialects.

On the other hand, if we chose, let us say, the Gothic form as basic, we could easily get to the Old English and Old Norse forms. In Old English we would then have, in addition to a shift of **þ* to *ð*, a common type of change involving the loss of a nasal after a vowel and before a consonant, with a lengthening of the vowel to compensate for the loss of the nasal. We can see changes like this in progress even in Modern English, where "cannot" has become "can't," and "can't," in many dialects, has lost the nasal consonant *n* with accompanying nasalization and lengthening of the vowel (phonetically [kãt], where [~] indicates a nasalized vowel). Furthermore, we may recognize this Old English change as part of a much larger phenomenon in which not just *n*, but all nasal consonants were lost before certain other consonants, with accompanying vowel lengthening. Compare OE *gōs* 'goose' with OHG *gans*, OE *ūs* 'us' with OHG *uns*, OE *fīf* 'five' with OHG *fimf*.

The Old Norse form can also be easily derived from the Gothic one, in this case by the *assimilation* of *þ* to the preceding consonant, that is, by a process in which the second sound becomes identical to the first. This, too, is a common type of sound change, and can be found in many languages of the world.

In the last two paragraphs I rather blithely assumed the Gothic form Vnþ to be basic. Could I not just as easily have taken the Old High German form Vnd, or for that matter a composite form *Vnð, with sounds from more than one of the daughter languages? Given the limited data above, the answer is a qualified yes. Especially in the case of the composite form *Vnð, most of the changes required to get to the daughter languages are reasonably natural. In the case of *Vnd, the required shift of *d to ð or þ is more problematic.

It should be remembered, however, that we already have a rule, based on the words for 'three' and 'thou', that changes *þ to d in Old High German. It is good methodology to use that rule here as well, as long as we can reasonably explain the difference between the proposed *þ that remains *þ in Old Norse and Old English and the *þ that changes to n or ð. And in fact we can. Those examples of *þ that remain are all found at the beginnings of words, whereas the ones that change are not.

For the words for 'could' and 'other', then, we reconstruct the proto-form *Vnþ, which is found unchanged in Gothic. Old Norse assimilates the second consonant to the first, Old English drops the nasal, lengthens the vowel, and changes *þ to ð, and Old High German simply changes *þ to d.

One important aspect of the comparative method, touched on immediately above, perhaps needs to be made more explicit. This is the assumption, borne out in actual analysis, that sound change is *regular*, that is, that the same sound in the same general environment will develop in the same way. We would not expect to find that in some language, for example, a p in one word has gone to f, in another to m, and in yet another to b, in a totally arbitrary fashion. If we find apparently arbitrary changes, in which the assumption of regularity of sound change appears to be false, we must consider whether we have missed something, whether there is something different about the environments of the p's in question that accounts for the different changes. In other words, there is some subregularity we have missed. It is clear that, in the example given above, a simple statement to the effect that Proto-Germanic *þ has sometimes remained þ in Old Norse, but has gone to n at other times, is not enough. The change or lack of change to n is regular, in the sense that if we define the environment of the change specifically enough (for example by saying that þ goes to n after another n), all indeterminacy is eliminated.

This methodological procedure has resulted in some very gratifying discoveries of subregularities that might otherwise have been missed. Perhaps the most famous example of this is the sound change known as

Verner's Law in Germanic, which was itself set up to explain certain apparent exceptions to a "law" formulated earlier, Grimm's Law.

Grimm's Law was initially formulated to explain certain correspondences between the Germanic family as a group and the numerous other language families thought to be related to it. These include the Slavic, Greek, Indic, Italic, and Celtic families, among others. The proposed parent language is known as Proto-Indo-European, or Indo-European for short.

What Grimm noticed was that the sounds we reconstruct as Proto-Germanic *f, *þ, and *x (which has the sound of the *ch* in German *ach*) corresponded quite regularly to *p*, *t*, and *k* in other Indo-European languages, as the words below show (Latin here represents the rest of Indo-European, and Gothic represents Proto-Germanic; Latin *c* represents the sound *k*, and Gothic *h* reflects Proto-Germanic *x):

Latin	Gothic	
portare	faran	'go'
tres	þreis	'three'
centum	hund	'hundred'

The part of Grimm's Law that accounted for these regularities assumed that in these words (and in many others, of course) the Indo-European parent language had the sounds *p, *t, and *k, as in the Latin cognates, and that they changed in Germanic to *f*, *þ*, and *x*, informally represented as follows:

$$\text{IE } {}^*p \rightarrow {}^*f$$
$$ {}^*t \rightarrow {}^*þ$$
$$ {}^*k \rightarrow {}^*x$$

Unfortunately, this "law" had many exceptions, as the following cognates show (Latin *x* represents the sequence *ks*):

Latin	Goth.	
septem	sibun	'seven'
centum	hund	'hundred'
dux	(OE heretoga)	'duke'

For years scholars didn't know what to do with these exceptions, until in 1875 the Danish linguist Karl Verner found the explanation. There was indeed a difference between the phonetic environments of those *p*'s that had gone to *b* (originally actually ƀ, a [v] formed with the upper lip rather than the upper teeth) and those that had gone to *f*. The crucial factor was not just the surrounding sounds, but what *accents* the words in question had had in Indo-European. On the basis of evidence from such other

Indo-European languages as Sanskrit and Greek, Verner was able to show that all the words in which IE *p had changed in Germanic to *f* either had that *p as the first sound in the word, or had the accent on the syllable immediately preceding the *p, as in the examples below:

IE *pətér- → Goth. fadar   'father'
  *népôt- → ON nefi   'nephew'

Those p's that changed in Germanic to ƀ, on the other hand, were those that had not stood in initial position and that had not had the accent on the immediately preceding syllable, as in the words below:

IE *sep(t)m̄ → Goth. sibun   'seven'
  *upéri   → OHG ubar   'over'

Subsequently, the accent shifted to the initial syllable in almost every word in Germanic, obscuring the original conditions for Verner's Law.

In this example, then, we can see the advantages of the assumption that sound change is regular. Something that initially seemed arbitrary proved, upon closer examination, to be highly predictable.

I could give more examples of the comparative method to show its amazing accuracy and dependability, but the discussion above will suffice. I will merely add that one can sometimes find independent confirmation of the results that comparative linguists have arrived at. For example, proto-sounds reconstructed by the comparative method have sometimes been confirmed by the discovery of another language related to those used in the reconstruction. The decipherment of the Hittite language early in this century enormously strengthened the likelihood of some reconstructions made on the basis of other Indo-European languages.

Use of the comparative method has enabled us not only to define precisely what we mean when we say that languages are related, but also to talk about *degrees* of relationship. Although Russian, French, German, and English can all be traced back to a common ancestor language, we would not want to leave it at that. German and English are clearly more related to each other than to the other two, and we would like to be able to express that fact. One popular device in historical linguistics for expressing degrees of relationship is the *family tree*. In Figure 1 below I give a somewhat abbreviated version of the Germanic tree. Though I have tried there to be fair to at least one suggested view of the Germanic branch of Indo-European, it should be noted that I am not trying to make any statement about the interrelationships among the various Indo-European language families. The basis for each postulated branching, from the highest to the lowest member, is a set of changes common to all the lan-

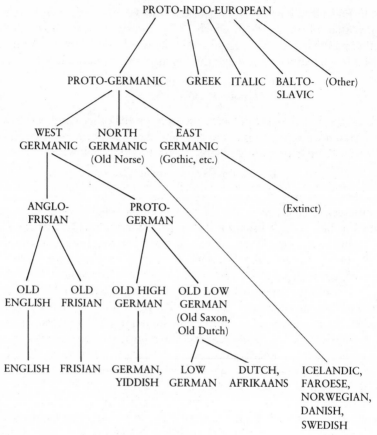

Fig. 1.   The traditional English family tree.

guages on that particular branch. For example, two of the characteristics
that set the Germanic family off from all other Indo-European family
branches are the above-mentioned accent shift to initial syllables and the
changes known as Grimm's and Verner's Laws.

Objections have frequently been raised both to the tree method of
representing relationships and to this particular Germanic tree. Some
scholars have argued that more branches should be put in (for example,
by grouping North and East Germanic together against West Germanic).
Other scholars have argued for fewer branchings, or for different branchings. In this regard, the West Germanic branch is especially embarrassing,

since in some cases the languages show similarities not to each other, as this branching would suggest, but to languages in entirely different groups. For example, certain similarities between Old High German and Gothic set them apart from all the other languages, and there are some features that the Anglo-Frisian languages, but not German, share with North Germanic.

What these sometimes fierce arguments tend to overlook is the fact that a branching on a tree diagram need not correspond to a physical separation between groups of speakers. Even when people speak different dialects, there is likely to be some communication between them, so that people of different dialect regions may still share some changes that cross over the dialect boundaries. This geographical fact is simply not captured by the abstraction of a tree diagram.

For all its faults, however, the tree diagram has been a very useful device for presenting many of the results arrived at by the comparative method. And though modern historical linguists recognize certain shortcomings in the method, it still plays an important role in the investigation of language relationship and language change.

Linguistics, Archeology, and History

Once we have established genetic relationships between languages, and once we have set up proto-languages from which the languages actually found can be derived, all sorts of other questions come crowding in. Can we locate the speakers of the proto-language in space and time? Do we know anything about their civilization? How did speakers of the daughter languages get to where they are now? Can we establish connections between the linguistic facts and the facts of archeology?

Scholars have tried long and hard to answer these and similar questions, especially for Indo-European and Germanic. In most cases the answers are sketchy or controversial, but I will try to give some idea of what possibilities exist. Before going on, however, I would like to throw out one warning: language groups should never be confused with ethnic groups. Though it is true that one way a language can spread is by the spread and increase of the people that speak it, it is perhaps just as common for a language to spread at the expense of another language; that is, people who at one point spoke language X as a group start speaking language Y. A perfect example of the latter type of spread is the present extent of the Romance languages. Most of the people who now speak these

Latin-derived languages are the descendants not of the original Latin speakers, but rather of other early ethnic groups that, for one reason or another, adopted Latin (or one of its derivatives) as their mother tongue. Most of France, for example, originally spoke Celtic dialects.

This warning given, we can go on to say something about whoever it was that originally spoke Indo-European or Germanic, where they lived, and what their culture was like.

Most of the evidence for Indo-European culture is in itself linguistic. For, after all, if one may use the comparative method to reconstruct the forms of words in the proto-language, what could be more natural than to attempt to reconstruct their meanings also? The persuasiveness of such attempts depends, of course, on the number and distribution of the languages used in the reconstruction, and on how much agreement the various cognates show in their meanings. Assuming a satisfactory grounding in the data, we may argue from the words we reconstruct for Indo-European, and the meanings associated with them, that the Indo-Europeans knew certain objects and not others, certain types of weather, a certain type of family system, and so forth.

The Indo-Europeans appear to have been organized into rather small groups or clans, for there is no widespread cognate with the reconstructed meaning 'king' (though a word for 'clan chieftain' is found). A study of reconstructed relationship terms seems to indicate also that women joined the families of the men, since, among other things, we have a common term meaning 'daughter-in-law' but none meaning 'son-in-law'.

The existence of many terms for domesticated and wild animals, and few for vegetables or specific grains, indicates a heavy reliance on hunting and animal husbandry for food. Metals were virtually unknown; at most, some Indo-European languages share a single term meaning variously 'metal, copper, bronze'. Of course, in this area as in those touched upon earlier, the absence of a word in the reconstructed proto-language is far less compelling evidence than the presence of a word: a lack of evidence is not itself sure evidence.

As for weather, because the Indo-European language is reconstructed with words for 'snow' and 'winter', we may conclude that its speakers did not live too far south. This conclusion has been combined with other arguments to try to place the Indo-Europeans geographically. Thus a term some have reconstructed with the meaning 'inland sea' has been used as evidence for placing the Indo-Europeans around the Black Sea or the Baltic. If, however, the term meant 'pond', as others maintain, it proves nothing of the sort.

Another argument for the location of speakers of Proto-Indo-European involves a supposed cognate, found in five of the Indo-European subfamilies, that has been reconstructed as meaning 'beech tree'. If this reconstruction is correct, then it is significant for the location of the Indo-European homeland, since in prehistoric times the beech was apparently not indigenous to any areas east of a line drawn from Kaliningrad (formerly Königsberg) in the western Soviet Union to the Crimea, north of the Black Sea.

One apparent difficulty with this theory is the fact that, even though the words in the five language families are cognate, they only mean 'beech' in two of the five: Germanic and Italic. In Greek, Iranian, and Slavic the words signify various kinds of oak, elm, or elder. This can be explained, the argument goes, by noting that in the areas settled by the Greeks, Iranians, and Slavs after their migration from the Indo-European homeland, there were no beeches to be found. Accordingly, the speakers of those languages took the term originally meaning 'beech' and applied it to other trees. The Germanic and Italic tribes, which remained in the beech-tree area, kept the word in its original meaning.

Taking reconstructions like the above together as a group, though not necessarily agreeing on the meanings of particular words in Indo-European, many scholars have come to the conclusion that the Indo-Europeans lived somewhere in eastern Europe, either in the north near the Baltic or in the south near the Black Sea. Still, all their arguments are really nothing but more or less persuasive conjectures. It would help a great deal to have archeological evidence that aided in pinpointing the Indo-European community. And indeed, one influential school of thought, closely associated with the name of Marija Gimbutas, believes that just such an archeological link can be found in the remains of a culture that was located north of the Black Sea after the fifth millennium B.C. Known as the "Kurgan Culture" for its burials in *kurgans* or barrows, in its archeological remains this group displays numerous characteristics that have been reconstructed for the Indo-European parent language, and its geographical expansion appears to correlate quite well with what we know from other sources about the spread of the Indo-Europeans.

This view may be widely held, but it is certainly not the only possibility. In recent work, for example, Colin Renfrew has argued quite persuasively for an entirely different location, namely *south* of the Black Sea in eastern Anatolia (now Turkey), and a much earlier starting point, before 6000 B.C.

Information about the early history of what are now called the Germanic peoples is also rather sketchy. The weight of evidence, however, points to an ancient homeland in modern Denmark and southern Sweden. As for when they got there from the Indo-European homeland, the evidence is primarily archeological. Although humans had inhabited this region since about 10,000 B.C., the Germanic tribes are usually associated with an archeologically distinct group, known as the "Battle-ax Culture," who invaded the area in the third(?) millennium B.C., carrying with them a number of artifacts that, on the basis of comparative reconstruction, philologists consider to be characteristic of Indo-European culture.

Only at a relatively late era is there evidence about the Germanic people that is neither linguistic nor archeological. About 200 B.C. we may discern the first faint allusions to the Germanic tribes in the writings of Greek and Roman historians, and after the second half of the second century A.D. we find documents written by the Germanic peoples themselves (though certainly not by historians). These are the so-called *runic* inscriptions, scratched on metal, stone, bone, and occasionally wood; I discuss them in some detail in Chapter 4.

From the available data, we may reconstruct a gradual splitting-up of the Germanic people and their languages, along with a migration southward out of their original homeland in southern Scandinavia. By 300 B.C., Germanic tribes had apparently spread across the area shown in Map 1, from northern Belgium in the west to the Vistula in the east, and south as far as the upper Elbe. Scholars sometimes make, at this point, a rough division of the Germanic tribes into five distinct groups, each of which eventually developed a distinct set of languages or dialects, although their languages were probably not very differentiated in 300 B.C. The people who remained in Scandinavia (most of which is not shown in Map 1) form the nucleus for the later North Germanic languages. To the east of the Oder river, and spread along the Baltic coast, lived a group of people who later formed the nucleus of the East Germanic language group, of which the only well-attested language is Gothic. Finally, west of the Oder, and spread out as far as modern Belgium, lived a conglomerate of people commonly referred to as West Germanic, comprising, on the map, the Ingvaeones, or North Sea Germanic group; the Istvaeones, sometimes called the Weser–Rhine group; and the Irminones, also called the Elbe group. These subgroups of West Germanic derive ultimately from the Roman historian Tacitus, who in his work *Germania*, written about A.D. 98, noted that the Germanic people themselves made this division, at that time probably based mainly on cultural differences.

The further fates of these five groups are discussed in more detail in

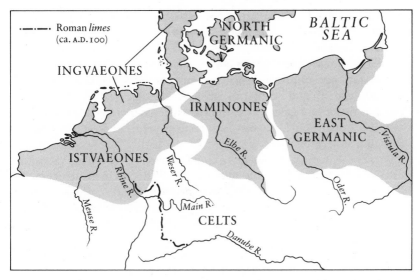

Map 1. Location of the Germanic tribes around 300 B.C. (After Frings [1957: 146], by permission)

later chapters, but the following short summary may be in order. The North Germanic people remained in Scandinavia, which is still the center of this subfamily. The East Germanic group, however, including tribes with such stirring names as the Vandals, the Goths, and the Burgundians, undertook an extensive series of migrations eastward, and later southward, to wind up in such distant places as modern Bulgaria, Italy, Spain, and even North Africa. Although they established some rather famous empires in these places, in the long run the East Germanic group was assimilated to other cultures and languages, and today not a single language descended from theirs still exists.

The Elbe Germanic group also migrated far southward. By different and often circuitous routes, tribes of this group, such as the Alamanni, the Langobardi, and the Marcomanni, settled southern Germany and northern Italy, pushing out Celts and Illyrians and crossing the Roman *limes*, a fortified wall that extended from the Rhine just above Koblenz southeastward to Regensburg near the Danube. Whereas the Langobardi were finally linguistically assimilated to the Romance dialects of northern Italy, the Alamanni and Marcomanni continued to speak Germanic dialects that can be roughly identified with the present Alamannic and Bavarian dialects of German, respectively. Another group of Elbe Germans with somewhat less wanderlust settled in what is now Thuringia, although their language was later to be heavily overlaid with Franconian characteristics.

The Weser–Rhine group moved mainly southwestward, occupying the western part of present Germany, most of the Netherlands, and large parts of Belgium and northern France. As the place names of the region suggest, this group gave rise to the Frankish federation that was to have a decisive effect on European history in general, and on German and French history in particular.

Finally, the North Sea group, or Ingvaeones, represents the source for our own language, English, and for the Frisian language, its closest relative. Elements of the North Sea Germanic tribes also merged with elements of other West Germanic groups to form the ancestral dialects of much of northern Germany and the Netherlands.

Dialects and Languages

I cannot end this chapter without briefly discussing the distinction between what are called "dialects" and what are called "languages." As I noted earlier when discussing the comparative method, one basic assumption of that method is that related languages began as nothing but dialects of an original proto-language, and in time diverged enough to be called languages in their own right. Comparative linguists, in fact, tend to refer to related languages as "dialects" of a particular language family, as when English, Frisian, German, Swedish, Gothic, and so on, are called dialects of Germanic.

It should also be noted that an endpoint on a family tree (such as the ones I have given for Modern German and English), and in fact probably each of the single points I have labeled with such terms as Proto-Indo-European, Proto-Germanic, West Germanic, and so on, disguises a diversity of speech variants as great as or greater than those we find in modern spoken English. So the question arises, for historical linguists as well as for modern students of dialectology: what distinguishes a dialect from a language?

Generations of linguistic study have not succeeded in giving a purely linguistic answer to this question. One can think of a number of criteria, among them how well speakers of two different variants can understand each other, how many common elements they share in their languages, and so forth. A look at actual speech situations, however, shows why these criteria fail. Take as an example two modern European cities where Germanic languages are still spoken, The Hague in the Netherlands and Bern in Switzerland. Now we know that these two cities speak languages quite different from one another, and in fact that people would characterize what is spoken in The Hague as a dialect of Dutch, and what is spoken in Bern as a dialect of German. Although the two dialects have quite a bit in common (they are both Germanic dialects, after all), they are also mutually incomprehensible: people from these two areas speaking their own dialects cannot understand each other.

But observe what happens when one tries to characterize all the intermediate dialects along a line drawn between the two cities. The dialects at any two adjacent points along the way turn out to be very similar, and almost perfectly comprehensible to each other. So where does one draw the absolute boundary line that would segregate the Dutch dialects from the German dialects?

One also finds examples of the following sort. If we look at the Germanic dialects still spoken in Scandinavia, namely Norwegian, Swedish, and Danish, we find a high degree of mutual comprehension between them: Norwegian and Swedish are mutually intelligible; Danes can usually understand both of the other two fairly well; and the other two can, with some difficulty, understand the Danes. And yet, we don't speak of these as being dialects of the same language, but rather as separate languages. Why?

The answer to this question appears to be more sociological than linguistic. In a sense, a certain variety of speech can be classified as being a dialect of one language, rather than another, when speakers of that variety think it is. Clearly, we have to do here with a question of cultural identity, rather than of linguistic fact. The reasons may be varied, but two that carry a great deal of weight are, on the one hand, political unity, and, on the other hand, a supraregional literature in something approaching a standard language. In tracing the history of the modern languages, then, we must pay special attention to these factors.

Organization of the Book

In the following chapters I present each of the older Germanic languages in the same way.

The first major section in each chapter is a brief history of the people who spoke the language treated in that chapter. I emphasize "brief," because not only *could* a book be written about the history of the Goths, say, or the Franks; several *have*. I have tried to restrict myself to some major facts about the various peoples, and in general the history ends at the end of the period of the corresponding language. Thus, the history of the Anglo-Saxons ends with the Norman invasion, because the language as written after this date is commonly characterized as Middle English, and differs considerably from the earlier form.

In the second section of each chapter I discuss, again briefly, the major texts found in the dialect under discussion. Frequently this brevity derives from the subject matter; some of these languages have very few sources. In other cases, such as Old Norse, there is a great wealth of texts. In such instances, an exhaustive list of texts would also be exhausting, and I have contented myself with a summary of the principal genres.

The third and central part of each chapter consists of two readings. In most of the languages, the first text is the New Testament parable of the Sower and the Seed, chosen because that text is found in so many of the languages, and because I can assume it is reasonably familiar to many of my readers. In Old Frisian and Old Low Franconian, unfortunately, this text does not exist. For these languages I have picked texts that have at least a chance of being known to the reader: the Ten Commandments for Old Frisian, two selections from the Book of Psalms for Old Low Franconian.

Although the Parable of the Sower and the Seed is found in many of our languages, it can hardly be called a typical text for most of them. I have therefore tried to balance it with other texts more representative of those found in the dialects in question. For example, for Old Norse I have picked one of the shorter episodes from Snorri's *Edda*, which has the additional virtue of being entertaining.

Because this is an introductory survey, I certainly do not expect readers to be able to breeze through even the most familiar texts in a language unknown to them. But I want them to *try*. To help this process, I have appended to the right of each selection a list of English or German words that are cognate with those found in the text (occasionally a word from some other language is given). Unless noted otherwise, cognates in roman type are English, and cognates in italics are German. To be as reasonable about this as possible, I have attempted first to find an English cognate fairly close in sense to the form in the reading, and only failing that to find a good German cognate. Even so, the cognates do not always mean exactly the same things as the words in the text, nor are they always grammatically parallel. I find this rather more of a virtue than a fault, since it forces readers to grapple with the reading a bit more energetically than they might otherwise do, which in turn leads to a greater sense of triumph than might emerge after an easy translation. Nevertheless, I have tried to avoid giving cognates that are so different in shape or meaning from the form in the text as to be useless. I have no doubt tended to err in the direction of obscurity, and for this I beg understanding. After all, someone out there will find it enlightening that Old Norse *barn* is cognate with Scots English "bairn."

No doubt some of the cognates I cite will fail to enlighten, and many words in the readings simply have no obvious cognates. I have therefore included after the reading texts in each language a complete glossary, in which every word in the readings is translated and every form is given a grammatical characterization.

For those who want to check up on their translations, or for those who are about to give up, I have included an appendix containing word-by-word translations of all the readings. But I implore the reader to wait a bit before resorting to these. If you read only the translations, in most cases you will at best learn something about the Bible, or about the frequently Latinate word order of its old Germanic translations.

Immediately following each chapter's reading selections and glossary is a fourth section on the orthography and grammar of its language. This is in no way a complete grammar of the language; such a grammar would be impossible in an introductory book. Rather, the grammatical sections point out characteristic features of the language under discussion, either those that uniquely characterize *this* language as against all others, or those that it shares with *some* languages and not others. In Chapter 10 I use many of these features to discuss the thorny issues surrounding the precise relationships among the older Germanic languages.

However, if the grammatical discussion in each chapter is more or less limited to a few salient characteristics, I would be cheating the reader if I did not give a fuller discussion somewhere of the general outlines of Germanic grammar. Similarly, the discussions of interesting phenomena in the individual languages would be virtually incomprehensible without some more general grammatical context. Thus I have attempted in Chapter 2 to summarize some major points of grammar that will help the reader to a clearer understanding of all the older Germanic languages. In this discussion I have included a guide to proper pronunciation of the letters used to write the various Germanic texts. Idiosyncratic pronunciation values must of course be handled in the chapters on individual languages, but certain general principles can be enunciated once for all.

The fifth and last major section of each chapter deals not so much with the language treated in that chapter as with questions of general interest to the student of Germanic, frequently questions that are raised by or related to the treatment of the particular language under discussion. Thus in the chapter on Old Saxon, it seemed to me imperative to offer some discussion of Germanic verse forms; although this topic clearly applies more generally than just to Old Saxon, the major texts of that language, which are exclusively poetic, cry out for such a discussion.

Chapter 10 differs from the preceding chapters, for it discusses not the individual Germanic languages but the relations among them, in the hope of reaching a sensible explanation for the similarities and differences remarked upon earlier. A number of theories that have been offered in the more or less recent past are sketched in that chapter, and a few final words on these topics round out the book.

FURTHER READING

Feist, Sigmund. *Kultur, Ausbreitung und Herkunft der Indogermanen.* Berlin: Weidmann, 1913.

Gimbutas, Marija. "Proto-Indo-European Culture." In G. Cardona, H. M. Hoenigswald, and A. Senn, eds., *Indo-European and Indo-Europeans: Papers Presented at the Third Indo-European Conference at the University of Pennsylvania,* pp. 155–97. Philadelphia: University of Pennsylvania Press, 1970.

Jespersen, Otto. *Growth and Structure of the English Language.* 9th ed. New York: Doubleday, 1955. [Reprint of the 1948 ed.; see esp. ch. 5.]

Lehmann, Winfred P. *Historical Linguistics: An Introduction.* 2d ed. New York: Holt, Rinehart & Winston, 1973.

Lockwood, W. B. *Indo-European Philology.* London: Hutchinson University Library, 1969.

Pedersen, Holger. *The Discovery of Language: Linguistic Science in the Nineteenth Century.* Bloomington, Ind.: Indiana University Press, 1962. [Reprint of the 1931 ed.; see esp. ch. 8.]

Renfrew, Colin. *Archaeology and Language: The Puzzle of Indo-European Origins.* London: Cape, 1987.

Schwarz, Ernst. *Germanische Stammeskunde.* Heidelberg: Winter, 1956. [See esp. chs. 2, 3.]

Skomal, Susan Nacev, and Edgar C. Polomé, eds. *Proto-Indo-European: The Archaeology of a Linguistic Problem. Studies in Honor of Marija Gimbutas.* Washington: Institute for the Study of Man, 1987.

Tschirch, Fritz. *Geschichte der deutschen Sprache.* 2d ed. Vol. 1, *Die Entfaltung der deutschen Sprachgestalt in der Vor- und Frühzeit.* Grundlagen der Germanistik, 5. Berlin: Schmidt, 1971. [See esp. ch. 1.]

Waterman, J. T. *A History of the German Language.* 2d ed. Seattle: University of Washington Press, 1976. [See esp. chs. 1, 2.]

2

Germanic: A Grammatical Sketch

Pronunciation

I begin with a brief outline of pronunciation rules that hold in general for the older Germanic languages. Thus although this section from time to time refers to language-particular phenomena, I do not discuss them in any great detail here, deferring a more complete presentation to the chapters on individual languages.

In order to talk about the pronunciation of letters at all, we must clearly distinguish between pronunciations and letters in our discussion. Thus in this book I consistently differentiate between orthographic forms, normally written in italics, and phonetic forms, normally written between square brackets [ ]. Frequently the same symbols may be found in both usages, as when I indicate orthographic *p* and phonetic [p]. This is no coincidence, of course. Ideally letters and sounds would correspond one to one, and it would make sense to choose the same symbols for both, still distinguishing between them theoretically.

Of course, we rarely find the ideal situation. Individual languages have their own odd discrepancies between letters and sounds, as when Gothic *g* is said to stand for sounds as distinct as [g], [ɡ], [x], and [ŋ] (see below for an explanation of these sounds). Even in the absence of discrepancies, different languages may choose different letters for the same sounds, some, say, choosing to represent [k] with *c*, others with *k*.

For clarity's sake, in the phonetic transcriptions I have chosen symbols that overlap as much as possible with actual spellings in Germanic languages. In some cases these are not the symbols most commonly used in linguistic transcriptions. It seems to me, however, that using the latter would simply complicate the situation for most readers. Thus for the *th-*

sound found in Modern English "thorn" I use the phonetic transcription [þ]. This far better represents the practice of old Germanic orthographies than does the commonly used [θ], which derives from Greek orthography.

Below I present the most commonly encountered sounds of Germanic in the following way. To the left appears, for each sound, the specific phonetic symbol that I use throughout the book. Immediately to the right, I give where possible a Modern English word containing that sound. In some cases it is necessary to describe the sound rather than to exemplify it. Finally, on the far right appear the symbols commonly used in Germanic spelling systems to capture that sound (though some languages use symbols I do not give here, as will be noted where appropriate). One of them is usually identical to the symbol I have chosen as the phonetic representation.

I begin with a list of the common consonants:

Phonetic symbol	English example	Germanic spelling
[p]	pin	p
[t]	tin	t
[k]	kin	k, c
[b]	bin	b
[d]	din	d
[g]	gold (*not* gin)	g
[f]	fin	f
[þ]	thin	þ, th
[s]	sin	s
[x]	(German *ach*)	h, ch
[h]	hint	h
[v]	van	u, v, (sometimes) f
[ƀ]	(A [v] formed with both lips, as in Spanish *caballo*)	ƀ, b, u, v
[ð]	then	ð, d, th, dh
[z]	Zen	s, (sometimes) z
[ɢ]	([g] spoken without complete closure in the mouth)	ǥ, g
[l]	lint	l
[r]	(Not like American [r]. Formed by tapping tip of tongue quickly	r

	against roof of mouth, as in "butter")	
[m]	mint	m
[n]	ninny	n
[ŋ]	sing	n (before *g* and *k*)
		g (in Gothic)
[w]	win	uu, u
[j]	yen	j, i

I have not given here all the consonants found in every Germanic language, but rather those found in a large number of them. Other consonants, and their phonetic symbols, are introduced in the individual chapters.

Further, although it is perhaps obvious, the reader should beware of taking symbols that are familiar from English as one would interpret them in Modern English. Thus although *z* does in fact represent [z] in Gothic, in Old High German it is pronounced [ts]. Similarly, *y* almost invariably represents a vowel in the oldest Germanic languages (see below), and it is *j* that is pronounced as we usually pronounce Modern English *y*.

Finally, I should point out that, whereas in Modern English we are used to so-called "silent" consonants—consonants that are spelled but not pronounced—in the older Germanic languages such things are unknown. If a letter is written, it is pronounced. This rule holds not only for such clusters as *kn*, even at the beginnings of words, but also for double consonants, which must be pronounced as *long* consonants. Thus the written sequence *gg* should be pronounced like the *g*'s in Modern English "big guns."

We turn now to the vowels. From the viewpoint of Modern English, surprisingly little is predictable about the pronunciation of the most commonly used Germanic vowel symbols. English spellings are not a guide to Germanic vowel sounds. From the viewpoint of other European languages, such as German or Italian, the old Germanic spellings are more understandable.

We may begin with the five basic vowel symbols *a, e, i, o, u.* In older Germanic texts these may appear either as shown, or modified in some way. Three common modifications are a superimposed circumflex (ˆ), a superimposed macron (-), and an acute accent (ˊ). Usually not found in the same language, the circumflex, the macron, and the acute accent mean the same thing, namely that the vowel in question is *long*, or articulated with greater muscular tension than an equivalent *short* vowel. Immediately below I have given the basic long vowels of Germanic, indicated with a circumflex in the phonetic transcription, and their approximate pronunciation equivalents from Modern English. Note that in practically no case are the English sample words spelled with the most commonly used Germanic letters:

Phonetic symbol	English example	Germanic spelling
[â]	"ahh!" or in some dialects the *o* in "bomb"	â, ā, á
[ê]	*ay* in "hay"	ê, ē, é
[î]	*ee* in "queen"	î, ī, í
[ô]	*o* in "bone"	ô, ō, ó
[û]	*oo* in "moon"	û, ū, ú

In some of the Germanic languages, these five common long vowels are joined by two others, also frequently spelled with the letters *e* and *o*, with or without modifications. These are pronounced with the mouth more open than when pronouncing [ê] and [ô]. I will symbolize them phonetically as [e:] and [o:]:

[e:]   Like the *e* of "bed," but longer
[o:]   Like English "aww!," with rounded lips

The short vowels in Germanic, represented by the same symbols *without* the circumflex, macron, or acute accent, were originally probably just that: shorter in duration than the long vowels, but otherwise articulated similarly. For something analogous to this in Modern English, compare the pronunciation of "beat" with "bead." The vowel of the first takes noticeably less time to pronounce than that of the second.

In most of the Germanic languages, however, the short vowels at some point became more than mere short equivalents of the long vowels (thus compare the vowel of "bit" with that of "beat"). I suspect that most scholars use this later pronunciation when they read old texts aloud. Thus the list below presents the later pronunciations, not least because the vowels then become more directly comparable to Modern English vowels:

Phonetic symbol	English example	Germanic spelling
[a]	*o* in "hot"	a
[e]	*e* in "get"	e
[i]	*i* in English "pin"	i
[o]	Many English speakers don't have this vowel: articulated with the mouth more open than in its long counter-	o

part. I have something
close to it in the word
"caught," or, better,
the first "oh" of
"oh-oh!"

[u]   *u* in English "put"   u

In addition to the long and short vowels, all the Germanic languages have diphthongs of various kinds, that is, combinations of two vowels together. In general, one may rely on the principle that each of the two symbols is pronounced as it would be separately, with the proviso that in the diphthong they belong to the same syllable. Thus *iu* is pronounced roughly like Modern English *eew*, *ai* like the English word "I," and so on. In some languages this rule fails, and I treat those cases in the chapters on individual languages.

One additional class of vowels should be noted in this section, especially since they do not exist in Modern English. This is the class of *front rounded vowels*. Characteristic of this class is a pronunciation similar to that of the *front* vowels [i], [î], [e], and [ê], but with concomitant lip rounding. Thus a vowel spelled *ü* or *y*, phonetically [ü], is pronounced like [i] with rounded lips, and the vowel symbolized as *ö* or *ø*, phonetically [ö], is pronounced like an [e] with rounded lips. These vowels too may sometimes be combined in diphthongs, in which case the principle that I stated in the last paragraph applies. More specific instructions for the individual languages, along with additional phonetic transcriptions where necessary, are found in later chapters.

Grammar

In the following sketch of Germanic grammar, I have left out a great deal. Two considerations have guided me in this. First, this book is meant to be an introduction, and a detailed description of minor noun classes or the intricacies of the various verb subclasses might only confuse the reader, who is in any case not expected to emerge from this book with a complete knowledge of the Germanic languages. Second, when scholars compare the older Germanic languages with one another in order to discern their relationships, they generally focus on a relatively small number of criteria. It is upon these criteria that I feel the emphasis in this book should lie. Thus, although the class of derived adverbs is interesting in and of itself, it does not normally play a role in comparing the older languages with each other, and I accordingly neglect it here.

Now a second warning is in order. Obviously, when one discusses a grammatical system, examples are necessary. One possibility would be to list the reconstructed Proto-Germanic forms for, say, the personal endings of the present tense of the strong verbs. Unfortunately, given the uncertainties inherent in comparative reconstruction, we cannot always tell what forms Proto-Germanic had, and indeed in some instances more than one form is possible. It might well be misleading if I simply chose one form for an illustration and neglected the other possibilities. But showing all the possibilities would detract from the major goals of the book. Thus I have chosen instead to illustrate Germanic paradigms with forms from Gothic. In a number of ways, this is quite appropriate, since Gothic frequently preserves archaic forms that the other dialects have lost. But it must be conceded that some characteristics of the Proto-Germanic grammatical system are better preserved in other dialects, and I will note several such cases.

Nouns

The grammatical distinctions reflected in the Germanic noun, that is, those for which it *inflects*, are *number* and *case*.

The category of number needs little elucidation. Like Modern English, all the Germanic languages distinguish *singular* and *plural*. Also as in Modern English, some nouns are not really pluralizable, as our word "wheat" is not, and others are only found in the plural, as is our word "pants." In general, however, any noun may appear in either the singular or the plural, as necessary.

Interestingly, there is one other number category found sometimes in Germanic, namely the *dual*. Opposed both to singular and plural, the dual refers to objects that come in pairs: for example, someone's hands. Although a number of Indo-European languages show a fairly free use of this number in many nouns, in Germanic the dual is not found in nouns at all, but only in the *pronominal* and *verbal* systems, as we will see below.

Case, too, is a very important category for Germanic. It is, however, probably the hardest one for monolingual speakers of Modern English to understand, for we have lost case distinctions almost entirely. Their primary function is to show the syntactic value of nouns in sentences; that is, cases make it clear whether a given noun (or actually noun phrase, often including associated adjectives, pronouns, or articles) is functioning as a subject of a verb, an object of a verb or preposition, or whatever. One of the reasons we can do without explicit case endings in Modern English is that our language has a comparatively rigid word order, and we may assess a noun's function quite dependably from where it is ordered with respect to other words of the sentence.

To make this discussion clearer, take the following sentence in Modern English:

> The boy gave his mother's wine to the girl.

We know the following things about this sentence: First, the subject of the sentence is "the boy," that is, it is the boy who is doing the giving. We know this principally because the phrase "the boy" precedes the verb "gave." Second, the direct object of the sentence is "his mother's wine," that is, the wine is the thing that is being given. This follows from the observation that this phrase follows the verb "gave." Third, in the phrase "his mother's wine" there is a relation between two noun phrases, namely "wine" and "his mother." Furthermore, the relationship is understood as one of possession, namely "his mother" possesses the "wine." The primary indication of this is the suffix -'s, which indicates a possessor (here, at least). This suffix comes closer to doing what Germanic case suffixes do. Finally, the recipient of the giving (the indirect object) is "the girl." This we know because this noun phrase follows the preposition "to."

Note that there are only a few things we can do to the elements of this sentence without changing the meaning or even producing an ungrammatical sentence. For example, "His mother's wine gave the boy to the girl" or "The boy gave the girl to his mother's wine" mean entirely different things than the original sentence, while "The boy gave wine his mother's to the girl" and "To the girl gave his mother's wine the boy" are not good sentences. Finally, "The boy gave to the girl his mother's wine" is all right, though stilted, and "The boy gave the girl his mother's wine" is perfectly good. In this case, it appears that if the verb is followed by two noun phrases neither of which stands after a preposition, we understand the first of them as the indirect object and the second as the direct object.

Now take the equivalent in Gothic:

> Magus gaf wein aiþeins seinaizôs maujai.

(Please note that this is a sentence invented to show as many relations as possible. It is not found in any Gothic texts, and the Gothic bishop Wulfila should not be held responsible.) In this sentence, the equivalent to "the boy" is *magus*. Whereas in English its function as subject can be deduced from its position, in Gothic this can be deduced from the *nominative* suffix *-us*. It would not matter where in the sentence we found *magus*: the fact that it is in the nominative case shows it is the subject.

The word *wein* 'wine', on the other hand, is in the *accusative* case, which marks it as direct object, again regardless of its position in the sentence. Thus even if we found the sentence *Wein aiþeins seinaizôs gaf magus maujai*, it would mean the same thing: the boy is giving the wine, not the wine the boy.

The phrase *aiþeins seinaizôs* 'of his mother' is in the *genitive* case, the case of possession, among other things. Note that in the English translation I have this time used the preposition "of," another way (besides the suffix -'s) to indicate the same relationship in English.

The word *maujai* 'to (the) girl', finally, is found in the *dative* case, or the case of the indirect object. The remarks made above about word order apply as well here: however we switched the order of words around, the sentence would mean the same thing. Note also that Gothic dispenses entirely with the preposition in this instance, with no loss in clarity.

To avoid oversimplifying, I must hasten to add that the nominative, accusative, genitive, and dative cases introduced above are also found in other functions besides subject, direct object, possessor, and indirect object. The nominative, for example, is also found as the case of a *predicate nominal*, or a noun phrase predicated of another noun phrase. Thus in the Gothic equivalent of "John is the king," both "John" and "the king" would be in the nominative case. The accusative is not only the case of the direct object, but also frequently the case required by a preposition. Thus the Gothic preposition *þairh* 'through' regularly requires that the noun it governs appear in the accusative. Similarly, a number of prepositions regularly require the genitive (e.g., Gothic *in* 'because of') or dative (*miþ* 'with'). Again, some Gothic verbs require what we would consider to be a direct object to appear with a dative or genitive inflection. Although this requirement is frequently hard to understand from the English point of view, we must admit the possibility that it was perfectly natural to a Goth. In fact, similar things still happen in Modern German.

I must mention here two other cases found in Germanic languages, though both of them are already somewhat rare even in the oldest attested stages of those languages. One of them is the *vocative*, or the case of address: thus the case of "father" in a sentence like "Father, we have some bad news for you." The only Germanic language showing this case is Gothic, and even there it is in all instances identical either to the nominative or to the accusative.

The other case (not found in Gothic) is a bit more robust. It is the *instrumental* case. As the name indicates, it is used to identify the instrument of an action, thus the case of "stone" in a sentence like "He broke the window with a stone." In most of the languages that have this case, it is more frequent in pronouns following certain prepositions than it is in nouns.

It would be useful if at this point I could round out the discussion by giving a single exemplary noun from Gothic or some other Germanic language and show how it inflects for number and case. Of course these categories intersect, so that we may speak of a *nominative singular* and a *nominative plural*, a *dative singular* and a *dative plural*, and so on. Unfortunately, and somewhat contrary to the expectations of a native speaker of English, the ending that expresses the dative singular of one noun is not always the same as the one that expresses the dative singular of another. Thus in the Gothic sentence above, the dative singular is expressed by the ending *-ai* in *maujai*, but if we had chosen another noun for the recipient of the wine we might easily have found a different ending. For example, the dative singular ending of the word for 'boy' is *-au*, as in *magau* 'to the boy'.

Part of the reason for this distressing lack of consistency lies in the existence of a grammatical category I haven't discussed yet—that of *gender*. I have ignored it until now, because for nouns this category is fundamentally different from those of number and case. Whereas any given noun may at one time or another appear in either number or in any case, the same does not hold for gender. Each noun has but a single gender associated with it, which remains constant whatever happens. Or to put it another way, gender is *inherent* in nouns.

Three genders are found in all the older Germanic languages: *masculine*, *feminine*, and *neuter*. As the names indicate, at some time in the past these categories may have had something to do with genuine biological gender, but by Germanic times such a connection is tenuous at best. Thus while one word for 'man' is masculine, at least one of the words for 'woman' is neuter in gender, and the association of the word for 'hand' with the feminine gender is quite obscure. It is better to think of these categories as arbitrary noun classes rather than as genuinely meaningful distinctions.

Although arbitrary and probably meaningless, the genders do exert a powerful influence in a number of different directions. Among other things, they regulate the forms of adjectives and articles accompanying nouns (we will discuss this regulation a bit later). They also to a certain extent regulate which specific forms of the case and number endings appear on the nouns.

I say "to a certain extent," because even if one knows that a given noun is masculine or feminine, one still cannot be sure what form, say, the dative singular will take. To illustrate this, let us return to the form *magau* 'to the boy', cited above. If one thought that *-au* was *the* masculine dative singular ending, one would be wrong. If we take another masculine noun, for example *wair* 'man', and put it into the dative singular, we find a different ending: *waira* 'to the man'.

Thus in addition to the three genders, we must reckon with another arbitrary subdivision of nouns: the inflectional classes. In fact, the older Germanic languages had upwards of twenty such classes, depending on how one counts them, each of which can be said to have its own unique set of case and number endings.

It would go far beyond the intent of this book to exemplify, or even to name, all these classes. Rather, below I have chosen a few classes to represent the many. Specifically, I have chosen to represent the classes that contain the vast majority of nouns, and to ignore those that either have very few members, or can be considered subvarieties of the major classes.

The traditional names for the Germanic noun classes contain the word "stem," as in *a-stems*, *ô-stems*, *n-stems*, and the like. The reasons for these names are less than obvious to beginning students of Germanic, since the *a*, *ô*, or *n* to which the names refer is frequently not evident. In fact, the notion of calling the classes "stem classes" is not terribly enlightening, even to the linguist, since the word "stem" refers to an inflectional system not found as such in any Germanic language, but only in the reconstructed Proto-Germanic and Proto-Indo-European. Nevertheless, I have used the traditional terms in the chart below precisely because they are traditional, and I would be foolish to invent new terms for them, which would only confuse the reader who wants to read on in the field.

	a-stems		*i*-stems	
	Masc. *dags* 'day'	Neut. *waurd* 'word'	Masc. *gasts* 'guest'	Fem. *ansts* 'grace'
		SINGULAR		
Nom.	dags	waurd	gasts	ansts
Acc.	dag	waurd	gast	anst
Gen.	dagis	waurdis	gastis	anstais
Dat.	daga	waurda	gasta	anstai
(Inst.)	(OHG tagu)	(OHG wortu)	(OHG gastu)	

PLURAL

Nom.	dagôs	waurda		gasteis	ansteis
Acc.	dagans	waurda		gastins	anstins
Gen.	dagê	waurdê		gastê	anstê
Dat.	dagam	waurdam		gastim	anstim

	ô-stems	n-stems		
	(Fem. only)	Masc.	Fem.	Neut.
	giba 'gift'	guma 'man'	tuggô 'tongue'	haírtô 'heart'

SINGULAR

Nom.	giba	guma	tuggô	haírtô
Acc.	giba	guman	tuggôn	haírtô
Gen.	gibôs	gumins	tuggôns	haírtins
Dat.	gibai	gumin	tuggôn	haírtin

PLURAL

Nom.	gibôs	gumans	tuggôns	haírtôna
Acc.	gibôs	gumans	tuggôns	haírtôna
Gen.	gibô	gumanê	tuggônô	haírtanê
Dat.	gibôm	gumam	tuggôm	haírtam

Pronouns

In a way, the category of pronoun is misnamed. Etymologically, the term *pronoun* means 'for a noun', that is, it denotes something that stands in for a noun that is missing. In many cases, pronouns do just that. Take a Modern English sentence like "He came in." If we ask what the word "he" stands for in this sentence, we are likely to get an answer like "John" or "the boy," both of which are nouns. Hence the application of the word "pronoun" to "he."

Traditionally, however, the term is also applied to words that may accompany nouns, especially, for example, to the form that in most Germanic languages plays the dual role of *article* and *demonstrative*. Take the Modern German phrase *der gute Mensch* 'the good person'. As I have translated the phrase, the word *der* is an article, translating as English 'the'. With a bit more emphasis, however, the word takes on more of a pointing, or demonstrative, function, and is then better translated by 'that', as in 'that good person'. Finally, both in German and in the older Germanic languages, it is possible to use a form like *der* without any accompanying noun at all. At that point such forms become genuine pronouns, translating into English as something like 'that one', or even 'he'.

There are several subclasses of Germanic pronouns that I will not discuss in detail—not because they are unimportant or uninteresting, but, again, because this is an introductory book, and the classes in question are not central when one compares the Germanic languages with one another.

As with nouns, the categories of case and number play an important role in the inflection of pronouns. This role appears clearly in the paradigms for the *first* and *second person personal pronouns* given below (the examples are from Gothic):

	First person	Second person
	SINGULAR	
Nom.	ik 'I'	þu 'thou'
Acc.	mik	þuk
Gen.	meina	þeina
Dat.	mis	þus
	DUAL	
Nom.	wit 'we two'	*jut 'you two'
Acc.	ugkis	igqis
Gen.	*ugkara	igqara
Dat.	ugkis	igqis
	PLURAL	
Nom.	weis 'we'	jus 'you'
Acc.	uns, unsis	izwis
Gen.	unsara	izwara
Dat.	uns, unsis	izwis

These paradigms, in contrast to those for nouns, show a three-way distinction for number rather than a two-way distinction: that is, the pronouns of the first and second persons distinguish singular, dual, and plural, rather than just singular and plural.

Pronouns of the third person do not distinguish dual and plural. However, they do distinguish genders (this should cause no hardship for speakers of Modern English). I give below the paradigms for the *third person personal pronoun* in Gothic:

	Masc.	Neut.	Fem.
		SINGULAR	
Nom.	is 'he'	ita 'it'	si 'she'
Acc.	ina	ita	ija
Gen.	is	is	izôs
Dat.	imma	imma	izai

PLURAL

Nom.	eis 'they'	ija	*ijôs
Acc.	ins	ija	ijôs
Gen.	izê	izê	izô
Dat.	im	im	im

Commonly grouped with the personal pronouns is the *reflexive* pronoun. Translated into Modern English with the words 'himself, herself, itself', the reflexive pronoun always refers back to the subject of the sentence in which it appears. The reflexive inflects neither for gender nor for number; it has only case distinctions. In a way this makes sense, for the gender and number of the noun that the reflexive refers to can always be told from the subject of the sentence.

	Reflexive
Nom.	—
Acc.	sik
Gen.	seina
Dat.	sis

It should also be noted that the absence of a nominative reflexive is systematic; since the reflexive refers back to the subject of a sentence, it can never *be* the subject of the sentence.

Like the personal pronouns, the demonstrative pronouns show a distinction between singular and plural, inflect for case, and come in three genders. Unlike the personal pronouns, the demonstratives may, and frequently do, appear with a noun as part of a noun phrase, just as in the Modern German example given above, *der gute Mensch* 'that good person'. With a noun, these pronouns are used as articles or as demonstrative adjectives. In this case the pronoun agrees with the noun in all these grammatical features—that is, if the demonstrative accompanies a feminine noun in the dative singular, it will itself show the feminine dative singular inflection:

	Masc.	Neut.	Fem.
	SINGULAR		
Nom.	sa	þata	sô
Acc.	þana	þata	þô
Gen.	þis	þis	þizôs
Dat.	þamma	þamma	þizai
(Instr.)	(OHG diu)	(OHG diu)	—

PLURAL

Nom.	þai	þô	þôs
Acc.	þans	þô	þôs
Gen.	þizê	þizê	þizô
Dat.	þaim	þaim	þaim

In a number of the older Germanic languages, the demonstrative pronouns illustrated immediately above may also serve as *relative pronouns*, that is, as pronouns that allow one to modify a noun with a whole clause, as in the English sentence "The man *who came in the door* immediately left again," where "who came in the door" modifies "man." In some of the Germanic languages, the demonstrative cannot function alone as a relative, but has to be accompanied by another form. In Gothic, for example, one must append the subordinating suffix *-ei* to make a demonstrative into a relative, as in the nominatives *saei, þatei, sôei* (and so on for other case forms).

Other pronominal forms, which I do not discuss here for want of space, are the *interrogatives*, corresponding to English "who? which? what?" the *indefinites*, corresponding to "some, one, each, every," and so on.

Adjectives

One way or another, adjectives are strongly associated with nouns. In some cases they may be *predicated* of nouns, as in "The grass is *green*." In other instances they are *attributes* of nouns, as in the phrase "the *green* grass."

In a language like Modern German, the distinction between predicate and attributive adjectives is significant, since the attributive, but not the predicate, adjectives must agree with their nouns. In Modern German, this means that predicate adjectives appear without any inflection at all, while attributive adjectives are inflected. In the older Germanic languages, this distinction is less important; even predicate adjectives may have to agree with the noun of which they are predicated.

In any case, one important fact about adjectives is that they usually must agree with the nouns they modify. What this means is that when a noun is in a certain number and case, its adjective must be also. In addition, adjectives must agree with the gender of their nouns. Thus, although any given noun will possess a certain gender under all circumstances, an adjective (which must be capable of appearing with nouns of any gender) inflects for all genders. This complication can be illustrated by the so-called *strong declension* of the Gothic word for 'blind', given below:

	Masc.	Neut.	Fem.
		SINGULAR	
Nom.	blinds	blind, -ata	blinda
Acc.	blindana	blind, -ata	blinda
Gen.	blindis	blindis	blindaizôs
Dat.	blindamma	blindamma	blindai
(Instr.)	(OHG blintu)	(OHG blintu)	—
		PLURAL	
Nom.	blindai	blinda	blindôs
Acc.	blindans	blinda	blindôs
Gen.	blindaizê	blindaizê	blindaizô
Dat.	blindaim	blindaim	blindaim

Unfortunately, the adjectives are even more complicated than this. Besides the strong declension shown above, all Germanic adjectives may also inflect according to the *weak declension*:

	Masc.	Neut.	Fem.
		SINGULAR	
Nom.	blinda	blindô	blindô
Acc.	blindan	blindô	blindôn
Gen.	blindins	blindins	blindôns
Dat.	blindin	blindin	blindôn
		PLURAL	
Nom.	blindans	blindôna	blindôns
Acc.	blindans	blindôna	blindôns
Gen.	blindanê	blindanê	blindônô
Dat.	blindam	blindam	blindôm

Unlike the markings for case, number, and gender, the use of strong or weak forms does not depend on the form of the accompanying noun. Rather, it in general depends on the presence of the definite article (which is identical to the demonstrative pronoun illustrated above). If the definite article is present, then the adjective is usually inflected weak; if the definite article is absent, then the adjective is inflected strong. Essentially this system is still found today in Modern German, as in *der gute Mann* (weak) but *ein guter Mann* (strong).

I will not spend much time on the final categories for which adjectives inflect, because they are familiar from every modern Germanic language. These are the categories of *comparative* and *superlative*, illustrated quite well by Modern English "sweet," "sweeter," "sweetest." It should be kept in mind that these categories intersect with the ones given above, so that the comparative and superlative must also agree with an accompanying noun in case, number, and gender, and may also appear in a strong or weak form (though in fact in many of the older Germanic languages the weak adjective declension is preferred or required at least for the comparative, and frequently also for the superlative).

Verbs

The inflectional categories of the Germanic verb system are *voice, mood, tense, number,* and *person.* Also commonly discussed with verbs are the forms known as *participles* and *infinitives,* which in the earlier Germanic languages are perhaps better seen as special kinds of adjectives and nouns derived from verbs.

There are two voices in Germanic, *active* and *passive.* When the verb is in the active voice, the subject of the sentence is in some sense the *agent* of the action, or at least the doer of the action. On the other hand, when the verb is inflected for passive, the subject of the verb is seen as the *patient,* or undergoer of the action. Take for example the Gothic verb *bairan* 'to carry'. When it is inflected actively, as in *bairiþ* '(he) carries', the subject is seen as carrying something. When it is inflected passively, however, as in *bairada* '(he) is carried', the subject is being carried by someone or something. Note that in Modern English I translate the passive with a phrase, 'be carried', consisting of an auxiliary or helping verb, "be," plus a past participle. Such a *periphrastic* formulation is, in fact, the normal way to express the passive in the Germanic languages. Indeed, original passive inflections of the verb are found in Gothic alone of all of the older Germanic languages and even there they are only found in the present tense.

The category of *mood* may be somewhat confusing for speakers of Modern English. In a general sense, mood has to do with the orientation of the speaker with respect to what he or she is saying. A command is usually in the *imperative* mood; a statement is in the *indicative*; a wish or an irreal statement (of a "condition contrary to fact") is in the *subjunctive.* There are more specific rules, especially for the use of the present or the past subjunctive, which it would be inappropriate to treat in an introductory work. It should also be pointed out that for obvious reasons the imperative appears only in the present tense.

Tense is easier to comprehend for a speaker of Modern English. The older Germanic languages really have only two tenses, as far as verb inflection goes, namely *present* and *preterite* (or *past*). This much is true even in Modern English: when we say "I run" or "I ran," we are actually

		Present		Preterite		Present	
INDICATIVE	Sg. 1	nima	lagja	nam	lagida	nimada	lagiada
	2	nimis	lagjis	namt	lagidēs	nimaza	lagiaza
	3	nimiþ	lagjiþ	nam	lagida	nimada	lagiada
	Dual 1	nimōs	lagjōs	nēmu	lagidēdu		
	2	nimats	lagjats	nēmuts	lagidēduts		
	Pl. 1	nimam	lagjam	nēmum	lagidēdum	nimanda	lagianda
	2	nimiþ	lagjiþ	nēmuþ	lagidēduþ	nimanda	lagianda
	3	nimand	lagjand	nēmun	lagidēdun	nimanda	lagianda
SUBJUNCTIVE	Sg. 1	nimau	lagjau	nēmjau	lagidēdjau	nimaidau	lagiaidau
	2	nimais	lagjais	nēmeis	lagidēdeis	nimaizau	lagiaizau
	3	nimai	lagjai	nēmi	lagidēdi	nimaidau	lagiaidau
	Dual 1	nimaiwa	lagjaiwa	nēmeiwa	lagidēdeiwa		
	2	nimaits	lagjaits	nēmeits	lagidēdeits		
	Pl. 1	nimaima	lagjaima	nēmeima	lagidēdeima	nimaindau	lagiaindau
	2	nimaiþ	lagjaiþ	nēmeiþ	lagidēdeiþ	nimaindau	lagiaindau
	3	nimaina	lagjaina	nēmeina	lagidēdeina	nimaindau	lagiaindau
IMPERATIVE	Sg. 2	nim	lagei				
	3	nimadau	lagjadau				
	Dual 2	nimats	lagjats				
	Pl. 1	nimam	lagjam				
	2	nimiþ	lagjiþ				
	3	nimandau	lagjandau				
INFINITIVE		niman	lagjan				
PARTICIPLE		nimands	lagjands	numans	lagiþs		

inflecting the verb, but when we say "I will run" or "I have run" or "I am running," we are using periphrastic constructions with auxiliary verbs. Such periphrastic constructions are much rarer in the older Germanic languages. Thus in Gothic, for example, we commonly find the present used also in a future meaning, and the preterite used also to express the *pluperfect*, as in Modern English "I had run."

Number in the Germanic verb is governed by the subject. Thus, when the subject is singular, the verb is inflected for the singular; when the subject is in the plural, the verb is also. In the first and second persons, there is also a dual inflection of the verb, which is used when the subject is understood or explicitly indicated to consist of two people.

Person, too, is a verbal category governed by the subject. Thus we find in the Germanic verb the categories of *first*, *second*, and *third* persons, equivalent respectively to Modern English forms appearing with "I," "you," and "he," "she," or "it."

When a verbal form inflects for the categories so far discussed, it is said to be a *finite* form of the verb. But alongside these paradigmatic forms there are also three *nonfinite* forms of most verbs. The first is the *infinitive* proper, which is essentially a noun formed from the present tense verbal stem; consider Modern English "to run." The second is the *present participle*, which is an adjective formed from the present stem, analogous to forms like Modern English "running." The third is the *preterite participle*, an adjective sometimes but not always based on the preterite stem of the verb, and etymologically identical with forms like "driven" in "I have driven" or "a driven man."

Again, it would be helpful if a single verb could illustrate how all the inflectional categories discussed above interact in actual verb inflection. Unfortunately, like the nouns, the verbs have a number of essentially arbitrary subclasses that inflect in different ways. We are familiar with such subclasses in Modern English, where we distinguish so-called *regular* verbs—"I kiss," "I kissed," "I have kissed"—and *irregular* verbs— "I sing," "I sang," "I have sung." The traditional names for the earlier versions of these two classes in Germanic are *weak verbs* and *strong verbs*, respectively. Even in the earliest stages of Germanic we can find further subclasses of each of these classes, and traditionally we distinguish between at least seven types of strong verb and four types of weak verb. It will no doubt relieve the reader to see that I am not giving an example of each subtype in the paradigm on the opposite page. Instead, I have taken one representative verb from the strong class, Gothic *niman* 'to take', and one from the weak class, Gothic *lagjan* 'to lay', and I hope that they will suffice to illustrate the inflection of the Germanic verb.

In the following chapters I will specify the various grammatical classes more closely, usually to point out distinctions between the older Germanic languages. For the moment, however, I hope that the preceding sketch has sufficed to orient the reader in a general way.

FURTHER READING

Braune, Wilhelm, and E. A. Ebbinghaus. *Gotische Grammatik*. 18th ed. Tübingen: Niemeyer, 1981.

van Coetsem, Frans. "Zur Entwicklung der germanischen Grundsprache." In L. E. Schmitt, ed., *Kurzer Grundriss der germanischen Philologie bis 1500*, vol. 1, *Sprachgeschichte*, pp. 1–93. Berlin: de Gruyter, 1970.

van Coetsem, Frans, and Herbert L. Kufner, eds. *Toward a Grammar of Proto-Germanic*. Tübingen: Niemeyer, 1972.

Keller, R. E. *The German Language*. Atlantic Highlands, N.J.: Humanities Press, 1978. [See esp. ch. 3.]

Krahe, H., and W. Meid. *Germanische Sprachwissenschaft*. 7th ed. 3 vols. Berlin: de Gruyter, 1967–69.

Meillet, A. *Caractères généraux des langues germaniques*. Paris: Hachette, 1917.

Prokosch, Eduard. *A Comparative Germanic Grammar*. Philadelphia: Linguistic Society of America, 1938.

3

GOTHIC

A Brief History of the Visigoths and Ostrogoths

Greek and Roman sources of the first and second centuries A.D. are the earliest written evidence we have for the Goths, under the names *Guthones*, *Gothones*, and *Gothi*. The sources agree in placing these people along the Vistula river, although whether they were on the coast or a bit inland is unclear.

Also not totally clear is the connection between these people and other tribal groupings of similar names found at that time and later in parts of south central Sweden (now Västergötland and Östergötland) and on the island of Gotland. If the legend recorded by the sixth-century Gothic historian Jordanes is accurate, the Goths came to the mouth of the Vistula from across the sea, displacing a number of Germanic tribes who were there before them, including the Vandals. The weight of scholarship appears to support this story, with (mainland) Götland being seen as the likely point of origin, and the early first century B.C. as the likely time.

Owing perhaps partially to population pressure, a large number of Goths subsequently left the Vistula in the mid-second century A.D. Around 170 they reached an area north of the Black Sea, where they settled between the Don and the Dniester rivers (Map 2). These people were joined by other migrating waves between A.D. 200 and 230.

The Goths were now, of course, on the borders of the Roman Empire, which they proceeded to harry unmercifully. In fact, their attack on the Roman province of Dacia (present-day Rumania) was so intense that the Romans were forced to abandon it after 270, and a large number of Goths soon settled there. From around this time we can discern a split between two large Gothic groups, the Ostrogoths in what is now the

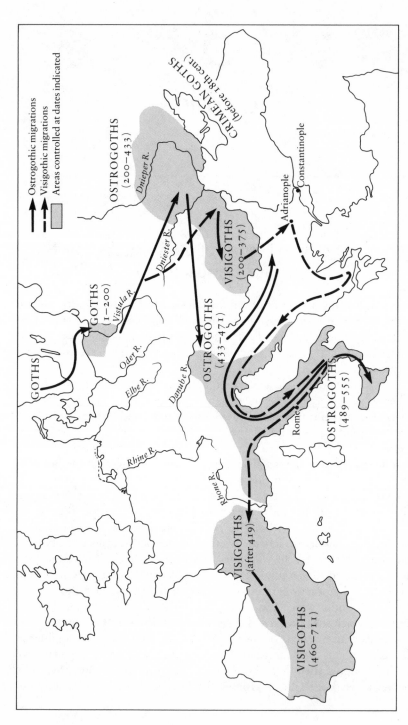

Map 2. Gothic migrations of the first through the eighth century A.D. (After Schwarz [1956: 84], by permission)

Ukraine and the Visigoths between the Danube and the Dniester rivers. The division may have gone back to the very earliest days of the Goths, or may have been due to a relatively recent rivalry between leading families.

Generally speaking, the Visigoths and the Ostrogoths led separate existences after about 270. While the Ostrogoths were consolidating their control over the barbarian tribes to their east and north, the Visigoths moved largely in the orbit of the Eastern Roman Empire, at times as allies, at times as enemies. They were the first Goths to be Christianized, primarily, but not exclusively, through the work of the Gothic bishop Wulfila, discussed below. He is said to have worked among the main body of Visigoths in Dacia for seven years, until around 347 he and his followers were driven from the area and forced to seek imperial protection south of the Danube in what is now Bulgaria. His group appears to have been reinforced between 369 and 372 by the survivors of a vicious persecution carried out by the conservative Gothic chieftain Athanaric, who saw both in Wulfila's Arian faith and in the orthodox Catholic faith of others a threat to traditional Gothic values and, not incidentally, a religion altogether too friendly to Rome.

In the year 375, the Goths were subjected to a massive invasion from the East by an aggressive non-Germanic group known as the Huns. Although the Ostrogoths were most immediately affected, the Visigoths too were hard pressed. After a decisive defeat in 376, most of the Visigoths fled south of the Danube, there to become dependents of Rome. Athanaric and a few dedicated followers escaped into the Carpathian mountains, all for nought—Athanaric was to die a refugee in Constantinople in 381.

Peace did not reign long, however. Irritated by a number of grievances against the empire, the Visigoths under their new leader Frithigern took up arms against the Romans in 378. After a great victory before the city of Adrianople, a victory in which the Eastern emperor Valens himself was killed, the Visigoths were granted the status of federates of Rome, which is to say, essentially independent rulers of their newly occupied territories.

For almost twenty years the Visigoths remained relatively quiet. Then, apparently convinced of greener pastures elsewhere, they set off westward in 395 under a new ruler, Alaric. Passing through Thrace, Macedonia, and Thessaly down into Greece, they succeeded in capturing a number of important Greek cities on the mainland and in the Peloponnesus before Roman armies drove them back in 397. In 401 and again in 408, Alaric moved against Italy, and in 410 his armies sacked Rome itself.

Alaric did not intend to stay in Italy for long. Instead he planned to move his people to North Africa, a plan that might well have succeeded had his ships not been destroyed by a storm. On the unplanned march back north, Alaric suddenly fell ill and died. He was succeeded by his brother-in-law Athaulf or Atawulf, who led the Goths first into southern Gaul, then into northern Spain.

Until 475, the Visigoths ruled, as off-again on-again federates of the Romans, over a large part of southern Gaul and northern Spain. By that date, in fact, they ruled most of the rest of Spain as well. In 451 they participated in the famous battle of the Catalaunian plains, which broke the back of the Hun Attila's advance through Europe. In this battle many of their foes were Ostrogoths (see below).

In 475 the Gothic king Euric declared the Gothic possessions a kingdom independent of Rome, but most of the Gallic part of that kingdom was stripped away from his son by the Franks in 507. From that date until 711, when the Moors invaded and conquered them, the Visigoths, stationary at last, ruled over most of the Iberian peninsula.

As for the Ostrogoths, before the advent of the Huns they had established a rather large empire east of the Dniester, parts of it stretching as far as the Baltic. Unlike the Visigoths, the Ostrogoths were highly centralized at an early date, under the rule of a true king. In 375 that king was the famed Ermanaric, a figure of legend in later Germanic literature.

The attack of the Huns in 375 proved the great fragility of this empire. Ermanaric is reported to have committed suicide when confronted with the hopelessness of his situation, and thereafter the main body of the Goths surrendered to the Huns. Others, however, fled south of the Danube to join the Visigoths, and still others of them settled in Roman Pannonia, a province incorporating parts of modern Austria, Hungary, and Yugoslavia.

The Ostrogoths seem not to have been too dissatisfied under the yoke of the Huns. Indeed, reports of emissaries to the court of Attila suggest that the Hunnish king held Gothic culture and the Gothic soldiery in high esteem. Certainly the Ostrogoths formed an important part of his armies, and they were there, fighting not only the Romans but also the Visigoths, when Attila was defeated in Gaul in 451. They even seem to have fought for the Huns under Attila's sons when most of the other subject Germanic tribes carried out a successful revolt in 454.

With the collapse of the Hunnish empire in 455, the main body of Ostrogoths settled as federates of the Romans in Pannonia. But they did not settle there for long. In 471, under their great leader Theodoric, a large number of Ostrogoths drifted south into the Balkans, where they were caught up in the politics of the Eastern Roman Empire, which often involved playing the various Germanic peoples and leaders off against each other.

Theodoric was outstandingly successful at these skirmishes. Joined by many of the remaining Ostrogoths, he soon built up a power base in Lower Moesia, a feat that could not but disturb the Eastern emperor Zeno. However, the Ostrogoths were not the only Germanic thorns in Zeno's side: Italy had fallen under the control of the mercenary soldier Odoacer, a fickle subject at best, and Zeno conceived the idea of replacing him with Theodoric. This fell in quite well with Theodoric's own wishes, and from 489 to 493 he waged a winning war against Odoacer, which ended in the latter's (probably treacherous) death and Theodoric's ascendancy.

Theodoric ruled Italy until his death in 526, but his kingdom was not fated to outlive him by many years. In 535 the emperor Justinian declared war on the Goths, a war that was to end with a total collapse of their power in 555.

The Goths of both branches ceased to be a distinct ethnic and linguistic group in Europe in the eighth century. In Spain and Italy they were assimilated into the native populations to become Spaniards and, along with the later Langobards, Italians. Only in the east are there some late echoes of their existence, as I explain further below.

Gothic Texts

Bible Gothic

Besides Wulfila's Bible translations (see below), there are very few sources for our study of the language. These few include:

1. The *Skeireins*, an eight-page commentary on the Gospel of Mark, perhaps a translation, but clearly not by Wulfila.

2. A three-page fragment from a translation of the Old Testament book of Nehemiah, probably too different in style and in the rendering of biblical names to be ascribed to Wulfila.

3. A fragment of a Gothic church calendar, containing parts of October and November.

4. Two Latin title deeds containing a number of Gothic names and words.

5. Three examples of the Gothic alphabet, with the names of the letters included, a few sample Gothic sentences with some kind of pho-

netic transcription above them, some Gothic numbers, and some comments on the pronunciation of Gothic.

6. A collection of Latin homilies with Gothic interpretations in the margins.

7. A possible Gothic toast contained in a Latin distich.

8. Gothic personal names in Greek and Latin texts.

9. A number of runic inscriptions that may or may not be Gothic.

By far the main source for our knowledge of Gothic remains the Bible translation ascribed to the Gothic bishop Wulfila (ca. 311–83), which has been preserved in a number of different fragmentary manuscripts. The most precious of these is the Codex Argenteus, now to be found in Uppsala, Sweden. This manuscript is written on purple parchment with silver and gold letters, and contains large fragments of the Gospels of Matthew, John, Luke, and Mark. Other manuscripts, many of them quite long, contain large segments of other New Testament books.

The ascription of a Bible translation to Wulfila comes from the Arian church historian Philostorgius, and it seems reasonable to maintain that the texts we are discussing here are precisely that translation. Both Philostorgius and the Byzantine scholar Socrates agree that Wulfila translated the entire Bible except for the Books of Kings, supposedly omitting these in order to avoid stirring up the warlike nature of the Goths. If this is true, we certainly have lost a lot; what survives is only about three-fourths of the New Testament.

The church historians also concur in the assertion that Wulfila was forced to invent an alphabet in order to write the translation. Scholars agree that his alphabet was based mainly on a Greek model, but in some cases it seems clear that Wulfila has helped himself out with Latin or even runic symbols. In Figure 2 we see three variants of the Gothic letters found in various manuscripts.

Little is known about Wulfila's life. His maternal grandparents may have been Christian Cappadocians captured in a Gothic raid around 264. Wulfila was probably born in 311, among the Visigoths along the Danube. Raised a Christian, he went to Constantinople in his twenties, where he trained under the Arians. These were followers of a variant of Christianity that was soon to be declared a heresy, believing that God the Father and God the Son are not of the same substance and that the Son is subject to the Father, and the Holy Spirit to the Son.

Consecrated a bishop in about 341, Wulfila returned to the Visigoths to convert them. After a great deal of persecution for his beliefs and preaching, Wulfila, along with many of his followers, was forced to take

Numerical value	cod. Ambros. B	cod. Vindob. 195	cod. arg. Hand I	Romanization
1	λ	⁊	Λ	a
2	Β	Ⴁ	Ꙗ	b
3	Γ	Γ	Γ	g
4	⅃	Ψ	⅁	d
5	F	(·)	Є	e
6	U	U	U	q
7	Ӿ	Ⴎ	Z	z
8	ƕ	ɳ	ɦ	h
9	ψ	Ψ	ψ	þ
10	ıı̈	ı̈	ı ı̈	i ı̈
20	Ƙ	Κ	Ƙ	k
30	λ	λ	λ	l
40	ɧ	ʜ	Μ	m
50	Ν	N	Ν	n
60	ʗ	Ⴑ	ʗ	j
70	ꞃꞃ	ꞃ	ɳ	u
80	π	π	π	p
90			Ч	–
100	⅃⅃	⅃⅃	Ƙ	r
200	Ɛ	Ⴀ	S	s
300	ꞇ	Τ	Τ	t
400	Υ	Υ	Υ	w
500	Ⴔ	ᴎ	Ⴔ	f
600	Χ	+	Χ	x
700	(·)	ᴗ ᴗ	Ο	ƕ
800	ꭗ	ꭗ	ꭗ	o
900		↑		–

Fig. 2. The Gothic alphabet. Note the use of letters to serve also as numbers. (After Braune and Ebbinghaus [1981: 14], by permission)

refuge south of the Danube in the Roman province of Moesia. From here he continued his missionary work, however, and by the time of his death, probably in 383, a large number of Goths had converted to Arian Christianity, in fact at a time when most of the rest of Christendom had rejected that creed. It is because of the Goths, and thus ultimately because of Wulfila, that Arianism survived as long as it did, a large obstacle to Christian unity.

Crimean Gothic

In 1562, the Flemish nobleman Oghier Ghislain de Busbecq, serving as ambassador of the Holy Roman Empire to the Ottoman Turks, penned a letter to an old school friend in Europe. In it, he reported meeting two men from the Crimea, where, as he had often heard, a group of people lived who exhibited Germanic traits in their appearance, customs, and language. Curious about this group, Busbecq spent several hours with the two, eliciting details about this Crimean culture and language. In his report on this conversation, he listed a number of words and short phrases with their Latin equivalents, eighteen cardinal numbers, and the three-line beginning of a song (without translation), in all 101 separate language forms.

Unfortunately, there are many problems in the linguistic evaluation of this small corpus. In the first place, according to Busbecq, though one of his informants was originally a native speaker of the language in question, he had lived so long among the Greeks that he had forgotten his own language. Thus most of Busbecq's information came from the other man, a native Greek who had apparently become fluent in the Germanic tongue of the Crimea. However fluent he may have been, though, we have to reckon with some interference from Greek.

Second, Busbecq was not a professional linguist, and he may not have been totally objective. Furthermore, in writing down the words he elicited, he used an idiosyncratic spelling system compounded of both Flemish and German orthographic conventions, and its interpretation is not always clear.

Third, our data come not from Busbecq's letter itself, but from a pirated French printing of it, which in turn most probably came from a manuscript copy of the original letter. This leaves room for a good many errors in transmission.

Even granting the inadequacy of the corpus, most scholars are reasonably confident in assigning this language to the East Germanic branch of the Germanic family, and its similarities to Wulfila's Visigothic language cannot be denied. There are, however, such important differences that one cannot consider Crimean Gothic to be descended from Wulfila's Gothic. Perhaps the most reasonable classification of this language is as a late Ostrogothic dialect; that would fit the geographical and historical facts also.

Ostrogothic or no, this language too no longer exists. The people who spoke it have been totally assimilated into the local populations, putting an end to the entire East Germanic subfamily of languages.

Readings

Parable of the Sower and the Seed

(Mark 4.1–9)

Jah aftra Iesus dugann laisjan at marein, jah	(be)gan, *lehren, Meer*
galesun sik du imma manageins filu, swaswe	(*Aus*)*lese, sich*, many, *viel*
ina galeiþandan in skip gasitan in marein;	*ihn, leiten*, ship, sit
jah alla so managei wiþra marein ana staþa	*wider*, (*Ge*)*stade*
was. Jah laisida ins in gajukom manag, jah	*lehrte*
qaþ im in laiseinai seinai: "Hauseiþ! Sai,	quoth, *Lehre, sein*, hear
urrann sa saiands du saian fraiwa seinamma.	ran, sow(er), sow
Jah warþ, miþþanei saiso, sum raihtis ga-	*ward*, some (= "one"), right
draus faur wig, jah qemun fuglos jah fretun	(be)fore, way, came, *Vogel, frassen*
þata. Anþaruþþan gadraus ana staina-	*ander*, steinig
hamma, þarei ni habaida airþa managa, jah	there, had, earth
suns urrann, in þizei ni habaida diupaizos	soon[?], deep
airþos; at sunnin þan urrinnandin ufbrann,	sun, then, up, burn(ed)
jah unte ni habaida waurtins, gaþaursnoda.	*Wurzel*, thirst
Jah sum gadraus in þaurnuns; jah ufarsti-	thorns, *überstiegen*
gun þai þaurnjus jah afƕapidedun þata, jah	
akran ni gaf. Jah sum gadraus in airþa goda,	acorn (= "fruit"), gave, good
jah gaf akran urrinnando jah wahsjando jah	*wachsend*
bar ain .l. jah ain .j. jah ain .r. Jah qaþ: saei	bore, one
habai ausona hausjandona, gahausjai."	have, ear(s), hear(ing), hear

Gabriel and Mary

(Luke 1.26–38)

Þanuh þan in menoþ saihstin insandiþs was	then, month, sixth, sent
aggilus Gabriel fram guþa in baurg Galei-	angel, from, God, *Burg*

laias sei haitada Nazaraiþ, du magaþai in — hight (= "named"), maid
fragibtim abin, þizei namo Iosef, us garda — name, gard(en)
Daweidis, jah namo þizos magaþais Ma-
riam. Jah galeiþands inn sa aggilus du izai — leiten, in
qaþ: "Fagino, anstai audahafta, frauja miþ — Gunst, mit
þus; þiuþido þu in qinom. . . ." Jah qaþ ag- — dir, queen
gilus du izai: "Ni ogs þus, Mariam, bigast — got
auk anst fram guþa. Jah sai, ganimis in kil- — nimmst, child (see Glossary)
þein jah gabairis sunu, jah haitais namo is — bear, son
Iesu. Sah wairþiþ mikils, jah sunus hauhis- — wird, much, highest
tins haitada, jah gibid imma frauja guþ stol — give(s), him, stool
Daweidis attins is. Jah þiudanoþ ufar garda — over
Iakobis in ajukduþ, jah þiudinassaus is ni
wairþiþ andeis." Qaþ þan Mariam du þamma — end
aggilau: "ƕaiwa sijai þata, þandei aban — how, sei
ni kann?" Jah andhafjands sa aggilus qaþ — know
du izai: "Ahma weihs atgaggiþ ana þuk, — weih(en), go
jah mahts hauhistins ufarskadweid þus, — might, overshadow
duþe ei saei gabairada weihs haitada sunus
guþs. . . ." Qaþ þan Mariam: "Sai, þiwi fraujins, wairþai mis bi waurda þeinamma." Jah — me, word
galaiþ fairra izai sa aggilus. — far

GLOSSARY

In alphabetizing Gothic, þ follows t; ƕ follows h; i representing [j] is listed as j. Unless specified otherwise, nouns and pronouns are nominative singular, adjectives are masculine nominative singular, and verbs are infinitives. The parenthetical identification of any form has reference only to the Readings, and is not necessarily an exhaustive list of all possible identifications of that form in the language.

aba 'man', aban (acc. sg.), abin (dat. sg.)
afƕapjan 'strangle', afƕapidedun (3 pl. pret. ind.)
aftra 'again'
aggilus 'angel', aggilau (dat. sg.)
ahma 'spirit'
ains 'one', ain (neut. nom. sg.)
airþa 'earth', airþa (acc. sg.), airþos (gen. sg.)
ajukduþs 'eternity', ajukduþ (acc. sg.)
akran 'fruit', akran (acc. sg.)

alls 'all', alla (fem. nom. sg.)
ana 'on'
andeis 'end'
andhafjan 'answer', andhafjands (pres. part., masc. nom. sg.)
ansts 'grace', anst (acc. sg.), anstai (dat. sg.)
anþaruþþan 'another then'
at 'at'
atgaggan 'go toward, come to', at-gaggiþ (3 sg. pres. ind.)
atta 'father' (cf. Attila 'Little Father'), attins (gen. sg.)

audahafts 'blessed, endowed', *audahafta* (fem. nom. sg.)
auk 'for, because'
auso 'ear', *ausona* (acc. pl.)

bairan 'bear', *bar* (3 sg. pret. ind.)
baurgs 'city', *baurg* (acc. sg.)
bi 'by, according to'
bigitan 'receive', *bigast* (2 sg. pret. ind.)

Daweid 'David', *Daweidis* (gen. sg.)
diups 'deep', *diupaizos* (fem. gen. sg.)
du 'to'
duginnan 'begin', *dugann* (3 sg. pret. ind.)
duþe 'so that'

ei, -ei (introduces subordinate clauses)

faginon 'rejoice', *fagino* (2 sg. imp.)
fairra 'far (from)'
faur 'beside'
filu 'much, many' (neut. nom. sg.)
fragibts 'engagement', *fragibtim* (dat. pl.)
fraitan 'eat' (used of animals), *fretun* (3 pl. pret. ind.)
fraiw 'seed', *fraiwa* (dat. sg.)
fram 'from'
frauja 'Lord', *fraujins* (gen. sg.)
fretun see *fraitan*
fugls 'bird', *fuglos* (nom. pl.)

gabairan 'bear', *gabairis* (2 sg. pres. ind.), *gabairada* (3 sg. pres. ind. pass.)
Gabriel 'Gabriel'
gadriusan 'fall', *gadraus* (3 sg. pret. ind.)
gaf see *giban*
gahausjan 'hear', *gahausjai* (3 sg. pres. subj.)
gajuko 'parable', *gajukom* (dat. pl.)
galaiþ see *galeiþan*

Galeilaia 'Galilee', *Galeilaias* (gen. sg.)
galeiþan 'go', *galaiþ* (3 sg. pret. ind.); *galeiþands* (pres. part., masc. nom. sg.), *galeiþandan* (masc. acc. sg.)
galisan 'gather', *galesun* (3 pl. pret. ind.)
ganiman 'conceive', *ganimis* (2 sg. pres. ind.)
gards 'house, family', *garda* (dat. sg.)
gasitan 'sit'
gaþaursnan 'dry up', *gaþaursnoda* (3 sg. pret. ind.)
giban 'give', *gibid* (3 sg. pres. ind.), *gaf* (3 sg. pret. ind.)
gods 'good', *goda* (fem. acc. sg.)
guþ 'God', *guþs* (gen. sg.), *guþa* (dat. sg.)

haban 'have', *habai* (3 sg. pres. subj.), *habaida* (3 sg. pret. ind.)
haitan 'call, name', *haitada* (3 sg. pres. ind. pass.), *haitais* (2 sg. pres. subj.)
hauhista 'the Highest', *hauhistins* (gen. sg.)
hausjan 'hear, listen', *hauseiþ* (2 pl. imp.), *hausjandona* (pres. part., neut. acc. pl.)

ƕaiwa 'how?'

ik 'I', *mis* (dat. sg.)
im, imma, see *is*
in 'because'
in 'in, on, into, among'
ina see *is*
inn 'inside'
ins see *is*
insandjan 'send', *insandiþs* (pret. part., masc. nom. sg.)
is 'he', *ina* (acc. sg.), *is* (gen. sg.), *imma* (dat. sg.), *ins* (acc. pl.), *im* (dat. pl.)
izai see *si*

.j. 'sixty'
jah 'and'
Iakob 'Jacob', *Iakobis* (gen. sg.)
Iesus 'Jesus', *Iesu* (acc. sg.)
Iosef 'Joseph'

kann see *kunnan*
kilþei 'womb' (cf. E. "child"), *kilþein* (acc. sg.)
kunnan 'have knowledge of, know', *kann* (1 sg. pres. ind.)

.l. 'thirty'
laiseins 'teaching', *laiseinai* (dat. sg.)
laisjan 'teach', *laisida* (3 sg. pret. ind.)

magaþs 'maiden, virgin', *magaþais* (gen. sg.), *magaþai* (dat. sg.)
mahts 'might, power'
manag, managa, see *manags*
managei 'multitude', *manageins* (gen. sg.)
manags 'much', *managa* (fem. acc. sg.), *manag* (neut. acc. sg., as adv.)
marei 'sea', *marein* (dat. sg.)
Mariam 'Mary'
menoþs 'month', *menoþ* (acc. or dat. sg.)
mikils 'great'
mis see *ik*
miþ 'with'
miþþanei 'while'

namo 'name', *namo* (acc. sg.)
Nazaraiþ 'Nazareth'
ni 'not, no'

ogan 'fear', *ogs* (2 sg. imp.)

qaþ see *qiþan*
qiman 'come', *qemun* (3 pl. pret. ind.)
qino 'woman', *qinom* (dat. pl.)
qiþan 'say, speak', *qaþ* (3 sg. pret. ind.)

.r. 'a hundred'
raihtis 'then, you see'

sa 'the, that' (masc. art. and dem. pro.), *þamma* (dat. sg.), *þai* (nom. pl.)
saei = *sa* + *-ei*
sah = *sa* + *-uh*
sai 'lo'
saian 'sow', *saiso* (3 sg. pret. ind.)
saiands 'sower'
saihsta 'sixth', *saihstin* (masc. dat. sg.)
saiso see *saian*
sei = *sa* + *-ei* or *so* + *-ei*
seins 'his', *seinai* (fem. dat. sg.), *seinamma* (neut. dat. sg.)
si 'she', *izai* (dat. sg.)
sijai see *wisan*
sik (refl. pro., acc.)
skip 'ship', *skip* (acc. sg.)
so 'the, that' (fem. art. and dem. pro.), *þizos* (gen. sg.)
stainahs 'stony', *stainahamma* (dat. sg.)
staþs 'shore', *staþa* (dat. sg.)
stols 'seat, throne', *stol* (acc. sg.)
sum 'some, one'
sunno 'sun', *sunnin* (dat. sg.)
suns 'soon'
sunus 'son', *sunu* (acc. sg.)
swaswe 'so that'

þai, þamma, see *sa*
þan 'then'
þandei 'since, given that'
þanuh = *þan* + *-uh*
þarei 'there, where'
þata 'the, that' (neut. art. and dem. pro.), *þata* (acc. sg.), *þis* (gen. sg.)
þaurnus 'thorn', *þaurnjus* (nom. pl.), *þaurnuns* (acc. pl.)
þeins 'thy, thine, your', *þeinamma* (neut. dat. sg.)
þis see *þata*

þiudanon 'rule', *þiudanoþ* (3 sg. pres. ind.)

þiudinassus 'kingdom', *þiudinassaus* (gen. sg.)

þiupjan 'bless, endow', *þiupido* (pret. part., fem. nom. sg.)

þiwi 'maiden'

þizei = *þis* + *-ei*

þizos see *so*

þu 'thou, you', *þuk* (acc. sg.), *þus* (dat. sg.)

ufar 'over'

ufarskadwjan 'overshadow', *ufarskadweid* (3 sg. pres. ind.)

ufarsteigan 'rise up over', *ufarstigun* (3 pl. pret. ind.)

ufbrinnan 'burn up', *ufbrann* (3 sg. pret. ind.)

-uh 'and' (or for emphasis)

unte 'because'

urrinnan 'go out, go up', *urrann* (3 sg. pret. ind.); *urrinnandin* (pres. part., masc. dat. sg.), *urrinnando* (neut. nom. sg.)

us 'from, out of'

wahsjan 'grow', *wahsjando* (pres. part., neut. nom. sg.)

wairþan 'happen, become', *wairþiþ* (3 sg. pres. ind.), *wairþai* (3 sg. pres. subj.), *warþ* (3 sg. pret. ind.)

was see *wisan*

waurd 'word', *waurda* (dat. sg.)

waurts 'root', *waurtins* (acc. pl.)

weihs 'holy'

wigs 'way, road', *wig* (acc. sg.)

wisan 'be', *sijai* (3 sg. pres. subj.), *was* (3 sg. pret. ind.)

wiþra 'against, next to'

Some Aspects of Gothic Grammar

In this section, and in the corresponding sections of subsequent chapters, I cannot give anything approaching a complete grammar of the language under discussion. In the first place, such a procedure would be out of place in an introductory book. In the second place, it would eventually become staggeringly redundant, since the Germanic languages share a great many features, a number of which I have noted in Chapter 2. Accordingly, in what follows I will treat phenomena that are unique to Gothic, or are shared with some, but not all, of its sister languages. Thus the phenomena considered are those that seem useful for determining the groupings and subgroupings of the Germanic family.

Spelling and Pronunciation

Consonants

Many of the correspondences of sounds and spellings in Gothic have already been treated in Chapter 2. Thus *p*, *t*, *k* are pronounced as their spelling indicates, as are *f*, *s*, *z*, *þ*, *l*, *m*, *n*, *r*, *j*. Gothic *q* is pronounced [kw], and does not necessarily precede a *u*. Gothic *b*, *d*, *g* are pronounced as the stops [b], [d], and [g] sometimes (namely at the beginnings of words and after consonants), and as the fricatives [ƀ], [ð], and [g] at other times (medially after vowels). The letters *b*, *d* are generally not found at the ends of words or before *t*, *s* (unless *b*, *d* follow consonants), being replaced in those positions by *f*, *þ*. Thus, the *b* in *bairan* 'bear' is pronounced [b], and the *d* in *diups* 'deep' is pronounced [d]. But the *b* in *giban* 'give' is pronounced [ƀ], and the *d* in *bidjan* 'ask' is pronounced [ð]. Further, the *b* of *giban* is replaced by *f* in the past tense: *gaf*. The *d* of *bidjan* is replaced by *þ* in the past tense: *baþ*.

Although one might expect *g* to act like *b*, *d*, it does not fully do so. The pronunciation as a stop [g] initially and after a consonant seems likely, as does the fricative pronunciation as [g] medially after a vowel, but the spelling *g* is also found in final position. Nonetheless, most scholars assume here a pronunciation something like [x], which would restore parallelism with *b*, *d*. Thus the *g* in *giban* is the stop [g], the *g* in *daga* ('day', dat. sg.) is the fricative [g], and the *g* in *dag* ('day', acc. sg.) is the fricative [x].

The letter *g* may have not only the sound values given above, but also at times a value like that of *ng* in Modern English *sing* (thus [ŋ]), specifically, before the letters *g* and *k* in Gothic. Thus the words *aggilus* 'angel' and *drigkan* 'drink' have pronunciations closer to their Modern English cognates than their spellings might imply. The reader should be warned, however, that not all instances of *gg* in Gothic should be read as [ŋg]. For example, in the words *triggws* 'true' and *skuggwa* 'mirror', *gg* is pronounced as a long stop consonant [gg].

The letter *h* is assumed to have two pronunciations, namely [h] at the beginnings of words (*haurn* 'horn'), but [x] elsewhere in the word (*nahts* 'night').

The letter *ƕ*, which is pronounced like *h* with concomitant lip rounding ([hʷ]), probably had the same kind of pronunciation variants as did *h*. Thus it would sound like British English *wh* in Gothic *ƕan*, but harder, as [xʷ], in *saƕ* 'saw'.

Finally, the letter *w* is in general pronounced as indicated in Chapter 2, as [w]. At the end of a word after a consonant or medially between consonants, however, it was probably pronounced like the vowel [u] (*waurstw* 'work').

Vowels

As far as their pronunciation is concerned, the simple (non-diphthongal) vowels of Gothic are generally as exemplified in Chapter 2. However, they sometimes differ markedly in their spelling. Below I indicate the values of the Gothic letters in terms of the phonetic transcriptions presented in the last chapter. We begin with the long vowels:

â	=	[â]	hâhan 'hang'
ê	=	[ê]	galêsun 'gathered'
ai	=	[e:]	saian 'sow'
ei	=	[î]	galeiþan 'go'
ô	=	[ô]	stôls 'seat, throne'
au	=	[o:]	staua 'court'
û	=	[û]	ût 'out'

It should be noted that except for *ei*, none of these vowels shows any indication of length (such as the circumflex) in the manuscripts of the language, a practice I follow in the Readings and Glossary. The circumflex I use on them here is a scholarly addition. At the end of this chapter, I will give some of the arguments for modifications of this sort. This is by no means the only modification found in the scholarly treatment of Gothic, as will be seen below.

The short vowels of Gothic are the following:

a	=	[a]	aggilus 'angel'
aí	=	[e]	baíran 'bear'
i	=	[i]	qiman 'come'
aú	=	[o]	waúrd 'word'
u	=	[u]	sunus 'son'

Again, the acute accents on *aí, aú* are scholarly diacritics, added to distinguish these vowel sounds from others that were spelled exactly the same way in the manuscripts, but are supposed to have been pronounced differently. For example, in the manuscripts the longs *ai* and *au* above are spelled identically to the short vowels.

Finally, there are three diphthongs in Gothic:

ái	=	[a] + [i]	láisjan 'teach'
áu	=	[a] + [u]	áuso 'ear'
iu	=	[i] + [u]	diups 'deep'

The acute accents on *ái, áu*, as one might expect, are not found in the manuscripts.

Phonology

This section does not discuss the sound values of Gothic letters. I take the pronunciations given above for granted, and the questions I address here have to do with the distribution of various sounds in the language, and especially how their distribution differs from that found in the other old

Germanic languages. I have by no means treated all the interesting phonological facts of Gothic, or even all the phenomena that set Gothic off
from the other dialects. Instead I have selected a few highly significant
differentiating criteria, to which I will return in every chapter.

    1. A large number of words in Gothic show a long [ê] where most of
the other languages systematically show an [â] or even an [ô]. This vowel
is assumed also to have existed in Proto-Germanic, probably with the
phonetic value of [æ̂], a lengthened version of the vowel in Modern English "bad." It is usually called $\hat{e}_1$ to distinguish it from another vowel,
called $\hat{e}_2$ ([ê]), which has few reflections in Gothic, but shows up as *ê* in
most other Germanic languages. To avoid confusion, in the rest of this
book I refer to these vowels by using letters corresponding to their presumed Proto-Germanic sound values, thus as *æ̂* and *ê* respectively. The
examples below contrast Gothic reflexes of *æ̂* with those found in Old
High German:

Goth.	OHG	
mênoþ	mânôd	'month'
qêmun	kâmun	'came' (3 pl.)

Besides the two given above, several other words in our texts contain this
vowel. It appears, for example, in *galêsun* 'gathered' and *frêtun* 'ate', as
their Modern German equivalents, *lasen* and *frassen*, indicate.

    2. The pronunciation section above depicted the short vowel system
of Gothic as having five distinct vowels. This would normally imply that
there exist words with different meanings whose only audible difference
is that between these vowels. Such is the case, for example, with Modern
English "pin," "pen," "pan," "pun." The normal implication is partly
wrong for Gothic, however, at least as far as the vowels *i* and *ai* are concerned, and similarly *u* and *au*. For the vowels in these pairs are virtually
in what linguists call *complementary distribution*. That is, in any phonetic context where one member of either pair may appear, the other
member cannot. Specifically, *ai* and *au* appear only before the consonants
h, *ƕ*, *r*, and *i* and *u* almost never appear there (there are a very few exceptions). Note the distribution of vowels in the following words:

filu	'much'	fugls	'bird'
skip	'ship'	guþ	'God'
is	'he'	sunus	'son'
baíran	'bear'	baúrgs	'city'
raíhtis	'you see'	daúhtar	'daughter'

There are two systematic exceptions to this rule. The reduplicating prefix (grammatically characterized in "Verbs," below) contains the vowel *aí* regardless of what consonant follows, and the emphatic suffix *-uh* does not show the expected form *-aúh*.

Because of this distribution rule in Gothic (which clearly represents a change from the distribution reconstructed for Proto-Germanic), numerous words show different forms in Gothic than they do in other Germanic languages. Here are a few examples:

Goth.	OHG	
niman	neman	'take'
gulþ	gold	'gold'
faíhu	fihu	'money, livestock'
baúrgs	burg	'city'

3. Some instances of *gg* in Gothic represent not [ŋg] as in English "longer," but long [gg]. These examples invariably precede the consonant *w*, and the entire sequence *ggw* represents a development from an original Proto-Germanic *ww* in the middle of words. This change, called *sharpening*, is otherwise found only in Old Norse. In addition to the sequence *ww*, sharpening affects the Proto-Germanic sequence *jj*, changing it in Gothic to *ddj*. Examples:

Goth.	OHG	
triggws	(gi)triuwi	'true'
twaddje	zweiio	'of two'

4. Despite the discussion in the last paragraph, a few instances of *ggw* in Gothic must still be interpreted as [ŋgw], for example in the words *aggwus* 'narrow' and *siggwan* 'sing'. As the Old High German equivalents *engi* and *singan* illustrate, most of the other Germanic languages have dropped the [w] in this sequence of sounds.

5. In all the Germanic languages except Gothic, original Proto-Germanic *z* has changed to *r*, by a process called *rhotacism*. Thus Gothic has *z*, or sometimes *s*, in words that show *r* in the other languages:

Goth.	OHG	
láisjan	lêren	'teach'
huzd	hort	'hoard'
wêsun	wârun	'were'

6. Alone among the Germanic languages, Gothic shows a sound sequence *þl-* at the beginnings of words, as in the word *þliuhan* 'flee'. All

the other Germanic languages show the original sequence, *fl-*, as in the
Old High German form, *fliohan*.

Nouns and Pronouns

The following facts about Gothic nouns and pronouns are of some interest, although they do not represent anything like a complete grammatical
characterization.

1. The original nominative singular ending of masculine *a*-stem
nouns in Proto-Germanic was **-az*. Of all the Germanic languages,
Gothic has remained closest to this, with its suffix *-s*: compare Goth.
dags 'day' with OHG *tag*.

2. The Gothic nominative plural of the same class has the ending
-ôs, which significantly differentiates Gothic from some, but not all, other
Germanic languages: for example, Goth. *fuglôs* 'birds' versus OHG
fogala.

3. As noted already in Chapter 2, Gothic shows a distinction in the
first and second person personal pronouns between dual and plural, not
just in the nominative case, which is illustrated below, but in the other
cases as well:

Dual	Plural
wit 'we two'	weis 'we'
*jut 'you two'	jus 'you'

4. The third person singular masculine personal pronoun in Gothic
is *is*. This form differentiates Gothic from a number of languages in
which that pronoun begins with *h-*; compare Old English *hē*.

5. Unlike some other Germanic languages, Gothic regularly distinguishes between the accusative and dative cases in first and second person
singular personal pronouns. Thus note the correspondences below (the
OE forms are those found in West Saxon prose, upon which the grammars of Old English are largely based):

	Goth.	OE	
Acc.	mik	mē	'me'
Dat.	mis	mē	'me'
Acc.	þuk	ðē	'thee'
Dat.	þus	ðē	'thee'

6. Unlike some other Germanic languages, Gothic has a reflexive pronoun, as explained in Chapter 2. The forms are *sik* (acc.), *seina* (gen.), *sis* (dat.). Correlated with this is the existence of the masculine possessive adjective *seins* 'his'.

Verbs

1. As I indicated in Chapter 2, Germanic verbs distinguish not just between strong and weak conjugations, but even between subclasses of these conjugations. The strong verb conjugation, for example, is traditionally said to have seven subclasses. Of these, the first six use some kind of vowel alternation in the root of the verb to capture tense distinctions, as in Modern English "sing" – "sang" – "sung," "ride" – "rode" – "ridden." The difference between the classes has to do with the specific vowel-alternation pattern chosen.

The seventh subclass is different, however, at least in Gothic. For here Gothic makes use of another process entirely, that of *reduplication*. A few examples will aid further discussion:

háitan	'call, name'	haíháit	(3 sg. pret. ind.)
fâhan	'catch'	faífâh	(3 sg. pret. ind.)
saian	'sow'	saísô	(3 sg. pret. ind.)
lêtan	'let'	laílôt	(3 sg. pret. ind.)

In these verbs, the past tense (preterite) is formed by repeating the first consonant (or in a few cases consonant cluster) of the root of the verb and appending after it the vowel *aí*. The resulting form attaches as a prefix to the basic root. Thus for *háit-* one takes the initial *h*, creates the form *haí-*, and prefixes it to the root to get *haíháit*. As the forms for 'sow' and 'let' above show, in some cases the vowel of the root changes also (always to *ô*).

Gothic is unique among the Germanic languages in preserving reduplication in the seventh class. In the other languages, members of this class generally show vowel-alternation patterns similar to those found in the first six classes. Thus in Old High German:

heizan	'be called'	hiaz	(3 sg. pret. ind.)
fâhan	'catch'	fiang	(3 sg. pret. ind.)
lâzan	'let'	liaz	(3 sg. pret. ind.)

On the other hand, Old High German *sâwen* 'sow' has fallen out of the strong system entirely, inflecting in that language as a weak verb (e.g., 3 sg. pret. ind. *sâta*).

2. As with the strong verbs, weak verbs in Germanic have sub-classes. Gothic is unique in having four such subclasses, and specifically in having the so-called fourth or -*nan* class. Formed in the present tense with a suffix -*n* or -*na*, in the preterite with a suffix -*nô*, these verbs are practically all derived from pure adjectives, or from preterite participles of strong verbs (as I indicated in Chapter 2, participles are also adjectives). In general, these derived verbs are characterized semantically as *inchoative*, that is, they signify the process resulting in the state the corresponding adjective describes. Thus note:

þaúrsus	'dry'	gaþaúrsnan	'become dry, wither'
fulls	'full'	usfullnan	'fill up'
*wakans	'awake'	gawaknan	'awaken'

3. Unlike most other older Germanic languages, Gothic shows the suffix -*t* as the marker of the second person singular in the preterite indicative of strong verbs. Compare *bigast* 'you received' from the verb *bigitan*, or *namt* 'you took' from the verb *niman*: Old High German, like most of the other languages, shows a suffix -*i* here, as in *nâmi* 'you took' from *neman*.

4. As I noted in Chapter 2, Gothic is unique among the Germanic languages in retaining a passive inflection for verbs, whereas the other languages must use periphrastic constructions. Two good examples from the Readings are *gabaírada* 'is born' from *baíran* 'to bear', and *háitada* 'is (will be) called' from *háitan* 'to call'.

5. In Gothic, as opposed to a number of other languages, the third person singular present indicative of the verb 'be' is *ist* with a final -*t*. Compare Old English *is*.

6. Unlike some of the other languages, Gothic distinguishes first, second, and third person endings in plural verb forms. Compare:

Goth.	OE	
baíram	berað	'we carry'
baíriþ	berað	'you carry'
baírand	berað	'they carry'

7. The verbs for 'stand' and 'go' in Gothic are *standan* and *gaggan* respectively. In some, but not all, of the other Germanic languages, we find, in addition to or instead of forms like these, *contracted* forms, such as Old High German *stân* and *gân*.

The Assignment of Sounds to Letters

In the discussion of Gothic pronunciation above, I noted that the texts do not show all the distinctions scholars make between Gothic sounds. For example, the Gothic letter sequences *au* and *ai* are frequently assigned at least three values each, while *u* and *a*, among the simple vowels, are assigned two each. Among the consonants, *b*, *d*, and *g* are usually assigned at least two readings, while *g* may have as many as four. How can this be justified?

These issues are merely part of the much wider issue of how the sound values of written symbols can be assigned at all, not only in Gothic but in all the old Germanic languages. I will attempt to address this question to some extent, although for a full discussion one must refer to the appropriate books and articles listed at the end of this chapter, and to the references found in them.

In a 1970 article on Gothic, James Marchand lists nine criteria that may be used to garner information about the pronunciation of written forms:

1. Comparison with other Germanic languages, and by extension with the proto-language;

2. The regular alternation of sounds within forms of the same word;

3. Data on the origin of the alphabet used;

4. The Gothic rendering of biblical names;

5. The spelling in Gothic of words borrowed from other languages (loanwords);

6. The spelling in other languages of loanwords from Gothic;

7. Scribal errors in the copying of manuscripts, and the scribal placement of word breaks;

8. Arguments from the linguistic structure of Gothic; and

9. The findings of universal phonetic and phonological investigations.

Marchand notes that the importance assigned to these sources is generally in the order listed, with 1 being given the most weight, and 9 least. He himself believes that only criteria 3, 4, and 8 should be given any serious attention.

Be that as it may, I will show below how each of these criteria has played some role in the scholarly treatment of Gothic. Gothic, of course, is a dead language, having produced no descendants that survive to the present. If it had survived, Marchand would have listed a tenth criterion, which plays some role in the resolution of similar issues in the other Germanic languages, namely:

10. Pronunciations found in later descendants of the language.

We will discuss these criteria one by one, then:

1. Marchand is absolutely correct when he calls this criterion the most important for much of past research. Perhaps the most obvious case is in the interpretation of the letter sequences *au* and *ai*. Each of these has three interpretations. First, they are read as the short vowels *aí* [e] and *aú* [o], essentially variants of *i* and *u* before the consonants *h*, *ƕ*, *r*. Second, they represent the diphthongs *ái* [ai] and *áu* [au]. Finally, they are interpreted as the long monophthongs *ai* [e:], *au* [o:], found only before vowels.

The etymological arguments for these assignments run as follows. Where we read short *aí* and *aú*, the related Germanic languages, and by reconstruction the proto-language, show short vowels. Thus Gothic *baíran* 'bear' corresponds to, among others, OHG *beran*, ON *bera*; Gothic *daúhtar* 'daughter' is cognate with OHG *tohter*, OE *dohtor*.

The diphthongs *ái* and *áu*, on the other hand, correspond to long vowels or diphthongs in the other languages, for which we reconstruct Proto-Germanic diphthongs: Gothic *háitan* 'call, name' corresponds to ON *heita*, OS *hêtan*, while Gothic *ráuþs* 'red' finds a parallel in ON *rauðr*, OHG *rôt*.

The long vowels *ai* and *au*, finally, are reflected in the other Germanic languages as long vowels, generally different from those that correspond to *ái* and *áu*. Note Gothic *saian*, *háitan*, opposite the distinct vowels in ON *sá* and *heita*, and Gothic *bauan* and *ráuþs* opposite ON *búa* and *rauðr*.

2. One illustration of the second source of evidence is again the word *saian* 'to sow'. For there is a clearly related word within Gothic that shows an undisputed long monophthong in the same position as the disputed *ai*, namely *sêþs* 'seed'. It seems that we have here a root *sê-*, the vowel of which becomes more open when it appears before another vowel.

A better example of the use of this criterion is provided by the interpretation of the letters *b* and *d*, however. I pointed out earlier that scholars suggest two pronunciations for these consonants, namely as the stops [b] and [d] at the beginnings of words and after consonants, and as the fricatives [ƀ] and [ð] between vowels. Now in some words that contain *b* and *d* between vowels, that *b* or *d* may, through grammatical inflection, come to stand in word-final position. When this happens, *b* is reflected as *f*, *d* as *þ*. These latter, of course, are definitely fricatives. That being the case, the argument goes, the *b* and *d* with which *f* and *þ* alternate must also be fricatives, since it is much easier to get [f] from something like [ƀ] than from hard [b], and analogously with *þ* and *d*. Examples are *gaf* 'gave' from *giban* 'give', *faúrbáuþ* 'forbade' from *faúrbiudan* 'forbid'.

One should note that the first criterion could also be applied to Gothic *giban*, since its cognates in the other Germanic languages frequently show a fricative, as even Modern English "give" illustrates. But this should not be surprising: it is not the case that each pronunciation is assigned on the basis of one single criterion. In the best case, all applicable criteria will point in the same direction.

3. The third criterion—the origin of the Gothic alphabet—obviously plays a major role in determining the pronunciation of Gothic. For example, the assignment to the letter *g* of a pronunciation [ŋ] in the Gothic sequences *gg* and *gk*, as in the words *siggwan* 'sing', *drigkan* 'drink', follows quite naturally from the similar use of the Greek letter from which Gothic *g* clearly derives. Similarly, the interpretation of the letter sequence *ei* as long [î], as in *steigan* 'climb', finds support in the fact that εɩ in the Greek of Wulfila's day had the same value.

4. If Gothic uses a different letter or letter sequence than Greek does in a biblical name, the fourth criterion comes into play. Thus the interpretation of Gothic *ai* sometimes as a short monophthong *aí* ([e]) and at other times as a long monophthong *ai* ([e:]) is in line with its use in biblical names both to capture Greek ε, as in the first and last vowels of *Aíleisabaíþ* 'Elizabeth', and to render Greek αɩ, at that time pronounced as a long monophthong; this is the case in the second syllable of *Haíbrai-us* 'Hebrew'.

5. Biblical names are, of course, one kind of loanword in Gothic. They are a bit more dependable than other kinds of loanwords because, we believe, they were all borrowed at the same time and by one man, namely Wulfila. For other loanwords we cannot be sure of the date or circumstances of the borrowing, and indeed their testimony is more equivocal. Nonetheless, it is of some interest for our speculations about the complementary distribution of *u* and *aú* in Gothic that loanwords from Latin containing short *u* in that language seem to be subject to the same rules as native vocabulary. Note the apparent lowering of the first vowel of Latin *urceus* 'jug' to the *aú* found in Gothic *aúrkeis*.

6. The same uncertainties about the circumstances of borrowing attach to arguments using loanwords from Gothic into other lan-

guages. Latin loanwords have been used as arguments both for and against the diphthongal pronunciation of *áu* in Gothic. Latin writers of around A.D. 300 write of the *Austrogoti*; those of around 400 write of the *Ostrogoti*.

7. Scribal errors in the copying of manuscripts may tell us something about the dialects of the scribes, but it is unlikely that they can tell us anything about Wulfila's language. Thus though Ostrogothic scribes occasionally spell *o* with *u* (as in *supuda* instead of *supoda* as the third singular present passive of *supôn* 'to spice'), this is likely to be an Ostrogothic phenomenon, uninformative for Wulfila's own case. This surmise is supported when one notes that Ostrogothic names in Latin sources also often show *u* for original *ô*.

8. Structural arguments about Gothic pronunciation have to do with linguistic relations between the Gothic sounds themselves. In this sense, the second criterion above is also a structural one, dealing as it does with alternations of sound in different forms of the same word. On a more abstract plane, we are applying the structural criterion of parallelism between phonetically related sounds when we propose for Gothic *g* the same pattern of sound distributions that we find for *b* and *d*, for example when we propose that *g* must have been pronounced as something like [x] in final position even though the scribes give no indication of this.

9. We may be said to apply universal phonological criteria to a particular spelling when we accept some theoretically possible phonetic interpretations of that spelling, and reject others, purely on the basis of our study of other (preferably many other) languages. In fact, of course, we are applying such criteria when, as in the eighth criterion, we assume the language has any structure at all, or when we look for parallelism between *b*, *d*, and *g*. But even the suggestion that these consonants are pronounced as stops initially and fricatives between vowels, rather than the reverse, gains support from our study of other languages of the world. The former arrangement is quite frequent—it happens, for example, in Spanish—but the latter is very rare.

10. The tenth criterion, as I noted above, cannot be applied to Gothic, which has no living descendants. It can, however, be used with texts in the other old Germanic languages. We speculate, for example, that the two instances of *c* in OE *cirice* 'church' were pronounced something like Modern English *ch* [č] precisely because we have the modern form of this word and many similar cases.

I noted earlier that Marchand downgrades the importance of all criteria except the third, fourth, and eighth. Without agreeing with him in all respects (I am less certain than he about the preeminence of biblical names, and find regular alternation of sounds more useful than he does), I can nonetheless agree with his objections to the first criterion. That a sound may once have been pronounced a certain way, or that certain distinctions between sounds may once have been made, says very little about Wulfila's Gothic. After all, we would not find persuasive an analysis of a Modern English text based on the way things were pronounced in Middle English.

The three-way split between *ái* and *áu*, *aí* and *aú*, and *ai* and *au* is easily the most troubling of these etymologically based distinctions. If such a distinct difference actually existed in contemporary Gothic, does it not seem likely that Wulfila, who otherwise did such an outstanding job of reducing the spoken language to writing, would have captured it with separate symbols? Many scholars have found this argument persuasive, and believe that there was at most a two-way distinction in *ai* and *au*, and that it was totally predictable: *ai* should be read as short [e] before consonants, and as a somewhat longer vowel of the same quality, [e:], before vowels. An analogous state of affairs holds for *au*: [o] before consonants; [o:] before vowels.

Nevertheless, there is a certain utility in making the three-way distinction when one is concerned with the comparison of Gothic with other languages, or with its development out of Proto-Germanic. After all, the suggested vowels *ái*, *aí*, and *ai* do come from three different sources, and at some time before Wulfila's day they must have been phonetically distinct. One solution to this problem, then, a solution embraced by a number of researchers, is to talk about a stage we may call Pre-Gothic, in which the distinctions we are interested in have not been neutralized. Pre-Gothic is then used in making comparisons between the various older Germanic languages, a practice I have in fact followed above.

FURTHER READING

Bennett, William H. *An Introduction to the Gothic Language.* Ann Arbor: Ullrich's, 1972.

Braune, Wilhelm, and E. A. Ebbinghaus. *Gotische Grammatik.* 18th ed. Tübingen: Niemeyer, 1981.

Marchand, James W. "Gotisch." In L. E. Schmitt, ed., *Kurzer Grundriss der germanischen Philologie bis 1500*, vol. 1, *Sprachgeschichte*, pp. 94–122. Berlin: de Gruyter, 1970.

Mierow, Charles Christopher. *The Gothic History of Jordanes.* Princeton, N.J.: Princeton University Press, 1915.

Musset, Lucien. *The Germanic Invasions: The Making of Europe, A.D. 400–600.* Trans. Edward James and Columba James. University Park, Pa.: Pennsylvania State University Press, 1975.

Owen, Francis. *The Germanic People.* New York: Bookman, 1960. [See esp. ch. 5.]

Penzl, Herbert. *Methoden der germanischen Linguistik.* Tübingen: Niemeyer, 1972.

Schwarz, Ernst. *Germanische Stammeskunde.* Heidelberg: Winter, 1956. [See esp. chs. 16, 17.]

Stearns, MacDonald, Jr. *Crimean Gothic: Analysis and Etymology of the Corpus.* Saratoga, Calif.: Anma Libri, 1978. [See esp. chs. 1, 3–6.]

Thompson, E. A. *The Visigoths in the Time of Ulfila.* Oxford: Clarendon Press, 1966.

4

OLD NORSE

A Brief History of the Norsemen

During the Age of Migrations, when many other Germanic groups were migrating from the ancestral homeland in the north, the ancestors of the speakers of Old Norse stayed close to home. There were some movements within that area, of course. The Danes moved south out of southern Sweden into Zealand and the Jutland peninsula, which after the departure of the Angles and other tribes was relatively empty. The Swedes, meanwhile, who at first were merely one of several tribal groups occupying modern Sweden, set about conquering their neighbors, the Geats, and slowly expanded their power base through central Sweden and Götland. And as reported by the *Ynglingatal*, an Old Norse genealogical poem, the royal house of Norway also originally came from Sweden to the Oslo region. It was not until late in the eighth century, however, that the rest of Europe came to hear much about these people. And when they did, the tidings brought little joy. For the northernmost Germanic peoples appeared on the world scene as vikings, professional pirates who attacked from the sea without warning and carried away any treasure they could get their hands on.

It was probably in the mid-eighth century that the vikings began their attacks and conquests in western Europe. For by the time the Norwegians attacked Ireland and England, it seems clear that they had already established bases in the Shetlands and Orkneys. Since it was the illiterate Picts that they took them from, no records of these conquests survive.

The further progress of the Norwegian vikings is better recorded. They seem to have been responsible for an exploratory raid in the south of England in 789, which resulted in the death of a sheriff, and for the

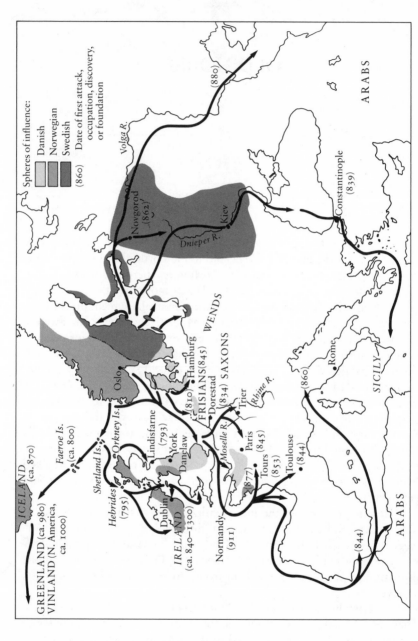

Map 3. Viking expeditions and settlements around A.D. 800–1000. (After Haugen [1976: 136], by permission)

sack of the Lindisfarne monastery in northeastern England in 793, to which the English reaction was nothing short of hysterical. In the main, however, the Norwegians concentrated on northern Scotland and the Hebrides, the Isle of Man, and the various coasts of the Irish Sea. In 836 they founded Dublin as a trading post and a military base for raids elsewhere, and Cork and Limerick also trace their origins to similar foundations. During the course of the ninth century, there arose a very distinctive Norse kingdom in Ireland, based on mixed Scandinavian and Celtic elements, which was effectively independent of any control from the Norwegian homeland. From this Irish base the Norwegian vikings carried out many of their later attacks, for example that on Muslim Spain in the mid-ninth century and the more lasting assault on northwest England in the early tenth century (Map 3).

The Danes first broke on the scene about forty years after the Norwegians, but from the outset they were more visible, primarily because the areas they attacked were far more central in the Europe of that time. Thus in 834 they attacked the important trading center of Dorestad on the Rhine in Frisia, with repeated attacks in later years. In 845 they attacked and looted Hamburg, and throughout the ninth century they were a scourge to the Low Countries and northern France especially, advancing up the Seine as far as Paris, and up the Rhine and Moselle as far as Trier.

The Danes made their most permanent impression on England, however. Although they had certainly raided off and on before that time, in the middle of the ninth century the character of their attacks on England changed. The Danes first wintered there in 851, and in 865 what the *Anglo-Saxon Chronicle* calls the "great army" arrived, with no intention of leaving soon. This host appears to have campaigned in the eastern, and especially the northeastern, part of England for the next ten years, and by 876 or 877 the kingdom of Northumbria and most of eastern Mercia was under Danish control, areas that were later to belong to the "Danelaw." In 878 the Danes briefly captured most of the last remaining Anglo-Saxon kingdom, Wessex, but Alfred the Great forced them to leave that kingdom later in the same year. They took East Anglia as a consolation prize.

The fighting between Wessex and the Danes continued for years. It achieved a respite when, in 886, the presence of the Danes in England was legitimized by a treaty between them and Alfred, which established the boundaries between the various spheres of influence in England, ceding most of the northeast to the Danes. With the advent of the Norwegians in the northwest in the early tenth century, there was very little territory left under Anglo-Saxon control.

In fact, however, the areas controlled by the Scandinavians were still largely populated by Anglo-Saxons. Furthermore, Alfred and his children were wily tacticians and politicians, setting up a series of strongholds in their own lands and then extending the chain into Danish-held lands year by year. With the defeat in 954 of Eric Blood-Axe, king of York, the boroughs of the Danelaw became part of the united kingdom of England under the kings of Wessex.

The Scandinavians were not finished with England, however. In the 980's, a large army of mixed Scandinavian nationalities under Danish kings began another series of devastating attacks both on the island kingdom and on the shores of France, attacks at least partially aimed at exacting large tributes from those kingdoms. These attacks led ultimately to an interruption of the Anglo-Saxon dynasty and the accession in 1016 of a Dane, Knut or Canute, to the throne of all England. Scandinavian hegemony lasted until 1042, not long before the Norman conquest of 1066. In a sense, of course, the Norman conquest itself could be called Scandinavian, as the name "Norman" indicates. For the duchy of Normandy was a creation of Danish vikings, perhaps under a Norwegian chief, to whom France had ceded the region in 911. By the time they took control of England, however, these descendants of the vikings were more French than Danish, though the ancestral relationship was still recognized.

The vikings were not only pirates; they were also explorers. Pushing westward far out of sight of the land, the Norwegians discovered the Faroe Islands and, in the late ninth century, Iceland. Their first settlement in Iceland is dated to 874, and by the mid-tenth century about 50,000 people were living there. Many of them were the descendants of aristocratic refugees from King Harald Fairhair, who in the period around 870 was establishing his control over all Norway, unifying that country for the first time. There was also apparently a substantial complement of Norwegians and Celts in Iceland from the Irish Sea settlements, and a number of settlers from other Norwegian colonies also.

Iceland became not a kingdom, but a kind of aristocratic republic, ruled by priest-chieftains (goðar). From 930 on, it had its own parliament (alþingi) under the chairmanship of a law-speaker. The alþingi had the authority to make law but no way of enforcing it, leaving that up to the offended individual—a situation that led to the writing of many a saga of bloody self-help.

Greenland was discovered in 981 by Eric the Red, who had been banished from Iceland for manslaughter. Having given the island an inaccurately attractive name to attract colonists, he settled there with fourteen ships full of people in 985 or 986. About the year 1000, Eric's son Leif, investigating a report of land farther to the west, discovered and explored "Vinland," which could be nothing other than some part of North America.

Although the Swedes did not participate to any great extent in the events described above, they were not inactive. If the Danes and Norwegians can be described as mercantile pirates, the Swedes are better characterized as piratical merchants. Even before the Viking Age, Swedes had established profitable trading towns on the Baltic, whence they carried out a trade in furs, cloth, spices, jewels, precious metals, and the like, with peoples as far away as Constantinople and Arabia. Their principal trading routes lay through what is now Russia, especially along the Dnieper and Volga rivers. Some have claimed that the Swedes (under the name *Rus*) are responsible for the founding of major cities such as Novgorod and Kiev, and thus for the earliest impetus toward a Russian state. Be that as it may, they clearly played an important role in this area in the ninth and tenth centuries, during the height of their trading activity.

The relationship of the Swedes with their trading partners was not always peaceful. From 860 on, Greek and Arab sources report occasional raids by vikings. Additionally, the Swedes, along with Norwegians and even Icelanders, frequently hired out as mercenaries. They formed the backbone of the Byzantine emperor's Varangian Guard in Constantinople.

Christianity came first to Denmark, where it was generally introduced by the mid-tenth century. It then arrived in Norway, being declared the state religion there in 995, and consolidating its hold in the early eleventh century. In Iceland, Christianity was declared the state religion at the alþingi in 1000. Finally, in Sweden, the new religion had real success only in the mid-twelfth century. With the conversion, the excesses of the Viking Age were moderated. And thanks to the introduction of the pen, many of that age's great successes could also now be documented.

Old Norse Texts

To devote to each Old Norse text the same amount of space I gave each Gothic text (though in some cases that is only a line) would take up the rest of the book and then some. To make the task easier, I have made two major exclusions in this section. First, since I discuss runic inscriptions in the last part of this chapter, I do not discuss them here. Second, I treat below almost exclusively Icelandic texts. This is by no means an arbitrary decision, since by far the largest and most interesting part of Old Norse literature was written in Iceland.

Even with these exclusions, I am forced to limit myself to a brief sketch, not of the major texts, but of the major types of texts we find in this language. For Old Norse is unique among the Germanic languages in the volume and richness of its literature.

1. Although not the first type to be written down, Eddic poetry probably represents the oldest preserved genre of Old Norse literature. These poems, preponderantly short, dramatic, stanzaic, and alliterative, are found primarily in a single manuscript written shortly after 1250. This is undoubtedly a copy of an older manuscript. Broadly speaking, the poems deal with two distinct but interrelated subjects: the gods and myths of Germanic heathendom, and the heroes of the Germanic Age of Migrations. Various scholars have assigned different poems to centuries ranging from the ninth to the thirteenth—from the Viking Age to the relatively settled age when the poems were actually written down. Their subject matter, of course, must be traced back to an even earlier period.

2. Related to Eddic poetry in subject, though not in style, is the *Prose Edda* of Snorri Sturluson. Written about 1220, this work has three parts. The first is a compilation of myths of the heathen world, told in prose with occasional poetic quotations. Its purpose, in Snorri's Christian time, was to give poets the necessary background to understand and use the mythological allusions so frequent in skaldic poetry (discussed below). Indeed, the second part of the work, on poetic speech, makes this goal yet more explicit, explaining a number of presumably obscure allusions and attempting something of a classification of types. The heart of the third section is one long poem written in honor of Snorri's noble benefactors, deliberately containing examples of all the skaldic meters Snorri could think of.

3. Skaldic verse was an ancient genre by the time Snorri got around to writing a textbook for it, and indeed it may not be a much later genre than Eddic poetry. But if Eddic poetry represented the cultural heritage of the general populace, skaldic poetry was definitely the province of the elite. Indeed, much skaldic poetry deals with the exploits of kings and other patrons, and was clearly meant as praise poetry. Unlike Eddic poems, skaldic poetry was episodic and descriptive, and supposedly, under the best circumstances, extemporaneous. Given its form, however, that last adjective is hard to believe. For skaldic poetry is easily among the most artificial forms of literature ever devised by human beings. It was subject to very rigid rules of meter, alliteration, and rhyme; it deviated consider-

ably from everyday syntax; and it used an extensive set of conventional words and expressions (kennings) that make it almost incomprehensible to the non-initiate.

Because its form is so strict and unmalleable, a skaldic poem would be very difficult to change in any significant way, even in oral transmission. For this reason, many writers, both in medieval Iceland and contemporary times, have considered skaldic poetry to be a better witness than most to the historicity of events and situations (assuming the original poet didn't fabricate the facts). Thus we find poems scattered throughout the prose writings of the early Icelanders, and particularly in the sagas (discussed below).

Besides the praise of benefactors, skaldic poetry had other functions, including epitaphs, love poetry, curses, and so on. From the twelfth century on, it was even used for religious purposes, for example in the celebration of saints' lives.

4. Almost from the beginning of vernacular manuscript writing in Iceland in the early twelfth century, we find a great interest in the history of that island and its inhabitants. The first notable historical work is the *Íslendingabók* (Book of the Icelanders), written around 1125 by Ari Þorgilsson, a priest. Unfortunately, we possess only a condensed version of the original work. In the extant version, Ari gives a brief history of Iceland from the first settlement to his own day, and a history of the Church in Iceland. He cites his sources very carefully, and in many cases draws from the oral testimony of contemporaries, setting an exacting standard for historical writing. Such high standards were very rare in his day, but they were to have a great influence on later Icelandic writing.

The original version of the *Íslendingabók*, Ari says, contained genealogies of Iceland's foremost families and a treatment of the lives of the Norwegian kings. Clear echoes of such writings appear in the later kings' sagas and family sagas (see below). Probably the later *Landnámabók* (Book of Settlement), which exists in a number of thirteenth- and fourteenth-century versions, is at least partly based on work done by Ari, either in the lost first edition of the *Íslendingabók* or elsewhere. The *Landnámabók* contains not only lists of the early settlers of Iceland, their landholdings, and their descendants, but also descriptions of many of the people and of significant incidents in their lives.

5. As one might expect, considering who did the first writing in Iceland, religious objectives played a significant role in Icelandic writing from the beginning. Many manuscripts are taken up with translated homilies, sermons, instructional treatises, and saints' lives. Since the date

and time of day were important in religious observances, a number of works on the calendar and astronomy have come down to us. And since reading and writing were an important means of propagation of the faith, we also have several grammatical works, one of which, the *First Grammatical Treatise*, stands up quite well even when compared with the works of modern linguists.

6. The strands of historical and religious interest came together in the second half of the twelfth century with the first of the *Konungasögur* (Kings' Sagas), which deal with the two Norwegian kings Olaf Tryggvason and St. Olaf Haraldsson. Similarly, the lives of two Icelandic bishops possessed of saintly qualities were put down in sagas, as were the lives of other slightly less holy but equally pious early clerics of Iceland.

Although the word *saga* etymologically means 'something said', it should be made clear from the start that a saga in the Icelandic tradition is a piece of prose literature, a deliberate composition by a particular author. While sagas may also have been meant to inform, their purpose was generally to entertain the reader, and in their later form this was clearly the main purpose. And while an individual saga may be based upon some core of oral tradition, the saga as a type is a written form par excellence.

The earliest religious sagas were followed very quickly by others dealing with less churchly topics. Other Norwegian kings were treated in kings' sagas, which reached their high point about 1230 in the *Heimskringla* (Globe of the World) by Snorri Sturluson. Yet another type of saga, perhaps closer to the typical Icelander's heart, dealt with the doings of the first settlers in Iceland during the period up to about 1030. Filled with tales of litigation, bloody feuds, and vindicated honor, these "family sagas" provide an alien but gripping experience for modern readers, and alone would assure the place of Old Norse in the pantheon of world literature.

More contemporary doings were the subject of *Sturlunga saga*, actually a collection of sagas dealing with events of the late twelfth and thirteenth centuries, and named after Snorri's family, the Sturlungs. Not surprisingly, these do not differ a great deal in style or subject matter from the family sagas, although they frequently have a great deal more detail. After all, essentially the same people were writing both types of sagas, and they clearly did not think human nature had changed a great deal in the intervening centuries.

Yet another type was the "legendary sagas," dealing with the Viking Age and even earlier periods. These usually made little pretense of historical authenticity; they were composed purely to entertain. The incidence of magic and monstrous creatures in them is correspondingly high.

7. Besides the indigenous literature, from the thirteenth century on there were genres in Iceland clearly influenced by literary developments on the Continent. Thus we find ballads, sagas of chivalry like *Tristrams saga* and *Ívents saga*, and other types, which herald the end of the classical period of Old Norse literature.

Readings

Parable of the Sower and the Seed

(Matt. 13.3–8)

Hinn er sá vill sæði sínu, þá ferr hann út. Ok meðan hann er á veginum, þá fellr sumt niðr í hjá veginum, ok koma fuglar at ok eta þat. En sumt fellr í þurra jǫrð ok grjótuga, en með því at þar var grunnlendi ok engi vǫkvi, þá rann skjótt upp, ok þornaði þá þegar af sólar ofhita. Sumt rann upp í millum klungra ok hagþyrna, ok af þeirra hvassleika þá fellr þat brátt niðr til jarðar ok fyrirfersk. En sumt kom í góða jǫrð ok varð at ávǫxti hundrað hlutum meira en hann sáði.

sow, will, seed, *sein*, fares, out, *auch*
is, on, way, *da*, falls, some, nether, in
come, *Vogel*, at, eat, that
dürr, earth, grit
there, *war* ('was'), land
ran, up, of
Sol, heat, middle
hawthorn
nether, till, earth
came, good, *ward*, wax, hundred
more, sowed

Thor and the Giant Skrymir

(from Snorri's *Edda*)

Þá mælti Skrýmir til Þórs at hann vill leggjask niðr at sofa, "en þér takið nestbaggann ok búið til náttverðar yðr." Því næst sofnar Skrýmir ok hraut fast, en Þórr tók nestbaggann ok skal leysa. En svá er at segja sem ótrúligt mun þykkja, at engan knút fekk hann leyst, ok engan álarendann hreyft svá at þá væri lausari en áðr. Ok er hann sér at þetta verk má eigi nýtask, þá varð hann reiðr, greip þá hamarinn Mjǫllni tveim hǫndum ok steig fram ǫðrum fœti at, þar er Skrýmir lá, ok lýstr í hǫfuð honum; en Skrýmir vaknar ok spyrr hvárt laufsblað nǫkkut felli í hǫfuð honum, eða hvárt þeir hefði þá matazk ok sé

lay
take, bag
bauen, night, next
fast, took
shall, loosen, so, say, un-, *trauen*
think, knot, *fing*
loose, end
were, looser, see(s), that
work, may, *nützen*, wroth, gripped
hammer, two, hand(s), *stieg*
from, other, foot, lay
head, him, waken(s)
spüren, leafblade, fell
they, had, *sei(en)*

búnir til rekkna. Þórr segir at þeir munu þá says
sofa ganga. Ganga þau þá undir aðra eik. Er [Scots] gang ('go'), under, other, oak
þat þér satt at segja, at ekki var þá óttalaust dir, sooth, -less
at sofa. En at miðri nótt, þá heyrir Þórr at mid, night, hear(s)
Skrýmir hrýtr svá at dunar í skóginum. Þá din
stendr hann upp ok gengr til hans, reiðir stand(s)
hamarinn títt ok hart ok lýstr ofan í miðjan hard, (von) oben
hvirfil honum; hann kennir at hamarsmuð- ken(s), mouth
rinn søkkr djúpt í hǫfuðit. En í því bili sink(s), deep
vaknar Skrýmir ok mælti: "Hvat er nú? Fell what, now, fell
akarn nǫkkut í hǫfuð mér? Eða hvat er títt acorn, me, (be)tide
um þik, Þórr?" En Þórr gekk aptr skyndiliga dich, ging, after
ok svarar at hann var þá nývaknaðr, sagði at (an)swer, new, wakened, said
þá var mið nótt ok enn væri mál at sofa. Þá mid, were, Mal
hugsaði Þórr þat, ef hann kvæmi svá í fœri that, if, came
at slá hann it þriðja hǫgg, at aldri skyldi hann slay, third, hew, should
sjá sik síðan; liggr nú ok gætir ef Skrýmir see, sich, seit(dem), lies
sofnaði fast. Ok litlu fyrir dagan þá heyrir little, (be)fore, day
hann at Skrýmir mun sofnat hafa; stendr þá have
upp ok hleypr at honum, reiðir þá hamarinn lope(s)
af ǫllu afli ok lýstr á þunnvangann þann er all, thin, Wange
upp vissi; søkkr þá hamarrinn upp at skapt- shaft
inu. En Skrýmir settisk upp ok strauk of set, stroke(d)
vangann ok mælti: "Hvárt munu fuglar nǫk- Vogel
kurir sitja í trénu yfir mér? Mik grunaði, er sit, tree, over, me, mich
ek vaknaða, at tros nǫkkut af kvistunum felli
í hǫfuð mér. Hvárt vakir þú, Þórr? Mál mun wake, thou
vera upp at standa ok klæðask. En ekki eigu stand, clothe
þér nú langa leið fram til borgarinnar er long, Burg
kǫlluð er Útgarðr." called

GLOSSARY

In alphabetizing Old Norse, ð follows d, and þ, æ, ǫ, ø, and œ follow z. Unless specified otherwise, nouns and pronouns are nominative singular, adjectives are masculine nominative singular, and verbs are infinitives. The parenthetical identification of any form has reference only to the Readings, and is not necessarily an exhaustive list of all possible identifications of that form in the language.

á 'on, at, to'
áðr 'before'
aðra see annarr
af 'from, with'

afl 'strength', afli (dat. sg.)
akarn 'acorn'
álarendi 'strap-end', álarenda (acc. sg.); álarendann = álarenda + -inn

aldri 'never'
allr 'all', *ǫllu* (neut. dat. sg.)
annarr 'other, another, second, one (of
two)', *ǫðrum* (masc. dat. sg.), *aðra*
(fem. acc. sg.)
aptr 'back'
at 'to, at'
at 'that' (conj.)
ávǫxtr 'yield', *ávǫxti* (dat. sg.)

bil 'moment', *bili* (dat. sg.)
borg 'fortress', *borgar* (gen. sg.);
borgarinnar = *borgar* + *-innar*
(see *in*)
brátt 'soon'
búa 'prepare', *búið* (2 pl. pres. ind.);
búnir 'ready' (pret. part., masc.
nom. pl.)

dagan 'dawn', *dagan* (acc. sg.)
djúpr 'deep', *djúpt* (neut. nom. sg.)
duna 'resound', *dunar* (3 sg. pres. ind.)

eða 'or'
ef 'if'
eiga 'have', *eiguð* (2 pl. pres. ind.);
eigu þér = *eiguð þér* (see *þú*)
eigi 'not'
eigu, eiguð, see *eiga*
eik 'oak', *eik* (acc. sg.)
ek 'I', *mik* (acc. sg.), *mér* (dat. sg.)
ekki 'not'
en 'and, but'
en 'than' (in comparisons)
engi 'no' (adj.), *engan* (masc. acc. sg.)
enn 'still'
er (rel. particle)
er see *vera*
er 'when'
eta 'eat', *eta* (3 pl. pres. ind.)

fá 'get', *fekk* (3 sg. pret. ind.)
falla 'fall', *fellr* (3 sg. pres. ind.), *fell*
(3 sg. pret. ind.), *felli* (3 sg. pret.
subj.)

fara 'go', *ferr* (3 sg. pres. ind.)
fast 'hard, fast'
fekk see *fá*
fell, felli, fellr, see *falla*
ferr see *fara*
fótr 'foot, side', *fœti* (dat. sg.)
fram 'forward'
fugl 'bird', *fuglar* (nom. pl.)
fyrir 'before'
fyrirfarask 'perish', *fyrirfersk* (3 sg.
pres. ind.)
fœri 'opportunity', *fœri* (acc. sg.)
fœti see *fótr*

ganga 'go', *gengr* (3 sg. pres. ind.),
ganga (3 pl. pres. ind.), *gekk* (3 sg.
pret. ind.)
góðr 'good', *góða* (fem. acc. sg.)
grípa 'grip', *greip* (3 sg. pret. ind.)
grjótugr 'stony', *grjótuga* (fem.
acc. sg.)
gruna 'suspect', *grunaði* (3 sg. pret.
ind.)
grunnlendi 'shallow soil'
gæta 'watch', *gætir* (3 sg. pres. ind.)

hafa 'have', *hefði* (3 pl. pret. subj.)
hagþyrnir 'hawthorn', *hagþyrna*
(gen. pl.)
hamarr 'hammer', *hamar* (acc. sg.);
hamarinn = *hamar* + *-inn, hamarrinn* = *hamarr* + *-inn*
hamarsmuðr 'end of hammerhead';
hamarsmuðrinn = *hamarsmuðr* +
-inn
hann 'he', *hann* (acc. sg.), *hans*
(gen. sg.), *honum* (dat. sg.), *þeir*
(nom. pl.)
hart 'hard'
hefði see *hafa*
heyra 'hear', *heyrir* (3 sg. pres. ind.)
hinn 'that one, the one' (masc. dem.
pro.)
hjá 'next to'

hlaupa 'run, leap', *hleypr* (3 sg. pres. ind.)

hlutr 'part', *hlutum* (dat. pl.)

honum see *hann*

hraut see *hrjóta*

hreyfa 'move', *hreyft* (pret. part.)

hrjóta 'snore', *hrýtr* (3 sg. pres. ind.), *hraut* (3 sg. pret. ind.)

hugsa 'consider', *hugsaði* (3 sg. pret. ind.)

hundrað 'hundred'

hvárt 'whether' (also introduces direct questions)

hvassleiki 'sharpness', *hvassleika* (dat. sg.)

hvat 'what?' (neut. interr. pro.)

hvirfill 'crown of the head', *hvirfil* (acc. sg.)

hǫfuð 'head', *hǫfuð* (acc. sg.); *hǫfuðit* = *hǫfuð* + *-it*

hǫgg 'blow', *hǫgg* (acc. sg.)

hǫnd 'hand', *hǫndum* (dat. pl.)

í 'in, on, into'; *í millum* 'in the middle of'

in 'the' (fem. art.), *-innar*, *-nnar* (gen. sg., suffixed to its noun)

inn 'the' (masc. art.), *-inn*, *-nn* (nom. sg., suffixed to its noun), *-inum*, *-num* (dat. sg. and pl.)

it 'the' (neut. art.), *it* (acc. sg.), *-it*, *-t* (acc. sg., suffixed to its noun), *-inu*, *-nu* (dat. sg.)

jǫrð 'earth', *jǫrð* (acc. sg.), *jarðar* (gen. sg.)

kalla 'call', *kǫlluð* (pret. part.)

kenna 'perceive, see', *kennir* (3 sg. pres. ind.)

klungr 'thorn bush', *klungra* (gen. pl.)

klæðask 'get dressed'

knútr 'knot', *knút* (acc. sg.)

koma 'come', *koma* (3 pl. pres. ind.), *kom* (3 sg. pret. ind.), *kvæmi* (3 sg. pret. subj.)

kvistr 'branch', *kvistum* (dat. pl.); *kvistunum* = *kvistum* + *-inum* (see *inn*)

kvæmi see *koma*

kǫlluð see *kalla*

lá see *liggja*

langr 'long', *langa* (fem. acc. sg.)

laufsblað 'leaf'

lauss 'loose', *lausari* (comp., masc. nom. sg.)

leggjask 'lie down'

leið 'journey', *leið* (acc. sg.)

leysa 'untie', *leyst* (pret. part.)

liggja 'lie', *liggr* (3 sg. pres. ind.), *lá* (3 sg. pret. ind.)

litlu 'a little'

ljósta 'strike', *lýstr* (3 sg. pres. ind.)

má see *mega*

mál 'time'

matask 'eat', *matazk* (pret. part.)

með því at 'because'

meðan 'while'

mega 'be able, can', *má* (3 sg. pres. ind.)

meira 'more'

mér see *ek*

miðr 'mid, the middle of', *miðjan* (masc. acc. sg.), *mið* (fem. nom. sg.), *miðri* (fem. dat. sg.)

mik see *ek*

millum see *í*

Mjǫllnir (name of Thor's hammer), *Mjǫllni* (acc. sg.)

munu 'will, must, may', *mun* (3 sg. pres. ind.), *munu* (3 pl. pres. ind.)

mæla 'speak', *mælti* (3 sg. pret. ind.)

náttverðr 'dinner', *náttverðar* (gen. sg.)

nestbaggi 'supplies bag', *nestbagga* (acc. sg.); *nestbaggann* = *nestbagga* + *-inn*

niðr 'down'

nótt 'night', *nótt* (dat. sg.)

nú 'now'

nýtask 'be of use'

nývaknaðr 'newly woke'

næst see *því næst*

nǫkkurr 'a, any, some', *nǫkkut* (neut. nom. sg.), *nǫkkurir* (masc. nom. pl.)

of 'over'

ofan 'from above'

ofhiti 'over-warmth', *ofhita* (dat. sg.)

ok 'and'

ótrúligr 'unbelievable', *ótrúligt* (neut. nom. sg.)

óttalauss 'fearless', *óttalaust* (neut. nom. sg.)

rann see *renna*

reiða 'swing', *reiðir* (3 sg. pres. ind.)

reiðr 'angry'

rekkja 'bed', *rekkna* (gen. pl.)

renna 'run', *rann* (3 sg. pret. ind.)

sá 'that, he' (masc. dem. pro.), *þann* (acc. sg.)

sá 'sow', *sáði* (3 sg. pret. ind.)

saðr 'true', *satt* (neut. nom. sg.)

sagði see *segja*

satt see *saðr*

sé see *vera*

segja 'say', *segir* (3 sg. pres. ind.), *sagði* (3 sg. pret. ind.)

sem 'as'

sér see *sjá*

setjask 'set', *settisk* (3 sg. pret. ind.); *setjask upp* 'sit up'

síðan 'afterwards'

sik (refl. pro., acc. sg.)

sinn 'his', *sínu* (neut. dat. sg.)

sitja 'sit'

sjá 'see', *sér* (3 sg. pres. ind.)

skal see *skulu*

skapt 'handle', *skapti* (dat. sg.); *skaptinu = skapti + -inu* (see *it*)

skjótt 'quickly'

skógr 'wood(s)', *skógi* (dat. sg.); *skóginum = skógi + -inum* (see *inn*)

Skrýmir (name of a giant, Thor's enemy)

skulu 'shall', *skal* (3 sg. pres. ind.), *skyldi* (3 sg. pret. subj.)

skyndiliga 'quickly'

slá 'hit'

sofa 'sleep' (v.)

sofna 'go to sleep', *sofnar* (3 sg. pres. ind.), *sofnaði* (3 sg. pret. subj.), *sofnat* (pret. part.)

sól 'sun', *sólar* (gen. sg.)

spyrja 'ask', *spyrr* (3 sg. pres. ind.)

standa 'stand', *stendr* (3 sg. pres. ind.)

stíga 'walk', *steig* (3 sg. pret. ind.)

strjúka 'stroke', *strauk* (3 sg. pret. ind.)

sumr 'some, one', *sumt* (neut. nom. sg.)

svá 'so, thus'

svara 'answer', *svarar* (3 sg. pres. ind.)

sæði 'seed', *sæði* (dat. sg.)

søkkva 'sink', *søkkr* (3 sg. pres. ind.)

taka 'take', *takið* (2 pl. pres. ind.), *tók* (3 sg. pret. ind.)

til 'to, for' (also adverbial particle appearing with verbs)

títt 'quickly'

títt 'the matter, going on'

tók see *taka*

tré 'tree', *tré* (dat. sg.); *trénu = tré + -inu* (see *it*)

tros 'droppings'

tveir 'two' (masc.), *tveim* (dat.)

um 'concerning, with'

undir 'under'

upp 'up'

út 'out'

Útgarðr 'Utgard' (a home of giants)

vaka 'be awake', *vakir* (2 sg. pres. ind.)

vakna 'wake up', *vaknar* (3 sg. pres. ind.), *vaknaða* (1 sg. pret. ind.)

vangi 'cheek', *vanga* (acc. sg.); *vangann* = *vanga* + *-inn*

var see *vera*

varð see *verða*

vegr 'way', *vegi* (dat. sg.); *veginum* = *vegi* + *-inum* (see *inn*)

vera 'be', *er* (3 sg. pres. ind.), *sé* (3 pl. pres. subj.), *var* (3 sg. pret. ind.), *væri* (3 sg. pret. subj.)

verða 'become', *varð* (3 sg. pret. ind.)

verk 'work'

vilja 'want, intend', *vill* (3 sg. pres. ind.)

vita 'be turned', *vissi* (3 sg. pret. ind.)

væri see *vera*

vǫkvi 'moisture'

yðr see *þú*

yfir 'over'

þá 'then'

þann see *sá* (pro.)

þar 'there'

þat 'it', *þat* (acc. sg.), *því* (dat. sg.), *þau* (nom. pl.; also used for groups of both sexes)

þegar 'immediately'

þeir see *hann*

þeirra 'their' (all cases)

þér see *þú*

þetta 'that' (neut. dem. pro.)

þik see *þú*

þorna 'dry up', *þornaði* (3 sg. pret. ind.)

Þórr 'Thor', *Þórs* (gen. sg.)

þriði 'third', *þriðja* (neut. acc. sg.)

þú 'you', *þik* (acc. sg.), *þér* (dat. sg.; nom. pl.), *yðr* (dat. pl.)

þunnvangi 'temple', *þunnvanga* (acc. sg.); *þunnvangann* = *þunnvanga* + *-inn*

þurr 'dry', *þurra* (fem. acc. sg.)

því see *þat*

því næst 'next'

þykkja 'seem, appear'

ǫðrum see *annarr*

ǫllu see *allr*

Some Aspects of Old Norse Grammar

Spelling and Pronunciation

Consonants

Although the spellings of Old Norse are generally like those discussed in Chapter 2, there are also quite a few surprises. Indeed, it seems that for Old Norse, as we understand it, the majority of consonant symbols have more than one value.

The letters *p*, *t*, *k* are in general pronounced as in Chapter 2, thus:

> *grípa* 'grip' has the consonant [p]
> *tré* 'tree' has the consonant [t]
> *kalla* 'call' has the consonant [k]

However, except for *t*, each of these letters has other pronunciations as well. Thus *p* is pronounced more like [f] when it is followed by *t* or *s*: *skapt* 'handle' is pronounced as if it were *skaft*.

Similarly, before any of the front vowels (long and short *i*, *e*, *y*, *ø*, long *œ* and *æ*), but especially before *i* and its consonantal counterpart *j*, *k* was pronounced with a distinct palatalization, as [kʲ]: *kenna* is pronounced like *kjenna*.

Old Norse *b* and *d*, fortunately, are relatively problem-free:

> *búa* 'prepare' begins with [b]
> *dagan* 'dawn' begins with [d]

The spelling *g*, however, is a bit more complex. Initially, after the nasal consonant *n*, and when doubled, it is pronounced [g], except when, like *k*, it is palatalized before a front vowel or *j* to [gʲ]:

> *góðr* 'good' begins with [g]
> *langa* 'long' contains the sequence [ŋg]
>
> *baggi* is pronounced as if it were *baggji*

Between vowels, *g* is pronounced as a fricative [ɣ]. As in Gothic, this is approximately the sound in German *ach* [x], with simultaneous vibration (*voicing*) of the vocal cords: *dagan* 'dawn' has [ɣ]. This fricative in turn may be palatalized before front vowels and *j*, yielding something that approaches [j] itself, except that it is accompanied by more turbulence in the mouth: *segja* 'say'.

Before *s* or *t*, *g* may be pronounced either as [k] when it follows *n* or another *g*, or as [x] when it follows a vowel:

> *langs* (masc. gen. sg. of *langr*) like *lanks*
> *dags* (gen. sg. of *dagr* 'day') with [x]

The fricatives *f*, *þ*, and *ð* are subject to an interesting rule in Old Norse. They appear as voiceless [f] and [þ] at the beginnings of words or in combination with another voiceless consonant, but as voiced [v] and [ð] otherwise. In the case of [þ] and [ð] the distinction in the symbols makes this clear:

> *þat* 'that', *þykkja* 'seem', but never *ðat*, *ðykkja*
> *saðr* 'true', *jǫrð* 'earth', but never *sapr*, *jǫrþ*

In the case of *f* the orthography does not show the distinction, but we are quite sure that it existed phonetically, thus:

> *fara* 'go' with [f]
> *hafa* 'have', *af* 'from' with [v]

In Old Norse, *h* is generally pronounced [h], but before *v* it was apparently harder, more like [x]:

> *hart* 'hard' with [h]
> *hvass* 'sharp' with something like [xw]

Unlike *f* and *þ*, *s* apparently was always voiceless: *s* in both *sofa* 'sleep' and *leysa* 'untie' is [s].

The consonants *m*, *n*, *l*, and *r* were pronounced in two ways. First, they might have voicing, as in English or German:

> *miðr* 'mid' with [m]
> *nǫtt* 'night' with [n]
> *langr* 'long' with [l]
> *fara* 'go' with [r]

But when clustered with one of the voiceless stops *p*, *t*, *k* or with *h* they often lacked voicing. These sounds are difficult for English speakers to produce. Try to whisper just these sounds plus the accompanying stops without whispering the vowels:

> *vakna* 'wake up' has voiceless [n]
> *hlaupa* 'run' has voiceless [l]
> *fótr* 'foot' has voiceless [r]

Old Norse *n*, as in other Germanic languages, is pronounced as [ŋ] before *g* or *k*: *langa* 'long' has [ŋg].

The consonant *v* was earlier something like the [w] of English "water," but during the history of Old Norse it moved first to [ƀ] (a *v* made with both lips), then to something like Modern English [v], at which point it fell together in pronunciation with Old Norse *f* (also, not incidentally, destroying the mutually exclusive distribution of voiced and voiceless *f*):

> *vera* 'be' ultimately with [v]
> *hǫggva* 'strike' also ultimately with [v]

The consonant *j* was pronounced [j]: *jǫrð* 'earth'.

Vowels

Old Norse possessed all the basic vowels introduced in Chapter 2, both long and short. Thus the five basic short vowels [i], [e], [a], [o], [u] all exist in this language, and are spelled with those very symbols:

> sitja 'sit'   duna 'resound'
> eta 'eat'   sofa 'sleep'
>   falla 'fall'

The five basic long vowels also exist, spelled in normalized texts with an acute accent rather than a circumflex:

> grípa 'grip'   búa 'prepare'
> tré 'tree'   hrjóta 'snore'
>   sjá 'see'

In addition to these simple vowels, and for reasons I will discuss below, Old Norse also possessed a number of vowels that have not been covered so far. These are called the *umlaut vowels*, both long and short. Among the shorts we have:

y, pronounced like *i* with lip rounding, phonetically [ü]: *þykkja* 'seem'
ø, pronounced like *e* with lip rounding, [ö]: *søkkva* 'sink'
ǫ, pronounced like *a* with lip rounding, [å]: *hǫnd* 'hand'

The longs are as follows:

ý, pronounced like *í* with lip rounding, [ǖ]: *nýtask* 'be of use'
œ, pronounced like *é* with lip rounding, [ȫ]: *fœri* 'opportunity'
æ, pronounced like the *a* of E. "man," but long, [ǣ]: *sæði* 'seed'

In addition, Old Norse has three diphthongs that are commonly cited (others are also mentioned, depending on one's definition of a diphthong):

au = ǫ + u: hlaupa 'run'
ei = e + i: eiga 'have'
ey = e + y: leysa 'untie'

Phonology

1. It may be recalled that the vowel *ê* in Gothic derived in most cases from Proto-Germanic *ǣ*, that is, *ê₁*, and usually corresponds with *â* or its equivalents in the other Germanic languages. For example, its cognate is *á* in Old Norse. Compare:

ON	Goth.	
sá	saian (from *sǣan)	'sow'
láta	lêtan	'let, put'
váru	wêsun	'they were'

2. In Gothic, there was a rule that certain short vowels appeared only before certain consonants, while other vowels never appeared in those positions. We ascribe this rule to a historical process whereby the consonants in question affected the articulation of vowels preceding them, making them more open, thus opening original [u] to [o], in Gothic *aú*, or [i] to [e], in Gothic *aí*.

In Old Norse, there is little sign of this consonantal conditioning of vowels. As if to make up for the lack, however, Old Norse has a highly visible process, called *umlaut*, whereby the quality of a vowel is influenced by the vowel or semivowel of the next syllable. Specifically, if the next syllable contained one of the vowels *i*, *u*, or *a*, whether long or short, or one of the semivowels *j* or *w* (ON *v*), the quality of the anterior vowel changed to become closer in quality to that of the following vowel.

Three varieties of umlaut in Old Norse are commonly distinguished:

a. Probably the oldest of these processes, *a*-umlaut lowered *i* to *e* and *u* to *o* before low vowels, most prominently *a*. Though the process is quite obscure by the time of the first written manuscripts, it still is reflected in a few word alternations, for example *niðr* 'down' – *neðan* 'from below'.

b. Another process, more clearly reflected in the texts, is *i*-umlaut. Probably as the oldest part of this process, *e* went to *i* before *i* or *j* in the next syllable, as the alternation between *meðal* 'between' and *miðja* 'middle' shows. By the era of our texts, however, the process has gone much farther, to the point where all the back vowels—short and long *a*, *o*, and *u*, the diphthongs *au* and *jú*, plus *ǫ*, itself the result of *u*-umlaut—were drawn towards the front articulatory position of the umlauting *i* and *j*:

> *u* and *û* became [ü] (spelled *y*) and [û̃] (spelled *ý*) respectively
> *o* and *ô* became [ö] (spelled *ø*) and [ỗ] (spelled *œ*) respectively
> *a* and *â* became [e] and [æ̂] (spelled *æ*) respectively
> *au* became [eü] (spelled *ey*)
> *jú*, itself derived from *iu* and *eu*, became [û̃] (spelled *ý*)
> *ǫ* became [ö] (spelled *ø*)

Besides resulting in a great number of forms that look quite different from their Gothic cognates, as in *þykkja* 'seem' opposite Goth. *þungkjan*, or *leggja* 'lay' opposite Goth. *lagjan*, umlaut also caused widespread alternations in the paradigmatic forms of many words, as is apparent in the Readings. Thus *hlaupa* 'run' has the third singular present indicative *hleypr*, which formerly had an *i* in the suffix; *fótr* 'foot' has the dative singular *fœti*; *hafa* 'have' has the third plural preterite subjunctive *hefði*, and so on.

c. The third process is *u*-umlaut. By this process, vowels that had no lip-rounding took on such rounding before a *u* or *v* in the following syllable. Only short vowels appear to have participated significantly:

> *i* became [ü] (spelled *y*)
> *e* became [ö] (spelled *ø*)
> *a* became [å] (spelled *ǫ*)

Again this leads to differences from Gothic (and in fact most of the other Germanic languages): *hǫnd* 'hand' opposite Goth. *handus*, OHG *hand*; *syngva* 'sing' opposite Goth. *siggwan*, OHG *singan*. In addition, this process too leads to alternations in the paradigms of Old Norse: neuter dative singular *ǫllu* opposite *allr* 'all', *jǫrð* 'earth' opposite genitive singular *jarðar*; in the latter case, *u* had earlier appeared in the nominative ending.

As may already be apparent from some of the examples, the workings of umlaut are not as clear in the Old Norse manuscripts as the consonantal conditioning is in Gothic. There are a number of reasons for this; most of them relate to the length of time between the original operation of the rules and the date of the first texts:

i. In some cases the vowel or semivowel that caused the umlaut has been lost. For example, the vowel of ON *horn* 'horn' actually derives from a *u* appearing in a syllable before an *a*, something like **hurna*, but the *a* has since disappeared.

ii. In other cases vowels that did *not* historically cause umlaut, say *e* or *o*, have themselves changed so that they look as if they should have. Thus the dative singular form *nagli* appears to be an exception to the rule that *a* changed to *e* before *i*, until one finds that the *i* in question used to be an *e*.

iii. In some cases where the operation of umlaut caused alternation between vowels in different forms of a word, the alternation was wiped out by *analogy*. That is, the alternating vowels gave way to one vowel in all forms; the vowel chosen could be either the umlauted or the non-umlauted variant. Thus the vowel of *verðr* 'you, he becomes' seems like an exception to umlaut, since the suffix *-r* used to contain an *i*. But the expected form *virðr* does not appear because of analogy to the other forms of the present tense, including the infinitive *verða*, which all show an *e*.

3. It may be remembered that a historical process in Gothic sharpened original medial *jj* and *ww* to *ddj* and *ggw* respectively. A very similar process took place in Old Norse, the main difference being that *jj* and *ww* here both become *gg* clusters, with *j* and *v* respectively:

ON	OHG	
tveggja	zweiio	'of two'
hǫggva	houwan	'strike'

4. Like Gothic, Old Norse preserves the *w* of the consonant cluster *ngw*, whereas most of the other Germanic languages get rid of it; Norse has only changed it to a *v*: ON *syngva* 'sing' opposite OHG *singan*.

5. Unlike Gothic, Old Norse has changed original Proto-Germanic *z* to *r*, by way of an intermediate sound symbolized *ʀ* (I discuss this be-

low in the section on runes, since these preserve a letter for *R* as a distinct sound):

ON	Goth.	
meira	maiza	'more'
váru	wesun	'were'
dýr	dius	'animal'

6. As in all the other Germanic languages except Gothic, original initial *fl-* is found as such in Old Norse; compare Gothic *þl-*, ON *flýja* 'flee' opposite Goth. *þliuhan*.

7. After short vowels, the consonants *g* and *k* were doubled, or *geminated*, before *j* and, sometimes, before *w*. Compare the Old Norse forms below with their Gothic equivalents:

ON	Goth.	
leggja	lagjan	'lay'
hyggja	hugjan	'think'

8. In Old Norse the consonant *n* is dropped before *s*. Compare:

ON	OHG	
oss	uns	'us'
gás	gans	'goose'

9. Old Norse has a number of "assimilatory" phenomena (wherein one sound becomes like or identical to an adjacent sound) shared as a group by no other Germanic language. A sample is given below:

[ht] becomes [tt]:	ON *þótti*	Goth. *þúhta*	'seemed'
[nþ] becomes [nn]:	ON *finna*	Goth. *finþan*	'find'
[ŋk] becomes [kk]:	ON *drekka*	OE *drincan*	'drink'
[lþ] becomes [ll]:	ON *gull*	Goth. *gulþ*	'gold'

Nouns and Pronouns

1. The ending **-az* of Proto-Germanic, used in the nominative singular both of masculine *a*-stem nouns and of most strong masculine adjectives, has been preserved in Old Norse as *-r*, by way of runic *-aR*:

ON	Goth.	OHG	
armr	arms	arm	'arm'
góðr	góþs	guot	'good'

2. The nominative plural of the same masculine *a*-stems (but not of the adjectives) is expressed by means of the suffix *-ar*:

ON	Goth.	OHG	
armar	armôs	arma	'arms'
fuglar	fuglôs	fogala	'birds'

3. The definite article of Old Norse (corresponding semantically to Modern English "the") stands out in two ways:

a. It has a different historical source from that found in the other languages: compare ON *inn* (masc.), *in* (fem.), *it* (neut.), with Goth. *sa, so, þata,* and OHG *der, diu, daz.*

b. It is regularly added to the ends of nouns as a suffix: compare ON *hamarrinn* with OHG *der hamar.*

4. Like Gothic, Old Norse shows a distinction between dual and plural in the first and second person personal pronouns:

> *vit* 'we two' but *vér* 'we'
> *it* 'you two' but *ér* 'you' (pl.)

5. In the masculine and feminine third person personal pronouns, Old Norse shows forms beginning in *h-*, unlike several of the other languages, including Gothic:

ON	Goth.	
hann	is	'he'
honum	imma	'him' (dat. sg.)
hon	si	'she'
hennar	izôs	'her' (gen. sg.)

6. Like Gothic, but unlike a number of the other languages, Old Norse normally shows a distinction between accusative and dative in the first and second person singular personal pronouns:

	ON	OE	
Acc.	mik	mē	'me'
Dat.	mér	mē	'me'
Acc.	þik	ðē	'thee'
Dat.	þér	ðē	'thee'

7. Old Norse has a reflexive pronoun *sik, sér, sín,* along with the associated possessive pronoun *sinn* 'his, her'.

8. Along with all the Germanic languages except Gothic, Old Norse has developed an "intensified" demonstrative pronoun (with a meaning something like 'this') by attaching an intensifying particle *-si* to the regular demonstrative, and then carrying out a series of analogical changes that render this origin obscure. The result, though, is two demonstratives, whereas Gothic has just one:

ON masc. nom. sg. *sá*   and *sjá*   opposite Goth. *sa*
    masc. nom. pl. *þeir*   and *þessir*   opposite Goth. *þai*
    neut. nom. sg. *þat*   and *þetta*   opposite Goth. *þata*
    neut. dat. pl. *þeim* and *þessum* opposite Goth. *þaim*

Verbs

1. I noted in the last chapter that Gothic is alone among the Germanic languages in preserving reduplication as a means for forming the preterites of verbs. In Old Norse there are still some signs of the original reduplication:

> *róa* 'row' has the 3 sg. pret. ind. *reri*
> *sá* 'sow' has the 3 sg. pret. ind. *seri* (*-r-* by rhotacism)

It is clear, however, that the original reduplication is no longer felt as such in Old Norse. Rather, from an ahistorical point of view, we seem to be dealing with a preterite suffix *-er*, which follows the initial consonant or consonant cluster of the root and precedes the personal endings, as the following forms make clear:

> *gróa* 'grow' has the 3 sg. pret. ind. *greri*
> *snúa* 'turn' has the 3 sg. pret. ind. *sneri*

In general, Old Norse has brought the verbs of the Gothic reduplicating class into line with the other strong verbs by introducing vowel alternation into them:

> *heita* 'be called' has the 3 sg. pret. ind. *hét* (Goth. *haihait*)
> *auka* 'increase' has the 3 sg. pret. ind. *jók* (Goth. *aiauk*)
> *halda* 'hold' has the 3 sg. pret. ind. *helt* (Goth. *haihald*)

2. In the last chapter, I pointed out that Gothic was unique in possessing four classes of weak verbs, and specifically in having a separate class of verbs with an *n*-suffix, the *-nan* verbs. Old Norse has no such independent morphological class with its own set of endings, but it does have a productive set of *-na* verbs clearly derived from the same source as the Gothic ones. As in Gothic, these verbs are primarily inchoatives. Examples from the texts above:

> *vakna* 'wake up'; compare ON *vaka* 'be awake'
> *sofna* 'go to sleep'; compare ON *sofa* 'sleep'

3. As in Gothic, the marker of the second person preterite indicative in strong verbs is *-t* in Old Norse: *namt* 'you took'; compare OHG *nâmi*.

4. Among the Germanic languages, only Gothic has a true passive, which it inherited from Proto-Germanic. But Old Norse has created a new *medio-passive* by combining verb forms with forms of the reflexive pronoun, although the latter have, through phonetic change, frequently become obscure by the time of the manuscripts. The medio-passive forms of verbs were used in a number of ways, most of them basically indicating that the subject of the verb was also included in the field of action of the verb. Principally the meaning was reflexive, as in *klæðask* 'clothe oneself' or *leggjask* 'lay oneself down'. In cases like *eignask* 'possess', the meaning was clearly never reflexive, but (somewhat redundantly) benefactive: 'to possess for oneself'. Other uses ranged from a reciprocal one when the subject was plural (as in *berjask* 'to fight each other') to some that strike at least Modern English speakers as purely passive: *lúkask* 'to be closed (by someone)'.

5. The third person singular present indicative of the verb for 'be' is *er* in Old Norse, without the *t* found in Gothic *ist*.

6. Like Gothic, Old Norse distinguishes the endings of the first, second, and third persons plural:

> berum 'we carry'
> berið 'you carry'
> bera 'they carry'

7. The verbs 'stand' and 'go' are *standa*, *ganga* in Old Norse, with no contracted forms such as those found in other languages.

The Runes

I have several times referred to runic inscriptions, without ever making it clear what they are or were. This section will rectify the situation to a certain extent, although the field of runology is so rich that I can only touch on a few main points.

The Older Futhark

The term *rune*, as used now, and even as used by the rune-makers themselves, refers to any member of a set of symbols found in a distinctive Germanic alphabet (now called the *futhark* after the sound values of the first six symbols). It was used primarily in northern Europe from probably the mid-first century on. I give below the 24 symbols found in the

oldest version of this alphabet, known as the *older futhark*, along with
their common Romanizations and probable Germanic names. (The chart
and the names are from Klaus Düwel [1968]; the names are originally
from Wolfgang Krause [1966].)

THE OLDER FUTHARK

Form	Romanization	Name	Meaning of name
ᚠ	f	*fehu*	cattle, possessions
ᚢ	u	*urûz*	aurochs
ᚦ	þ	*þurisaz*	ogre
ᚨ	a	*ansuz*	god
ᚱ	r	*raidô*	journey, wagon
ᚲ	k	*kaunan*	sickness
ᚷ	g	*gebô*	gift
ᚹ	w	*wunjô*	joy
ᚺ	h	*haglaz*	hail
ᚾ	n	*naudiz*	tribulation
ᛁ	i	*îsaz*	ice
ᛃ	j	*jêran*	(good) year
ᛇ	i	*îwaz*	yew tree
ᛈ	p	*perþô*	fruit tree
ᛉ	z (R)	*algiz*	elk
ᛋ	s	*sôwilô*	sun
ᛏ	t	*Tîwaz*	(god's name)
ᛒ	b	*berkanan*	birch twig
ᛖ	e	*ehwaz*	horse
ᛗ	m	*mannaz*	person
ᛚ	l	*laukaz*	leek
ᛜ	ng	*Ingwaz*	(fertility god's name)
ᛞ	d	*dagaz*	day
ᛟ	o	*ôþalan*	inherited property

A number of comments are necessary regarding this chart. As to
pronunciation:

• There is little doubt that the runes for *b, d, g* had two pronunciations, namely as the stops [b], [d], [g], and as the fricatives [ƀ], [ð], [g], as
in Gothic.

• At least two values must also be assigned to each of the vowel
symbols, since the runes show no distinction between long and short
vowels, but the distinction obviously existed in the language itself.

• The letter R, given in parentheses after *z*, is actually the only value
we posit for the rune ᛉ in the inscriptions that have survived. It represents a sound somewhere between [z] and [r], as in the Czech composer's
name Dvořák. This is the original Germanic sound [z], which, it should

be remembered, is rhotacized in all the Germanic languages except Gothic. The surviving runic inscriptions, which still distinguish this sound from original [r], show us an intermediate stage in the rhotacism.

• It should be noted that there are two symbols that are assigned the letter value *i*. These were originally different vowels, namely **ei* for the first *i*-rune and **i* or **î* for the second. Since original **ei* and **î* are generally supposed to have fallen together in the pronunciation [î] by the mid-first century in all the Germanic languages, this apparent redundancy is sometimes used to date the original development of runic writing at some time before the linguistic merger. However, it should be pointed out that the second *i*-rune is rare.

A comparison of the sound values assigned to the runes with their proposed names will show that the rune-users followed the *acrophonic* principle found in many other alphabets. That is, in almost all cases the first sound of the name of the rune is the sound symbolized by the rune. The only exceptions to this are the names for ᛦ R and ᛜ *ng*, which for structural reasons could never appear in word-initial position (R, in fact, is found only in word-final position in the existing inscriptions). For these two sounds, names were found that at least contained them.

A good deal has been written on the reconstructed names of the runes, and not all scholars agree with Wolfgang Krause's proposals. The problem is that the runic inscriptions themselves do not name the runes. Instead, names for them are found rather haphazardly in a number of medieval scholarly manuscripts, and more systematically in four "rune poems," also preserved in medieval manuscripts, which clearly carry on an ancient mnemonic tradition. The reconstructions of Krause and others are based on a comparison of these poems (ranging in date from the ninth to the fifteenth centuries) with each other and with a tenth-century list of Gothic letter-names. Although the latter deals with a different alphabet, it seems to have made use of many of the same words as the rune-users.

One obvious question to be asked about the rune names is whether they represented something more than just mnemonics. Specifically, did they have some kind of religious or magical significance? In this brief summary, I will not discuss any of the various proposals advanced, beyond pointing out that this collection of names for gods, men, animals, plants, and meteorological phenomena (plus a few other things) strikes one as a good sample of the heathen conceptual world.

The order of the runes in the futhark is relatively certain, both from the later rune poems and from a number of inscribed rune-lists. A few of these rune-lists also document the subdivision of the 24 runes into three groups of eight runes each: the groups are referred to as *ættir* ('families') in later Icelandic manuscripts, a term possibly derived originally from the word *átta* 'eight'.

Age and Origin of the Runes

The earliest surviving runic inscriptions date from the second half of the second century, and are found primarily on materials, such as metal or stone, that resist decomposition reasonably well. It is very likely, however, that the runes were originally devised to be carved in wood, as their forms suggest by their avoidance of curves and horizontal lines. The first runic inscriptions, then, were probably made much earlier than the surviving ones, possibly as early as the first half of the first century A.D., but have since rotted away. This is supported, as I mentioned above, by the linguistic testimony of the two *i*-runes.

Although later Icelandic literary sources ascribed the runic writing system to Odin, most runologists have sought a more prosaic origin, and specifically have sought a connection with the writing systems of the more civilized parts of Europe. Some have sought to show a connection between the runes and variants of the Greek alphabet; others have argued for a Latin model. Still others have maintained that the precursor should be sought in the North Italic alphabets used by the Etruscans, themselves developed from Latin and Greek models. Especially the Latin and North Italic theories can point to similarities in the shapes of a number of letters, and the Etruscans even provide a probable source for the *boustrophēdon* (literally 'as the ox turns' in plowing) writing of many runic inscriptions—that is, the writing may proceed from left to right in one line, return from right to left in the next, then again left to right, and so on.

An integral part of many of the origin theories is the proposal of one or another Germanic tribe as the bringers of the runes to their fellow barbarians. Thus the theory of Greek origin relies heavily on the Goths as transmitters, while other theories ascribe this function to the Cimbri, the Marcomanni, and the Heruleans. The fact is, however, that the runes might just as easily be the creation of a single individual, drawing, of course, on Latin or North Italic sources or both. The unknown inventor might well have lived far beyond the borders of the Roman Empire, in present-day Denmark. This would correlate rather nicely with the distribution of inscriptions in the older futhark, which center overwhelmingly on the Danish islands and surrounding territories.

Texts in the Older Futhark

If the runes were indeed developed for writing on wood, then we have lost a great deal. Inscriptions on wood or bone have been preserved only under the most favorable circumstances, for example when they ended up in marshes. Such finds include wooden lance shafts and boxes and bone scraping-knives and combs.

Metal and stone are more durable, and most of the surviving runic inscriptions are found on these materials. Movable items marked with runes include spear blades, fibulas (clasps), combs, amulets, boxes, rings, horns, medallions, and whetstones. Immovable items include stone cliffs and large commemorative stones.

Although I have used the term "writing" for the runic inscriptions, they were of course not written in the standard sense. The term *writan* was indeed used by the rune-writers, but in the old meaning 'carve' or 'inscribe' (cf. Modern German *reissen, ritzen*). Another term in use was *faihjan* 'paint', most likely referring to the practice of coloring the scratched lines. Verbs for 'do' and 'make' round out the rune-users' characterization of what it was they were doing.

There are relatively few inscriptions in the older futhark. Einar Haugen places the number surviving from before the year 550 at around 125. He is clearly not including the so-called bracteates (medallions) in this number, which were mass-produced in the late fifth and sixth centuries in imitation of fourth-century Roman medallions, and were worn or kept as good-luck talismans or for other magical purposes. Only 128 of these contain runic inscriptions at all; a number of them clearly come from the same stamp, and most seem to use runes for pure ornament, rather than to represent words.

Of the remaining inscriptions, most contain only one or two words. When it is only a single word, this is frequently a descriptive term or name, as in the following inscription found on a spear blade in Norway: *raunijaʀ* 'tester'.

With two words we may find short phrases, again usually descriptive, as on a memorial stone in Norway: *hnabudas hlaiwa* 'Hnabud's grave' (the inscription itself does not show word division). We may also find short sentences, as on a fibula from North Jutland: *bidawarijaʀ talgidai* 'B. cut' (the runes).

There are, of course, longer inscriptions, though these too mostly seem to serve the purposes of naming objects, naming the owners of

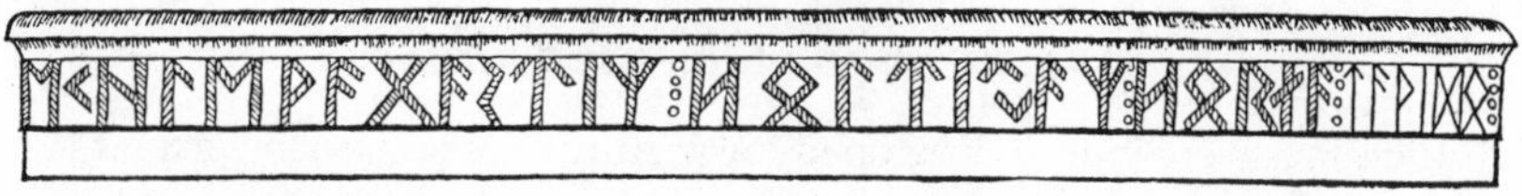

Fig. 3. The inscription of the Golden Horn of Gallehus. (Courtesy National-museet, Copenhagen)

objects, naming the carver of the runes, naming the person memorialized, or some combination of the above. The most famous runic inscription of all, that on the now-lost Golden Horn of Gallehus (given in runic form in Fig. 3), though not the longest, may serve as an example: *ek hlewagastiʀ holtijaʀ horna tawidô* 'I, Hlegest of Holt, made the horn' (note the word divisions found here).

The runes could be used not only for epigraphic purposes, but also for magical ones, as the other ancient meaning of the Old Norse word *rún* shows: 'secret, mystery, whispering'. Magical use could take the form of real sentences with magical content, sentences or phrases containing magical words, or even strings of runes that may have had some magical implication but are quite opaque to modern research.

The Language of the Older Futhark

Obviously one cannot build up a grammar of a language based on 125 inscriptions, especially considering how many of them contain one or two words. Nevertheless, a few characteristics of the early runic language can be pointed out:

1. Phonologically, the inscriptions show characteristics common to North and West Germanic, but not Gothic, such as the change of Proto-Germanic *$æ$ to *$â$, or the rhotacism of *z*. They do not show any characteristics unique to either North or West Germanic until the mid-sixth century at the earliest.

2. The morphology of the inscriptions is quite archaic, containing phenomena (such as full endings in nominative singulars like *hlewagastiʀ*) that none of the later literary languages have preserved.

3. The word order of the inscriptions, wherever there are enough words to make it out, seems freer than in the later languages.

4. The vocabulary, though restricted, does not seem to point to any particular later Germanic language as a descendant.

The language of the older futhark is traditionally referred to as Proto-Norse. Recent scholarship has suggested that this is an inappropriate designation, inasmuch as the forms in the inscriptions could just as easily be early German as, say, early Norwegian or Danish (ignoring, of course, the fact that the overwhelming majority of the inscriptions are found in Scandinavia, with a few scattered through Germany, England, and Eastern Europe). Thus many take the runic inscriptions from before about 550 as evidence for a surprisingly late breakup of Common Germanic (excluding East Germanic) into North and West Germanic, and thence into the various dialects treated in this book.

The younger futhark, to which we now turn, is a different matter. This is clearly a purely Scandinavian development, and records dialects that are recognizably Scandinavian.

The Younger Futhark

One danger of the acrophonic principle is that when sound change takes place, as it invariably does, the name of a letter may come to be pronounced differently. And if the change affects the first sound in that name, one has three choices: abandon the acrophonic principle; bring in a new name that begins with the desired old sound; or assign a new value to the letter. The rune-writers invariably took the third choice. Thus when a sound change eliminated the sound [j] before vowels at the beginnings of words, the Proto-Scandinavian rune name *jára* was affected too; the Old Norse form is *ár*. Furthermore, the signification of the rune changed also, and it was now used for the sound [a]. As for the original *a*-rune, it came to be used for a nasalized [ã] (as in French *ans*) because of changes in the initial sound of its name.

When one considers these changes together with many others that occurred in Proto-Scandinavian from the sixth century on—for example, umlaut, which greatly increased the number of vowels to be spelled—one might expect sweeping changes in the futhark. Indeed, during the eighth century a marked change did take place: the number of runic symbols was *reduced* from 24 to 16 (at least in Scandinavia; I will not discuss here the use of runes in England, where they played a far less important role).

No one has yet given a satisfactory explanation for this reduction in the inventory of runic symbols at the same time that the inventory of sounds increased drastically. Yet by the year 800 all runic inscriptions use this reduced alphabet (which, it should be noted, had a number of different variants, both geographically and historically). Thus a single symbol could stand for half a dozen significantly different sounds.

This reduction in the number of available symbols by no means correlates with a paucity of texts. On the contrary, inscriptions in the younger futhark run into the thousands. This was the era of the vikings, and the many memorial stones attest to the momentous activities not only of the emerging kings, but also of pirates and merchants who had traveled all over the known (and even the unknown) world.

The art of rune-carving did not die out completely, even after the introduction of writing in Latin letters on parchment. In some remote areas, the practice survived into the sixteenth or seventeenth century. The recent discovery in the Norwegian city of Bergen of approximately five hundred runic inscriptions from the thirteenth and fourteenth centuries attests not just to the staying power of this method of writing, but also to its popularity among the common people. Written mostly on wooden objects, these inscriptions range from love poetry to commercial documents, from the religious to the fleshly. Unlike most of the earlier runic inscriptions, many of those of Bergen appear to have been genuine communications, records, literary compositions, and the like. The implications of these inscriptions have yet to be fully digested into runology, but certainly our ideas about the uses of runes, at least in later times, will have to be revised somewhat. One must also ask what picture we would have of the use of runic inscriptions in earlier times, even in the older futhark, if more inscriptions on wood had survived. After all, it is much easier to send someone a letter written on a stick than one written on a rock.

FURTHER READING

Almgren, Bertil, et al. *The Viking.* Gothenburg: Tre Tryckare, 1966.

Düwel, Klaus. *Runenkunde.* Stuttgart: Metzler, 1968.

Gordon, E. V. *An Introduction to Old Norse.* 2d ed. Rev. A. R. Taylor. Oxford: Clarendon, 1957.

Haugen, Einar. *The First Grammatical Treatise: The Earliest Germanic Phonology. An Edition, Translation and Commentary.* 2d ed. London: Longman, 1972.

———. *The Scandinavian Languages.* Cambridge, Mass.: Harvard University Press, 1976. [See esp. chs. 8–10.]

Noreen, Adolf. *Altisländische und altnorwegische Grammatik: Laut- und Flexionslehre.* 4th ed. Halle (Saale): Niemeyer, 1923.

Owen, Francis. *The Germanic People.* New York: Bookman, 1960. [See esp. pp. 209–25.]

Sawyer, P. H. *The Age of the Vikings.* 2d ed. New York: St. Martin's, 1971.

Schwarz, Ernst. *Germanische Stammeskunde.* Heidelberg: Winter, 1956. [See esp. chs. 38, 39.]

Turville-Petre, E. O. G. *Myth and Religion of the North: The Religion of Ancient Scandinavia.* London: Weidenfeld and Nicolson, 1964.

————. *Origins of Icelandic Literature*. Oxford: Clarendon, 1967. [Reprint of the
    1953 ed.]
Valfells, Sigrid, and James E. Cathey. *Old Icelandic: An Introductory Course*. Ox-
    ford: Oxford University Press, 1981.
de Vries, Jan. *Altnordische Literaturgeschichte*. 2 vols. Berlin: de Gruyter,
    1964–67.

5

OLD SAXON

A Brief History of the Saxons

The Saxons Before Charlemagne

The name of the Saxons first appears in the mid-second century, in the works of the Greek geographer Ptolemy. It was the name of a tribe inhabiting the North Sea coast to the east of the lower Elbe, in what is now Holstein, and also three islands in the Elbe estuary. They were named after their characteristic short sword, called a *sahs*, a word still found as the second component of the German word *Messer* 'knife'.

Since the later distribution of the Saxons is so much broader, it is a little strange that they occupied such a small area in the second century. The answer to this problem appears to be that they didn't: Ptolemy most likely based his description on Roman reports from about A.D. 5. In any case, by the third century the Saxons had probably merged with a number of other Germanic peoples to form a greater unity, also called Saxons. The major contributors to this new grouping were almost without a doubt the Chauci, who had earlier lived on or near the North Sea coast between the Ems and the Elbe, and whose name nearly disappears in the third century. A single reference in the fourth century describes them as "part of the Saxons."

How the merger came about is an open question. Most scholars appear to feel that the joining was amicable, but some find this unlikely, given the rather violent later history of the Saxons. Those in favor of the subjugation theory can quote later Saxon historians, who describe an invasion by Old Saxons on the North Sea coast between the Elbe and the Weser in the second half of the second century, resulting in the reduction of the natives to bondsman status. Only by assuming such an invasion, these scholars claim, can one understand the extraordinary differences between nobles and bondsmen in later Saxon law (on which see below). Those who argue that the alliance was friendly, and therefore did not involve the long-term invasion of a large number of original Saxons in Chauci territory, point to the archeological evidence, which shows no major cultural shifts in the supposedly invaded areas at the time of the supposed invasion. They also note that the center of political gravity in the later Saxon alliance was in an area earlier occupied by Chauci, while the homeland east of the Elbe in fact played a rather peripheral role in most of the later doings of the Saxons.

Be that as it may, all concede that some of the later tribal assimilations into the Saxon alliance were friendly, but that most were bloody. With the departure of the Langobards from the lower Elbe around A.D. 400, the remaining Bards appear to have joined the Saxon alliance willingly. Other areas were taken forcibly from their inhabitants, including territory on the upper Ems River taken from the Angrivarians at the end of the fourth century, and territory south of the middle Lippe seized from the Boruktuarians at the beginning of the eighth century. In almost all cases, the natives were reduced to bondsman status. In 531 the Saxons participated with the Franks in the destruction of the Thuringian kingdom, getting the northern part of that area and the associated populations as their share of the spoils.

Although there had been some earlier contacts, the Saxons first forced themselves upon the attention of the Romans in the latter part of the third century, when they harassed the coasts of northern Gaul and southeastern England. Their attacks were so severe that a special coastal defense was set up in these areas, known as the *Litus Saxonicum* 'Saxon Shore', around the beginning of the fourth century. If the purpose of the special defense was to keep the Saxons out, however, it ultimately failed. By the middle of the fifth century, the northern coasts of Gaul had a large number of permanent Saxon settlers, as did some parts of the western coasts (although the former were more important). Ultimately, all these Saxons were to be assimilated into the Franks, in a way that their stay-at-home cousins were not.

From the mid-fifth century on, England too got its share of permanent Saxon settlers, as the term "Anglo-Saxon" implies. I will discuss their further fate in the next chapter.

Although the relations between the Saxons and the neighboring Franks must have been reasonably amicable in 531, when they jointly destroyed the kingdom of Thuringia, on the whole their relationship was troubled. Even after the joint venture in Thuringia there appears to have been some friction, for the newly settled Thuringian Saxons were obliged to pay a yearly tribute to the Frankish kingdom, not the kind of thing one expects from an erstwhile ally. This tribute was a sore point for the Saxons in later years, since they thought it demeaning.

For approximately the next hundred years, we have reports of on-again, off-again wars between at least a part of the Saxons and the Franks. In 556 the Thuringian Saxons defeated the Frankish king Chlotar and had the tribute-obligation lifted, only to have it reimposed later in the same year. In 632–33, however, the Saxons fought on the side of the Franks against the invading Wends (a Slavic people), and the tribute-obligation was again lifted.

In the early eighth century, the Merovingian Frankish kingdom was shaken by confusion following the death of Pippin, the mayor of the palace, and in 715 the western Saxons took advantage of the situation by invading the lower Rhenish areas of the kingdom. Three years later Charles Martel pushed the invading Saxons out, and followed up with a victorious push all the way to the Weser. He was forced to enter western Saxony again in 720 and 738, and from this latter war we hear not only that he was victorious, but also that he devastated the countryside, exacted pledges of tribute, and took hostages for good behavior.

In 743 the eastern Saxons allied with the Bavarian Duke Odilo in his revolt against Frankish overlordship. After Odilo's defeat, Carloman turned against the Saxons and defeated them. In 748, however, the Thuringian Saxons again rose up, this time allied with a disgruntled claimant to the Frankish throne. After a defeat at the hands of Pippin the Younger, these Saxons were forced to reinstitute the traditional tribute-obligation lifted more than a century before.

The western Saxons, who since 738 had also been obligated to pay the Franks tribute, revolted again in 753; Pippin put them down with the customary devastation, exaction of tribute, and taking of hostages. The scenario was repeated in 758.

Saxon Society Before Charlemagne

Before I turn to the events that led at last to the fall of Old Saxony as an independent state, it would probably be useful to sketch some of the characteristics of that state. The information comes from a variety of medieval sources, including Anglo-Saxon, Frankish, and Saxon descriptions, laws, treaties, and histories from the seventh through the tenth centuries. Even

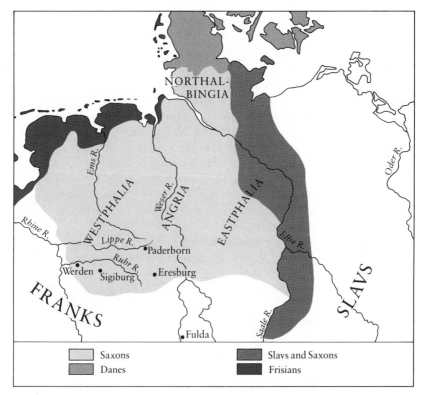

Map 4.   Saxony in the ninth century A.D.

with so much documentation, some of what I present here is speculative, and scholars disagree even on major points.

By the end of the eighth century, Saxony resembled a large, almost equilateral triangle two hundred miles on a side. The rather blunt point consisted of a stretch of North Sea coast from the Weser to the Elbe and, beyond the Elbe, Holstein and Ditmarsch. To the northwest, the Saxons abutted on the Frisians; to the west and south they bordered Frankish territories; to the east, across the Saale and Elbe rivers, they faced the Slavs.

The Saxon state was loosely organized into three major provinces: Westphalia to the west, Angria in the center (on the Weser), and East-phalia to the east. A significant subdivision of Eastphalia was the area north of the Elbe, known as Northalbingia. It is not clear to what extent these provinces had any permanent government, although they certainly had military leaders in times of war. The basic units of Saxon political life appear to have been the *Gaue*, relatively small areas containing several villages and corresponding in size, though not necessarily in boundaries, with the later counties.

Head of each Gau was the *Fürst*, literally 'first', who was in all cases a member of the aristocracy. He was the local leader in time of war, and exercised judicial and priestly functions also (the Saxons worshipped the old Germanic gods, such as Wotan and Donar, and their own patron god Sahsnot). The Fürst did not inherit the office, but was officially appointed by a kind of national assembly (to be discussed below).

The Saxons possessed four hereditary social classes: nobles, freemen, bondsmen, and slaves. Since members of the last class were considered property, not people, only the first three were considered relevant to the makeup of Saxon society.

There is some disagreement about whether the nobles represent descendants of the original Saxon invaders of the expanded territories, or simply the old Germanic nobility, augmented by the addition of rich freemen. It seems to me that the following facts are in favor of the first notion, or at least of the notion that the nobles largely represent the original invading Saxons plus Chauci. First, the nobility was a far more numerous class in Saxony than elsewhere. Second, in the proposed original homeland of the Saxons, Northalbingia, the class of nobles appears not to have existed; neither did that of bondsmen. There were just greater and lesser freemen. Third, the place of the nobility as against the freemen was much higher in Saxony than elsewhere: the *wergeld*, or death price, of a noble was six times that of a freeman.

The nobles appear to have been large landholders, and the bondsmen were the people who did their farming for them. The freemen were probably small independent farmers whose independence was hardly secure.

As I mentioned before, even though the size of the nobility was large, its relative standing was nonetheless greater than in other Germanic groups. The gulf between nobles and other classes was, if anything, widened by the relatively good standing that bondsmen had in Saxony: they had a wergeld amounting to three-fourths that of a freeman, bore arms, and had a voice in the assembly. Their elevation implies an effective lowering of the standing of freemen.

The law appears to have strictly enforced these social gulfs. The death penalty was prescribed for any man who married above his station, and marriage with a woman beneath one's station had no legal standing.

The laws and customs were surprisingly grim in other ways, too. Things like cattle theft or breaking and entering, which were punished with fines elsewhere, brought the death penalty in Saxony. Pregnant unmarried women and adulterous married women were whipped from village to village and finally put to death.

Unlike most other Germanic tribes, the Saxons had not gone over to a monarchical form of government by the eighth century. Instead, they had a form of representative republic, with yearly meetings of the all-Saxon assembly at a designated point on the Weser. Thirty-six representatives were designated from each Gau, of whom twelve were nobles, twelve freemen, and twelve bondsmen. Although this appears to be a surprisingly fair arrangement on the surface, in fact it was much to the advantage of the nobles, on whom the bondsmen depended and to whom they owed service. Indeed, the nobles seem sometimes to have made almost a conscious effort to play the freemen and bondsmen off against each other.

If the nobles protected their privileged status against threats from below, they also did their best to guarantee that there would be no monarchy above. The leadership necessary during times of war was not determined, as it had been in other Germanic tribes, by vote of the assembly. (This custom, in those other tribes, frequently led to the establishment of popularly elected tyrannies that refused to go away in times of peace.) Instead, the war leader (*heritogo*) was selected from among the hundred or so Gau leaders by lot.

It should be emphasized that the Saxons did not represent the kind of unified nation that, for example, the Franks did. Even in times of war, the individual Gaue and provinces retained a great deal of independent initiative; in dealings with the Saxons, it was rare that one dealt with the nation as a whole. There is little doubt that the Frankish kings found this more than a little frustrating.

The Frankish Annexation of Saxony

I have shown above that long before the time of Charlemagne, relations between the Franks and Saxons were not particularly friendly. The Frankish kings had led armies into Saxony a number of times, but their victories had produced only fleeting results. Frankish settlements near the borders were exposed to constant harassment from the Saxon side.

The year 772 marked the beginning of the final series of wars that was to spell Saxony's end as an independent state. For in that year the

imperial council in Worms officially declared war on the Saxons, and
Charlemagne moved immediately to implement it.

This first push into Saxony came from the south, and was directed
against the Angrians, presumably in order to drive a wedge between eastern and western Saxony. The attack was in all respects successful. The
Frankish army succeeded in taking and garrisoning the fortress of Eresburg. Afterwards they pushed on to one of the holiest places in Saxon
religion, a place in the forest containing the *Irminsul* or "Pillar of the
World," a large upright log serving as a focus for the worship of the heathen gods. This the Franks totally destroyed, taking the treasures found
there as booty. They then pushed on to the Weser, where they forced the
Saxons to sue for peace. Twelve hostages were taken from the Saxons,
and clearly other agreements were reached, although the sources are not
very explicit as to their content. They surely involved at least an agreement that the Saxons would allow Christian missionaries free access to
the land.

But this was neither a total war nor a secure victory. Only the Angrians had really been affected by this war, and not even all of them.
In any case, most of Saxony apparently did not feel it had agreed to
anything. So much became clear when Charlemagne was forced to turn
his attentions to northern Italy to protect his interests and those of the
Church. In 774, when the Frankish king and a good part of his forces
were across the Alps, the Saxons rose up, took the Eresburg by storm,
and then crossed the borders into Franconia, where they did a great deal
of damage.

The satisfaction of this revenge was brief, however. When Charlemagne got back from Italy, he again declared war against the Saxons, this
time resolving not to stop until the Saxons were completely subjected to
his authority and to the Christian religion. In 775 he entered Saxony
from the west. Within three months he had fought all the way to the
Oder, beaten the armies of all three provinces, and forced the Saxons to
their knees. In addition to giving Charlemagne hostages, the Saxons
pledged fealty to him, a first step on the way to vassalage. The fortress
at Eresburg was rebuilt, and a new garrison was installed at Sigiburg on
the Ruhr.

It seems that at this point many, if not most, of the Saxon nobility
were content to cease warring against the Franks. It is at least true that
the leaders of the Eastphalians and the Angrians, Hessi and Brun, respectively, are not mentioned again as leaders of the Saxon resistance. This is

not to say that Saxon resistance ceased, however. For on the occasion of Charlemagne's next trip into Italy in late 775 and early 776, the Frankish garrisons at Eresburg and Sigiburg were attacked in force, and the former was again destroyed.

Charlemagne attacked again on his return from Italy, and again he was quickly victorious. This time nobles from all over Saxony pledged fealty, many conversions were made, and some of the worst trouble-makers were deported to other areas of the empire. For the first time we find explicit mention of an agreement whereby the Saxons not only were to admit missionaries, they were to convert to Christianity as a nation.

At the imperial assembly in 777 in Paderborn, without any inter-vening war, a great number of Saxon nobility repeated their pledges of fealty, a rash of conversions occurred, and a synod of bishops determined the best way to go about Christianizing Saxony. Charlemagne might well have assumed that his conquest of Saxony was complete.

One important member of the nobility was not to be found at Paderborn, namely Widukind of the Westphalians, who had fled to Den-mark. It was probably Widukind who had led the Westphalians in 775, and also he who had led the attacks against the Frankish garrisons in 776. In any case, from 777 on he was clearly the leader of the Saxon resis-tance. And resistance there was. In 778 Charlemagne was called off to Spain on another imperial war, and the Saxons used this occasion to institute a ferocious attack not only on the Frankish garrisons, but on Franconia itself. Up and down the Rhine they raged, burning, plundering, and looting. When they were forced to retreat by the advent of Frankish troops, they attempted to attack the monastery at Fulda, the major stepping-off place for the Christianization of Saxony, and were prevented from doing so only in the nick of time. According to contemporary re-ports, during this period the Saxons were not only fighting the Franks, but also taking reprisals within their own country against the many Saxon nobility who remained faithful to Charlemagne.

As usual, Charlemagne returned and quelled the disturbances with little trouble. In 779 and 780 he imposed further restrictions on the Sax-ons. And in 782, finally, he officially completed the annexation of Saxony to the Frankish empire by bringing in Frankish institutions at all levels. Most notably, he employed the administrative system of placing districts under counts, who were officials of the Frankish court. He imposed a number of rather draconian laws enforcing Frankish hegemony and im-posing legal and financial obligations to the Church. In an obvious concession to his Saxon allies, the countships were all filled with Saxon nobles, and the existing Saxon legal system, which so clearly favored the nobility, was allowed to continue unaltered, insofar as it did not conflict with the new laws.

Clearly some Saxons were not totally happy with the new order. When Widukind returned from another journey to Denmark and sent out a call for arms, it was answered. There were uprisings all over Saxony; monasteries and churches were destroyed, and many officials were forced to flee. In a major battle on the Weser, a large Frankish force was defeated. By the time Charlemagne had hurried up to the scene of the battle with reinforcements, however, Widukind had departed for Denmark and his army had dispersed. Enraged, Charlemagne demanded that those who had participated in the uprising be handed over to him, and the Saxon nobility complied. Forty-five hundred Saxons were beheaded at Werden.

The uprisings that followed this act lasted until 785, when Widukind, aware of the hopelessness of his cause, at last allowed himself to be baptized, and relative peace was achieved in most of Saxony. Individual regions of Saxony resisted Frankish overlordship for quite a long time, however, sometimes quite forcefully, and the last of the battles between Franks and Saxons took place in 804. From then on the history of the Saxons was linked with that of the Holy Roman Empire. After the end of the Carolingian dynasty, they even contributed their own dynasty to the imperial throne.

Lintzel (1933) has noted that the real losers of the Frankish-Saxon wars were not the Saxon nobility, but the freemen and peasants. He argues that even before the wars, the nobility was threatened by unrest among the oppressed lower classes, and that the nobles saw both Christianity and the Frankish presence as ways to preserve their privileged status. It was they who made the treaties with Charlemagne, but the peasants who broke them. Although the nobles must have been distressed by the increasing stringency of the accords they struck with the Franks, he argues, in general they sided with the invaders against the insurrectionists. Civil war went hand in hand with the foreign one.

This thesis of class war in Saxony seems to be supported by further events in that region. Specifically, in the mid-ninth century a powerful league of peasants arose there, dedicated to a restoration of ancient liberties and native Saxon custom. This was the famous *Stellinga*, which, during the wars of succession between Charlemagne's grandsons, almost succeeded in throwing the nobility out of the country. Ultimately, it was ruthlessly suppressed by Louis the German.

The only noble who stands out from the pack here is Widukind, but Lintzel does not ascribe particularly admirable motives to him, either. If the Saxon uprisings had succeeded, Lintzel argues, Saxony might easily have become a kingdom like the other Germanic kingdoms, with Widukind, a popularly supported tyrant, on the throne. And this, he suggests, was Widukind's motivation. What was denied to him by the Saxon constitution he tried to win through insurrection.

Old Saxon Texts

Aside from the biblical epics (about which more below), our knowledge of Old Saxon comes from several smaller sources of various types. The connected texts include, among others, a number of benedictions, exegeses of psalms, confessions of faith, tax rolls, a translation of an Old English homily, an inscription on a coin, and the famous *Hildebrandslied* (which is by no means pure Old Saxon). In addition to these, there are Saxon glosses of words in Latin texts, in some cases so frequent that they approach word-for-word interlinear translations. A number of different kinds of Latin texts are so treated, ranging from Vergil to the Gospels and from saints' lives to a description of plants and fish. Finally, we find Old Saxon words and expressions in Latin texts, especially several from the monastery of Werden.

The major Old Saxon document is the *Heliand*, an alliterative epic poem of almost six thousand long lines, which recounts the story of Jesus in a form that combines the contributions of all four Gospels into a single narrative. This poem is notable for the way it translates the story not only into a Germanic verse form, but also into a Germanic conceptual framework. In the *Heliand*, the setting is clearly not the far-off Holy Land but rather the plains and marshes of northern Germany, while the characters and the relations between them reflect Saxon reality more than they do the original Jewish one. One often-quoted example is that in the Old Saxon version the men to whom the angels announce the birth of Christ are tending not sheep but horses.

There are several scholarly theories about the date and place of composition of the original manuscript, the origin of the author, his motivation for writing, and the natural or artificial quality of his language.

One reason for the lack of agreement is that the *Heliand* comes down to us in four separate manuscripts, two more or less complete and two fragmentary, all found in different places and exhibiting more or less significant differences in language. Further confusing the picture is the interpretation of statements in two Latin prefaces, presumably to the *Heliand* but preserved quite separately from the epic itself.

The date of composition is commonly set a little after 830, although others have placed it as late as 850 (it depends on which Emperor Louis the prose preface is talking about). The place of composition is generally believed to have been the East Franconian monastery of Fulda, where a great deal of Old High German literary activity took place, including the translation of Tatian's gospel harmony, which clearly preceded and influenced the *Heliand*. Some scholars, however, believe that most or all of the writing of the *Heliand* took place in the monastery of Werden on the Ruhr.

According to the preface, the *Heliand* was written at the urging of Emperor Louis, probably Louis the Pious, Charlemagne's son, presumably as part of the effort to Christianize Saxony. Several scholars have doubted this motivation, and characterize the work more as an individual offering to Christ, whose story it is, or as an intentionally literary work made for an elite group of Christian cognoscenti. As for who the artist was, the speculations range all over the map: he was a layman; he was a cleric; he was an Anglo-Saxon; he was Frisian; he was a Saxon from Westphalia, from Eastphalia, and so on.

Finally, scholars disagree about whether the *Heliand* reflects an actually spoken language or not, and, if it does, exactly how it reflects Saxon speech. The focus of argument has been primarily on the supposed Anglo-Frisian and Old High German characteristics of the texts (about which more below), and whether they reflect true dialectal conditions in the Old Saxon territories, or mere scribal conventions and influences. There are too many suggested possible permutations to give here.

The other major Old Saxon text is a fragment of a ninth-century epic poem, the *Genesis*. The existence of this work, most probably inspired by the success of the *Heliand*, was suspected even before the actual fragments were discovered in 1894: the German scholar Eduard Sievers had proposed in 1875 that the Anglo-Saxon *Genesis* had been based on an Old Saxon original. Indeed, when the Old Saxon fragments were discovered, there was a close correspondence between the passages they had in common (only 25 lines in all). The Old Saxon *Genesis* runs to just 330 long lines, but when one adds the 590 Anglo-Saxon lines that have no

Saxon equivalents and allows for the complete loss of other sections, one sees that the original must have been quite long.

Readings

Parable of the Sower and the Seed
(Heliand 2378–2412)

Hê stôd imu thô bi ênes uuatares staðe,   *he, stood, him, by, one, water, Staden*

ni uuelde thô bi themu gethringe   *wollte, dem, throng*

  oƀar that thegno folc   over, thane, folk

an themu lande uppan   thea lêra cûðean,   land, up, *die, Lehre, kund*

ac geng imu thô the gôdo   ging, the, good

  endi is iungaron mid imu,   and, his, younger, *mit*

friðubarn godes,   themu flôde nâhor   *Friede*, [Scots] bairn, God, flood, *näher*

an ên skip innan,   endi it scalden hêt   on, ship, in, it, *hiess*

lande rûmor,   that ina thea liudi sô filu,   *Raum, -er, ihn, Leute, so, viel*

thioda ni thrungi.   Stôd thegan manag,   *dringen*, many

uuerod bi themu uuatare,

  thar uualdand Crist   there, wield

oƀar that liudio folc   lêra sagde: that, said

"Huat, ik iu seggean mag," quad he,   what, *ich*, you, say, may, quoth

  "gesîðos mîne,   mine

huô imu ên erl bigan   an erðu sâian   how, earl, began, earth, sow

hrêncorni mid is handun.   *rein*, corn, hand(s)

  Sum it an hardan stên   some, hard, stone

oƀanuuardan fel,   erðon ni habda,   *oben*, -wards, fell, had

that it thar mahti uuahsan   *möchte, wachsen*

  eftha uurteo gifâhan,   root, *fangen*

kînan eftha biclîƀen,   cleave

  ac uuarð that corn farloren,   *ward, verloren*

that thar an theru lêian gilag.   *der*, lay

  Sum it eft an land bifel,

an erðun aðalcunnies: bigan imu aftar thiu   *edel*, kin, began, after

uuahsen uuânlîco   endi uurteo fâhan,   *Wahn, -lich*

lôd an lustun: uuas that land sô gôd,   *Lust*, was, so

frânisco gifêhod.   Sum eft bifallen uuarð   fallen

an êna starca strâtun,   thar stôpon gengun,   *eine, stark*, street, step(s)

hrosso hôfslaga   endi heliðo trâda;   horse, hoof, *Schlag, Held, tret(en)*

uuarð imu thar an erðu   endi eft up gigeng, — *up*
bigan imu an themu uuege uuahsen; — *way*
   thô it eft thes uuerodes farnam, — *des, vernahm*
thes folkes fard mikil   endi fuglos alâsun, — *Fahrt, [Scots] mickle, Vogel, lasen*
that is themu êcsan uuiht   aftar ni môste — *aught, must*
uuerðan te uuillean, — *werden, to, will*
   thes thar an thene uueg bifel. — *den*
Sum uuarð it than bifallen,
   thar sô filu stôdun
thiccero thorno   an themu dage; — *thick, thorn, day*
uuarð imu thar an erðu   endi eft up gigeng,
kên imu thar endi cliƀode. — *cleaved*
   Thar slôgun thar eft crûd an gimang, — *schlugen, Kraut, among*
uueridun imu thene uuastom: — *wehrten, Wachstum*
   habda it thes uualdes hlea — *Wald*
forana oƀarfangan, — *(be)fore*
   that it ni mahte te ênigaro frumu uuerðen, — *might, einig, werden*
ef it thea thornos sô   thringan môstun.” — *if, dringen*

The Lord's Prayer
(Heliand 1600–1612)

Fadar ûsa   firiho barno, — *father, our*
thû bist an them hôhon   himila rîkea, — *thou, bist, high, Himmel, Reich*
geuuîhid sî thin namo   uuordo gehuuilico. — *geweiht, sei, thine, name, word, welch*
Cuma thîn   craftag rîki. — *come, kräftig*
UUerða thîn uuilleo — *werde*
   oƀar thesa uuerold alla, — *over, this, world, all*
sô sama an erðo,   sô thar uppa ist — *same, up, is*
an them hôhon   himilo rîkea.
Gef ûs dago gehuuilikes râd, — *give, Rat*
   drohtin the gôdo,
thîna hêlaga helpa, — *holy, help*
   endi alât ûs, heƀenes uuard, — *lass, heaven, ward*
managoro mênsculdio, — *manch, Schuld*
   al sô uue ôðrum mannum dôan. — *we, other, man, do*
Ne lât ûs farlêdean   lêða uuihti — *ver-, lead, Leid, wight*
Sô forð an iro uuilleon, — *forth, ihr*
   sô uui uuirðige sind, — *worthy, sind*
ac help ûs uuiðar allun   uƀilon dâdiun. — *wider, evil, deed(s)*

GLOSSARY

In alphabetizing Old Saxon, ƀ and ð follow b and d, respectively; c is treated as k, and uu is listed separately after u. Unless specified otherwise, nouns and pronouns are nominative singular, adjectives are masculine nominative singular, and verbs are infinitives. The parenthetical identification of any form has reference only to the Readings, and is not necessarily an exhaustive list of all possible identifications of that form in the language.

aðalcunni 'noble sort', *aðalcunnies* (gen. sg.)

aftar 'afterwards'; *aftar thiu* 'after that'

ac 'but'

al 'just'

alâsun see *alesan*

alâtan 'absolve', *alât* (2 sg. pres. imp.)

alesan 'glean, pick up', *alâsun* (3 pl. pret. ind.)

all 'all', *alla* (fem. acc. sg.), *allun* (fem. dat. pl.)

an 'on, in, onto, to, according to'; *an gimang* 'in and among'

barn 'child', *barno* (gen. pl.)

bi 'by, next to, with'

bifallan 'fall', *bifel* (3 sg. pret. ind.), *bifallen* (pret. part.)

biginnan 'begin', *bigan* (3 sg. pret. ind.)

biclîƀen 'hold fast'

bist see *sîn, uuesan*

dâd 'deed', *dâdiun* (dat. pl.)

dag 'day', *dages* (gen. sg.), *dage* (dat. sg.), *dago* (gen. pl.)

dôan 'do', *dôan* (3 pl. pres. ind.)

drohtin 'lord'

ef 'if'

eft 'afterwards'

eftha 'or'

êcso 'owner', *êcsan* (dat. sg.)

ên 'a, an' (masc. art.)

ên 'a, an' (neut. art.), *ên* (acc. sg.), *ênes* (gen. sg.)

êna 'a, an' (fem. art.), *êna* (acc. sg.)

endi 'and'

ênes see *ên* (neut.)

ênig 'any', *ênigaro* (dat. sg.)

erða 'earth', *erðun* (acc. sg.), *erðon* (gen. sg.), *erðu, erðo* (dat. sg.)

erl 'man'

fadar 'father'

fâhan 'get'

fallan 'fall', *fel* (3 sg. pret. ind.)

fard 'traffic, journey, way'

farlêdean 'lead astray'

farliosan 'lose', *farloren* (pret. part.)

farniman 'destroy, take away', *farnam* (3 sg. pret. ind.)

fel see *fallan*

filu 'much, many'

firihos 'people', *firiho* (gen. pl.)

flôd 'flood', *flôde* (dat. sg.)

folc, folk 'people, folk', *folc* (acc. sg., folkes* (gen. sg.))

forana 'from the beginning'

forð 'forth'

frânisco 'splendidly'

friðubarn 'child of peace'

fruma 'advantage, good thing', *frumu* (dat. sg.)

fugal 'bird', *fuglos* (nom. pl.)

gangan 'go', *geng* (3 sg. pret. ind.), *gengun* (3 pl. pret. ind.)

geƀan 'give', *gef* (2 sg. pres. imp.)

gehuuilic 'every', *gehuuilikes* (masc. gen. sg.), *gehuuilico* (neut. inst. sg.)

geng, gengun, see *gangan*

gesîð 'companion', *gesîðos* (nom. pl.)

gethring 'crowd(ing)', *gethringe* (dat. sg.)

geuuîhid see *uuîhian*

gifâhan 'get, acquire'

gifêhon 'equip', *gifêhod* (pret. part.)

gigangan 'go', *gigeng* (3 sg. pret. ind.)

giliggian 'lie', *gilag* (3 sg. pret. ind.)

gimang see *an*

god 'God', *godes* (gen. sg.)

gôd 'good', *gôdo* (masc. nom. sg. weak), *gôd* (neut. nom. sg. strong)

habda see *hebbian*

hand 'hand', *handun* (dat. pl.)

hard 'hard', *hardan* (acc. sg.)

hê, he 'he', *ina* (acc. sg.), *is* (gen. sg.), *imu* (dat. sg.), *iro* (gen. pl.)

hebbian 'have', *habda* (3 sg. pret. ind.)

heban 'heaven', *hebenes* (gen. sg.)

hebenes see *heban*

hêlag 'holy', *hêlaga* (fem. acc. sg.)

helið 'man, hero', *heliðo* (gen. pl.)

help see *helpan*

helpa 'help', *helpa* (acc. sg.)

helpan 'help', *help* (2 sg. pres. imp.)

hêtan 'call, order', *hêt* (3 sg. pret. ind.)

himil 'heaven', *himila, himilo* (gen. pl.)

hlea 'covering'

hôfslaga 'hoofbeat', *hôfslaga* (nom. pl.)

hôh 'high', *hôhon* (neut. dat. sg. weak)

hrêncorni 'wheat', *hrêncorni* (acc. sg.)

hross 'horse', *hrosso* (gen. pl.)

huat 'what?' (neut. interr. pro.), *huat* (acc. sg.)

huô 'how'

ik 'I', *uue, uui* (nom. pl.), *ûs* (acc. and dat. pl.)

imu see *hê, he*

ina see *hê, he*

innan 'in, into'

iro see *hê, he*

is see *hê, he*; see also *it*

ist see *sîn, uuesan*

it 'it', *it* (acc. sg.), *is* (gen. sg.)

iu see *thû*

iungaro 'disciple', *iungaron* (nom. pl.)

kînan 'sprout', *kên* (3 sg. pret. ind.)

clibon 'hold fast', *clibode* (3 sg. pret. ind.)

corn 'seed, corn'

craftag 'powerful', *craftag* (neut. nom. sg.)

Crist 'Christ'

crûd 'weed', *crûd* (nom. pl.)

cûðean 'make known'

cuman 'come', *cuma* (3 sg. pres. subj.)

land 'land', *land* (acc. sg.), *lande* (dat. sg.)

lâtan 'allow, let', *lât* (2 sg. pres. imp.)

lêd 'evil', *lêda* (acc. pl.)

lêia 'rock', *lêian* (dat. sg.)

lêra 'teaching', *lêra* (acc. sg.)

liodan 'grow', *lôd* (3 sg. pret. ind.)

liodio see *liudi*

liudi 'people' (nom. pl.), *liodio* (gen. pl.)

lôd see *liodan*

lust 'joy', *lustun* (dat. pl.)

mag, mahte, mahti, see *mugan*

man 'man', *mannum* (dat. pl.)

manag 'many (a)', *managoro* (gen. pl.)

mannum see *man*

mênsculd 'offense', *mênsculdio* (gen. pl.)

mid 'with'

mikil 'great', *mikil* (fem. nom. sg.)

mîn 'my', *mîne* (nom. pl.)

môste, môstun, see *môtan*

môtan 'be able, can', *môste* (3 sg.
   pret. ind.), *môstun* (3 pl. pret. ind.)
mugan 'be able, can', *mag* (3 sg. pres.
   ind.), *mahte* (3 sg. pret. ind.), *mahti*
   (3 sg. pret. subj.)

nâh 'near', *nâhor* (comp., masc.
   nom. sg.)
namo 'name'
ne, ni 'not'

oƀanuuardan 'from above'
oƀar 'over'
oƀarfâhan 'cover', *oƀarfangan* (pret.
   part.)
ôðar 'other', *ôðrum* (dat. pl.)

queðan 'speak', *quad* (3 sg. pret. ind.)

râd 'aid', *râd* (acc. sg.)
rîki 'kingdom', *rîkea* (dat. sg.)
rûmo 'far', *rûmor* (comp.)

sagde see *seggean*
sâian 'sow'
sama 'same' (neut. nom. sg.)
seggean 'say', *sagde* (3 sg. pret. ind.)
sîn, uuesan 'be', *bist* (2 sg. pres. ind.),
   ist (3 sg. pres. ind.), *sind* (1 pl. pres.
   ind.), *sî* (3 sg. pres. subj.), *uuas*
   (3 sg. pret. ind.)
scalden 'push off'
skip 'ship', *skip* (acc. sg.)
slahan 'strike, push', *slôgun* (3 pl.
   pret. ind.)
sô 'so, as, thus, if'
staƀ 'shore', *staƀe* (dat. sg.)
stân, standan 'stand', *stôd* (3 sg. pret.
   ind.), *stôdun* (3 pl. pret. ind.)
starc 'strong, hard', *starca* (fem.
   acc. sg.)
stên 'stone', *stên* (acc. sg.)
stôd, stôdun, see *stân, standan*
stôpo 'step, tread', *stôpon* (nom. pl.)

strâta 'street', *strâtun* (acc. sg.)
sum 'some, one'

te 'to, according to'
than 'then'
thar 'there, where'
that 'so that, that' (conj.)
that 'that (one)' (neut. dem. pro.),
   thes (gen. sg.)
that 'the' (neut. art.), *that* (acc. sg.),
   thes (gen. sg.), *themu, them*
   (dat. sg.)
that 'that, which' (rel. pro.)
thê, the 'the' (masc. art.), *thene* (acc.
   sg.), *thes* (gen. sg.), *themu, them*
   (dat. sg.), *thea* (nom. pl.)
thea see *thê, the;* see also *thiu*
thegan 'man', *thegno* (gen. pl.)
them, themu, see *that* and *thê, the*
thene see *thê, the*
theru see *thiu*
thes see *that* and *thê, the*
thesa see *thius*
thiccero see *thikki*
thikki 'thick', *thiccero* (gen. pl.)
thin, thîn 'your, thy' (2 sg. poss. pro.),
   thîn (nom. sg. neut.), *thîna* (acc.
   sg. fem.)
thîna see *thin, thîn*
thioda 'people'
thiu 'the' (fem. art.), *thea* (acc. sg.),
   theru (dat. sg.)
thius 'this' (fem. dem. pro.), *thesa*
   (acc. sg.)
thô 'then, when, thereupon'
thorn 'thorn', *thornos* (nom. pl.),
   thorno (gen. pl.)
thringan 'crowd', *thrungi* (3 sg. pret.
   subj.)
thû 'you', *iu* (dat. pl.)
trâda 'step', *trâda* (nom. pl.)

uƀil 'evil', *uƀilon* (dat. pl.)
up 'up'

uppa, uppan 'above'
ûs see *ik*
ûsa 'our'

uuahsan, uuahsen 'grow'
uuald 'forest', *uualdes* (gen. sg.)
uualdan 'rule'; *uualdand* 'mighty'
    (pres. part., masc. nom. sg.)
uualdes see *uuald*
uuânlîco 'prosperously'
uuard 'protector'
uuarð see *uuerðan, uuerðen*
uuas see *sîn, uuesan*
uuastom 'growth', *uuastom* (acc. sg.)
uuatar 'water', *uuatares* (gen. sg.),
    uuatare (dat. sg.)
uue see *ik*
uueg 'way, path', *uueg* (acc. sg.),
    uuege (dat. sg.)
uuelde see *uuillian*
uuerðan, uuerðen 'become' (also pass.

auxiliary), *uuerða* (3 sg. pres.
    subj.), *uuarð* (3 sg. pret. ind.)
uueridun see *uuerien*
uuerien 'hinder, prevent', *uueridun*
    (3 pl. pret. ind.)
uuerod 'people, folk', *uuerodes*
    (gen. sg.)
uuerold 'world', *uuerold* (acc. sg.)
uui see *ik*
uuiðar 'against'
uuîhian 'consecrate, hallow', *geuuîhid*
    (pret. part.)
uuiht 'demon', *uuihti* (acc. pl.)
uuiht 'something, anything'
uuilleo 'will, wish, desire', *uuillean,*
    uuilleon (dat. sg.)
uuillian 'want', *uuelde* (3 sg. pret. ind.)
uuirðig 'worthy', *uuirðige* (masc.
    nom. pl.)
uuord 'word', *uuordo* (inst. sg.)
uurt 'root', *uurteo* (gen. pl.)

Some Aspects of Old Saxon Grammar

Spelling and Pronunciation

Consonants

Old Saxon comes down to us in a number of different manuscripts whose spelling systems sometimes differ markedly. In this section I restrict myself to the letters used in normalized editions of the *Heliand*, and to the sounds modern scholars have traditionally assigned to these letters. Where spelling deviations in other texts may point to significant pronunciation variants, I indicate this.

In general, the spellings of Old Saxon correspond quite well to those given in Chapter 2. The letters *p, t, k* are pronounced as one would expect:

> *skip* 'ship' with [p]
> *watar* 'water' with [t]
> *folkes* 'folk's' (gen. sg.) with [k]

As in Modern English, *c* is also usually pronounced [k]:

> *clibon* 'hold fast' begins with [k]

Only before *i* and *e* does *c* have another pronunciation, namely [ts]:

crûci 'cross' with [ts]

The letters *b* and *d* are in general pronounced as in Modern English, but in word-final position and before voiceless consonants like *t* or *s*, they are probably pronounced [p] and [t]:

bi 'by' with [b]
dôan 'do' with [d]

lamb 'lamb' with final [p]
flôd 'flood' with final [t]

As in other Germanic languages, *g* is pronounced in a number of ways. At the beginnings of words, medially after *n*, and when doubled, it is pronounced as [g]:

gôd 'good' begins with [g]
gangan 'go' has the sequence [ŋg] as in English "finger"
seggean 'say' contains [gg] as in the English phrase "big guns"

Word-finally after *n*, *g* is pronounced as [k]:

lang 'long' with final [ŋk]

As in Gothic and Old Norse, one pronunciation of *g* in Old Saxon is as a voiced fricative, [ɣ], namely medially before a back vowel (*a*, *o*, *u*, etc.), or before a voiced consonant:

dages 'day's' (gen. sg.) with [ɣ]
fuglôs 'birds' with [ɣ]

As in Old Norse, a more *j*-like voiced fricative [ɣʲ] is found medially before front vowels (*i*, *e*, etc.):

wege 'way' (dat. sg.) with [ɣʲ]

Word-finally, *g* is pronounced as [x]:

dag 'day' with final [x]

The letter *f* is pronounced as one would expect:

fallan 'fall' with [f]

The voiced equivalent of *f* in Old Saxon—thus, the letter that is pronounced [v]—is the letter *ƀ*:

clibon 'hold fast' with [v]

Note that in normalized spelling these two letters do not generally appear in the same positions: *ƀ* appears medially between voiced sounds (especially vowels); *f* appears initially, finally, and before voiceless consonants.

Instead of *þ*, Old Saxon uses the letter sequence *th*. As in Modern English, this is pronounced sometimes as voiced [ð] (as in E. "bathe"), sometimes as voiceless [þ] (as in E. "bath"). The voiced pronunciation occurs medially between voiced sounds; the voiceless pronunciation initially, finally, and before voiceless consonants. The letter *ð* is found in all positions where *th* is found, except initially, and has the same sound values:

> *thikki* 'thick' with initial [þ]
> *wirthig* or *wirðig* 'worthy' with [ð]

The letter *s* has the same distribution of sound values as does *th*. Thus it is pronounced as [z] medially between voiced sounds, as [s] otherwise:

> *seggean* 'say' with [s]
> *wesan* 'be' with [z]

Old Saxon *h* has two pronunciations. Initially and medially before vowels, it is pronounced [h]. Finally and medially before consonants, it is pronounced [x]:

> *heƀan* 'heaven' with [h]
> *slahan* 'strike' with [h] as in E. "peahen"
> *nâh* 'near' with [x]

The letters *r*, *l*, *m*, *n* are all pronounced as expected:

> *riki* 'kingdom' with [r]
> *lust* 'joy' with [l]
> *man* 'man' with initial [m]
> *namo* 'name' with initial [n]
> *thringan* 'crowd' with [ŋg] as in E. "finger"

The combination *uu* (frequently listed in dictionaries as *w*) is pronounced [w]. Sometimes, and especially before the vowel *u*, this sound is symbolized with a single *u*:

> *uuatar* 'water' with initial [wa]
> *uurt* 'root' with initial [wu]

The sound [j] is usually represented by the symbol *i* in Old Saxon, but sometimes by the letter sequence *gi*:

> *iungaro* or *giungaro* 'disciple' with initial [j]

After consonants this sound is also frequently captured with the letter *e*:

> *seggean* 'say' with [j] following the *gg*

Vowels

On the face of it, the Old Saxon vowels of normalized texts present us no problems. There are five short vowels, *i*, *e*, *a*, *o*, *u*, and five longs, *î*, *ê*, *â*, *ô*, *û*. In general they are pronounced as one might expect from Chapter 2. Specifically, *i*, *a*, *o*, *u*, *î*, *â*, *û* are commonly considered to be pronounced exactly as explained there. On the basis of arguments like those given for the threefold value of Gothic *ai*, however (see Chapter 3), and additionally because of the pronunciation of modern North German dialects, the letters *e*, *ê*, *ô* are said to be ambiguous as to sound value in Old Saxon.

First, *e* is normally assigned two values. One of them (representing the umlaut of earlier *a*) is higher, more in the direction of *i*: something like the vowel of E. "way," but shorter. This may then be given, in philological presentations rather than normalized texts, the symbol *ę*, and the phonetic symbol may as well be [ę]. The other *e* (sometimes spelled *ë*) is pronounced more like the vowel in E. "get," thus [e]:

> *seggean* 'say' has the vowel [ę]
> *weg* 'way' has the vowel [e]

Similarly, *ê* has a distinction between higher and lower pronunciations. The higher (original *ê₂* or [ê]) is the vowel I have been symbolizing as [ê], while the lower is the vowel I have symbolized as [e:]. This latter represents the development in Old Saxon of the original diphthong *ai*:

> *hêt* 'was called' has the vowel [ê]
> *hêtan* 'be called' has the vowel [e:]

As the two examples show, some rather important distinctions—here between the present and past tense of a verb—hinge on distinguishing these two pronunciations, even though the manuscripts do not normally represent them differently.

Finally, *ô* has an analogous distinction between higher and lower pronunciations, with [ô] being high, [o:] being low (the latter comes from Germanic *au*):

> *gôd* has the vowel [ô]
> *hôh* has the vowel [o:]

Although this is not emphasized in the handbooks, it seems highly likely that, besides [ę], Old Saxon possessed other umlaut vowels not symbolized in the manuscripts, namely front rounded vowels like [û̈], [ü], [ô̈]. Certainly the later dialects possess them, and since the factors that caused these vowels to develop from the back vowels (namely [i], [î], [j] in the next syllable) had mostly disappeared by the end of Old Saxon times, the umlaut change itself must have operated during those times. It seems probable, then, that *thrungi* was actually pronounced [þrüŋgi], with a vowel like [i] with rounded lips, and that *hôrian* 'hear' would have sounded like [hôrjan], with a sound like rounded [ê].

Phonology

1. In Old Saxon, as in Old Norse, original *æ* has become long *â*:

OS	Goth.	
lâtan	lêtan	'allow'
alâsun	lêsun	'they gleaned'
dâd	gadêþs	'deed'

2. Like Old Norse, Old Saxon shows umlaut. In Old Saxon, however, the process is much less apparent. In the first place, there are no signs at all of *u*-umlaut like that found in Old Norse. Second, *a*-umlaut (which lowered *i* to *e* and *u* to *o*) is at least as obscure in Old Saxon as in Old Norse. That is to say, while one can sometimes see its effects by comparing Old Saxon with Gothic (cf. OS *gold* 'gold' with Goth. *gulþs*, the OS form showing the effects of a former *a* in the ending), within Old Saxon itself the alternations created by *a*-umlaut have mostly been leveled: *gold* 'gold'–*guldin* 'golden' is one of the few clear alternations left. Note the past participles *gidriban* 'driven', *gigripan* 'gripped' as examples where *i* has apparently not been lowered before *a*.

Even *i*-umlaut appears to be limited in Old Saxon when compared with Old Norse. The only vowel that is regularly fronted before an *i* or *j* of the next syllable is short *a*, as seen in the following alternations:

gast 'guest' – gesti (nom. pl.)
slahan 'strike' – slehis (2 sg. pres. ind.)

But as I argued above briefly in the pronunciation section, *i*-umlaut must have had a far greater effect than the orthography of Old Saxon texts shows, since the later dialects all have regular umlaut of both long and short vowels.

3. Unlike Gothic and Old Norse, Old Saxon shows a development of the older diphthongs *ai* and *au* to monophthongs, specifically [e:] and [o:]. Although, as we will see, Old High German and Old Low Franconian do this too under certain circumstances, Old Saxon does it virtually without exception:

OS	Goth.	ON	OHG	
mêr	mais	meir	mêr	'more'
dôd	dauþs	dauðr	tôt	'dead'
stên	stains	steinn	stein	'stone'
dôpian	daupjan	deypa	toufan	'baptize'

4. In addition to creating the new monophthongs [e:] and [o:], Old Saxon has held on to the older long *ê* (that is, *ê₂*) and *ô*. The distinction I have made here between the older and newer monophthongs is based on later dialect evidence, rather than on the Old Saxon manuscripts themselves.

While it is true that Old Saxon manuscripts do not distinguish between newer and older monophthongs, some manuscripts regularly write expected *ê* as *ie*, and *ô* as *uo*. These spellings are highly reminiscent of Old High German, and indeed a number of scholars have suggested that they were simply imported from the Old High German scribal tradition. But in fact, it seems more likely that they represent dialectal variants of Old Saxon:

OS	Goth.	OHG	
hêr, hier	hêr	hier	'here'
stôd, stuod	stôþ	stuont	'stood'

5. Unlike both Gothic and Old Norse, Old Saxon shows no evidence of sharpening in the old semivowel clusters *jj* and *ww*:

OS	ON	
tweio	tveggja	'of two'
triuwi	tryggr	'true'

6. Again unlike Old Norse and Gothic, Old Saxon loses the *w* of the cluster *ngw*: compare OS *singan* 'sing' with Goth. *siggwan*.

7. Like Old Norse and unlike Gothic, Old Saxon has changed original Germanic *z* to *r*:

OS	Goth.	
mêro	maiza	'greater'
lêrian	laisjan	'teach'

8. It may be remembered that Old Norse doubled the consonants *g* and *k* after a short vowel and before *j* (or sometimes *w*). This phenomenon, called *gemination*, has a far greater scope in Old Saxon, and indeed in all the languages described in subsequent chapters. In the first place, in Old Saxon all consonants can be doubled, except for *r*. In the second

place, the doubling takes place not just before *j* and sometimes *w*, but also quite frequently before *r* and *l*, and occasionally before *m* and *n*. Old Saxon is unique among the so-called West Germanic languages in that it usually still shows the conditioning *j*:

OS	Goth.	OE	
biddian	bidjan	biddan	'ask'
huggian	hugjan	hycgan	'think'
luttil	leitils	lȳtel	'little'
akkar	akrs	æcer	'field, land'

9. Like Old Norse, Old Saxon does not show the initial cluster *þl-*. Instead it shows *fl-*: compare OS *fliohan* 'flee' with Goth. *þliuhan*.

10. In Old Norse we noted that the consonant *n* is dropped between a vowel and *s*. In Old Saxon, as also in Old English and Old Frisian, this loss of a nasal, along with compensatory lengthening of the preceding vowel, is much more general. Indeed, it occurs before any of the voiceless fricatives *f*, *þ*, and *s*:

OS	Goth.	
fîf	fimf	'five'
sîð	sinþs	'way'
ûs	unsis	'us'
cûð	kunþs	'known'

11. In (4) above I noted that some scholars have attributed the *ie* and *uo* found in some manuscripts for older *ê* and *ô* to Old High German scribal influence. Though in this case there appear to be good arguments for ascribing the symbols (and their pronunciations) to dialect variation, in other cases the argument for genuine outside interference is stronger. These include the following phenomena characteristic of Old English or Old Frisian, or both:

a. The occasional use of *e* for expected *a*, and *ê* for expected *â*: *gles* instead of *glas* 'glass'; *gêr* instead of *iâr* 'year';

b. The use of *o* for *a* before nasals, and of *ô* for *â* under the same conditions: *hond* for expected *hand* 'hand'; *mônoth* for *mânoth* 'month';

c. The use of *â* for expected *ê* or *ô* (from Germanic *ai* and *au*: *hâlag* for *hêlag* 'holy'; *bâm* for *bôm* 'tree';

d. The apparent palatalization of *k* before *e*, symbolized with an orthographic *i* between the two: *kiennian* instead of *kennian* 'know'.

Among Old High German interferences can be counted the occasional substitution of *ei* or *ou* for expected *ê* and *ô*, the presence of the nasal in words like *uns* 'us', and occasional forms that show the High German Consonant Shift (see Chapter 9).

Nouns and Pronouns

1. The masculine nominative singular ending *-az* of Germanic, found both in *a*-stem nouns and in strong adjectives, disappears completely in Old Saxon. This contrasts with both Gothic and Old Norse, where the ending is kept as *-s* and *-r* respectively:

OS	Goth.	ON	
dag	dags	dagr	'day'
gôd	gôþs	góðr	'good'

2. The nominative plural of the masculine *a*-stem nouns in Old Saxon is *-os*: OS *fuglos* 'birds' opposite Goth. *fuglôs*, OHG *fogala*.

3. Like Old Norse and Gothic, Old Saxon has a distinction between dual and plural in first and second person personal pronouns:

OS *wit* 'we two' but *wî, we* 'we'
git 'you two' but *gî, ge* 'you' (pl.)

4. The masculine third person personal pronoun in Old Saxon shows forms beginning in *h-* in the nominative singular, with much less frequent occurrence of such forms in other cases. Although this feature distinguishes Old Saxon clearly from Gothic, the Saxon forms are also different from Old Norse, which shows much more widespread use of *h-*:

OS	Goth.	ON	
hê	is	hann	'he'
imu	imma	honum	'him' (dat. sg.)
siu	si	hon	'she'
ira	izôs	hennar	'her' (gen. sg.)

5. Most Old Saxon texts do not distinguish between accusative and dative in the first and second person singular personal pronouns:

	OS	Goth.	
Acc.	mî	mik	'me'
Dat.	mî	mis	'me'
Acc.	thî	þuk	'thee'
Dat.	thî	þus	'thee'

6. Old Saxon has no reflexive pronoun, using forms of the personal pronouns instead. Numerous examples of this appear in the texts above (although many of the reflexives used there are clearly pleonastic):

geng imu 'went'   kên imu 'sprouted'

In connection with this, Old Saxon does not have the possessive pronoun *sîn* 'his', which we find derived from the genitive reflexive in Gothic and Old Norse: *ên erl bigan . . . sâian . . . mid is handun* (not *mid sînen handun*).

7. Like Old Norse, Old Saxon has the intensified demonstrative pronoun derived from the regular demonstrative plus *-si*:

OS masc. nom. sg. *thê*   and *these*   opposite Goth. *sa*
   fem. acc. sg.   *thia* and *thesa* opposite Goth. *þô*
   neut. dat. pl.   *thêm* and *thesun* opposite Goth. *þaim*

Verbs

1. Like Old Norse, Old Saxon has given up reduplication as a means of forming the past tense of verbs. Most members of the former reduplicating class now show vowel alternation as in the rest of the strong verbs:

OS	Goth.	
hêtan ([e:]) – hêt ([ê])	haitan–haihait	'call–called'
fâhan–feng	fâhan–faifâh	'catch–caught'

Several former members of this class now inflect weak: *sâian–sâida* 'sow–sowed'; compare Goth. *saian–saisô*.

2. The class of *-na* verbs, so frequent in Gothic and Old Norse, is absent in Old Saxon. The inchoative meaning of 'become X', where X stands for some state, is captured by periphrastic phrases using auxiliary verbs. In this connection, compare the Old Saxon phrase *gewîhid sî thin namo* 'thy name be made holy' with its Gothic equivalent *weihnai namo þein* 'may thy name become holy', the Gothic showing the *-na* verb *weihnan* 'become holy'.

3. In Old Saxon, the second person singular preterite indicative form of strong verbs shows the ending *-i*. Furthermore, the root vowel of the verb in this form is that of the preterite plural, not that of the other preterite singular forms. Both of these characteristics distinguish Old Saxon from Gothic and Old Norse:

OS	Goth.	
niman	niman	'take' (inf.)
nam	nam	(1 and 3 sg. pret. ind.)
nâmi	namt	(2 sg. pret. ind.)
nâmun	nêmum	(1 pl. pret. ind.)

4. Old Saxon has neither a morphological passive nor a medio-passive. Intead it makes use of auxiliary verbs like *werðan* 'become', as in *ac warð that corn farloren*.

5. The third person singular present indicative form of the verb 'be' in Old Saxon is most commonly *is*, but we also find *ist*. Interestingly, the texts that show the most occurrences of *ist* also show other phenomena characteristic of Old High German, such as *uo* for *ô* and *ie* for *ê*.

6. Old Saxon differs significantly from several of the other Germanic languages in having a single verb ending for all persons of the plural, although the specific ending may vary with tense and mood. Thus the present indicative has *wî, gî, sia kiosad* 'we, you, they choose' opposite Gothic *kiusam, kiusiþ, kiusand*, the preterite indicative *wî, gî, sia kurun* opposite Gothic *kusum, kusuþ, kusun*, and so on.

7. In addition to the long forms *standan* 'stand' and *gangan* 'go', familiar from Gothic and Old Norse, Old Saxon shows contracted forms *stân* and *gân*, although the long forms are more frequent.

8. Unlike Gothic and Old Norse, but like all the languages we will discuss in the following chapters, Old Saxon has developed the verbal infinitive into something approaching a true noun (the so-called gerund). This verbal noun may then function as subject or object of a verb, or object of a preposition, and may show case forms (those of the neuter singular). The nominative and accusative have no endings anyway, but in the dative and genitive real nominal endings show up on the infinitive. In Old Saxon the genitive is rare, being restricted to one text. The dative is more common: *faranne*, dative of *faran* 'go'; *duonne*, dative of *duon* 'do'.

Germanic Alliterative Verse

Earliest Forms

In the discussion above I characterized the Old Saxon *Heliand* and *Genesis* as poetic epics. This was not to say that the lines in these poems rhyme, or indeed that they can be scanned in any way familiar from modern English poetry. For Old Saxon poetry, and Germanic poetry in general, makes use of a different set of principles than most modern readers are used to. This section lays out very roughly what these principles are, and what kind of verse they led to in two different geographical areas of the Germanic world, namely the north (especially in Icelandic) and the west (especially in the continental dialects, and particularly Old Saxon), before they were replaced partially or entirely by poetic forms borrowed from Romance languages.

Perhaps the earliest preserved snatch of Germanic verse is the inscription on the Golden Horn of Gallehus, cited earlier:

> ek hlewagastiʀ holtijaʀ   horna tawidô

Following Lehmann (1956), we may note the following facts about the line, all of which are typical of early Germanic verse.

• It can be divided into two half-lines, each of which has two prominent syllables or "lifts" (German *Hebungen*: *hle-* and *hol-* in the first half-line, *hor-* and *ta-* in the second).

• The line is bound together by alliteration, that is, by the recurrence of some identical element at the beginning of lifts, in this case *h*.

• The metrically most important syllable in the line is the first lift of the second half-line (here *hor-*), since this is the one syllable that *must* carry the alliteration.

• The number of syllables between or after the lifts, in the so-called drops or *Senkungen*, is not restricted, varying from one to three in the line above.

• Weakly stressed syllables are permitted before the first lift, as with *ek* in the first half-line; this is known as "anacrusis," or in German *Auftakt*.

• The last lift does not alliterate.

To remove any residual doubt that the Gallehus inscription is a poetic one, one may cite a strikingly similar line from the Old Saxon Parable of the Sower and the Seed.

> hrosso hôfslaga   endi heliðo trâda

Note that it meets all of the same restrictions and shows all of the same freedoms, a remarkable fact considering these two lines were composed more than four centuries apart.

There are a few further facts about the Germanic "long line" (the technical term for the metrical unit formed by two half-lines). In the first place, the assignment of prominence to syllables is not at all arbitrary. Rather, metrical prominence follows word stress, and a syllable that is not stressed in everyday language cannot be stressed in poetry. Additionally, the earliest Germanic poetry shows a tendency in the lifts to avoid certain classes of words (verbs, for example) that normally do not bear as much emphasis as others. Indeed, as the examples above show, nouns and noun compounds are favored in these positions, as are adjectives under certain circumstances.

Prominence in the poetic line was not simply a matter of stress, however. Scholars have noted a strong tendency for prominent syllables to be not only stressed but also *long* (i.e., to contain *either* a long vowel or a diphthong, *or* a short vowel plus one or more consonants). Short syllables ending in a single short vowel were not commonly given metrical prominence even if stressed.

I use words like "tendency" and "commonly" in the paragraph above because the correlation between syllable length and prominence never approached the status of an absolute rule. Since many of the weakly stressed endings of earlier Germanic contained long vowels (as in *tawidô* above), it is clear that long syllables could be found in the drops. And the requirement that the lifts be filled by long syllables could be circumvented by the process of *resolution*, in which a short stressed syllable followed by another short could replace a long, as in *hlewa-* above.

Because of these exceptions, and because of the freedom allowed in the number of syllables filling a drop, Germanic alliterative verse had a characteristically choppy and irregular rhythm, far removed from what modern English poetry readers are used to. Nevertheless there was a system to the distribution of lifts and drops in the half-lines. I have listed below the five patterns that the German scholar Eduard Sievers (1893) has suggested underlie all half-lines in Germanic verse. They are listed in order of decreasing frequency. It should be noted that acute accent (´) stands for main stress, grave accent (`) for secondary stress, and × for weak stress. For each ideal type I have cited an example (frequently less than ideal) from the *Heliand*. The first three come from the texts in the Readings, but in Types D and E I have drawn in new material. For the sake of the presentation I have chosen lines as short and as clear as possible:

A: ´ × ´ ×	lande rûmor 'farther from land'
B: × ´ × ´	thar waldand Crist 'there where mighty Christ'
C: × ´ ´ ×	an ên skip innan 'onto a ship'
D: ´ ´ ` × *or* ´ ´ × `	man mislîko 'men variously'
E: ´ ` × ´ *or* ´ × ` ´	wârfastun word 'true words'

Old Saxon in fact simply seems to have too many syllables in most half-lines to show Sievers' patterns clearly. I will return to this point below, but for the moment the lines above should be taken as typical for early Germanic types.

The actual organizational principle of Germanic verse, of course, was alliteration, the recurrence of an identical element at the beginnings of lifts. Usually, the element was a consonant, as with the *h* in the lines above. Although the alliterating consonants had to be identical, it was not a problem if one of them was the first element of an initial cluster: *hle-* alliterates with *hol-* above. The only exception to this rule was that *sp*, *st*, and *sk* were treated as single consonants, and could only alliterate with themselves, as in:

> an êna starca strâtun   thar stôpon gengun

Vowels clearly were secondary elements in Germanic verse. Even though vowel alliterations were rather common, any vowel could alliterate with any other. Indeed, in the earliest verse compositions it seems to have been considered incorrect to alliterate identical vowels.

As for which of the four lifts carried the alliteration, the one that *had* to alliterate was the first lift of the second half-line. This syllable then determined alliteration for the other alliterating lifts, a fact that aids the modern reader greatly. In the first half-line, there was a distinct tendency for both lifts to alliterate, as in the two long lines given above. But neither of them absolutely had to, as long as the other did. When only one alliterated, there was a tendency for it to be the first. Finally, as noted above, only in rare cases was there alliteration in the fourth lift (the second of the second half-line).

The earliest forms of Germanic verse do not appear to have made use of any alliterative unit longer than a single long line. And even in later developments, such as skaldic verse, the larger units, such as stanzas, are metrical and content units rather than alliterative ones.

It would appear that even on the content level the long line was the chief unit in early Germanic poetry. That is, major syntactic breaks almost invariably corresponded with the end of the long line, while the breaks between half-lines reflected lesser linguistic boundaries.

In terms of genre, the earliest Germanic poetry beyond the level of the magical charm or the riddle was probably the short lay, recounting, with interspersed dialogue, significant incidents in the life of a god, an ancient Germanic hero, or a benefactor. Of surviving poetry, probably some of the Eddic poems of Old Norse come closest to the original type.

Many of the criteria for Germanic verse mentioned above remained characteristic until the very end of the form both in the north and in the south. Nonetheless, the two areas developed very different types of poetry on this common base, and it is the task of the following two sections to make the differences clear.

Alliterative Verse in the North

In form as well as content, many of the older Eddic poems remain rather close to the original Germanic verse form sketched above. Yet there are still a few developments worth noting.

There is a notable terseness about these poems, which sets them off from the alliterative verse of the south. This terseness is expressed primarily in the rather small number of syllables in the drops of the half-lines. While three or more unstressed syllables in a row are not unheard of, Eddic verse usually gets by with two, seems to aim for one, and sometimes dispenses with unstressed syllables almost entirely, as in the following line from the *Hávamál*:

> Deyr fé, deyja frændr   'Die cattle, die kin'

Lehmann, quite rightly I believe, ascribes this terseness to a number of linguistic factors. First, Old Norse retains a very strong primary stress (stress was weakened a great deal in the south, especially on the Continent). Second, Old Norse has a relatively large number of long syllables. Third, linguistic changes in the endings of Old Norse words shortened them significantly. In addition, Old Norse grammar required few of the unstressed function words, like the article 'the' or the auxiliary verbs 'have' and 'be', that so padded the sentences of the more southerly Germanic languages.

Another development, found even in the earliest Eddic verse, is the poetic form known as the stanza. This was, initially at least, a relatively irregular grouping of lines or half-lines to form a subsection of the larger poem. The grouping was primarily done on the basis of content, with the end of the stanza corresponding to a major syntactic break, and stanzas could vary greatly in size, even in the same poem. The later Eddic poems show a far greater regularity in this respect, and the skaldic poems, here as in other areas, tolerate virtually no irregularity at all.

In some Eddic poems we also find a purely metrical development of units longer than the Germanic long line. This was the *ljóðaháttr* stanza form, whose odd-numbered lines consisted of the expected two half-lines linked by alliteration, but whose even-numbered lines were so-called full lines, with three (or sometimes two) lifts and their own alliterative pattern. Note Frey's lament in *Skírnismál*:

Lǫng er nótt,   lǫng er ǫnnur,
hvé mega ek þreyja þrjár?
Opt mér mánaðr   minni þótti
en sjá half hýnótt.

'Long is a night,   long is a second,
How can I stand three?
Oft to me a month   less seemed
Than such a half bridal night.'

The strangest development of the original Germanic verse form may be found in skaldic poetry. Besides the metrical types found in the Eddic poems, the poetry of the skalds exhibits some in which half-lines (or, in the technical terminology for skaldic, "verses") regularly consist of three lifts, and others in which they must contain four. In addition, we find that the spareness of Eddic poetry leads in the skaldic style to actual counting of syllables. In one type of poem, for example, the stanzas show a fairly traditional metrical pattern (each verse consisting of two lifts), but every odd-numbered verse must contain three syllables, while each even-numbered one must have four. In the *dróttkvætt* form, with three lifts per verse, not only must each verse contain six syllables, the last two must come in the order stressed–unstressed (a so-called feminine ending).

Even by itself, this may seem somewhat restrictive, compared to earlier forms. But syllable-counting was merely one aspect of skaldic poetry. Another, seemingly quite alien to Germanic poetry, was rhyme (a feature perhaps borrowed from Irish verse). It was not, at least in most cases, the kind of end-rhyme with which we are acquainted in Modern English, but rather rhymes between syllables in the same verse. These rhymes were of two types. First, the consonant or consonant-cluster following the vowel in one syllable could be repeated with a different vowel in a following syllable; this was incomplete rhyme or *skothending*—compare Modern English "mustard" with "fasting." Second, the consonant or consonant-cluster could be repeated with the same preceding vowel; this was complete rhyme or *aðalhending*—compare "faster" with "lasting." Very soon after its introduction this innovation too was regulated: skothending was used in odd lines, aðalhending in even lines.

If skaldic poetry at this point begins to seem somewhat contrived, that would not be an unfair impression. Lehmann's comparison of skalds with jugglers, intent as much on play as on communication, seems apt. The complexity is further compounded by two additional factors.

First, instead of using alternative nouns of a more prosaic nature, skaldic verse uses *heiti* and *kennings*. Heiti are poetic nouns, archaic, newly coined, or shifted from normal usage, which substitute for a common term, as when I use "steed," "land-strider," or "stallion" in place of "horse." Kennings are noun phrases or compounds that do the same thing, as when I call a camel "the ship of the desert," or a sword "the blood-drinker." Many of the kennings used by the skalds require much more esoteric knowledge, however, as when gold is called "Freyja's tears," or the earth "the mother of Thor." It was precisely such knowledge that Snorri tried to preserve in his *Edda*.

Second, given the many rules they did follow, it is surprising how little attention the skalds seem to have paid to the syntactic patterns of their own language. Indeed, they clearly delighted in linguistic obscurity. Thus not only is word order strained, it is frequently difficult to figure out what sentence or phrase a given word belongs to, since parts of several different syntactic units were frequently intermixed in a stanza.

To illustrate all these characteristics, I give below the first two long lines of Einarr skálaglamm Helgason's *Vellekla*, taken from Lehmann (1956: 45), and including his free translation, intended to give the flavor of the original:

> Hugstóran biðk heyra
> (heyr jarl Kvasis dreyra)
> foldar vǫrð á fyrða
> fjarðleggjar brim dreggjar.

> 'O lord, let now be heard
> the lore of Kvasir's gore,
> fair words set forth, oh sire,
> the firth-men's song, earth-king.'

Lehmann gives as a more concise translation: "I ask the land's courageous ward to hear my poem."

Despite the advanced technical development of Germanic verse in the north, there appears to have been little change in function. Poetry was used for short lays, songs of praise, laments, even occasional lyric outpourings, but it was not typically used to narrate longer stories. For this, the preferred medium in the north was prose, specifically the saga, which I discussed in Chapter 4.

Alliterative Verse in the South

In the south, the picture is quite different. There are some few examples of other genres there—the Old High German *Ludwigslied* as a song of praise, the Old English *Fight at Finnsburg* as a short epic, occasional magic charms and other lesser types—but most of the surviving poetry consists of long epics, such as the Old English *Beowulf* and the Old Saxon *Heliand*. It seems likely that this genre of vernacular poetry was modeled on Latin traditions, as even its preponderantly religious subject matter indicates.

As one might expect, the main differences between short epics and long epics correlate with their length. Where the short epics gave little background for their stories, describing their characters' deeds only in certain significant events or situations, the long epics elaborated endlessly on background and environment, showing not only the historical and tribal situation, but also the motives and moods of the characters, the physical characteristics and atmosphere of the setting, and so on. One need only compare the Old Saxon sower parable with the others in this book to get an idea of how much elaboration was involved.

As with content, so with form. If the Old Norse verse forms are terse, the Old Saxon ones are expansive, indeed almost to the point of dissolution. Although still technically adhering to the metrical principles of Germanic verse given above, the southern epic pushed some of those principles to the limit—especially the one allowing any number of unstressed syllables in the drops. It should be pointed out, in the poets' defense, that most of the responsibility for these developments can be laid at the door of linguistic change. Lehmann notes that the north retained a strong word stress favorable to the alliterative principle, and that such stress weakened considerably in the south, with a corresponding increase in the importance of sentence stress. In addition, the southern languages, especially on the Continent, did not see nearly the reduction in unstressed endings that Old Norse did. In fact, a number of southern linguistic developments went in exactly the opposite direction: weakly stressed vowels were inserted to break up certain consonant clusters, and the number of function words, like 'the' and 'have', increased.

We may see the effects of these changes quite easily in the section of the *Heliand* given in the Readings. Below I give examples of some of the most obvious differences from the Old Norse poems.

Many Old Saxon half-lines show an amazing number of unstressed syllables:

Hê stôd imo thô bi ênes watares staðe

Here we find, besides the requisite two stressed syllables, *eleven* unstressed ones, of which eight are in anacrusis (the first lift of the half-line being on *watar-*). Note how many of the unstressed syllables are function words.

The *Heliand* tends to give metrical prominence to classes of words, such as verbs and pronouns, that rarely receive it in Old Norse, or even Old English:

> kên imu thar endi clibode (lifts on *kên* and *clibode*)
> an themu dage (lift on *themu*)

As Lehmann points out, Old Saxon is far freer to shift words between the alliterating and non-alliterating lifts than other languages. Thus in the first line below, the word *gôdo* bears the alliteration, while in the second it doesn't—the alliteration there is on *d*:

> ac geng imu thô the gôdo
> drohtin the gôdo

By contrast, the word *gôd* alliterates 33 out of the 35 times it occurs in *Beowulf*, according to Lehmann.

Whereas in earlier verse, and outside Old Saxon, it is considered bad form to rhyme the vowel following an alliterating consonant, or to use rhyming vowels when the alliteration is non-consonantal, in Old Saxon this is clearly felt to be desirable:

> huô imu ên erl bigan   an erðu sâian   (*erl* and *erðu*)
> hrêncorni mid is handun.   Sum it an hardan stên   (*handun* and *hardan*)

Given the increasing dissolution of the Old Saxon long line, this feature may be seen as something of a prophylactic measure, meant to increase the prominence of the alliterations.

There are two further important developments in southern verse, which have less to do with meter and rhythm than with matters of larger form.

First, the development of kennings in the north, when one thinks about it, goes along quite well with the characteristic terseness of northern verse. Metrically, the collocation of nouns in a kenning enables one to produce two lifts with few or no intervening syllables. Stylistically, kennings allow a wealth of meaning in a few words.

In the south, with its far more expansive style, kennings, though known, are far less frequent, especially on the Continent. The task was not to say things in as few words as possible, but to elaborate on them. Thus was developed the "variation," a predominantly nominal construc-

tion that restated in different words something already said, thereby pad-
ding the narrative. The *Heliand* is rife with such variations, as the lines
below show:

> ac geng imu thô the gôdo   endi is iungaron mid imu,
> friðubarn godes   (different words for 'Jesus')

> Sum it eft an land bifel,
> an erðun aðalcunnies   (different words for 'earth')

Variation, of course, is only one of the many strategies that the *Heliand*
poet and others use to delay the action by restating the same thing over
and over again. Our *Heliand* reading selection, as padded as it may seem,
is comparatively conservative in this respect.

Second, study of the variations in the *Heliand* text reveals that
many of them appear in the first half-line, before a major syntactic boundary. This syntactic effect of variation was probably intentional, for the
southern epic displays a strong tendency for syntactic breaks to come in
the middle of the long line, as opposed both to earlier and to northern
practice. This feature of southern poetry, known as *enjambment*, was one
way of ameliorating what Lehmann calls the "stichic rigidity" of the Germanic alliterative line. It should be noted, however, that this syntactic solution to the problem was not paralleled by the creation of larger metrical
units, as in the north. In form, the southern epic is little more than a very
long string of essentially independent long lines.

In the discussion above, I have concentrated on Old Norse and Old
Saxon, and have neglected two other older languages with substantial
amounts of poetry, namely Old English and Old High German. Yet given
the limitations of this book, such a procedure seemed warranted. Old English verse can be seen as intermediate between the Old Norse and Old
Saxon forms. Although it shares many linguistic developments with Old
Saxon it is closer to Old Norse in other ways, such as the retention of a
strong primary stress. In addition, both tradition and a closer contact
with the north allowed Old English to resist many of the changes that
affected Old Saxon verse.

In Old High German, finally, virtually all the changes that affected
Old Saxon had taken place even earlier. As a result, except for two rather
short poems (the mixed-dialect *Hildebrandslied* and the Bavarian *Muspilli*) and some verses from minor genres, Old High German poetry is of
the borrowed type with end-rhyme.

Of course, sooner or later all the Germanic languages were to suc-
cumb to the new structural principles. On the Continent, the change hap-

pened early, in the ninth century, with regular rhythms and end-rhyme replacing alliteration. In the north, the change was late, in the thirteenth century, and end-rhyme never entirely replaced alliteration; it simply became central, while alliteration became more peripheral. English, as might be expected, took a middle position, with end-rhymed verse becoming predominant only in the eleventh century, and isolated examples of alliterative poetry appearing long after that time.

FURTHER READING

Eichhoff, Jürgen, and Irmengard Rauch, eds. *Der Heliand*. Wege der Forschung, 321. Darmstadt: Wissenschaftliche Buchgesellschaft, 1973.

Frank, Roberta. *Old Norse Court Poetry: The Dróttkvætt Stanza*. Ithaca, N.Y.: Cornell University Press, 1978.

Gallée, Johan Hendrik. *Altsächsische Grammatik*. 2d ed. Halle: Niemeyer, 1910.

Holthausen, F. *Altsächsisches Elementarbuch*. 2d ed. Heidelberg: Winter, 1921.

Krogmann, Willy. "Altsächsisch und Mittelniederdeutsch." In L. E. Schmitt, ed., *Kurzer Grundriss der germanischen Philologie bis 1500*, vol. 1, *Sprachgeschichte*, pp. 211–52. Berlin: de Gruyter, 1970.

Lehmann, Winfred P. *The Alliteration of Old Saxon Poetry*. Norsk Tidsskrift for Sprogvidenskap, Supplement 3. Oslo: Universitetsforlaget, 1953. [Reprinted in Eichhoff and Rauch, eds. (q.v.), 144–76.]

———. *The Development of Germanic Verse Form*. Austin, Tex.: University of Texas Press, 1956.

Lintzel, Martin. *Der sächsische Stammesstaat und seine Eroberung durch die Franken*. Historische Studien, 227. Berlin: Ebering, 1933. [Reprint, Vaduz: Kraus, 1965.]

———. *Zur altsächsischen Stammesgeschichte*. Berlin: Akademie-Verlag, 1961.

Mühlbacher, Engelbert. *Deutsche Geschichte unter den Karolingern*. Darmstadt: Wissenschaftliche Buchgesellschaft, 1959. [Reprint of the 1896 ed.; see esp. ch. 6, section 1.]

Schmidt, Ludwig. *Geschichte der deutschen Stämme bis zum Ausgang der Völkerwanderung*. Vol. 1, *Die Westgermanen*. Munich: Beck, 1938. [See esp. pp. 33–70.]

Schwarz, Ernst. *Germanische Stammeskunde*. Heidelberg: Winter, 1956. [See esp. chs. 22, 25.]

Thompson, James Westfall. *Feudal Germany*. Chicago: University of Chicago Press, 1928. [See esp. ch. 4.]

de Vries, Jan. *Altnordische Literaturgeschichte*. 2 vols. Berlin: de Gruyter, 1964–67.

6

OLD ENGLISH

A Brief History of the Anglo-Saxons

I noted in the last chapter that by the third century the Saxons had become a force to be reckoned with along the shores of northern Gaul and southeastern England. Archeological evidence supports the notion that some Germanic settlers were already well established in East Anglia in the latter part of the fourth century, although these were probably Angles rather than Saxons. But both the historical sources and the archeological evidence seem to agree that the major influx of Germanic immigration into England came in the mid-fifth century. The historical sources refer to a British (i.e., Celtic) "proud tyrant" (whom the eighth-century Northumbrian monk and scholar Bede calls Vortigern), who invited the Saxons, under leaders Bede calls Hengest and Horsa, into the country to help his people resist attacks from the barbarian Picts and Scots of the north.

If this story is true, the invitation was a gross miscalculation. Reinforced by others of their countrymen who were attracted by the living apparently to be made in Britain, the Germanic tribes soon turned against their erstwhile employers, becoming more of a threat than the peoples they had been brought in to fight. The latter half of the fifth century is marked by Germanic attempts to move inland out of the southern and eastern coastal zones to which they had originally been limited, and by British attempts to keep them there. At a great battle fought sometime around 500 at "Mount Badon" (a location not definitely pinpointed in modern times), the British, perhaps under a king called Arthur, succeeded in stopping Anglo-Saxon expansion for a time. But in the latter part of the sixth century, after an apparently important victory in 571, the pace of Anglo-Saxon conquest speeded up again, and by the year 600 a great deal of southern Britain was in Anglo-Saxon hands, the areas under British rule having been reduced to a few distant corners of the west, such as Wales and Cornwall.

According to Bede, the forebears of the Anglo-Saxons of his day came from three great Germanic groups on the Continent: the Saxons; the Angles, who lived north of the Saxons on the Jutland peninsula, in modern Schleswig; and the Jutes, who are supposed to have lived north of the Angles, also on the Jutland peninsula. Modern research suggests two rather large revisions of this picture.

In the first place, it seems unlikely that the Jutes came directly from Jutland, if at all; rather, their archeological remains bear a striking resemblance to those of the Ripuarian Franks of the middle Rhine. The second revision, which has support from some old sources, would include large numbers of Frisians among the invading tribes. (See Chapter 7 for more details on the Frisians.) It is certain that many of the invaders had spent time on the Frisian coast before moving on to Britain, as Frisia's geographically intermediate position would suggest.

Again according to Bede, each of the tribal groupings formed the background for one or more of the English kingdoms of his day (Map 5). Thus the kingdom of Kent, the Isle of Wight, and the coastal zones facing the Isle of Wight were said to be Jutish; Essex, Sussex, and Wessex were inhabited by Saxons; and Angles predominated in East Anglia, Middle Anglia, Mercia, and Northumbria. No doubt there is a great deal of truth in Bede's reconstruction, but most scholars now feel that he exaggerated the distinctions between the various groups and their settlement areas. Although the invading Germanic tribes were far from an undifferentiated mass, the later clear distinctions, for example in dialect, are probably due to political divisions that arose after the invasions.

Although the Germanic invaders must at first have had little greater organization than isolated war bands, they quickly united into larger territorial groups under kings. Map 5 shows the approximate extent of the greater kingdoms by about 600, although in some places, especially Mercia, full consolidation lay some years in the future. Any idea of a larger political unity was at this time notably absent.

There were, however, more and less influential kings and kingdoms, depending mostly on the power and connections of individual men. In the earliest days of the Anglo-Saxons, power appears to have rested in the south and east, specifically (according to Bede) under Aelle of Sussex, Ceawlin of Wessex, Aethelberht of Kent, and Raedwald of East Anglia. We are not sure why the first two have such influence ascribed to them, but of Aethelberht (ca. 560–616) we know that he maintained relations

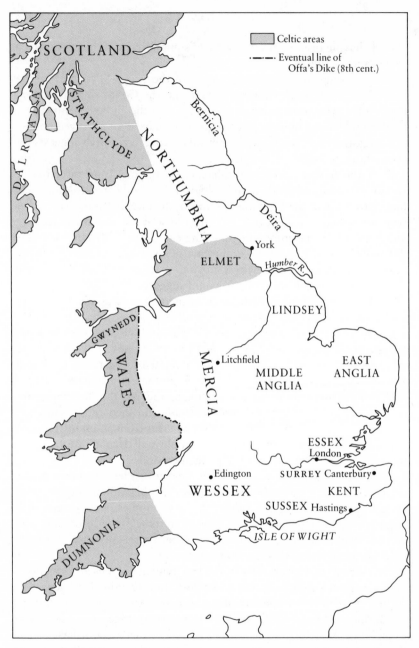

Map 5.   Anglo-Saxon political divisions around A.D. 600. (After Fisher [1973: 111], by permission)

with the Frankish court (he married the Frankish king's daughter, in fact), paved the way throughout England for Augustine of Canterbury's Christianization of the Anglo-Saxons, and was capable of imposing his will far outside the boundaries of his own kingdom. Raedwald (d. 624) at first seems to have accepted Aethelberht's supremacy, but later, because of the wealth and unity of his kingdom and its apparent control of the sea, he was able to advance his own pretensions to overlordship. He was even able to defeat and kill the founder of the united kingdom of Northumbria, Aethelfrith (d. 616), and put his own ally, Edwin, on its throne.

Ultimately, however, the centers of power in Anglo-Saxon England were to rest successively in the three kingdoms of Northumbria, Mercia, and Wessex. These were the kingdoms on the northerly and westerly frontiers of the area under Anglo-Saxon control, and only these kingdoms had any real room to expand. Their constant border wars with Picts, Scots, and British, not to mention each other, also kept their armies in fighting trim, and made them fearsome opponents for the older kingdoms of the south and east.

It was in fact under that Aethelfrith later killed by Raedwald of East Anglia that Northumbria (Anglo-Saxon England north of the Humber river) was first forged out of the two earlier kingdoms of Bernicia and Deira. (The Bernician Aethelfrith married the daughter of the old king of Deira, and drove out his son Edwin.) The boundaries of the new kingdom of Northumbria were both enlarged and strengthened by Aethelfrith's victories over the Scots of Dalriada, who had constantly threatened the Anglo-Saxon settlers of the Scottish lowlands, and the British of Gwynedd, who reportedly were harboring Edwin of Deira.

Upon the death of Aethelfrith, in 616, Edwin of Deira took control of the combined kingdom, and for the next fifty years or so Northumbria, despite its internal problems, was the effective center of power in Anglo-Saxon England. To the north and west, Edwin carved out new areas of Anglo-Saxon control, and according to Bede he exercised authority also over all the kingdoms of the south except Kent. His authority did not remain unchallenged, however. Eventually it was perceived to be so threatening to the newly emerging kingdom of Mercia that the latter, under its ruler Penda, allied with the British of Gwynedd to fight and finally kill Edwin in 633. Initially his death led to a falling-apart of the Northumbrian kingdom into its two components, Bernicia and Deira, but this respite was short. Oswald, a son of Aethelfrith, drove the British out of Northumbria in 634, and Northumbrian pressure on Mercia soon resumed. Oswald died in 641 in battle against the Mercians, but was succeeded by his brother Oswiu, under whom Northumbria reached the apogee of its power. Oswiu made tributaries of most of the Pictish and Scottish kingdoms to the north, and after a great battle in 655, in which (or soon after which) the Mercian king Penda met his death, he was also undisputed overlord of the southern Anglo-Saxon kingdoms.

With Oswiu's death in 670, Northumbria's primacy was quickly eclipsed. His successor, Ecgfrith, was decisively defeated by the Mercians in 678, and was killed in 685 while campaigning against the Celtic kingdoms of the north. For the next fifty years no English kingdom exercised any consistent authority over the others.

When next a clear overlordship emerged, it was in Mercia, under Aethelbald (716–57). Under him and his successor Offa (d. 796), Mercia reached heights of supremacy such as Northumbria had never realized. A number of kingdoms that had been relatively independent (such as East Anglia, Lindsey, and Essex) completely lost their independence during these years, and the others fell subject to much tighter control than ever before. Especially under Offa, Anglo-Saxon England became an international presence: Charlemagne attempted to cement a political alliance with Mercia by marrying one of his sons to one of Offa's daughters, and for the first time in two centuries England was graced with the presence of papal legates, who fell in with Offa's plan (ultimately abortive) to establish an archbishopric within Mercia, in Litchfield. Offa is also credited with the building of that huge earthwork on the Mercian border with Wales now known as Offa's Dike, and with the creation of a standard English currency that was to survive until after the Norman conquest.

Events after Offa's death in 796 proved that dominion in England was still very much a function of the power of individual kings, rather than of their institutions. For all that Offa had styled himself king of all the English people, and had even had his son anointed king by the Church in 787, thereby presumably establishing a dynasty, Mercia's supremacy fell apart in the early ninth century. Kent, Northumbria, and Wessex soon rebelled against Offa's successors, and only Kent was retaken after two years of fighting. Under Egbert (802–39), Wessex became as strong as Mercia. In 825, after defeating a large force under Beornwulf of Mercia, Egbert offered his own authority as a counter to Mercia's in southern England, and this offer was quickly taken up by Kent, Surrey, Sussex, and Essex, with East Anglia also appealing to him for protection. In 829, Egbert even succeeded momentarily in setting himself up as king of all the English, driving out the new Mercian king Wiglaf and receiving the submission of the Northumbrians. His brief supremacy came to an end in 830, with Wiglaf returning to the throne of Mercia, while the southern kingdoms remained part of Wessex's sphere of influence.

For a time thereafter, there was a balance of power between Mercia and Wessex, a balance that might have gone on indefinitely had it not been for the vikings. The first viking attacks on England had already taken place at the end of the eighth century, in fact while Offa was king. These attacks remained rather isolated, however, until after 835; they then increased gradually in frequency and intensity. More ominously, the vikings in 851 began to spend their winters on small islands off the English coast, establishing a year-round presence. Finally, in 865, a "great army" of Danes, as the *Anglo-Saxon Chronicle* calls them, came to mainland England to stay. Ironically, this viking presence ultimately was to lead to a permanently united English kingdom under Wessex.

It didn't look that way at first, of course. By 877, the Danish army (by that time several separate armies) had taken over and settled Northumbria and eastern Mercia, and had smashed the East Anglian kingdom. The Danes had made attempts on Wessex before, and in 878, under Guthrum, they succeeded for a time in actually occupying it, forcing its king, Alfred, to flee with members of his household into the marshes. In a remarkable reversal of fortunes, however, later in the same year Alfred succeeded in rallying his forces and defeated the Danes decisively at Edington, whereupon the invaders sued for peace. After giving hostages in pledge of peace, the Danes returned to the shattered kingdom of East Anglia and settled there.

Although there were frequent skirmishes between English and Danes, the next important event of Alfred's reign was his retaking of London in 886. London was strategically important, as the Danes had frequently used it up to then as a point of entry into the country. With this victory, Alfred was freely recognized as the overlord of all the English not subject to the Danes, thus guaranteeing him the support especially of the western Mercians. He also at this time entered into a formal treaty with the Danes, in order to extract from them the best possible treatment of the English living in Danish-dominated territories, but also formally recognizing Danish authority in the occupied lands.

The acceptance of Alfred's authority in western Mercia was not grudging. By marrying the daughter of a Mercian nobleman, by giving his daughter in marriage to the effective sovereign of English Mercia, Aethelred, and especially by ceding the newly recaptured London to

Aethelred rather than annexing it to Wessex, Alfred succeeded in ingratiating himself with the Mercians in a way hitherto atypical, and, as it turned out, more effective than conquest.

Under Alfred's children Edward (d. 924) and Aethelflaed (d. 918; the widow of Aethelred and ruler of Mercia after him), all the Danish territories south of the Humber were recaptured, and in 920 Edward received at least the nominal submission of all the sovereigns of England, Scotland, and Wales. Though he was still far from true overlordship, he had made at least a first stab at true unity in the whole of Great Britain.

Edward's successors Athelstan (924–39) and Edmund (940–46) succeeded in consolidating and even adding to the gains made under Edward, first gaining, then losing, then retaking southern Northumbria from its Danish and Norwegian overlords, and ceding a part of the north to the Scots in exchange for their help. In the reign of Eadred (946–55), the Northumbrians seceded again for a period, preferring Scandinavian rule; but with the death in 954 of Eric Blood-Axe, the Norwegian ruler at York, the subjection of Northumbria to the greater English state was complete.

Until 975, when Edgar the nephew of Eadred died, there was an uneasy peace in the newly unified land. Then things went downhill precipitously. After the brief reign of Edward, treacherously murdered in 978, England was subjected to the long and inglorious kingship of a man dubbed by his contemporaries *unræd*, loosely 'ill counsel', now known as Aethelred the Unready. Harassed by a new wave of Scandinavian invasions, Aethelred proved himself unready indeed, appointing incompetent commanders and advisers, trying to buy the invaders off with increasing quantities of Danegeld, ordering an ill-advised and unworkable execution of all Danes in the country. Even his rare intelligent moves, such as his marriage to Emma, sister of the duke of Normandy, were later to have disastrous consequences. In 1013, when a large army of Danes under King Swein invaded England (motivated at least partly by Aethelred's killing of Swein's sister), resistance was minimal, and Aethelred was forced to flee to Normandy.

Swein died only a few months later, and Aethelred returned to England, having promised through his son Edward to be a better king than before. The promise turned out to be rather rash. By 1015, when Canute the Great, son of Swein, reinvaded England, he confronted a divided and alienated kingdom, which he had no difficulty in pacifying. Aethelred died in 1016, and his oldest surviving son, Edmund, soon afterwards, leaving Canute in sole control of England.

Canute ruled as king of England until 1035, cementing his rule by, among other actions, marrying Aethelred's widow, Emma of Normandy, thereby forestalling the duke of Normandy from taking action on behalf of Aethelred's and Emma's sons. His own sons (by different wives) Harald Harefoot and Hardecanute ruled after him until Hardecanute's death in 1042.

In 1042, the dynasty of Alfred was briefly restored in the person of Edward, son of Aethelred and Emma of Normandy, and also Hardecanute's adoptive heir. His upbringing and part of his ancestry were Norman, and most modern scholars agree that at some point he promised the English throne to Duke William of Normandy. Upon his death in 1066, however, Harold Godwinson, earl of Wessex, was acclaimed king by the English, a position he held for only nine months. On October 14, 1066, Harold fell in battle against the Normans at Hastings, and the Anglo-Saxon state was at an end.

Old English Texts

Old English is second only to Old Norse in the volume and variety of texts. Thus in the following discussion I have restricted myself to a discussion of genres rather than of specific works, though in some cases certain preeminent texts must be mentioned.

Poetry

A notable fact about Old English poetry is that most of it is found in four manuscripts dating from around the year 1000. Some of these are real hodgepodges, containing poems of vastly differing type and quality. Additionally, because of where and when the manuscripts were compiled, the dialect of Old English in which they are written is predominantly Late West Saxon, with occasional Anglian and Northumbrian forms betraying a poem's composition in a different area of the country. The original date of many of the poems is a matter of scholarly controversy, and thus in the following discussion I have classified them by content rather than by period.

It seems that if one knows nothing else about Old English, one knows that it is the language of the famous heroic poem *Beowulf.* The central character is the legendary Geatish hero for whom the poem is named, and its central episodes are three fights that Beowulf has with various monsters in order to save allies, kin, and country. The insights that the poem gives into the Germanic heroic ethos are far too complex to discuss here, and I won't cheapen them by trying. Suffice it to say that *Beowulf*'s preeminent position in Germanic poetry is richly deserved.

In addition to *Beowulf*, there are a number of other (shorter) examples of secular heroic poetry in Old English. These include a fragment dealing with a battle between Danes and Frisians (also told as a brief digression within *Beowulf*), known as the *Fight at Finnsburg*; another fragment dealing with the story of Walter of Aquitaine, known as the *Waldere*; and two later poems dealing with historic battles against Anglo-Saxon enemies, one, *The Battle of Brunanburh*, embedded in the *Anglo-Saxon Chronicle* (see below under "Prose"), and the other, *The Battle of Maldon*, independent of the *Chronicle* but clearly related to its entry for the year 991.

This section should also mention the famous *Widsith*, which is not an epic in itself, but which, with its lists of personalities, countries, genealogies, and the like, could easily serve as the source of many. Many of the people it lists are indeed independently documented in other sources, both poetic and not.

For the Christian Anglo-Saxons, the works of the Christian saints, and of Christ himself, were no less heroic than those of secular heroes, and perhaps more so. Thus we find a fairly large body of poetic texts dealing with religious heroes. These include *Andreas*, *Juliana*, and *Elene*, *The Fates of the Apostles*, and two poems dealing with the Anglo-Saxon saint Guthlac; three poems (frequently linked and called *Christ I, II, and III*) dealing with the Advent, the Ascension, and Judgment Day; the famous and affecting *Dream of the Rood*, dealing with the Passion of Christ; and a number of miscellaneous poems dealing with Judgment Day, the descent into Hell, Christ's temptation by Satan, and so forth.

Also frequently couched in the heroic mode are some Old English poems on Old Testament and related topics, such as *Genesis A* and *B* (the latter goes back to an Old Saxon original), *Exodus*, *Judith*, and parts of *Daniel*.

An important genre for Old English poetry is the *elegy*. These lyric poems, often in dramatic monologue form, usually dwell on the contrast between past happiness and present misery, emphasizing the transitoriness of wealth, happiness, and glory, and sometimes, but not always, pointing to a religious resolution of the dilemma. The individual themes vary within this framework: *The Ruin* describes the present decay of a once-glorious city; *The Wanderer* and other poems deal with the fallen condition of an individual; *The Wife's Lament* considers the unhappy end of a love relationship. *The Husband's Message*, sometimes grouped with *The Wife's Lament*, is really more of a counter-elegy: things were bad before, but now the speaker has found happiness in exile, and wants his wife to join him.

In addition to the major types of poetry mentioned above, there are numerous minor genres, and some individual poems that are difficult to classify. The more secular pieces include charms (against dwarfs, for fruitfulness of the land, etc.), gnomic verse (maxims, proverbs), riddles, instructional dialogues, and a rune poem of the type mentioned in Chapter 4. The more religious or learned poems include prayers like the *Lord's Prayer* and the *Gloria Patri*, psalms, poetic fasting calendars, short homilies, a bestiary, a metaphorical poem about the phoenix, and Alfred's translation of Boethius's *Meters*.

Prose

Unlike Old English poems, the prose works in that language are fairly easy to group chronologically. Indeed, many of them are attributable to specific authors, and even to specific periods in their lives. Thus in the discussion below I have ordered the works according to chronological periods, of which scholars recognize roughly three, associated especially with the names of Bede, Alfred, and Aelfric.

Before the reign of King Alfred the Great (871–99), prose writing in Anglo-Saxon England was primarily in Latin. The earliest work of the pre-Alfredian period, Gildas's *De Excidio Britanniae* (ca. 540), was not even written by an Anglo-Saxon, but by a Celtic Briton. A combination of history and homily, it is of value primarily as an early overview of the first years of the Anglo-Saxons in Great Britain, of their wars with the Britons, and of their great but temporary defeat by the Britons at Mount Badon under a king later frequently identified as Arthur.

When the Christianization of the Anglo-Saxons commenced at the end of the sixth century, Latin writing began among the English. The earliest extensively documented texts are epistles and saints' lives (the latter especially being important for later vernacular prose). In the early eighth century, there was a virtual literary explosion, closely associated with the Venerable Bede (ca. 673–735), a Northumbrian monk. Although it is reported that Bede wrote in the vernacular, none of that work has survived. What we do have is an enormous body of his work in Latin. Besides his own epistles and saints' lives, Bede wrote treatises on Latin grammar, metrics, and rhetoric, commentaries on the Scriptures, and studies of the calendar and of the units of time. Most important, however, are his histories, especially the *Ecclesiastical History of the English People*. In this work, Bede gives far more than a history of the Church in England, though that is his primary goal. Using Gildas's work and other sources, he gives a remarkably detailed account of the early history of the Anglo-Saxons, an account that still serves as one of the major sources of our knowledge of that period.

Bede is important in Anglo-Saxon literary history for a number of reasons. One of them, of course, is simply the literary merit of his work, which is great. Another reason is that, when the Anglo-Saxons finally began writing their own language in any substantial way, Bede's were among the first works translated (especially the *Ecclesiastical History*). Finally, to the Anglo-Saxons of a later, rougher, and less literate period, he was an unparalleled example of scholarly and literary excellence, and a spur to the educational programs of Alfred, to whom we now turn.

Disturbed by much internal jockeying for power and by the depredations of vikings, the early and mid-ninth century saw in England an alarming drop in scholarship and literary activity, not to mention the outright loss of a large number of precious manuscripts from an earlier time. Thus when Alfred the Great of Wessex had finally achieved a relatively stable relationship between the Anglo-Saxons and the Danes, and asserted his own authority over all Anglo-Saxons not actually living in the Danelaw (see "History," above), one of his most important tasks, as he saw it, was the revitalization of English learning. An important part of this revitalization, as he notes in the preface to his translation of Pope Gregory the Great's *Pastoral Care*, was the translation of Latin works into the vernacular in order to make them more accessible.

Alfred himself was probably responsible for a large number of these translations. In addition to the *Pastoral Care*, which deals with the concept of the ideal bishop, Alfred is usually credited with the translation of philosophical works by Boethius and St. Augustine, Orosius's *Compendious History*, and a number of psalms. Other texts, such as a translation of Gregory's *Dialogues* and of Bede's *Ecclesiastical History*, though not by Alfred, were clearly a part of his program.

Also ascribed to Alfred's time, or shortly thereafter, though not necessarily to his literary circle, are the medical text called *Bald's Leechbook*, the Mercian *Life of St. Chad*, and a Mercian martyrology. But in many ways the most striking literary product credited to Alfred's time is the *Anglo-Saxon Chronicle*. Many scholars feel that this work was begun before Alfred, but there is little doubt that it flourished greatly under him. It is nothing less than a capsule history of the Anglo-Saxons beginning with the birth of Christ, and continuing, in one version at least, to the year 1154. This diary-like work, in which the entries are for years rather than days, is found in seven widely divergent versions. Their relationships to one another are unclear, though their earliest entries clearly all derive from some common source. The later entries differ substantially in content and emphasis, depending on where the versions were written, making their collective title, with the word *Chronicle* in the singular, somewhat misleading.

The entries in the *Chronicle* are by no means uniform. Some are short descriptive statements, some longer stories such as our reading selection, "Cynewulf and Cyneheard," for the year 755. Some again are poetic accounts. We can by no means suppose that the entries were all written immediately after their years were past (this is obvious in the case of the earliest entries), and in some cases there are evident insertions. Yet it is to the *Chronicle*, as well as to Bede's *History*, that we owe our remarkably detailed knowledge of Anglo-Saxon history.

Except for the *Chronicle*, no outstanding texts are ascribed to the period immediately after Alfred. It was only under his descendant Edgar (959–75) that England experienced a significant new spurt of literary activity, a beneficial side effect of the monastic reforms of that time. The most important names associated with this period are those of the monks Aelfric, Wulfstan, and Byrhtferth. Especially Aelfric deserves mention here, as many consider him the greatest literary stylist of the Anglo-Saxon period, and his brand of Late West Saxon is often used as the standard for the description of the Old English language. His vernacular writings include especially a number of homilies and lives of saints, and numerous translations of or commentaries on sections of both the Old and the New Testaments. His contemporary Wulfstan is responsible not only for a number of homiletic writings, but also for works on law, politics, and the relationship of church and state. Byrhtferth's name, finally, is associated with a number of scientific writings of the period, including commentaries on the scientific works of Bede and his own *Manual*, a philosophical work with a mathematical and humanistic slant.

Also associated with this late Old English period are a number of anonymous homilies and saints' lives, the so-called *West Saxon Gospels* (from which we take the Parable of the Sower and the Seed, below), an anonymous translation of Latin proverbs, and several works that reveal an increased interest in Oriental scenes and themes, such as the romance *Apollonius of Tyre*, the dialogue *Solomon and Saturn*, and other lesser works.

Readings

Parable of the Sower and the Seed

(Mark 4.1–9)

And eft hē ongan hī æt þǣre sǣ lǣran. And him wæs mycel męnegu tō gegaderod, swā þæt hē on scip ēode, and on þǣre sǣ wæs; and eall sēo męnegu ymbe þā sǣ wæs on lande. And hē hī fela on bigspellum lǣrde, and him tō cwæð on his lāre, "Gehȳrað: Ūt ēode sē sǣdere his sǣd tō sāwenne. And þā hē sēow, sum fēoll wið þone weg, and fugelas cōmon and hit frǣton. Sum fēoll ofer stānscyligean, þǣr hit næfde mycele eorðan, and sōna ūp ēode; and for þām hit næfde eorðan þiccnesse, þā hit ūp ēode, sēo sunne hit forswǣlde, and hit forscranc, for þām hit wyrtruman næfde. And sum fēoll on þornas; þā stigon ðā þornas and forðrysmodon þæt, and hit wæstm ne bær. And sum fēoll on gōd land, and hit sealde ūppstīgendne and wexendne wæstm; and ān brōhte þrītigfealdne, sum syxtigfealdne, sum hundfealdne." And hē cwæð, "Gehȳre, sē ðe ēaran hæbbe tō gehȳranne."

and, after, he, (be)gan, at sea, lehren
was, much, Menge, to, gathered, so
that, on, ship, der
all, um
land, viel, Beispiel[?]
quoth, his, lore, hear, out
seed, sow
some, fell, with, den, way, Vogel
came, it, frassen, over
stone, there, earth
soon
thickness, sun
shrank
Wurzel, thorns
stiegen
Wachstum, bore
good
wax(ing), one, brought, thirtyfold
sixtyfold, hundredfold
ear(s), have

Cynewulf and Cyneheard

Hēr Cynewulf benam Sigebryht his rīces ond Westseaxna wiotan for unryhtum dǣdum, būton Hamtūnscīre. Ond hē hæfde þā oþ hē ofslōg þone aldormon þe him lengest wunode, ond hiene þā Cynewulf on Andred ādrǣfde ond hē þǣr wunade oþ þæt hiene

here, benahm, his, Reich
for, un-, right, deed(s)
but, had
slew, alderman, longest
wohnte, ihn

ān swān ofstang æt Pryfetes flōdan; ond hē   swain, stung, flood
wræc þone aldormon Cumbran.   wreak

Ond sē Cynewulf oft miclum gefeoh-   oft, [Scots] mickle, fight
tum feaht uuiþ Bretwālum. Ond ymb XXXI   Brit(ish), Wales
wintra þæs þe hē rīce hæfde, hē wolde ādræ-   winter, *wollte*
fan ānne æþeling sē wæs Cyneheard hāten;   one, *Edeling*, hight
ond sē Cyneheard wæs þæs Sigebryhtes brō-   brother
þur. Ond þā geāscode hē þone cyning lȳtle   ask, king, little
werode on wīfcȳþþe on Merantūne ond hine   wife, town
þær berād ond þone būr ūtan beēode ær   rode, bower, ere
hine þā men onfunden þe mid þām kyninge   men, found, *mit*
wǣrun. Ond þā ongeat sē cyning þæt, ond   were, get
hē on þā duru ēode ond þā unhēanlīce hine   door(s)
werede oþ hē on þone æþeling lōcude, ond   *wehren*, looked
þā ūt rǣsde on hine ond hine miclum gewun-   races, wounded
dode; ond hīe alle on þone cyning wǣrun   all
feohtende oþ þæt hīe hine ofslægenne   slain
hæfdon.

Ond þā on þæs wīfes gebǣrum onfun-   found
don þæs cyninges þegnas þā unstilnesse, ond   thanes, stillness
þā þider urnon swā hwelc swā þonne gearo   thither, run, so, which, then, yare
wearþ, ond radost. Ond hiera se æþeling
gehwelcum feoh ond feorh gebēad, ond hiera   fee, *bieten*
nǣnig hit geþicgean nolde: ac hīe simle feoh-   (not) any
tende wǣran oþ hīe alle lǣgon būtan ānum   lay, one
Bryttiscum gīsle, ond sē swīþe gewundad wæs.   British, wounded

Þā on morgenne gehīerdun þæt þæs   morrow, heard
cyninges þegnas þe him beæftan wǣrun, þæt   aft(er)
se cyning ofslǣgen wæs. Þā ridon hīe þider,   *ritten*
ond his aldormon Ōsrīc ond Wīferþ his þegn
ond þā men þe hē beæftan him lǣfde ǣr,   left
ond þone æþeling on þǣre byrig mētton þǣr   -bury (in place names), met
se cyning ofslǣgen læg. Ond þā gatu him tō   gate(s)
belocen hæfdon, ond þā þǣrtō ēodon. Ond   lock, thereto
þā gebēad hē him hiera āgenne dōm fēos ond   own, doom
londes, gif hīe him þæs rīces ūþon, ond him   if
cȳþdon þæt hiera mǣgas him mid wǣron,   *künd(igen)*
þā þe him from noldon. Ond þā cuǣdon hīe
þæt him nǣnig mǣg lēofra nǣre þonne hiera   *lieber*, than
hlāford, ond hīe nǣfre his banan folgian   lord, never, bane, follow

noldon, ond þā budon hīe hiera mǣgum þæt
hīe gesunde from ēodon. Ond hīe cuǣdon   sound
þæt tæt ilce hiera gefērum geboden wǣre þe   ilk
ǣr mid þām cyninge wǣrun; þā cuǣdon hīe
þæt hīe þæs ne onmunden "þon mā þe ēowre   mind, mo(re), your
gefēran þe mid þām cyninge ofslǣgene
wǣrun." Ond hīe þā ymb þā gatu feohtende
wǣron oþ þæt hīe þǣrinne fulgon ond þone   therein
æþeling ofslōgon ond þā men þe him mid   slew
wǣrun, alle būtan ānum: sē wæs þæs aldor-
monnes godsunu ond hē his feorh generede,   godson, *nährte*
ond þēah hē wæs oft gewundad.   though

    Ond sē Cynewulf rīcsode XXXI wintra
ond his līc līþ æt Wintanceastre, ond þæs   *Leiche*, lieth
æþelinges æt Ascanmynster; ond hiera
ryhtfæderencyn gǣþ tō Cerdice.   right, father, kin, goeth

GLOSSARY

In alphabetizing Old English, *æ* and *ę* are treated as *a* and *e*; *þ* and *ð* follow *t*. Unless specified otherwise, nouns and pronouns are nominative singular, adjectives are masculine nominative singular, and verbs are infinitives. The parenthetical identification of any form has reference only to the Readings, and is not necessarily an exhaustive list of all possible identifications of that form in the language.

ac 'but'
ādrǣfan 'expel', *ādrǣfde* (3 sg. pret.
  ind.)
āgen 'own', *āgenne* (masc. acc. sg.)
aldormon 'nobleman', *aldormon*
  (acc. sg.), *aldormonnes* (gen. sg.)
alle see *eall*
ān 'one, a', *ānne* (masc. acc. sg.), *ānum*
  (masc. dat. sg.)
and, ond 'and'
Andred (place name)
ānum see *ān*
ǣr 'earlier, before'
Ascanmynster 'Axminster' (place
  name)
æt 'at'
æþeling 'prince', *æþeling* (acc. sg.)

bana 'murderer', *banan* (dat. sg.)
bær see *beran*
beæftan 'behind'
beēode see *begān*
begān 'surround', *beēode* (3 sg. pret.
  ind.)
belūcan 'lock up', *belocen* (pret. part.)
beniman 'deprive', *benam* (3 sg. pret.
  ind.)
bēodan 'offer', *budon* (3 pl. pret. ind.)
bēon, wesan 'be', *wæs* (3 sg. pret. ind.),
  wǣrun, wǣron, wǣran (3 pl. pret.
  ind.), *wǣre* (3 sg. pret. subj.)
berād see *berīdan*
beran 'bear', *bær* (3 sg. pret. ind.)
berīdan 'overtake', *berād* (3 sg. pret.
  ind.)

bigspell 'parable', bigspellum (dat. pl.)
Bretwālas 'Britons' (nom. pl.), Bretwālum (dat. pl.)
bringan 'bring', brōhte (3 sg. pret.
ind.)
brōþur 'brother'
Bryttisc 'British', Bryttiscum (dat. sg.)
budon see bēodan
būr 'bower', būr (acc. sg.)
būton, būtan 'except for'
byrig 'fort', byrig (dat. sg.)

Cerdic (personal name), Cerdice
(dat. sg.)
cōmon see cuman
cuǣdon see cweðan
cuman 'come', cōmon (3 pl. pret.
ind.)
Cumbra (personal name), Cumbran
(acc. sg.)
cweðan 'say, speak', cwæð (3 sg. pret.
ind.), cuǣdon (3 pl. pret. ind.)
Cyneheard (pers. name)
Cynewulf (pers. name)
cyning 'king', cyning (acc. sg.),
cyninges (gen. sg.), kyninge,
cyninge (dat. sg.)
cȳþan 'make known', cȳþdon (3 pl.
pret. ind.)

dǣd 'deed', dǣdum (dat. pl.)
dōm 'judgment', dōm (acc. sg.)
duru 'door', duru (acc. sg.)

eall 'all', eall (fem. nom. sg.), alle
(masc. nom. and acc. pl.)
ēare 'ear', ēaran (acc. pl.)
eft 'again, afterwards'
ēode, ēodon, see gān
eorðe 'earth', eorðan (acc. and
gen. sg.)
ēower 'your' (pl.), ēowre (masc.
nom. pl.)

feaht see feohtan

feallan 'fall', fēoll (3 sg. pret. ind.)
fela 'much'
feoh 'cattle, money', feoh (acc. sg.),
fēos (gen. sg.)
feohtan 'fight', feaht (3 sg. pret. ind.),
feohtende (pres. part., masc.
nom. pl.)
fēolan 'penetrate', fulgon (3 pl. pret.
ind.)
fēoll see feallan
feorh 'life', feorh (acc. sg.)
fēos see feoh
flōda 'flood', flōdan (dat. sg.)
folgian 'follow'
for 'for'
forscrincan 'wither', forscranc (3 sg.
pret. ind.)
forswǣlan 'scorch, burn', forswǣlde
(3 sg. pret. ind.)
for þām 'because'
forðrysmian 'choke', forðrysmodon (3
pl. pret. ind.)
fretan 'devour, eat' frǣton (3 pl. pret.
ind.)
from 'from, away from, away'
fugel 'bird', fugelas (nom. pl.)
fulgon see fēolan

gān 'go', gǣþ (3 sg. pres. ind.), ēode
(3 sg. pret. ind.), ēodon (3 pl. pret.
ind. and subj.)
gatu see geat
gǣþ see gān
gearo 'ready'
geāscian 'discover', geāscode (3 sg.
pret. ind.)
geat 'gate', gatu (acc. pl.)
gebǣre 'cry', gebǣrum (dat. pl.)
gebēodan 'offer', gebēad (3 sg. pret.
ind.), geboden (pret. part.)
gefeoht 'battle', gefeohtum (dat. pl.)
gefēra 'companion', gefēran (nom.
pl.), gefērum (dat. pl.)
gegaderian 'gather', gegaderod (pret.
part.)

gehīerdun see *gehȳran*

gehwilc 'each', *gehwelcum* (dat. pl.)

gehȳran 'hear, listen', *gehȳranne* (dat. of the inf.), *gehȳrað* (2 pl. imp.), *gehȳre* (3 sg. pres. subj.), *gehīerdun* (3 pl. pret. ind.)

generian 'save', *generede* (3 sg. pret. ind.)

gesund 'sound, safe', *gesunde* (masc. nom. pl.)

geþicgean 'take, receive'

gewundian 'wound', *gewundode* (3 sg. pret. ind.), *gewundad* (pret. part.)

gif 'if'

gīsel 'hostage', *gīsle* (dat. sg.)

gōd 'good', *gōd* (neut. acc. sg.)

godsunu 'godson'

habban 'have, hold', *hæbbe* (3 sg. pres. subj.), *hæfde* (3 sg. pret. ind.), *hæfdon* (3 pl. pret. ind.)

Hamtūnscīre 'Hampshire' (place name)

hātan 'be called', *hāten* (pret. part.)

hē 'he', *hine*, *hiene* (acc. sg.), *his* (gen. sg.), *him* (dat. sg. and pl.), *hīe*, *hī* (nom. and acc. pl.), *hiera* (gen. pl.)

hēr 'here'

hī, *hīe*, *hiene*, *hiera*, *him*, *hine*, *his*, see *hē*

hit 'it', *hit* (acc. sg.)

hlāford 'lord'

hundfeald 'hundredfold', *hundfealdne* (masc. acc. sg.)

hwelc see *swā hwelc swā*

ilce 'same', *ilce* (neut. acc. sg.)

kyninge see *cyning*

lǣfan 'leave', *lǣfde* (3 sg. pret. ind.)

læg, *lægon*, see *licgan*

land 'land', *land* (acc. sg.), *londes* (gen. sg.), *lande* (dat. sg.)

lār 'teaching, lore', *lāre* (dat. sg.)

lǣran 'teach', *lǣrde* (3 sg. pret. ind.)

lengest 'longest'

lēofra 'dearer'

līc 'body'

licgan 'lie, lie dead', *līþ* (3 sg. pres. ind.), *læg* (3 sg. pret. ind.), *lægon* (3 pl. pret. ind.)

līþ see *licgan*

lōcian 'look', *lōcude* (3 sg. pret. ind.)

londes see *land*

lȳtel 'small, little', *lȳtle* (neut. dat. sg.)

mǣg 'kinsman', *mǣgas* (nom. pl.), *mǣgum* (dat. pl.)

men see *mon*

menegu 'multitude'

Merantūn 'Merantown' (place name), *Merantūne* (dat. sg.)

mētan 'meet, find', *mētton* (3 pl. pret. ind.)

micel, *mycel* 'great', *mycel* (fem. nom. sg.), *mycele* (fem. acc. sg.), *miclum* (neut. dat. pl.)

miclum 'greatly'; see also *micel*, *mycel*

mid 'with'

mon 'man', *men* (nom. and acc. pl.)

morgen 'morning', *morgenne* (dat. sg.)

mycel, *mycele*, see *micel*, *mycel*

næbban = *ne habban*

næfde = *ne hæfde*; see *habban*

nǣfre 'never'

nǣnig 'none, no'

nǣre = *ne wǣre*

ne 'not'

nolde = *ne wolde*

noldon = *ne woldon*

ofer 'over, onto'

ofslēan 'slay', *ofslōg* (3 sg. pret. ind.), *ofslōgon* (3 pl. pret. ind.), *ofslægen* (pret. part., masc. nom. sg.), *ofslægenne* (pret. part., masc. acc. sg.), *ofslægene* (pret. part., masc. nom. pl.)

ofstingan 'stab to death', *ofstang* (3 sg. pret. ind.)

oft 'often'

on 'on, onto, to, in, at'

ond see *and*

onfindan 'discover', *onfundon* (3 pl. pret. ind.), *onfunden* (3 pl. pret. subj.)

ongan see *onginnan*

ongietan 'perceive', *ongeat* (3 sg. pret. ind.)

onginnan 'begin', *ongan* (3 sg. pret. ind.)

onmunan 'care for, wish', *onmunden* (3 pl. pret. subj.)

Ōsrīc (pers. name)

oþ 'until'

Pryfet 'Privet' (pers. name), *Pryfetes* (gen. sg.)

radost 'most quickly'

rǣsan 'rush', *rǣsde* (3 sg. pret. ind.)

rīce 'kingdom', *rīce* (acc. sg.), *rīces* (gen. sg.)

rīcsian 'reign', *rīcsode* (3 sg. pret. ind.)

rīdan 'ride', *ridon* (3 pl. pret. ind.)

ryhtfæderencyn 'paternal lineage'

sǣ 'sea', *sǣ* (acc. and dat. sg.)

sǣd 'seed', *sǣd* (acc. sg.)

sǣdere 'sower'

sāwen 'sow', *sāwenne* (dat. of the inf.), *sēow* (3 sg. pret. ind.)

scip 'ship', *scip* (acc. sg.)

sē 'who' (masc. rel. pro.)

sē, se 'that, that one, the' (masc. art., nom. sg.), *þone* (acc. sg.), *þæs* (gen. sg.), *þām* (dat. sg.), *þā, ðā* (nom. and acc. pl.)

sellan 'give', *sealde* (3 sg. pret. ind.)

sēo 'that, the' (fem. art., nom. sg.), *þā* (acc. sg.), *þǣre* (dat. sg.)

sēow see *sāwen*

Sigebryht (pers. name), *Sigebryht* (acc. sg.), *Sigebryhtes* (gen. sg.)

simle 'always'

sōna 'soon'

stānscylig 'stony, stone-shelly', *stānscyligean* (acc. pl.)

stīgan 'climb, rise', *stigon* (3 pl. pret. ind.)

sum 'some, one'

sunne 'sun'

swā hwelc swā 'whoever'

swā þæt 'so that'

swān 'swineherd, swain'

swīþe 'very'

syxtigfeald 'sixtyfold', *syxtigfealdne* (masc. acc. sg.)

tæt = *þæt* after preceding *t*

tō 'to'

þā 'then, when'; see also *sē, se*, and see *sēo*

ðā see *sē, se*

þām see *sē, se*; see also *þæt, ðæt*

þǣm see *þæt, ðæt*

þār, þǣr 'there, where'

þǣre see *sēo*

þǣrinne 'into there'

þǣrtō 'to there'

þǣs see *sē, se*; see also *þæt, ðæt*

þæs þe 'after'

þæt 'that' (conj.)

þæt, ðæt 'that, the' (neut. art., nom. sg.), *þæt* (acc. sg.), *þæs* (gen. sg.), *þǣm, þām* (dat. sg.)

þe, ðe 'who' (rel. particle)
þēah 'nevertheless'
þegn 'thane, servant', *þegnas*
    (nom. pl.)
þiccnes 'thickness', *þiccnesse* (acc. sg.)
þider 'thither'
þon mā þe 'any more than'
þone see *sē, se*
þonne 'then, than'
þorn 'thorn', *þornas* (nom. and
    acc. pl.)
þrītigfeald 'thirtyfold', *þrītigfealdne*
    (masc. acc. sg.)

unheānlīce 'nobly'
unnan 'grant', *ūþon* (3 pl. pret. subj.)
unriht 'unjust', *unryhtum* (dat. pl.)
unstilnes 'disturbance', *unstilnesse*
    (acc. sg.)
ūp 'up'
ūppstīgan 'climb up', *ūppstīgendne*
    (pres. part., masc. acc. sg.)
urnon see *yrnan*
ūt 'out'
ūtan 'from without'
ūþon see *unnan*

wǣran, wǣre, wǣron, wǣrun, wæs,
    see *bēon, wesan*
wæstm 'fruit, growth', *wæstm*
    (acc. sg.)
wearþ see *weorðan*

weaxan 'grow', *wexendne* (pres. part.,
    masc. acc. sg.)
weg 'way', *weg* (acc. sg.)
weorðan 'become', *wearþ* (3 sg. pret.
    ind.)
werian 'defend', *werede* (3 sg. pret.
    ind.)
werod 'band of men', *werode*
    (dat. sg.)
Westseaxe 'West Saxons' (nom. pl.),
    Westseaxna (gen. pl.)
wexendne see *weaxan*
wīf 'woman', *wīfes* (gen. sg.)
wīfcȳþþ 'company of a woman',
    wīfcȳþþe (dat. sg.)
Wīferþ (personal name)
willan 'want', *wolde* (3 sg. pret. ind.),
    woldon (3 pl. pret. ind.)
Wintanceaster 'Winchester' (place
    name), *Wintanceastre* (dat. sg.)
winter 'winter', *wintra* (gen. pl.)
wiota 'counselor', *wiotan* (nom. pl.)
wið, wiþ, uuiþ 'against, next to'
wolde, woldon, see *willan*
wrecan 'avenge', *wræc* (3 sg. pret.
    ind.)
wunian 'remain, stay by', *wunode,*
    wunade (3 sg. pret. ind.)
wyrtruma 'root', *wyrtruman* (acc. sg.)

ymbe, ymb 'around, after'
yrnan 'run', *urnon* (3 pl. pret. ind.)

Some Aspects of Old English Grammar

Spelling and Pronunciation

Consonants

As in the languages we have previously considered, the pronunciation of
Old English can be determined in general by applying the rules given in
Chapter 2 to the spelling of the texts. As with the other languages, how-
ever, there are some anomalies.

The letters *p* and *t* are pronounced much as in Modern English (again one should be careful, in the case of *t* between vowels, not to pronounce it as [d], as many American dialects do):

ūp 'up'   þæt 'that'

The letter *k*, found only rarely, is no more than a variant for *c*, which has two values: before or after the original (non-umlaut) vowels *i* and *e*, whether long or short, it has the value of Modern English [č] in "church"; elsewhere it has the value of [k], and *k* occasionally replaces it.

rīce 'kingdom' with [č]
cyning 'king' with [k]; also written kyning.

The consonants *b* and *d* are also uncomplicated:

būr 'bower' with [b]
gōd 'good' with [d]

As in Old Saxon, *g* is a bit more complex. It is pronounced as in modern "good" only when it follows *n* or is doubled:

cyning 'king' has the cluster [ŋg] as in modern "longer"
frogga 'frog' is pronounced like modern "frog got," with [gg]

Otherwise *g* is pronounced as a fricative. Before the front vowels *i* and *e*, after them at the end of a syllable, and also in a few instances where [j] or [i] had once followed the *g* in question (which of course the texts do not show), *g* is pronounced like the *y* in modern "yes," that is, as [j]:

ofslægen 'slain' (compare the modern pronunciation)

Elsewhere, *g* is pronounced as a back fricative [ɡ], as in the Germanic languages previously discussed: *gatu* 'gates' with [ɡ].

The letter sequence *cg* is pronounced like the first sound in modern "giant," symbolized [ǰ]:

geþicgean 'take' with [ǰ]
ecg 'edge' with [ǰ]

The letter sequence *sc* is pronounced like Modern English *sh*, phonetically [š]: *scip* 'ship' with [š].

The fricatives *f*, *s*, and *þ/ð* (*þ* and *ð* are interchangeable in Late Old English) have two values each. Between voiced sounds (usually vowels) they are pronounced as [v], [z], and [ð]:

hlāford 'lord' with [v]
wesan 'be' with [z]
brōþur 'brother' with [ð]

Elsewhere—that is, initially, finally, doubled—they are pronounced as [f], [s], and [þ]:

> *feallan* 'fall' with [f]
> *þiccnesse* 'thickness' with [s]
> *cwæð* 'said' with [þ]

In Old English, *h* is pronounced as [h] initially and before vowels, but as [x] before consonants and finally:

> *hēr* 'here' with [h]
> *feohtan* 'fight' with [x]

The letter *x* is pronounced as [xs], not [ks]:

> *Westseaxna* 'of West Saxons' with [xs]

Old English *r*, *l*, *m*, *n*, and *w* are pronounced as one might expect from Chapter 2. However, *u* is occasionally used for [w], as in *cuædon*.

Vowels

Like most of the other Germanic languages, Old English shows the five vowels *i*, *e*, *a*, *o*, *u*, both long and short. I will not discuss them further, since they show the pronunciations assigned to these letters in Chapter 2. But in addition to these vowels, Old English has the following others.

The letters *æ* and *ǣ* are pronounced like the vowels of Modern English "bat" and "bad" respectively, wherein the second vowel is a lengthened version of the first:

> *hæfde* 'had' with [æ]
> *lǣrde* 'taught' with [ǣ]

Old English *y* and *ȳ* are pronounced [ü] and [û] respectively:

> *cyning* 'king' with [ü]
> *gehȳran* 'hear' with [û]

Compared with Old Saxon, Old English shows a large number of diphthongs. The spellings *io* and *īo*, *eo* and *ēo*, and at least in the early texts *ie* and *īe*, are pronounced as one would expect, by combining the individual vowels. The sequences *ea* and *ēa*, however, are pronounced more like *æ* or *ǣ* followed by *a*, or even by the unstressed vowel of Modern English "sofa," [ə]:

> *eall* 'all' with [æə]
> *ēare* 'ear' with [ǣə]

However, I should point out that scholars have long debated what the exact values of these diphthongs were.

Phonology

Especially in the vowels, Old English shows a great number of changes not found in the languages discussed thus far. The discussion that follows presents only a few, and in some cases is less specific about the conditions for the changes than it might have been. Some of the changes are more widespread in the Old English dialects than others, and even within a given dialect, some changes are more complete than others. I have limited my discussion almost entirely to the West Saxon dialect, as is traditional—and, given the paucity of texts in the other dialects, practical.

1. As did the other Old Germanic languages besides Gothic, Old English originally changed the vowel *ǣ* to *â*. While this intermediate *â* is found written as *ā* under certain circumstances in some texts (especially before *w*), under most circumstances in Old English it returns to *ǣ*:

OE	Goth.	
sāwen	saian (from *sǣan*)	'sow'
sǣd	sêþs	'seed'
frǣton	frêtun	'ate' (pl.)
dǣd	gadêþs	'deed'

2. In line with this change of *â* to *ǣ*, Old English in most cases changes original short *a* to *æ*. Except before nasal consonants, this change systematically fails to take place only when the *a* in question is followed by a single consonant plus *a*, *o*, or *u*: OE *gæt* 'gate' but *gatu* (nom. pl.); *dæg* 'day' but *daga* (dat. sg.).

3. Before nasal consonants, in many cases both the long *â* and the short *a* just discussed become not *ǣ* and *æ* respectively, but *ō* and *o*:

OE	Goth.	
mon	manna	'man'
mōnað	mênoþs	'month'

4. Like Old Norse and Old Saxon, Old English shows umlaut. Again the original lowering effects of *a* are less than obvious, having been obscured by analogy. As usual, we do find some reflection of *a*-umlaut in derivationally related pairs like the by-now familiar alternation of *gold* 'gold' with *gylden* 'golden' (the latter showing the effects of *i*-umlaut).

As the example of *gylden* shows, Old English spelling regularly represents the changes brought about by *i*-umlaut. The basic changes are given below:

æ (from *a*) becomes *e*
ǣ (from *â*) remains *ǣ*
ā becomes *ǣ*
o and *ō* become *e* and *ē* respectively
u and *ū* become *y* and *ȳ* respectively
ea, eo, io become *ie, i* (in Late West Saxon, *y*)
ēa, ēo, īo become *īe, ī* (in Late West Saxon, *ȳ*)

As usual, in many cases the original conditioners of the change have become somewhat obscure by the time of the texts. We may, however, note the following examples from our reading selections:

> *gehȳran* 'hear' from **gehēarian*; compare Goth. *hausjan*
> *lǣran* 'teach' opposite *lāre* 'teaching'
> *men* 'men' opposite *mon* 'man'

Old English also shows *u*-umlaut, though less extensively in the "standard" West Saxon dialect. The effect, too, is different from that of *i*-umlaut. With *u*-umlaut, rather than simply shifting to another position, vowels "break" into diphthongs. Thus *a* can go to *ea*, *e* to *eo*, *i* to *io*. The first is *very* rare in West Saxon prose, the only consistent example being *ealu* 'ale' from **alu*. The others, too, are subject to a number of restrictions, and are frequently undone by analogy, but we do find more numerous reflexes, such as *smeoru* 'grease' from earlier **smeru*, and *mioluc* 'milk' from **miluk*.

5. In general, the instances in the texts of *ea*, *eo*, and the like, are the result not of umlaut but of consonantal influence. This phenomenon is the one more correctly called "breaking," and may be generally summarized as follows. When one of the vowels *i*, *e*, or *æ* (from older *a*) appears before the consonant *h*, or before an *r* followed by any consonant, or in some cases before an *l* followed by a consonant, it is broken, to *io* in the case of *i*, *eo* in the case of *e*, and *ea* in the case of *æ*. Some examples from the texts:

OE	OS	
eorðe	erða	'earth'
feoht	fehta	'battle'
wearþ	warð	'became'

6. The reflexes of the older diphthongs *ai* and *au* in Old English are quite distinctive. *ai* becomes *ā*, and *au* becomes *ēa*:

OE	Goth.	
stān	stains	'stone'
hātan	haitan	'be called'

(ge)bēad	bauþ	'offered'
ēare	auso	'ear'

7. Like Old Saxon, Old English shows no examples of sharpening. Thus we find *twēg(e)a* 'of two' (where the *g* stands for [j], as we saw above), *trēowe* 'true'.

8. The cluster *ngw* has lost its *w* in Old English: *singan* 'to sing'.

9. As in Old Norse and Old Saxon, rhotacism has taken place in Old English: OE *lǣran* 'teach'; compare Goth. *laisjan*.

10. Consonant gemination is as widespread in Old English as in Old Saxon, though the conditions are no longer as clear, *j* having dropped out in many cases. Thus all consonants except *r* are doubled before original *j* after a short vowel, and gemination sometimes takes place before original *r* or *l*:

OE	Goth.	
sellan	saljan	'give'
bittor	baitrs	'bitter'

11. Old English shows the initial consonant sequence *fl-* rather than *þl-* as in Gothic: *flēon* 'flee', opposite Gothic *þliuhan*.

12. Old English shares with Old Saxon the loss of a nasal before any of the voiceless fricatives *f*, *þ*, *s*:

OE	Goth.	
fīf	fimf	'five'
sīð	sinþs	'way'
ūs	unsis	'us'
cūð	kunþs	'known'

13. A phenomenon that southern Old English (and thus the standard West Saxon) shares only with Old Frisian among all the Germanic languages is the *assibilation* of the earlier stops *k* and *g* (the latter found as a stop only when doubled or after a nasal). What "assibilation" means is that before (and in some cases after) original long and short *i* and *e*, and also before *j*, the stop *k* became [č], as in modern "church," while the stop *g* or *gg* became [ǰ], as in modern "drudge." Unfortunately, the symbol for [č] is *c* in most Old English texts, which does not distinguish it from the sound [k]. (The [ǰ] does have a special symbolization, namely *cg*.) Later dialects make the pronunciation as [č] likely, however. For the first two examples below, compare the modern translation:

OE	OS	
cirice	kirika	'church'
rīce	rîki	'great, rich'
geþicgean	thiggian	'accept, take'

14. Another sound change that Old English shares only with Old Frisian to any extent is the *metathesis* of *r* in sequences of a consonant plus *r* plus a vowel. In effect, *r* and the vowel trade places:

OE	OS	
hors	hros	'horse'
beornan	brinnan	'burn'

Nouns and Pronouns

1. Like Old Saxon, Old English has completely lost the old Germanic ending *-az*, originally found in the nominative singular of *a*-stem masculine nouns, and in the nominative singular of masculine strong adjectives:

OE	Goth.	
weg	wigs	'way'
gōd	gôþs	'good'

2. The nominative plural of the masculine *a*-stem nouns in Old English is *-as*: OE *fugelas* 'birds'; compare Goth. *fuglôs*, OHG *fogala*.

3. Old English shows a distinction between dual and plural in first and second person personal pronouns:

> *wit* 'we two' versus *wē* 'we'
> *git* 'you two' versus *gē* 'you' (pl.)

4. In the third person pronouns, Old English shows forms beginning with *h-* throughout:

OE	Goth.	
hē	is	'he'
him	imma	'him' (dat. sg.)
hēo	si	'she'
hiera	izôs	'her' (gen. sg.)
hit	ita	'it'

5. Old English (in the West Saxon dialect) does not in most instances distinguish between the accusative and dative in the first and second person singular personal pronouns. The distinction exists as an archaism in poetry, but the general prose forms are as follows:

	OE	Goth.	
Acc.	mē	mik	'me'
Dat.	mē	mis	'me'
Acc.	ðē	þuk	'thee'
Dat.	ðē	þus	'thee'

6. Old English has no reflexive pronoun like *sik*, substituting forms of the personal pronoun instead. Note clauses like *hē . . . hine werede* 'he defended himself', indistinguishable from 'he defended him'. Furthermore, Old English does not have any possessive pronoun like Gothic *seins*, using instead the genitive of the personal pronoun, as in *his aldormon* 'his nobleman'.

7. Like Old Norse and Old Saxon, Old English has the intensified demonstrative pronoun:

> OE masc. nom. sg. *sē* and *ðes* opposite Goth. *sa*
>   dat. pl. *ðǣm* and *ðissum* opposite Goth. *þaim*

Verbs

1. Old English, like Old Norse, does not have a reduplicating class of verbs, though it does show some relic forms originally derived from reduplicated ones. Thus the preterite of *hātan* 'be called' is *heht*, and the preterite of *lācan* 'play' is *leolc*. Most of the other verbs that reduplicate in Gothic show a new vowel alternation in Old English:

OE	Goth.	
slǣpan–slēp	slêpan–saislêp	'sleep–slept'
sāwan–sēow	saian–saisô	'sow–sowed'

2. The class of *-na* verbs is absent in Old English.

3. Like Old Saxon, Old English shows the ending *-e* from *-i* in the second person singular preterite indicative of strong verbs, rather than the *-t* of Gothic and Old Norse. It also shows the root vowel (or sometimes the umlaut of a root vowel) of the preterite plural, rather than that of the preterite singular:

OE	Goth.	
beran	bairan	'bear' (inf.)
bær	bar	(1 and 3 sg. pret. ind.)
bǣre	bart	(2 sg. pret. ind.)
bǣron	bêrum	(1 pl. pret. ind.)

4. Old English has neither a morphological passive nor a medio-

passive, and must make do with periphrastic constructions (see the last section of this chapter). Interestingly, there is one verb in Old English that still shows remnants of the present passive inflection found in Gothic. The first person singular present indicative form of *hātan* 'be called' is *hātte*, corresponding to Gothic *haitada*.

5. The third person singular present indicative of the verb *bēon* 'be' is *is* in Old English, without a *-t*.

6. Like Old Saxon, Old English shows the same verb ending in all persons of the plural. Note the present tense indicative plural *bindað* 'we, you, they bind'.

7. Old English shows both long and short forms of the verb for 'go' (*gongan* and *gān*), but the short form predominates. The verb for 'stand' shows only the long form, *stondan*.

8. Also as in Old Saxon, Old English shows an inflected gerund, found quite clearly in our biblical passage: *to sāwenne* 'to sow', with dative inflection of the infinitive *sāwen*.

Selected Topics in Germanic Syntax

In describing the Germanic languages discussed so far, I have primarily been concerned with their phonological and morphological properties. Nor do I intend to deviate from that practice in future chapters. The fact is that more is known about the phonology and morphology of many of these languages than about their syntax. Even a moment's thought will suggest that syntax is at a disadvantage in comparison to the other subfields of linguistics when we are confronted with such limited evidence as we find for the older Germanic languages. A good syntactic description of any language necessarily treats not only what *is* in that language, but what *may be*; that is, it deals with patterns rather than inventories, patterns that can be used to create sentences never before produced in the language. When studying a modern language, the linguist may freely experiment with the patterns he or she believes appear in that language, inserting new material, modifying existing sentences, and then checking with a native speaker to see if the result is a grammatical sentence. But with archaic languages, of course, there are no native speakers to tell us what is grammatical and what is not. We are left with our hypotheses, and a fervent wish that somebody would discover substantial new texts containing a large number of precisely the kind of sentences required to test our guesses (not impossible, but extremely unlikely).

Even worse, many of the texts that do exist are undependable witnesses to the syntax of their languages. A majority of the translations from Greek and Latin originals are almost totally worthless as examples of native word order, government, use of participles and cases, and so on. Additionally, many indigenous poetic works are also somewhat suspect, given their propensity to violate grammatical rules in the service of a higher, esthetic standard. Descriptions of earlier language stages based upon an indiscriminate collection of examples from all available texts may thus significantly distort the true state of affairs in the languages involved.

Finally, with all the changes that have taken place in syntactic theory within the past few decades, and that are still going on, we are not at all sure about the correct way to present what we think we do know. Lacking a stable framework suitable for language description, few scholars wish to concern themselves with the detailed description of even a living language, far less a dead one.

As a result of all these factors, we are far less sure about the syntax of many of the older Germanic languages than about their phonology and morphology, though Old English is a bright spot in this regard. It follows that we are even less certain about the syntax of the parent language. Nevertheless, some work has been done, more programmatic than comprehensive, and I draw from this work in the following discussion.

The discussion takes as its point of departure the Readings found in this chapter, of course "The Sower and the Seed," but especially "Cynewulf and Cyneheard." From these Old English texts we will range backwards to Proto-Germanic and sideways to the other old Germanic languages, looking for origins and parallel developments respectively.

I have divided this brief discussion into three parts. The first deals with the word order of Old English and the other Germanic languages, principally the placement of the finite (inflected) verb with respect to the other major sentence constituents. Such a discussion necessitates considering a number of other ordering phenomena also.

The second section deals with the development in English and other Germanic languages of periphrastic verb forms to supplement the rather meager number of inflectional categories inherited from Proto-Germanic. The emphasis is upon the development of new forms for the future, the passive, and the perfect, all categories that in several other Indo-European languages have their own morphological realizations.

Finally, I discuss the development of clause subordination in the various Germanic languages, dealing here not only with clauses that function as complements to a superordinate verb (thus as subjects, objects, and so on), but also with those that modify nouns or pronouns (relative clauses).

Here more than elsewhere I must emphasize the incompleteness of the presentation. I have chosen these three topic areas because I find them interesting, not because they in any way cover the field. The interested reader should consult the works listed in "Further Reading" for a more comprehensive discussion.

Word Order

A glance at this chapter's Readings will show several sentences that appear to have the verb in the same position as in Modern English, that is, after the subject and before any objects:

> And sum fēoll on gōd land
> 'And one fell on good land'

> Cynewulf benam Sigebryht his rīces
> 'Cynewulf deprived Sigebryht of his kingdom'

However, frequently the verb does not immediately follow the subject, even when the verb is the second major constituent in the sentence. Rather, the element that precedes it may be some object or adverb that has been "topicalized":

> Þa on morgenne gehīerdun þæt . . . þegnas
> 'Then in the morning the retainers heard that . . .'

Very commonly, in this text, the verb may also be preceded simply by an introductory particle þā, a word order virtually equivalent to that in which the sentence begins with the verb:

> Ond þā gebēad hē him hiera āgenne dōm
> 'And then he offered them their own assessment'

In commands and direct yes-or-no questions, the verb begins the clause, as in Modern English. Our Readings give us no examples of the latter, and of direct commands we have only two different instances of 'Listen!' Since these verb positions are familiar from the modern language, however, I refrain from bringing in outside examples.

In subordinate clauses, the ordering is quite different. Typically, the verb is at the end of its clause:

gif hīe him þæs rīces ūþon
'if they granted him the kingdom'

Sometimes it is almost at the end of the clause, with a "heavy" sentence constituent following:

þæt him nǣnig mǣg lēofra nǣre þonne hiera hlāford
'that no relative was dearer to them than their lord'

With a few exceptions, such word-ordering patterns seem familiar from Modern German, which thus appears to be much more archaic than Modern English in this respect. Not familiar from Modern German, however, is the pattern in which the verb appears clause-final, or nearly clause-final, in *independent* clauses:

and eall sēo menegu ymbe þā sǣ wæs on lande
'and all the multitude was around the sea on the land'

ond hē on þā duru ēode ond þā unhēanlīce hine werede
'and he went to the door and then valiantly defended himself'

It should be noted that such verb-final independent clauses in Old English are almost always found non-initially in a sequence of narrative clauses, the *first* of which normally has the verb in second position. Thus note the clause that immediately precedes the second example above:

Ond þā ongeat se cyning þæt 'And then the king perceived that'

Most scholars now agree that the neutral position of the verb in Proto-Germanic, and in Indo-European, was in fact final, or, to use a popular typological classification, that these languages were SOV languages—that is, subject–object–verb, as exemplified for very early Germanic by the famous runic inscription *ek hlewagastiʀ holtijaʀ horna tawidô*, discussed earlier. There were two types of exceptions to the rule of verb-last. First, a small class of "light" verbs (short and usually somewhat redundant, such as the verb 'be') could shift to a position immediately after the first stressed element in the clause (thus to second position). The frequency of such verbs was increased quite a bit in Germanic by the growing use of auxiliary verbs such as 'have' and 'become' (see below). Second, much like other sentence constituents, verbs could be emphasized by putting them in first position in the clause.

Developments in all the Germanic languages tended to increase the number of verbs found in non-final position and to make them less exceptional, or in some instances, such as imperatives and interrogatives, to grammaticalize their exceptionality. The basic development can be characterized, then, as one from SOV to SVO, through a stage in which, as in Old English and Modern German, something other than the subject may precede a verb in second position. The Old English of our second reading passage above, indeed, seems to reflect an even older situation, with final verbs found in independent, non-initial narrative clauses.

The different Germanic languages have carried out this development at different rates. English and the Scandinavian languages have gone the farthest, German less far. A number of scholars have speculated that this difference, and indeed the whole motivation for the change to SVO order, must be sought in the variably paced breakdown of the case system that in the earlier languages served to distinguish subjects and objects.

Pioneering work done by Greenberg, and elaborated on for Germanic by Hopper, Lehmann, and Vennemann, has shown that a great number of other ordering phenomena can be correlated with the basic position of the verb in the clause. Thus SOV languages tend to have, among other features, adjectives preceding nouns, genitive attributes preceding nouns, the standard of comparison preceding the comparative adjective, and postpositions (prepositions following their nouns). SVO languages tend to have the opposite orders.

We might expect, then, to find in all the Germanic languages a historical development not only in verb position, but in these other orderings also. Given that the change of verb order has progressed quite far in all the older Germanic languages, of course, we might not necessarily expect to find SOV-related patterns predominating, but we might hope to find at least some relics.

And indeed, this situation obtains even in the Readings above. For adjectives preceding nouns, for example, we find:

> unryhtum dǣdum 'unlawful deeds' (dat.)
> miclum gefeohtum 'great battles' (dat.)

Genitives precede nouns in:

> þæs wīfes gebǣrum 'the woman's outcry'
> þæs cyninges þegnas 'the king's thanes'

Postpositions appear in:

> him mid 'with him'
> him from 'from him'

These orders differ wildly in frequency in Old English. Adjective before noun is the rule even in Modern English, as it is in Modern German (a fact that itself needs explaining, if it is so uncharacteristic of SVO languages; see the noun—adjective order of French for a more typical example). Old Norse shows both preceding and following adjectives.

Genitive before noun is also still common in English, at least when the genitive indicates possession, though note the widespread postposed "of" construction as in "the trunk of the car" or "the sack of the city" ("the city's sack" is at least highly unusual). Genitive after noun is the rule in Modern German, except for personal names. Again, Old Norse shows a relative freedom of position.

Postpositions are actually quite uncommon in Old English, and are found perhaps only with pronouns. Otherwise prepositions are the rule; note *mid þām kyninge* in "Cynewulf and Cyneheard" above. The same is true for Old High German, although Modern German shows a very recent development of some few postpositions, for example *gegenüber*. Old Norse, on the other hand, uses postpositions relatively freely, in phrases like *órom hǫllom frá* 'out of our halls'.

Not only can we find no examples of the standard of comparison preceding the comparative adjective in the texts above (rather the contrary, cf. *lēofra . . . þonne hiera hlāford* 'dearer than their lord'), they are virtually impossible to find in any Germanic language but Old Norse. There the order of standard before comparative adjective is quite frequent (as in *sólo fegra* 'fairer than the sun'), but comparative particle constructions like those in Old English are already replacing it.

On balance, it seems that the older Germanic languages are in transition, not only as regards verb placement, but also with respect to the correlated phenomena. Some things are a bit baffling, of course. For example, why does Old Norse, which shows the fewest examples of verb-final clauses among the Germanic languages, also show the most examples of such SOV-related phenomena as postpositions and standard before comparative? Why don't English and German ever develop a predominant pattern of noun before adjective? I leave these questions to the specialists.

Periphrastic Verb Inflections

Compared with many of its Indo-European relatives, Proto-Germanic had inherited a remarkably reduced verbal system from the parent language. There were two tenses, present and preterite. Of these, the present had to serve for the future, and the preterite had not only to express past time, but also past perfect time: "I had seen" as well as "I saw." Additionally, *aspectual* distinctions, which many other languages observed, such as those between completed or uncompleted, punctual or ongoing actions, were only poorly captured in Germanic. Finally, except for Gothic, the Germanic languages had all lost the distinctive Indo-European passive inflection, and even Gothic only retained it in the present tense.

Some features of this relatively impoverished (or perhaps just streamlined) system may be seen in all the older languages, and even some of the modern ones. German is still frequently content with the present tense in a future meaning, as in *Ich sehe dich morgen* 'I'll see you tomorrow', where only the adverb *morgen* makes the futurity clear. And note the following sentence from the story of Cynewulf, wherein the present has been narratively transposed into the past, but the same principle holds:

> budon . . . þæt hīe gesunde from ēodon
> 'offered . . . that they should get out unharmed'

Again, in our text as in others, the preterite must stand for a pluperfect:

> þone aldormon þe him lengest wunode
> 'the nobleman who had stayed with him the longest'
>
> þā men þe hē beæftan him lǣfde ǣr
> 'the men whom he had left behind him earlier'

Note, in the latter case, the apparent need for an adverb 'earlier'. Without such a disambiguating word, and in the absence of any other context, the clause could just as easily have meant 'whom he left behind him', or even 'whom he was leaving behind him'.

Evidently the speakers of the various Germanic languages felt that in some instances more was needed to make the meaning clear than some adverbial term of time or manner. For we find a growing tendency to use semantically rather colorless verbs like 'be' and 'have', in combination with the deverbal nouns known as infinitives and the deverbal adjectives known as participles, to create new verbal complexes capable of carrying the desired shades of meaning.

Tendencies in this direction must have been aided by the prior existence of a small group of verbs that, in combination with an infinitive, gave to the verbal content of that infinitive an additional meaning, in these cases mostly modal. I refer to the verbs meaning variously 'must', 'be necessary', 'want', and so on, commonly called *modal auxiliaries*, which gained their auxiliary function quite early.

By virtue of their modal function, many of these verbs carried futurity as a part of their meaning. Thus the auxiliary *willan* in Old English, which means 'want' or 'intend', can easily shift in the direction of pure futurity, as can *sculan* 'have an obligation to'. Indeed, as their Modern English cognates 'will' and 'shall' show, in the history of English they gave up their original modal meaning almost entirely. The following sentence from "Cynewulf" shows what may have been a transitional form:

> ond hīe nǣfre his banan folgian noldon
> 'and they never would (wanted to) follow his slayer'

The Scandinavian languages followed the same path, using the modal 'shall'. While both 'shall' and 'will' are quite frequent future auxiliaries in earlier German, they have been replaced in the modern standard language by the auxiliary *werden*, which originally had only the meaning 'become'. Even in the earliest texts this verb can be found used with a present participle (similar to its usage with other adjectives), as in this Old High German example from Otfrid's *Evangelienbuch*:

> thô ward mund sîner sprehhantêr
> 'then his mouth at once became speaking (began to speak)'

Given a tendency for *werden* to be used as the future of *sîn* 'be' (as even in Modern German: *er wird Bundeskanzler* 'he will be prime minister'), such verbal phrases were easily reinterpreted as consisting of a future auxiliary plus a participle, resulting in loss of the adjective inflection on the participle, among other things. For reasons that are not totally clear—perhaps phonetic change in some dialects, perhaps analogy with the modals discussed above—*werden* early on could be accompanied not only by the present participle, but also by the infinitive, which is today the only correct form.

Our reading selections document quite well one of the ways that the periphrastic perfect came to exist in the Germanic languages. Note the following clauses:

> oþ þæt hīe hine ofslægenne hæfdon
> 'until they had him (in a state of being) killed'

> Ond (hīe) þā gatu him tō belocen hæfdon
> 'And (they) had the gates closed against them'

As I have tried to express with my word ordering, the origin of the perfect in "have" rests in the main meaning of that verb, namely 'possess'.

In each instance the past participle is an adjective with passive meaning describing the object of that verb, and it agrees with the noun in gender, case, and number. This is clear in the first sentence, which shows a genuine inflection, but not so clear in the second, where the inflection is *zero*. Indeed, the existence of such zero inflections (which make the adjective look less adjectival) probably was instrumental in allowing the construction to be reinterpreted as auxiliary verb + main verb rather than main verb (+ noun) + adjective. That is, to use the first example above, 'they had killed him' rather than 'they had him (in a) killed (state)'.

It should be noticed that the perfect in "have" arises from transitive verbs, which are precisely those whose preterite participles evince passive meaning. For intransitive verbs, another periphrasis with the verb 'be' or 'become' evolved. Note the following sentence from our biblical text:

> And him wæs mycel męnegu tō gegaderod
> 'And a great multitude was gathered to him'

Here again the preterite participle is probably an adjective with zero inflection, this time modifying the subject with active meaning. Again it is easy to interpret this sentence as containing a perfective auxiliary plus a main verb. The perfect in 'be' remained quite robust throughout the Old English period, but then gradually gave way to the perfect in 'have,' remaining today only in archaisms like "Christ is risen." In German, both have remained to this day, albeit with some changes in distribution.

In most of the older Germanic languages, but especially in Old English, there is a *progressive* periphrasis that makes use of the verb 'be' plus an adjectival present participle:

> ond hīe alle on þone cyning wærun feohtende
> 'and they all kept on fighting against the king'

In one way or another, this construction is the ancestor of our modern progressive aspect in "-ing," as the translation shows.

Forms of 'be' or 'become' were also important in the formation of a passive periphrasis, as the following examples from "Cynewulf" show:

> ond sē swīþe gewundad wæs
> 'and that one was badly wounded'

> Ond hīe cuædon þæt tæt ilce hiera gefērum geboden wære
> 'And they said that the same had been offered to their companions'

> ēowre gefēran þe mid þām cyninge ofslægene wærun
> 'your companions that were killed with the king'

Of the three, the first would strike the modern reader as the most likely to contain a main verb 'be' + adjective, with the adjective describing a state resulting from the action of wounding; the last two seem more like verbs. Yet it is the third that shows a clear adjective inflection (on *ofslægene*), while the first two can be seen as ambiguous between a zero adjective inflection and no adjective inflection, which would make them more like verbs. Clearly this text documents an intermediate stage in the development.

While Old English used the verb 'become' as well as 'be' for the passive periphrasis, ultimately 'be' was the clear winner. In German, also, the forms *werden* 'become' and *sîn* 'be' competed, but here *werden* was ascendant.

Clause Subordination

In both the Readings in this chapter, and indeed in early Germanic texts in general, many clauses that we would now subordinate to others are found as independent sentences, with little or no formal marking of their logical relationship to other (preceding or following) sentences. Note the following string of clauses:

Ond þā on þæs wīfes gebǣrum onfundon þæs cyninges þegnas þā unstilnesse, ond þā þider urnon swā hwelc swā þonne gearo wearþ, ond radost.
'And then from the woman's cries the king's thanes discovered the disturbance, and there ran thither whoever then became ready, and fastest.'

We might be more inclined to translate this as follows:

'And when the king's thanes heard the uproar from the woman's outcry, those who got ready most quickly ran there.'

We may still, of course, string sentences together the way the Old English text does, but on the whole we prefer to make the relations between them explicit, in many cases by incorporating one sentence into another, as I did above.

All the surviving Germanic languages show a development from predominantly paratactic constructions, in which independent sentences follow one another in the text, to hypotactic ones, in which some clauses are made syntactically dependent on others. Our Old English texts exhibit several of the ways in which this development may have taken place. I discuss a few of them below.

Logically speaking, some clauses may function as the subjects or objects of other clauses. Thus while I may see an object, like "a dog," I may also see an entire action, like "John running down the street." How can I express this fact? One way is shown by the following two sentences from the Cynewulf text:

> Ond þā geāscode hē þone cyning . . . ond hine þǣr berād ond þone būr ūtan beēode. . . . One þā ongeat sē cyning þæt.
> 'And then he discovered the king . . . and overtook him there and surrounded the bower from without. . . . And then the king perceived that.'

In this clearly paratactic construction, the neuter demonstrative pronoun refers not to an object, but to the preceding sentence.

Now note the following sentence:

> ond him cȳþdon þæt hiera mǣgas him mid wǣron
> 'and told them that their relatives were with him'

This construction, which is clearly hypotactic, has *þæt* as an introductory conjunction, a form that is clearly identical with the neuter demonstrative pronoun. It is extremely unlikely that this usage is a coincidence, and indeed scholars are rather sure that 'that' constructions of the sort found in the last example, where the 'that' begins the subordinate clause, originally derive from a type of paratactic construction in which the 'that' belonged to the first clause and was immediately followed by the clause it referred to, thus something like:

> ond him cȳþdon þæt: hiera mǣgas him mid wǣron
> 'and told them that: their relatives were with him'

However, cases like the following make it quite clear that the reassignment of the pronoun to the subordinate clause had already taken place by the time the Cynewulf text was written:

> Þā on morgenne gehīerdun þæt þæs cyninges þegnas . . . , þæt se cyning ofslægen wæs
> 'Then in the morning the king's thanes heard that . . . , that the king was slain'

Sentences may serve not only as subjects or objects of verbs, but also as objects of prepositions. Again we find 'that' introducing such clauses, and may postulate a similar origin (*oþ* is a preposition meaning 'up to, until'):

> ond hē þǣr wunade oþ þæt hiene ān swān ofstang
> 'and he lived there until a swineherd stabbed him to death'

Compare this with the main-clause prepositional phrase found in the following sentence from the *Chronicle* for 871:

ond on feohtende wæron oþ niht 'and kept fighting until night'

Compare also the causal clause below, which uses the dative form of 'that', with the causal phrase after it, using the dative of a noun:

> and hit forscranc, for þām hit wyrtruman næfde
> 'and it withered, because it had no roots'

> benam Sigebryht his rīces . . . for unryhtum dǣdum
> 'deprived Sigebryht of his kingdom . . . for unlawful deeds'

As our Readings show, we may also find instances of conjunctions consisting of the simple preposition, without the word 'that':

> oþ hē ofslōg þone aldormon
> 'until he killed the nobleman'

> ǣr hine þā men onfunden (otherwise ǣr þǣm)
> 'before the men found him'

Whether this conjunctional usage of the preposition by itself developed from constructions containing 'that', or independently, I leave an open question.

All the Germanic languages have ways of forming relative clauses, that is, sentences that modify a nominal or pronominal element in the main clause. Below I give some instances of this in our reading passages:

> þone aldormon, þe him lengest wunode
> 'the nobleman who stayed with him the longest'

> ānne æþeling sē was Cyneheard hāten
> 'a prince who was called Cyneheard'

> hiera mǣgas . . . , þā þe him from noldon
> 'their relatives . . . , who didn't want to leave him'

A type of relative clause not found in our texts, and indeed very rare in Old English, is exemplified in the following Old High German sentence from Otfrid:

> in droume sie in zelitun then weg sie faran scoltun
> 'in a dream they told them the way they should go'

Some scholars believe that this latter type, in which the two clauses are simply linked by a shared element that is not repeated in the subordinate clause, is the oldest type. But it should be pointed out that such clauses, well known in Modern English and the Nordic languages, were almost unknown in the earliest stages; only German, in which the construction *decreased* in frequency, seems to be going the right direction.

Be that as it may, the other three examples represent well-documented types. In the first, we find an uninflected particle *þe* marking the relative clause. This type of relative marker is paralleled in one way or another in all the Germanic languages, though often with different particles: Gothic has *ei*, Old Norse *er*. The introduction of relative particles lies so far back that it is difficult to trace the course of development.

The nature of the relative marker in the second sentence is a bit clearer. It is formally identical to the demonstrative pronoun 'that, the', and inflects for both number and case. There are several theories about how this pronoun came to be used as a relative. One of them holds that the starting point came with sentences like the fourth one above, in which, however, the linking word is a demonstrative, thus of the form of the following example from Otfrid's Old High German:

> thô liefun sar . . . thie nân minnotun meist
> 'then ran immediately . . . those (who) loved him most'

The pronoun *thie*, which originally belonged to the main clause, but which by its nominative plural inflection could also belong to the subordinate clause, is then reinterpreted as in fact belonging to the subordinate clause. This new type of clause then gets used in other relative constructions.

Another theory derives the relative pronoun from the demonstrative of a formerly independent sentence. Thus the second relative sentence above might derive from an original construction of the following sort:

> Hē wolde ādrǣfan ānne æþeling. Sē was Cyneheard hāten.
> 'He wanted to exile a prince. That one was called Cyneheard.'

The third relative sentence above (*hiera mǣgas . . . þā þe . . .*), which is indeed of a form very common in all the Germanic languages, consists of a (former) demonstrative plus a particle. Whatever its source —possibly the reinterpretation of a main-clause demonstrative followed by a subordinate-clause particle?—it clearly serves to distinguish relative pronouns from demonstrative pronouns in the later language.

In this section I have barely scratched the surface of the syntactic phenomena of the older Germanic languages. I have totally neglected the use of cases and of the subjunctive; I have ignored the extremely interesting development of infinitive constructions; I have not even mentioned a large number of subordinate-clause types. As usual, the scope of this book has dictated my omissions. The reader is encouraged most heartily to explore the books and articles listed under "Further Reading."

FURTHER READING

Blair, Peter Hunter. *An Introduction to Anglo-Saxon England.* 2d ed. Cambridge: Cambridge University Press, 1977.

Cassidy, Frederic G., and Richard N. Ringler. *Bright's Old English Grammar and Reader.* 3d ed. New York: Holt, Rinehart & Winston, 1971.

Ebert, Robert Peter. *Historische Syntax des Deutschen.* Stuttgart: Metzler, 1978.

Fisher, D. J. V. *The Anglo-Saxon Age: C. 400–1042.* London: Longman, 1973.

Greenberg, Joseph H. "Some Universals of Grammar, with Particular Reference to the Order of Meaningful Elements." In J. H. Greenberg, ed., *Universals of Language*, 2d ed., pp. 73–113. Cambridge, Mass.: M.I.T. Press, 1966.

Greenfield, Stanley B. *A Critical History of Old English Literature.* New York: N.Y.U. Press, 1965.

Hopper, Paul J. *The Syntax of the Simple Sentence in Proto-Germanic.* The Hague: Mouton, 1975.

Lehmann, Winfred P. "Proto-Germanic Syntax." In F. van Coetsem and H. Kufner, eds., *Toward a Grammar of Proto-Germanic*, pp. 239–68. Tübingen: Niemeyer, 1972.

Lockwood, W. B. *Historical German Syntax.* Oxford: Clarendon, 1968.

Mitchell, Bruce, and Fred C. Robinson. *A Guide to Old English.* Rev. ed., with texts and glossary. Oxford: Blackwell, 1982.

Sievers, Eduard. *An Old English Grammar.* 3d ed. Trans. Albert S. Cook. New York: Greenwood, 1968. [Reprint of the original translation of 1903.]

Stenton, Frank M. *Anglo-Saxon England.* 3d ed. Rev. Doris M. Stenton. Oxford: Clarendon, 1971.

Traugott, Elizabeth C. *A History of English Syntax.* New York: Holt, Rinehart & Winston, 1972.

Vennemann, Theo. "Topics, Subjects, and Word Order: From SXV to SVX via TVX." In J. M. Anderson and C. Jones, eds., *Historical Linguistics*, vol. 1, pp. 339–76. Amsterdam: North-Holland, 1974.

7

OLD FRISIAN

A Brief History of the Frisians

According to the historian Tacitus, when the Roman general Drusus first crossed the lower Rhine in 12 B.C., ultimately in search of the mouth of the Ems, he encountered a tribe named the Frisii. Apparently he subjugated them with little trouble, and for the next three hundred years the Frisii were very much under the sway of the Roman Empire.

What kind of people the Frisii were is not totally clear. Although the designation *Frisii* is clearly the same as the later designation *Frisian*, and the latter clearly refers to a Germanic subgroup, some scholars feel that the people called Frisii in Drusus's time may have been a non-Germanic group who were later to merge with Germanic elements, lending their name to the newly formed population.

The lack of clarity on this point is not remedied by any agreement on the origin and etymology of the name. Speculations range from Germanic roots reconstructed with the meanings 'friends', 'free men', 'edge dwellers', and 'curly-haired ones', to roots of non-Germanic origin.

Similarly unclear is the original geographic distribution of the Frisii. In the southwest they seem to have lived as far down as the Rhine (the "Old Rhine," that is, which flows into the North Sea at Katwijk in the Netherlands), or even the Scheldt. In the northeast, they may have lived as far as the Ems, but perhaps only as far as the Lauwers.

Whatever their farthest extension, the heartland of the Frisii, as of the later Frisians, was the North Sea coast approximately from Alkmaar in the modern province of North Holland, across the lake at the mouth of the IJssel that later turned into the Zuider Zee, and along the west and north coasts of the present provinces of Friesland and Groningen to the mouth of the Ems. Here they lived almost exclusively on natural or artificial mounds of earth, *terpen*, which protected them from the frequent floodings of the landscape by the encroaching sea. This coastal area, which frequently lay below sea level, was crisscrossed by waterways and filled with lakes, while the less inhabited areas farther inland were mainly moors. The Frisians were herders rather than farmers, their cattle grazing on the meadows surrounding the terpen. What produce they had was principally imported rather than grown in the marshy soil.

The history of the Frisii under the Romans is sparse, but reasonably clear. From the invasion of Drusus on, the Frisii appear to have supplied provisions and even soldiers to the Roman army, and Frisii were no doubt part of the Roman garrisoning of Britain. In A.D. 28, there was a Frisian revolt, because of unfairly high taxation, which succeeded in shaking off the Roman overlordship. But Frisian independence lasted only until 47, when the general Corbulo subjugated them again. At this time any Frisii (probably very few) living in the zones immediately north of the Rhine from around Utrecht to Katwijk were removed, creating a *cordon sanitaire* between the Frisii and their more civilized neighbors to the south.

Of the Frisii we know little more. Though they are known to have participated in the Batavian uprising against the Romans from 59 to 71, and we have some report of them as late as the early fourth century, the historical records are essentially silent for the next three centuries. This silence clearly masks some rather important events. For one thing, the fifth century marks the beginning of the Anglo-Saxon invasions of England.

For the Frisians this meant two things. First, since the Angles and Saxons could hardly avoid going through Frisian territory to get to Britain, the Frisians were undoubtedly affected by the great migration. Some scholars have gone so far as to claim that the Frisians were in fact totally absorbed by the invaders, and that the later Frisians represent an amalgam of Angles, Saxons, and earlier Frisians. This claim is probably wildly exaggerated, but it seems beyond doubt that some intermixture occurred at this time, with some Angles and Saxons remaining behind on the mainland, and some Frisians participating in the settlement of England. Second, the departure of the Angles and the Saxons left the coastal areas east of the Frisians at least partially empty, and the Frisians had a little room to expand. And expand they apparently did, during the fifth and sixth centuries. By the end of that time, the Frisians appear to have occupied the coastal area all the way to the mouth of the Weser.

We have some documentation of a further expansion of the Frisians in the first half of the seventh century. This time they expanded to the south (Map 6). Specifically, the Frisians appear to have expanded into the

Map 6.   Past and present Frisian language areas.

area south of the modern IJsselmeer, all the way down to Dorestad, south-east of Utrecht. For a short period at least, this so-called *Frisia Magna* represented the farther expansion of the Frisian people. Then came the Franks.

Before discussing the Frisians under the Frankish emperors, I should touch on one other Frisian expansion, namely that into North Friesland, which is the coastal zone on the western side of the Jutland peninsula, in present-day Schleswig, plus a number of islands facing that coast. There is a great deal of disagreement about when Frisians first settled these areas, and indeed about whether the two parts of North Friesland (the islands and the mainland) ever really had much to do with one another. One theory holds that the islands were settled very early, during the age of the folk migrations, while the mainland was settled from the south at a much later date. Another theory holds that both the islands and the mainland were settled quite late, the islands from the seventh century on, the mainland from the tenth. In any case, North Friesland is rather peripheral in the later doings of the Frisians, and provides no documentation of Old Frisian. I will discuss it no further here.

Like most other continental Germanic groups, the Frisians came into conflict with the Franks. For the Frisians, this conflict essentially started in the seventh century, with attempts to retain Frisia Magna in the face of Frankish pressure from the south. The most famous figure in their long resistance is without doubt their king Redbad or Radbod, who was defeated by the Merovingian Pippin at Dorestad in 689. Although in 714, after the death of Pippin, Redbad recovered some of the territory lost in that defeat and subsequently, he was definitively defeated in 719 by Charles Martel, and died that same year.

In the course of the next decades, the Frisians were gradually annexed to the Frankish empire. Charles Martel conquered all of Friesland up to the Lauwers, and in 785, during the Saxon wars, Charlemagne succeeded in pushing his imperial boundaries all the way to the Elbe, thus including the eastern Frisian territories.

Along with Frankish domination, of course, came gradual Christianization. Begun under Wilfred, Archbishop of York, in the southern parts of Frisia Magna in 678, and continued there under Willibrord (d. 739), the missionary activity was expanded to present-day Friesland by St. Boniface, martyred near the Lauwers in 754. Under Willehad and the Frisian Liudger, this work continued after a pause of a few years, spreading also to the regions east of the Lauwers (a task made easier by Charlemagne's incorporation of these regions during the Saxon wars). By the beginning of the ninth century the Christianization of Friesland was effectively complete.

From the beginning of the Frankish domination, we may usefully distinguish between three different parts of the formerly independent Frisian territory: the northern part of the modern province of North Holland (West Friesland), the present-day province of Friesland and the coastal areas of present-day Groningen to the mouth of the Ems (Middle Friesland), and finally the coastal areas between the Ems and the Weser (East Friesland). Each of these was ultimately to suffer a different fate.

Although Frisia was a part of the Frankish and later the Holy Roman Empire, it was on the periphery of those empires. As a result it was subject to less control, but also received less protection from outside enemies. The lack of protection became quite apparent in the early ninth century, with the advent of the vikings. Indeed, so hopeless was the task of protecting Friesland against the vikings that Charlemagne's grandson found it easier simply to cede Dorestad and a considerable part of the coast of modern northern Holland to the Dane Rorik, expecting in return that he would protect the regions against his countrymen. Another Dane, Godfred, was given the same regions under the same conditions by the emperor Charles III. Godfred's death in 885 ended this Norman domination, however, and the Scandinavian period in Friesland had no permanent influence on the history and culture of the area.

Indirectly, however, it did. For in that North Holland kernel of the area granted to Rorik in the mid-ninth century, the coastal zone of Kennemerland, the Frankish counts of Holland subsequently grew in power and influence, asserting especially a claim to West Friesland, and this area finally fell to them in 1289. Though there are still a few language phenomena in North Holland that attest to an earlier Frisian-speaking population there, on the whole we find a complete absorption into the Dutch culture and language.

The counts of Holland were not content with West Friesland. They had designs on other Frisian territories as well, as did a number of other feudal lords. These designs remained unrealized for a very long time, however. Technically, these remaining areas of Friesland owed allegiance to the Holy Roman Emperor, and thus to his legal representatives, but in fact they possessed a degree of autonomy almost unheard of in the Middle Ages. Essentially, throughout the thirteenth and fourteenth centuries, Middle and East Friesland consisted of a number of small farmers' republics that totally regulated their own administration, public works, legislation, and justice, without outside interference. Though obviously not on a regular basis, these separate regions occasionally achieved a certain degree of pan-Frisian unity through meetings at Upstalsbom, an ancient law-mound near Aurich in East Friesland. At these meetings they established common Frisian law and reaffirmed their freedom and independence from external rulers.

Their independence was always shaky, however. The subsequent history of Middle and East Friesland is one of gradual splintering and retreat. German East Friesland was ultimately given in 1464 to the Low German–speaking counts of Cirksema, and, aside from a few North Frisian dialects, the Frisian language is represented in Germany today only in the small landlocked area known as the Saterland. The northern areas of the province of Groningen, too, ultimately went over to using Low German. Even the heartland of Frisia, as its present status as a province of the Netherlands indicates, came increasingly under the thumb of the counts of Holland. And although the Frisian language has managed to assert itself far better in Holland, there is no question that it is under heavy pressure from the Dutch standard language. The prognosis for the continued health of Frisian is thus not good.

Old Frisian Texts

In this section I can give neither an exhaustive list of texts in Old Frisian, nor a breakdown by genre. The first would be impossible, as there are well over 1,300 more or less separate texts. The second would be pointless, since virtually all the important texts are legal documents. I will try instead to give a feel for what types of documents are left to us from the Old Frisian period, and for what issues they have raised among modern scholars.

Not surprisingly, the first attestations of the Frisian language are Frisian names and words in Latin texts, and perhaps (though this is disputed) in a few runic inscriptions. What is surprising is that the oldest surviving connected Frisian texts date from the latter half of the thirteenth century. Thus the language we know as Old Frisian is on the whole contemporaneous with the *middle* period of the other Germanic languages (though there is at least some overlap in time with Old Norse). There must have been earlier texts, indeed texts in areas other than the law, but these have been lost. No doubt many were lost during the viking incursions noted in the last section.

Sjölin (1969, and following him, Markey 1981) has divided the most important Old Frisian texts into 25 separate categories, most of them containing but a single item. The only exception to this is the last, virtually a wastebasket category, which lumps together 1,300 late West Frisian legal documents, letters, chronicles, and so forth. Of the other 24 items, three are found in unique manuscripts, namely the *Basel Confessional Oaths* (ca. 1445), *Thet Freske Riim* (17th-century copy of a late 15th-century poem chronicling the legendary origin of the Frisians and their ancient privileges), and the *Sneek Legal and Administrative Statutes* (1490–1517). The remaining items are duplicated in one or another of seventeen different manuscripts.

The oldest of these seventeen, the First Brokmer Manuscript, was compiled after 1276; the latest, the Codex Furmerius, around 1600. Most of these manuscripts are collections of laws, privileges, and statutes, applying either to Friesland as a whole or to parts of it. Several contain in addition relatively extraneous material, such as *The Fifteen Signs Before the Last Judgment*, definitely not a legal text, or material bearing upon the right of the Frisians to freedom and to their own legal system. Such material includes various texts dealing with Charlemagne's putative granting of these rights for (again putative) aid against the Saxons, the Danes, and so on.

The 21 texts found in these manuscripts are in many cases clearly older than the manuscripts themselves. For example, the text known as the *Seventeen Privileges*, found in a large number of the manuscripts, apparently goes back to the eleventh century, and is probably based on even earlier Carolingian texts in Latin. Again, the text known as the *Magistrates' Law* may go back to the eleventh century.

I will not give here a breakdown of the various laws, statutes, and privileges in the Frisian texts. I would like, however, to make two points about them. First, with their volume and explicitness, these texts far surpass the legal texts of any other old Germanic language. Second, despite their relatively late date, they reveal a singularly Germanic point of view about the righting of wrongs, specifically an emphasis on monetary compensation rather than corporal punishment of the offender. This point is illustrated in my second reading selection.

One of the traditional questions about the Old Frisian texts is whether they reveal significant dialect differentiation. Certainly the texts show great differences in phonology and morphology, and these differences do correspond to a great extent with the putative eastern or western origins of the texts. It is also true, however, that the (amazingly uniform) eastern texts are almost without exception older than the western texts. (The eastern texts run from approximately 1275 to 1475; the western texts from 1475 to approximately 1600.) Thus the traditional designations of the two groups of language variants as "Old East Frisian" and "Old West Frisian" seem to be giving way to the designations "Classical Old Frisian" and "Post-Classical Old Frisian," a practice I endorse. Both the reading texts that follow are classical, and the linguistic description of Old Frisian that follows them, though cognizant of post-classical variants, is primarily based on Classical Old Frisian.

Another issue that has taxed Old Frisian scholars concerns the origins of the texts. The interrelated questions begin with why the extant texts are almost exclusively legal. And why were they compiled at such a late date? The time was inauspicious: the Frisians were strongly threatened, both politically and linguistically, by the Low Germans and the Dutch. And why were they accompanied by such specious (in fact invented) appeals to privileges granted by ancient authorities?

As I have formulated them, the questions suggest their own answers. These texts were compiled precisely in order to strengthen the case of the Frisians against encroaching outside authority. Although many of the laws had existed in oral form for several centuries, and had even been translated into Latin during the Carolingian period, their setting down, or even retranslation, during the fourteenth and fifteenth centuries represented a last gasp of Frisian independence in the face of overwhelming force. Markey, for one, links the beginning of the compilation of most of the Old Frisian legal texts with the final meetings of the Upstalsbom Union from 1323 to 1327.

Readings

As I noted above, both of our passages are from older (eastern) Classical Old Frisian texts. The first is from the beginning of the so-called *Asegabook* or First Rüstringer Manuscript, compiled sometime around 1300. The second, a typical legal text, is from the *Brokmer Letter*, extant in two different manuscripts.

The Ten Commandments

Thit riuht skrêf God selua, ûse hêra, thâ thet — right, *schrieb*, self, our, *Herr*, that
was thet Moyses lâtte thet Israhêliske folk — was, led, Israel(ite), folk
thruch thene râda sê, and of there wilda — through, *den*, red, sea, and, over, wild
wôstene, andse kômon tô tha berge, ther is — *Wüste*, *sie*, came, to, the, *Berg*, is
ehêten Synay. Thâ festade Moyses twîa — *(ge)heissen*, fasted, two
fiuwertich dega and nahta; thêr efter jef God — forty, day, night, there, after, gave
him twâ stênena tefla, thêr hi on eskriuin — two, stone, table, he, on, *(ge)schrieben*
hede tha tian bodo, tha skolde hi lêra tha — had, ten, *(Ge)bot*, should, *lehren*
Israhêliska folke.

Thet was thet êrost bod: Thîn God thet — *erst*, thine
is thi êna, ther skippere is himulrîkes and — one, *Schöpfer*, *Himmelreich*
irthrîkes, tham skaltu thianja. — earth, *dem*, shalt, thou, *dienen*

Thet was thet ôther bod: Thu ne skalt — other
thînes Godes noma nâwet îdle untfâ; thêr — name, not, idle, *empfangen*
mithi send ti urbeden alle mênêtha. — *mit*, sind, *Meineid*

Thet was thet thredde bod: Thu skalt — third
firja thene hêlega Sunnandî. . . . — *feiern*, *den*, holy, Sunday

Thet was thet fiarde bod: Thu skalt	fourth
êrja thînne feder and thîne môder, thet tu	ehren, father, mother, desto
theste langor libbe.	longer, live
Thet was thet fîfte bod: Thu ne skalt	fifth
nênne monslaga dûa.	man, slaughter, do
Thet was thet sexte bod: Thu ne skalt	sixth
nên hôr thâ nên overhôr dûa, bûta mith	whore, over, but
thînere âfta wîue skaltu godilîke libba.	wife, godlike
Thet was thet sivgunde bod: Thu ne	seventh
skalt nêne thiuvethe dûa, and ne skalt nâwet	theft
jerja ova thînes ivinkerstena haua, ther thi	(be)gehren, even, Christian, Habe
fon riuchta nâwet wertha ne mugun.	von, werden, may
Thet was thet achtunde bod: Thu ne	eighth
skalt nên onriucht tiuch dûa.	un-, Zeug(nis)
Thet was thet niugunde and thet tiande	ninth, tenth
bod: Thu skalt minnja God thînne skippere	(be)minnen
mith rênere hirta and thînne ivinkerstena	mit, rein, heart, like
lîke thi selva. Thesse tuâ bodo beslûtath alle	these, (ein)schliessen, all
tha ôthera bodo.	
Thet send tha tian bodo ther God urjef	
Moysese, and hi forth lêrde tha Israhêliska	forth, lehrte
folk (thesse bodo hîldon hia tha fiuwertich	held
jêra thâse andere wôstene wêron) and le-	years, were, (ent)ledigen
thogade hia fon monigere nêde and lâttese	many, need
an thet lond thet flât fon melokon and fon	land, flow, milk
hunige—thet was thet hêlege lond tô	honey
Jhêrusalem. Alsâ lât ûse hêra God alle tha tô	so
tha himulrîke, ther tha riuchte folgjath, and	follow
alle tha ther thet riuht jeftha ênich riuht	any
brekth (hit ne sê thet ma hit thruch nâtha	break, it, sei, man, Gnade
dûe, thruch thet tha nâtha send mârra thâ	more, than
thet riuht), sâ bislût hia God andere hille,	Hell
âlsa hi bislât tha Egypta liode anda râda sê,	Leute
thâse sîne liodon skathja weldon, tha Isra-	scathe, willed
hêliska folke.	

On the Man Who Flees into a Church

Jef hîr ên mon fliûth inna tsyureka, and tha	if, here, flee, church
fiund hine thêr on gêlath, al thet hi thenna	Feind, ihn, then
bîre nêdwere dêth, thet lidse gresfelle.	bei, der, Notwehr, do(th), lie, grass

Wirgath ma hine thêr on, sâ geldema hine — *würgen* ('worry'), *man, Geld*
mith fîfta halwe jelde, and tha liudem hun- — half, hundred
der merca, and thet hûs thera liuda. Nêl hi — *Mark*, house
thenna naut of unga, alsâ tha fiund fon un- — not
gath bi hêlgena monna, and bi rêdgewena — *Rat*, give
worde, sâ rêsze hi alsâ stôr, alsâ thi ther tha — word, reach
tsyurka bifêth. And hwasâre ênne mon âsleyt — slay
innâre tsyurika, sâ rêsze hi hunder merca
tha liudem and sexthech tha hêlegum; nêl- — sixty
lath hia of there tsyurka nauvet unga, thêrre
thenne on send, sâ unga thi rêdja, ther ur tha — *sind*
tsyurka sueren hêth, and kêthese of. Nêllet — sworn, hath
hia nâwet of unga, sâ berne hi thet forme — burn
bêken bi achta merkum thes selwa deis; and — beacon, eight, day
ne ungat hia thenna naut of, sâ berne alle
sîne sîthar tha bêkene thes letera deis and — *sein*, later
sogenje tha liude, alrec hira bî achta mercum;
and hôc hira sâ tha bêkene naut ne bernt
and sîne liude naut ne brench, sâ lêdema — bring, lead
oppa hine alra êrest, and fiuch hi with tha — *erst*, fight
sîthar, sâ felle hît a tuira wegena. — way

GLOSSARY

Unless specified otherwise, nouns and pronouns are nominative singular, adjectives are masculine nominative singular, and verbs are infinitives. The parenthetical identification of any form has reference only to the Readings, and is not necessarily an exhaustive list of all possible identifications of that form in the language.

a tuira wegena 'double'
acht 'eight', *achta* (dat. pl.)
achtunde 'eighth', *achtunde* (neut. nom. sg.)
âft 'legal', *âfta* (fem. dat. sg.)
all, al 'all', *alle* (masc. nom. and acc. pl.; neut. acc. pl.), *alra* (masc. gen. pl.)
alrec 'each'
alsâ 'just as, just so, so, as, when'
an 'on, to, in, until'
and 'and'
anda = *an* + *-da*; see *thi*
andere = *an* + *-dere*; see *thiu*

andse = *and* + *-se*; see *hi*
âslâ 'strike', *âsleyt* (3 sg. pres. ind.)

bêken 'beacon fire', *bêken* (acc. sg.), *bêkene* (acc. pl.)
berg 'mountain', *berge* (dat. sg.)
berna 'burn', *bernt* (3 sg. pres. ind.), *berne* (3 sg. and 3 pl. pres. subj.)
beslûtath see *bislûta, beslûta*
bî, bi 'by, in, at, with (a penalty of)'
bifâ 'attack, enter, occupy', *bifêth* (3 sg. pres. ind.)
bîre = *bî* + *there*
bislûta, beslûta 'close up, encompass',

bislût (3 sg. pres. ind.), *beslûtath* (3 pl. pres. ind.), *bislât* (3 sg. pret. ind.)

bod 'commandment', *bodo* (nom. and acc. pl.)

breka 'break', *brekth* (3 pl. pres. ind.)

brenga 'bring', *brench* (3 sg. pres. ind.)

bûta 'rather, besides'

dei 'day', *deis* (gen. sg.), *dega* (acc. pl.)

dêth see *dûa*

dûa 'do, commit', *dêth* (3 sg. pres. ind.), *dûe* (3 sg. pres. subj.)

efter see *thêr efter*

Egypta 'Egyptian', *Egypta* (neut. acc. pl.)

ehêten see *hêta*

ên 'one, a' (masc. nom. sg. strong), *êna* (masc. nom. sg. weak), *ênne* (masc. acc. sg.)

ênich 'any', *ênich* (neut. acc. sg.)

enne see *ên*

êrja 'honor'

êrost, êrest 'first', *êrost* (neut. nom. sg.)

eskriuin see *skrîva*

feder 'father', *feder* (acc. sg.)

fella 'pay (for), be fined (for)', *felle* (3 sg. pres. subj.)

festa 'fast', *festade* (3 sg. pret. ind.)

fiarde 'fourth', *fiarde* (neut. nom. sg.)

fîfta half 'four and a half', *fîfta halwe* (dat. sg.)

fîfte 'fifth', *fîfte* (neut. nom. sg.)

fîrja 'celebrate, observe'

fiuchta 'fight', *fiuch* (3 sg. pres. ind.)

fiund 'enemy', *fiund* (nom. pl.)

fiuwertich 'forty'

flât see *fliata*

flîa 'flee', *fliûth* (3 sg. pres. ind.)

fliata 'flow', *flât* (3 sg. pret. ind.)

fliûth see *flîa*

folgia 'follow', *folgjath* (3 pl. pres. ind.)

folk 'folk, people', *folk* (acc. sg.), *folke* (dat. sg.), *folk* (acc. pl.)

fon 'from, by, of, out, away'

forma 'first', *forme* (neut. acc. sg.)

forth 'further'

gêla 'hunt', *gêlath* (3 pl. pres. ind.)

gelde see *jelda*; *geldema* = *gelde* + *ma*

God 'God', *God* (acc. sg.), *Godes* (gen. sg.)

godilîke 'in accord with God, godly'

gresfelle 'uncompensated'

halda 'hold, keep', *hîldon* (3 pl. pret. ind.)

hava, haua 'possession', *haua* (acc. pl.)

hebba 'have', *hêth* (3 sg. pres. ind.), *hede* (3 sg. pret. ind.)

hêleg 'holy' (in masc. pl. also 'saints, church'), *hêlega* (masc. acc. sg.), *hêlegena, hêlgena* (masc. gen. pl.), *hêlegum* (masc. dat. pl.), *hêlege* (neut. nom. sg.)

hêra 'Lord'

hêta 'call, name', *ehêten* (pret. part.)

hêth see *hebba*

hi 'he', *hine* (acc. sg.), *him* (dat. sg.), *hia, -se* (nom. and acc. pl.), *hira* (gen. pl.)

hîldon see *halda*

hille 'Hell', *hille* (dat. sg.)

him see *hi*

himulrîke 'Heaven, Kingdom of Heaven', *himulrîkes* (gen. sg.), *himulrîke* (dat. sg.)

hine see *hi*

hîr 'here'

hira see *hi*

hirte 'heart', *hirta* (dat. sg.)

hît = *hi hit*

hit 'it', *hit* (acc. sg.)

hôc 'whichever'

hôr 'fornication', *hôr* (acc. sg.)
hunder 'a hundred'
hunig 'honey', *hunige* (dat. sg.)
hûs 'house'
hwasâ 'whoever, anyone';
   hwasâre = *hwasâ ther*

îdle 'idly'
inna 'in, into'
innâre = *inna there*
irthrîke 'Earth', *irthrîkes* (gen. sg.)
is see *sîn*
Israhêlisc 'Israelite', *Israhêliske* (neut.
   acc. sg.), *Israhêliska* (neut. dat. sg.
   and acc. pl.)
ivinkerstena 'fellow Christian',
   ivinkerstena (acc. and gen. sg.)

jef 'if'; see also *jeva*
jeftha 'or'
jeld, geld 'money, wergeld, death
   price', *jelde* (dat. sg.)
jelda, gelda 'pay (for)', *gelde* (3 sg.
   pres. subj.)
jêr 'year', *jêra* (acc. pl.)
jerja 'covet'
jeva 'give', *jef* (3 sg. pret. ind.)
Jhêrusalem 'Jerusalem'

kêtha 'order', *kêthe* (3 sg. pres. subj.);
   kêthese = *kêthe* + *-se* (see *hi*)
kuma 'come', *kômon* (3 pl. pret. ind.)

lang 'long', *langor* (comp.)
lât, lâtte, see *lêda*; *lâttese* = *lâtte* +
   -se (see *lêda* and *hi*)
lêda 'lead', *lât* (3 sg. pres. ind.), *lêde*
   (3 sg. pres. subj.), *lâtte* (3 sg. pret.
   ind.); *lêdema* = *lêde* + *ma*
lêra 'teach', *lêrde* (3 sg. pret. ind.)
leter 'later, last, next', *letera* (masc.
   gen. sg.)
lethogia 'free, release', *lethogade*
   (3 sg. pret. ind.)
libba 'live', *libbe* (2 sg. pres. subj.)

lidsja 'lie', *lidse* (3 sg. pres. subj.)
lîke 'like, as'
liode, liude 'people' (nom. pl.), *liode*
   (acc. pl.), *liuda* (gen. pl.), *liodon,*
   liudem (dat. pl.)
lond 'land', *lond* (acc. sg.)

ma 'one, a person'
mârra 'more'
melok 'milk', *melokon* (dat. pl.)
mênêth 'false oath', *mênêtha*
   (nom. pl.)
merc 'mark', *merca* (acc. pl.),
   mercum, merkum (dat. pl.)
minnja 'love'
mith 'with'
mithi see *thêr mithi*
môder 'mother', *môder* (acc. sg.)
mon 'man', *mon* (acc. sg.), *monna*
   (gen. pl.)
monig 'many, much', *monigere* (fem.
   dat. sg.)
monna see *mon*
monslaga 'murder', *monslaga*
   (acc. sg.)
Moyses 'Moses', *Moysese* (dat. sg.)
muga 'be able, can', *mugun* (3 pl.
   pres. ind.)

naht 'night', *nahta* (acc. pl.)
nâthe 'grace, kindness', *nâtha* (nom.
   and acc. pl.)
naut, nauvet, nâwet 'nought'
ne, ni 'not'
nêd 'danger, suffering', *nêde* (dat. sg.)
nêdwere 'defense', *nêdwere* (dat. sg.)
nêl = *ni will*
nêllath = *ni willath*
nêllet = *ni wellet*
nên 'no, none, any', *nênne* (masc. acc.
   sg.), *nên* (neut. acc. sg.), *nêne* (fem.
   acc. sg.)
ni see *ne, ni*
niugunde 'ninth', *niugunda* (neut.
   nom. sg.)

noma 'name', *noma* (acc. sg.)

of 'from, out, away'
on 'in, on'
onriuht, onriucht 'false', *onriucht*
   (neut. acc. sg.)
oppa 'against, upon'
ôther 'second, other', *ôther* (neut.
   nom. sg.), *ôthera* (neut. acc. pl.)
ova 'above, over, concerning'
overhôr 'adultery', *overhôr* (acc. sg.)

râd 'red', *râda* (masc. acc. and
   dat. sg.)
rêdgeva, rêdjeva, rêdja 'judge',
   rêdgewena (gen. pl.)
rên 'pure', *rênere* (fem. dat. sg.)
rêsza 'pay', *rêsze* (3 sg. pres. subj.)
riuht, riucht 'law', *riuht* (acc. sg.),
   riuchte, riuchta (dat. sg.)

sâ 'so, thus'
sê 'sea', *sê* (acc. and dat. sg.)
sê see *sîn*
self '-self, same', *selva, selua* (masc.
   nom. and acc. sg.), *selwa* (masc.
   gen. sg.)
send see *sîn*
sexte 'sixth', *sexte* (neut. nom. sg.)
sexthech 'sixty'
sîn 'be', *is* (3 sg. pres. ind.), *send* (3
   pl. pres. ind.), *sê* (3 sg. pres. subj.),
   was (3 sg. pret. ind.), *wêron* (3 pl.
   pret. ind.)
sîn 'his', *sîne* (masc. nom. and
   dat. pl.)
sîth 'colleague', *sîthar* (nom. and
   acc. pl.)
sivgunde 'seventh', *sivgunde* (neut.
   nom. sg.)
skalt see *skela*; *skaltu* = *skalt thu*
skathja 'harm, injure'
skela 'shall, should', *skalt* (2 sg. pres.
   ind.), *skolde* (3 sg. pret. ind.)
skippere 'creator', *skippere* (acc. sg.)

skolde see *skela*
skrîva 'write', *skrêf* (3 sg. pret. ind.),
   eskriuin (pret. part.)
sogenja 'gather, collect', *sogenje* (3 pl.
   pres. subj.)
stênen '(of) stone', *stênena* (fem.
   acc. pl.)
stôr 'much'
suera 'swear, affirm', *sueren* (pret.
   part.)
Sunnandî 'Sunday, Sabbath',
   Sunnandî (acc. sg.)
Synay 'Sinai' (place name)

tefle 'tablet', *tefla* (acc. pl.)
tha see *thi*; see also *thet* and *thiu*
thâ 'than, or'
thâ 'then, when'
tham see *thi*
thâse = *thâ* + *-se*; see *hi*
thene see *thi*
thenne, thenna 'then'
ther 'who, which, that' (rel. particle)
thêr 'there, where'
thêr efter 'after that'
thêr mithi 'with that'
thera see *thi*
there see *thiu*
thêrre = *ther thêr*
thes see *thi*
thesse see *thit*
theste 'all the (more)'
thet 'the, that' (neut. art. and dem.
   pro.), *thet* (acc. sg.), *tha* (dat. sg.
   and acc. pl.)
thet 'which, that' (neut. rel. pro.)
thet 'so that'
thet 'that' (conj.)
thi see *thu, tu*
thi 'the, that' (masc. art. and dem.
   pro.), *thene* (acc. sg.), *thes* (gen. sg.),
   tham, tha, -da (dat. sg.), *tha* (nom.,
   acc., and dat. pl.), *thera* (gen. pl.)
thianja 'serve'

thîn 'thy, your', *thînne* (masc. acc. sg.), *thînes* (masc. gen. sg.), *thîne* (fem. acc. sg.), *thînere* (fem. dat. sg.)

thit 'this' (neut. dem. pro.), *thit* (acc. sg.), *thesse* (nom. and acc. pl.)

thiu 'the' (fem. art.), *tha* (acc. sg. and nom. pl.), *there*, *-dere* (dat. sg.)

thiuvethe 'theft', *thiuvethe* (acc. sg.)

thredde 'third', *thredde* (neut. nom. sg.)

thruch 'through'

thu, tu 'thou, you', *thi* (acc. sg.), *thi, ti* (dat. sg.)

tian 'ten'

tiande 'tenth', *tiande* (neut. nom. sg.)

tiuch 'witness', *tiuch* (acc. sg.)

tô 'to'

tsyurka 'church', *tsyureka, tsyurika, tsyurka* (acc. and dat. sg.)

tu see *thu, tu*

twâ, tuâ 'two' (fem. and neut.)

twîa 'twice'

unga 'go, come', *ungat, ungath* (3 pl. pres. ind.), *unga* (3 sg. pres. subj.)

untfâ 'receive, take'

ur 'over, with respect to'

urbiada 'forbid', *urbeden* (pret. part.)

urjeva 'present', *urjef* (3 sg. pret. ind.)

ûse 'our'

was see *sîn*

weldon, wellet, see *willa*

wêron see *sîn*

wertha 'become, be coming'

wîf 'wife, woman', *wîve* (dat. sg.)

wild 'wild', *wilda* (fem. dat. sg.)

willa 'want, will', *will* (3 sg. pres. ind.), *willath, wellet* (3 pl. pres. ind.), *weldon* (3 pl. pret. ind.)

wirgja 'kill', *wirgath* (3 sg. pres. ind.)

with 'with, against'

wîve see *wîf*

word 'word, command', *worde* (dat. sg.)

wôstene 'desert', *wôstene* (dat. sg.)

Some Aspects of Old Frisian Grammar

Spelling and Pronunciation

Consonants

In general, the Old Frisian consonants are spelled as might be expected, given the rules of Chapter 2. But while *p* and *t* need no comment, *k*, as in English, is a bit trickier. Thus, as in English, the letter *c* may be used for this sound except before the front vowels *i* and *e*. Unlike Old English, however, Old Frisian often uses *k*, and it is indeed required before *i* and *e*. Note *mercum* and *merkum* in variation for 'marks' (dat. pl.) in the Readings, but invariably *kêtha* 'order'.

As in English, original *k* has in Old Frisian in many instances been palatalized to a sound like [ts] or even the [č] in "church." The resulting sound ultimately came to be written with a number of different combinations of consonant symbols, including *ts*, *sz*, and so on: *tsyurka, szurka, tszurka* 'church'; cf. OS *kirika*.

Though *b* and *d* are unexceptional, *g*, like *k*, may become an affricate, [dz] or [ǰ], usually spelled *ds*, *dz*, and so forth: *lidsja* 'lie'; cf. OS *liggian*.

Before *e* at the beginning of a word, *g* frequently alternates with *j*, indicating a fricative pronunciation [gʲ] in this position: *jelda* or *gelda* 'pay (for)'.

As in other languages, there is variation in Old Frisian between *v* medially and *f* elsewhere:

> *hava* 'possession' with [v]
> *feder* 'father' with [f]

The same variation can be assumed for the letter sequence *th*, although the writing system does not show it:

> *ôther* 'second' with [ð]
> *thiuvethe* 'theft' with [þ]

Similar variation can also be assumed for *s*.

With Old Frisian *h*, things are a bit more complicated. Basically, we can posit a pronunciation as [h] before vowels, but as the [x] of *ach* elsewhere:

> *hi* like English "he"
> *naht* like German *Nacht*

The rest of the consonants are essentially without problems.

Vowels

The vowels of Old Frisian present no problems at all, given the overview in Chapter 2. There are five short vowels, *i*, *e*, *a*, *o*, *u*, and five longs, *î*, *ê*, *â*, *ô*, *û*. Our use of the circumflex to indicate length, while traditional, is not from the manuscripts, which, if they indicate length at all, do so by doubling the vowel or following it with *e*, *i*, or *y*.

In addition to the ten monophthongs, Old Frisian has at least four diphthongs, *ai*, *ia*, *ei*, *iu*, pronounced as their component vowel symbols would suggest.

Phonology

As with Old English, the changes I discuss below are not presented as completely as they might be, especially for the vowels. In some cases the conditions for change are more complex than presented here: there are differences between the Old Frisian dialects, and even in a given dialect a change may have numerous exceptions. The dialects on which I have based the description, and from which I have drawn the reading texts, are those frequently referred to as Old East Frisian (Markey's Classical Old Frisian).

1. Much like Old English, Old Frisian has reversed the change, common to all Germanic languages except Gothic, of *æ̂* to *â*. Except before nasals (see [3] below), this vowel regularly becomes *ê* in Old Frisian:

OF	OHG	
rêda	râtan	'advise'
wêron	wârun	'were'

2. Like Old English, Old Frisian shows a parallel change of short *a* to *e* under most circumstances:

OF	OHG	
gres	gras	'grass'
festa	fastôn	'fast'
feder	fater	'father'

This change does not take place before nasals, and is found only infrequently before *h*, *l*, or *r*: OF *naht* 'night', *all* 'all'.

3. Both older *â* (from *æ̂*) and short *a* go to *ô* and *o*, respectively, before nasals:

OF	OHG	
kômon	quâmun	'came'
lond	land	'land'

4. Old Frisian, too, shows umlaut. Again the word *gold* 'gold' shows the lowering of an original *u* to *o* by *a*-umlaut, but in this case there is no alternating form showing the original *u*. Instead we find the form *gelden* 'golden' from older **guldin*.

As *gelden* shows, the *i*-umlaut of older *u* is *e*; indeed, in Old Frisian the *i*-umlaut of *a* is also *e*. (For reasons I need not go into here, the remaining short back vowel, *o*, could not appear before *i*-umlaut factors.) And in parallel fashion, the umlauts of *û*, *ô*, and *â* are all *ê*:

> *bed* 'bed' from **badi*
> *bikêma* 'complain'; compare OS *kûmian*
> *grêne* 'green' from **grôni*
> *hêra* 'hear' from **hârja*; compare Goth. *hausjan*

Like Old English, Old Frisian has a kind of *u*- or *w*-umlaut, and again as in Old English, its occurrence is restricted. Specifically, *i* can be umlauted to *iu* before a *u* preceded by *g*, or a *w* preceded by *k* or *ng*:

> *niugun* 'nine'; compare OS *nigun*
> *siunga* 'sing'; compare ON *syngva*

5. Like Old English, Old Frisian shows breaking. Thus *i* and *e* become *iu* before *ch(t)* or *h(t)*, and perhaps before the sequence *rk* in 'church':

> *riuht* 'law'; compare OE *reht*
> *tsyurka* 'church'; compare OS *kirika*

6. The reflexes of older *ai* and *au* in Old Frisian are partly like those in Old English, and partly different. While in Old English original *ai* becomes *ā* in all cases, in Old Frisian it becomes *â* sometimes, and *ê* at other times:

> *lâre* 'teaching'; compare OE *lâr*
> *mên* 'false'; compare OE *mân*

Unlike in Old English, in Old Frisian *au* has become *â* under all circumstances: *râd* 'red'; compare OE *rēad*.

7. Like Old Saxon and Old English, Old Frisian shows no sharpening; compare *triûwe* 'true', Goth. *triggws*.

8. The cluster *ngw* has lost its *w* in Old Frisian. Note *siunga* 'to sing' (though the *w* has clearly had an effect before being lost, as described in [4] above).

9. Rhotacism has taken place in Old Frisian, as in all Germanic languages besides Gothic: compare *mârra* 'more', Goth. *maiza*.

10. Consonant gemination has taken place in Old Frisian, as in Old Saxon and Old English. The conditions are no longer clear, since the conditioning *j* has usually dropped out:

> *hille* 'Hell'; compare OS *hellia*
> *ekker* 'acre'; compare Goth. *akrs*

11. Old Frisian shows the initial consonant sequence *fl-*, rather than *þl-* as in Gothic: *flia* 'flee', Goth. *þliuhan*.

12. Old Frisian, like Old Saxon and Old English, shows loss of a nasal before *f*, *þ*, and *s*:

OF	Goth.	
fîf	fimf	'five'
ûs	unsis	'us'
kûth	kunþs	'known'

13. Like Old Norse, Old Frisian shows loss of final *n* in all endings. All the infinitives in the Readings attest to this.

14. Like the West Saxon dialect of Old English, Old Frisian shows

assibilation, whereby *k* becomes [ts] and *g* becomes [dz] under certain circumstances. Specifically, *k* becomes [ts] initially before *i* and *e*, and medially before *i* and *j*:

OF	OS	
tsyurka	kirika	'church'
bretze	bruki	'break'

The development of *g* is a bit more complex, as indeed it is in Old English. For again, it was only after a nasal or when doubled that Old Frisian *g* represented a stop, at least originally. And only this "hard" *g* became an affricate [dz] when before *i* or *j*: *lidsja* 'lie'; compare OS *liggian*.

15. Like Old English, Old Frisian frequently shows metathesis of the sequence C*r*V to CV*r*: *berna* 'burn'; compare OS *brennian*.

Nouns and Pronouns

1. Like Old Saxon and Old English, Old Frisian shows no ending for the nominative singular of masculine *a*-stem nouns, nor for the nominative singular of masculine strong adjectives:

OF	Goth.	
wei	wigs	'way'
gôd	gôþs	'good'

2. The nominative plural ending of the masculine *a*-stem nouns is variable in Old Frisian. In the older eastern texts we find a rather consistent *-ar* or *-er*, sometimes alternating with *-a*.

sîthar 'colleagues'   dega 'days'

In the younger, western dialects we find no *-ar* or *-er*, but *-a* and *-an* or *-en*.

3. Possibly because of the texts in which it is transmitted, Old Frisian shows no dual pronouns, though modern North Frisian dialects have them.

4. As in Old English, in Old Frisian we find third person personal pronouns beginning with *h*- throughout:

OF	Goth.	
hi	is	'he'
him	imma	'him' (dat. sg.)
hiu	si	'she'

hire   izôs   'her' (gen. sg.)
hit   ita   'it'

5. Old Frisian does not distinguish the dative and accusative cases in the first and second person singular personal pronouns:

	OF	Goth.	
Acc.	mi	mik	'me'
Dat.	mi	mis	'me'
Acc.	thi	þuk	'thee'
Dat.	thi	þus	'thee'

6. Old Frisian has no reflexive pronoun, but does show *sîn* as a possessive form for the masculine and neuter singular: *alle sîne sîthar* 'all his colleagues'.

7. Like all the Germanic languages except Gothic, Old Frisian shows an intensified demonstrative pronoun:

OF masc. nom. sg. *thi* and *this* opposite Goth. *sa*
           dat. pl. *tham* and *thissem* opposite Goth. *þaim*

Verbs

1. Old Frisian does not show a reduplicating class of verbs. Instead we find either a new vowel alternation, or reassignment to the weak class:

OF	Goth.	
halda–hîld	haldan–haihald	'hold–held'
lêta–lêtte	lêtan–lailôt	'let–let'

2. The class of *-na* verbs is absent in Old Frisian.

3. The ending of the second person singular preterite indicative in Old Frisian is *-st*, differentiating Old Frisian from all the other older West Germanic languages, which have endings in *-i* (on the significance of this difference, see the last section of this chapter): *cômest* '(you) came'; compare OHG *kâmi*.

4. Old Frisian shows neither a morphological passive nor a mediopassive, and must make do with periphrastic constructions.

5. The third person singular present indicative of the verb 'be' is almost exclusively *is* in Old Frisian, without a *-t*.

6. Like Old Saxon and Old English, Old Frisian shows the same verb ending in all persons of the plural. Thus *folgjath* 'we, you, they follow'.

7. Old Frisian shows both long and short forms of the verbs 'go' and 'stand', though the long forms predominate. Thus *gân* and *gunga*, *stân* and *stonda*.

8. Also as in Old Saxon and Old English, Old Frisian has a gerund derived from the infinitive, although the gerund has frequently taken on the form of the present participle.

On Being a Younger Older Language

Each of these chapters on individual Germanic languages has listed a number of linguistic criteria, both phonological and grammatical, characteristic of each language. At most points, some comparison has been made among the various languages, with an eye to determining their interrelationships more closely in Chapter 10.

What has not been discussed in these comparisons is the difference in age between the languages being compared. Yet it is certainly not clear that one can directly compare a fourth-century Gothic form with a thirteenth-century Frisian form, and ascribe the differences entirely to their membership in different subfamilies of Germanic. What would a thirteenth-century Gothic form have looked like, or a fourth-century Frisian one?

All the languages I am considering in this book, except for Gothic—the oldest of them all, not counting a few runic inscriptions—contain the word "old" in their names. For many of those languages, their "old" forms contrast terminologically with their "middle" and "new" or "modern" forms. Yet the temporal implication of this parallel terminology for the different languages is quite misleading. Old English, for example, is documented already in the late seventh and early eighth centuries, but Old Frisian only begins to be documented half a millennium later, at a time when English is already in its "middle" period. Old High German, Old Saxon, Old Low Franconian, and Old Norse fall between these extremes, with Old High German being attested not much later than Old English and the bulk of texts in Old Norse preceding those in Old Frisian by a scant century.

When comparing these languages, then, we must take the time of attestation into account. For any given feature that appears to differentiate a significantly younger language from an older one, we should ask whether the presence of that feature is truly evidence of an early language differentiation, or only a later development explainable on other grounds.

Similarly, features that appear to *link* a significantly younger language with an older one should not automatically be accepted as proof of early close relationship.

Three common types of changes may obscure older connections between languages. All three are well documented in Old Frisian, and indeed can be found in some of the linguistic characteristics given in the last section.

In the section on nouns and pronouns, I noted that the nominative plural ending of masculine *a*-stem nouns is quite consistently *-ar* or *-er* in the older, eastern texts of Old Frisian. This is actually rather remarkable. In many other respects Old Frisian resembles Old English and Old Saxon, but this type of plural is otherwise found only in Old Norse; Old English and Old Saxon show *-as* and *-os* respectively. Does this mean that Old Frisian has some ancient connection with Old Norse not shared by Old English and Old Saxon?

Probably not. In the first place, by the time Old Frisian was being written down, the *-os* plural of Old Saxon was also no longer visible; it had generally been replaced before the middle period (apparently analogically) by *-a* or *-e*. Many scholars assume a similar development in Frisian, at a time well before the stage we know as Old Frisian; thus *-as* was present at an earlier period in that language as well.

As a result of the replacement of *-as* by *-a*, Old Frisian would have shown no distinction, in these nouns, between the nominative and accusative plural on the one hand, and the genitive plural on the other. In this theory, the *-ar* and *-er* nominative and accusative plural endings of documented Old Frisian were introduced at a relatively late period to restore the lost case distinction. And a likely source for the new suffixes is not difficult to find. Given the rather close interaction between the Frisians and the Scandinavian peoples during the viking period, the new suffix is explained as a borrowing from North Germanic.

To reiterate, then: originally the ancestor to the language we know as Old Frisian showed the same plural suffix as that found in Old Saxon and Old English. The *-ar* and *-er* actually found in the older texts of Old Frisian, which appear to point to a close genetic relationship between Old Norse and that language, are merely the result of a relatively late borrowing.

Another feature that distinguishes Old Frisian from Old English and Old Saxon, and indeed from all the other old Germanic languages, is the ending *-st* of the second person singular preterite indicative of strong verbs. Is this significant?

Again, not really. The ending *-st* is identical to the ending of the second person singular *present* indicative, and has clearly been analogically based on it. Again we must assume that pre–Old Frisian looked more like Old English and Old Saxon, with their second person singular preterite indicative ending -*i*, but that this ancient connection has been obscured by an analogy of an extremely common type. Indeed, both English and German carried out the same analogy, but not in the period we label "old."

There is another characteristic of Old Frisian treated in the last section that is reminiscent of Old Norse, namely the loss of final -*n* in endings, such as that of the infinitive. No other Germanic language shows such a change in its oldest period. Is this, then, evidence for an early close relationship between Old Norse and Frisian?

In this case, it's a little hard to tell. We have no way of dating the loss of final -*n* in Frisian, since the earliest texts (which, it must be remembered, are late) show consistent application of the change. But the change itself is of a type frequently found, at various stages, in most Germanic languages. For one characteristic of all the Germanic languages is a consistent strong accent on the root syllables of words, and a correspondingly weak one on ending syllables. With the passage of time, this results in a sloughing-off of vowels and consonants in those endings. Modern English shows a particularly advanced stage of the process (note that Modern English has *no* infinitive ending). In Modern Dutch as spoken in the Netherlands, final -*n* in unaccented syllables is virtually never pronounced, and the same is true of many German dialects (though not in the pronounced standard language).

These observations should make us wary of postulating any particularly close connection between Old Frisian and Old Norse on the basis of this one phenomenon. Instead, most scholars would probably be inclined to see the loss of final -*n* as a "drift" phenomenon—that is, the reflection of a general tendency in the Germanic language family, which operates independently of any genetic closeness or linguistic contact.

The above is not meant to imply that drift is unimportant as a sign of genetic relatedness, since such drift is presumably based upon some common (and in this case obviously inherited) linguistic predisposition. The point is, rather, that *all* the Germanic languages inherited this predisposition: if Gothic were spoken today, it would probably show tendencies in the same direction.

In the section on consonants, I noted that Old Frisian, like the West Saxon dialect of Old English, characteristically assibilates *k* and *g* to [ts] and [dz] respectively before *i* and *j*. While a few scholars believe that this common assibilation must have been carried out before the Anglo-Saxons

left the Continent (and thus when they were still in direct contact with
the Frisians), most believe that this distinctive sound change took place
many centuries later in both Old English and Old Frisian. If so, then this
change may well be another instance of drift based on a common predisposition, perhaps an inherited tendency to give *k* and *g* extremely pal-
atal pronunciations, [kʲ] and [gʲ], before *i* and *j*. In this case, however, the
predisposition is clearly *not* shared by all the Germanic languages, and
may still be seen as support for an ancient connection between English
and Frisian.

In this section I have touched on types of change that may obscure
earlier connections between languages or dialects by making them appear
either more distinct or more similar than they originally were. I have used
Old Frisian as an example principally because it is the youngest of the
older Germanic languages, and the recentness of the changes in question
makes them more visible to the scholar. There is no question, however,
that the processes of borrowing, analogy, and parallel phonetic drift are
active at all historical periods, and thus must be assumed for the periods
preceding the earliest documentation of the Germanic languages. Many
of the characteristics that scholars cite as proof for early connection or
divergence between the Germanic languages must thus be taken with a
grain of salt, or in some cases a whole shaker. Indeed, as the discussion in
Chapter 10 should show, at this late date it is virtually impossible to explain in a completely satisfactory way all the overlapping similarities and
differences between the various older Germanic languages.

FURTHER READING

Alberts, W. Jappe. "Friesland und die Friesen im ersten Jahrtausend." In V. H.
    Elbern, ed., *Das erste Jahrtausend: Kultur und Kunst im werdenden Abend-
    land an Rhein und Ruhr*, Textband 2, pp. 634–52. Düsseldorf: Schwann,
    1964.
Buma, W. J. *Die Brokmer Rechtshandschriften*. The Hague: Nijhoff, 1949.
Cummins, Adley H. *A Grammar of the Old Friesic Language*. London: Trüb-
    ner, 1887.
van Helten, W. L. *Altostfriesische Grammatik*. Leeuwarden: Meijer, 1890.
Hutterer, Claus Jürgen. *Die germanischen Sprachen: Ihre Geschichte in Grund-
    zügen*. Budapest: Akadémiai Kiadó, 1975.
Markey, T. L. *Frisian*. The Hague: Mouton, 1981.
Ramat, Paolo. *Das Friesische*. Innsbrucker Beiträge zur Sprachwissenschaft, 14.
    Innsbruck: Institut für Sprachwissenschaft der Universität, 1976.
Sjölin, B. *Einführung in das Friesische*. Stuttgart: Metzler, 1969.

8

OLD LOW FRANCONIAN

A Brief History of the Franks

At the beginning of the Christian era, it seemed as if the Romans were poised to take over the heartland of the continental Germanic tribes and make it simply another part of their empire. The Romans had Gaul pacified, and had reached the Danube in the south and the Rhine in the west. Under Drusus (d. 9 B.C.) they had won significant victories against Germanic tribes across the Rhine, and indeed had established, at least nominally, a Roman province of Germania, which reached all the way to the Elbe.

In the northwest, the Romans were firmly allied with a number of Germanic tribes: the Batavians, who lived on the islands formed by the Lek and Waal rivers in the Rhine delta, the Caninefates to their north (Kennemerland in present-day North Holland bears their name), and the Frisians. To the east of the Batavians, however, and all along the right bank of the Rhine, were Germanic tribes whose relations with the Romans were far less friendly, and whose desire for land focused their attention quite regularly on the territories to the west.

In A.D. 9, Roman dreams of a German province east of the Rhine were permanently dashed when the Roman general Varus, at the head of three legions, was bloodily defeated in the Teutoburg forest by an alliance of several Germanic tribes under the leadership of Arminius, a chief of the Cherusci. The Frisians and the Batavians were not in this alliance, however, and territories to the west of the Rhine and in the Rhine delta remained secure.

For the next two centuries, the Rhine border was an effective though porous one—porous, because it was not uncommon for the Romans to allow small or even large groups of barbarians to settle in Roman territory in return for their defense of the borders against other barbarians.

With the decay of Roman power in the third and fourth centuries, the pressure against the Rhine increased, led by the newly formed Frankish federation, an initially rather loose alliance of a large number of tribes between the Rhine and the Weser. We can distinguish three major subdivisions of this confederation: the Salians, to the east of where the IJssel river flowed into what was to become the Zuider Zee; the Ripuarians, along the middle Rhine; and the Hessians to their south, on the Main. Until the end of the reign of Constantine I (d. 337), these attempts on northern Gaul were repulsed, though a good number of Franks were resettled in Gaul by the Romans themselves.

In the mid-fourth century, however, the Frankish advance became a great deal more systematic. Cologne fell to the Ripuarians in 355, and the Salians succeeded in taking the Batavian islands and most of present-day North Brabant in 358. Although Cologne was retaken by the Romans, the Salians were allowed to remain on the lands they had taken, now as federates of Rome. Though technically a part of the Roman Empire, they were allowed to govern themselves, their major obligation to the empire being to defend their new territory against other Germanic groups. This legal sleight-of-hand worked for a while, but the Salians were better aggressors than they were defenders. In 428, under their leader Clodion, they broke across the Scheldt River into modern Brabant and even farther south. The Romans succeeded in stopping them, but did not push them back, and the "federates" wound up with even more territory to "protect."

In the course of the fifth century, the advance of the Franks was steady. In addition to the Salian move southward, we can discern a southwestward push on the part of the other Franks. Cologne fell permanently into the hands of the advancing hordes, as did Trier and the Moselle valley.

In some ways, the Salian Franks especially represented some kind of order in a situation that approached total chaos. Gaul was the object of many invasions (Burgundian, Alamannic, Visigothic, Hunnish), and the Salians' status as federates of Rome frequently put them on the side of the defenders. Franks (perhaps under Merovech; see below) stood with the Romans against the Huns in the famous battle of the Catalaunian plains in 451, which finally broke the back of the Hunnish invasion of Europe.

Of Merovech we know little, though he was a figure of legend to the Merovingian kings, whose dynasty bears his name. His son, Childeric (d. 482), is better known, and his grave, discovered in 1653, is an impor-

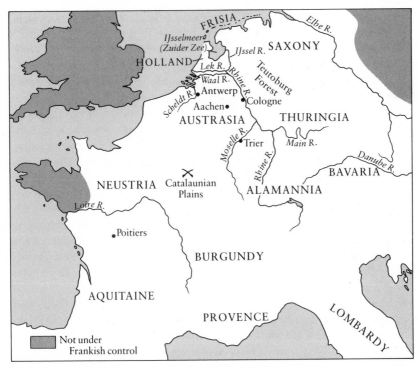

Map 7.   Western Europe under the Franks around A.D. 800.

tant resource for archeologists and historians. But it is Childeric's son
Clovis (Chlodwig) who is universally recognized as the greatest of the
Merovingians. By dint of treachery and assassination, he eliminated the
leaders of all the subtribes of the Salians and Ripuarians and made himself undisputed king of all the Franks. He eliminated the last vestiges of
Roman rule in Gaul, and under him the Franks controlled present-day
France down to the Loire. Other Germanic groups such as the Goths, the
Alamanni, and the Thuringians were taught to respect his power, the Alamanni in particular suffering a crushing defeat at his hands in 496. Clovis
also made the wise strategic move of converting to the Catholic faith of
his Burgundian wife, which made it easier for his Gallo-Roman subjects
to see him as the champion of Christianity against the heretical Arian
faith of most Goths and Burgundians.

Thus when he died in 511, Clovis left behind a strongly unified and
rather large kingdom. By ancient Frankish custom, however, this patri-

mony had to be divided equally among his four sons, a device not calcu-
lated to promote unity and stability. A great deal of skulduggery went
on before the death of Childebert in 558 enabled the last of the four,
Chlotar I, to rule again as undisputed king. Nonetheless, in the meantime
the Franks had extended their rule as far south as the Garonne and conquered the Burgundians, Thuringians, and Bavarians.

This, as it turned out, was the high point of the Merovingian dynasty. Upon Chlotar's death in 561, his four sons again split the kingdom.
This time the family feud *cum* civil war was extremely fierce and protracted, so protracted that there existed no single king of all the Franks
again until the accession of Chlotar II in 613. The intrigues, betrayals,
and disasters of the intervening period make extremely fascinating reading, but would be out of place in an overview like this.

By the time of Chlotar II, the Frankish nobility had already become
quite disenchanted with the Merovingians, and had taken many of the
trappings of power upon themselves. Increasingly important were the so-
called "Mayors of the Palace," the noble administrators of the three relatively autonomous districts of Austrasia in the northeast (including the
original Germanic homeland of the Franks), Neustria in the west, and
Burgundy in the southeast. Although initially these positions were held
by nobles of different families, one line, that founded by Pippin I, mayor
of Austrasia (d. 639), came to preeminence. Indeed, in the latter part of
the seventh century his grandson Pippin II of Heristal assumed control
over the entire kingdom, still nominally under the Merovingian kings. By
this time the latter were nothing but figureheads, living on country estates
and totally removed from any real power.

Pippin was succeeded by his illegitimate son Charles Martel, perhaps the greatest of the mayors. Besides strengthening the internal bonds
of the kingdom, he was largely responsible for putting a decisive end to
the Muslim expansion northward into Europe at the battle of Poitiers in
732. He also expanded the Frankish sphere into Frisia, and exacted tribute from the powerful Saxons.

It was Charles's son Pippin the Short who finally put an end to the
sham that the Merovingians had become. With support from the pope, he
deposed the last of their line, Childeric III, and had himself anointed the
king of the Franks.

This Carolingian dynasty of course reached its apogee in Pippin's
son, Charlemagne, crowned Holy Roman Emperor on Christmas Day,
800, after many years of conquest and consolidation. Any account of
Charlemagne's deeds here, determining as they did not just the future of
the Franks, but of all Europe, would be impossible in a discussion of this

scope. I should just note that Charlemagne, like Alfred in England, was interested not only in conquest, but also in culture, and it is ultimately to him that we owe the atmosphere that permitted, even required, the writing down of many of the texts discussed in this book.

Before I discuss the texts found in Old Low Franconian, I should make it clear that this language is not the only one connected with the Franks. Beyond the perhaps obvious fact that Old French, too, was a language spoken by Franks and influenced by their original Germanic idiom, there are also a number of dialects in Old High German that bear the name "Franconian." Thus we have the odd situation that even from the earliest surviving documents, one might be led to think of the Franks as speaking two different Germanic languages. This of course is not the case. The different dialects spoken by the Franks during this period surely showed no more differentiation than, say, the Old English or the Old High German dialects did, and perhaps less. It simply happens that one of the factors distinguishing Franconian dialects from one another, namely the presence or absence of the sound change known as the *High German Consonant Shift* (see Chapter 9), is considered by scholars to be the single most important test of whether a dialect should be called Old High German or not. Thus ultimately the problem is a terminological or classificatory one, not one of fact. This confusion is only deepened by the tendency to project backwards in time the more or less politically determined state of affairs we find in the modern era. Thus since Old Low Franconian has developed into a dialect of Dutch, while Old Central Franconian has developed into a dialect of German, and those are certainly separate languages, it seems to follow that the older dialects also represented separate languages. This is faulty reasoning.

Old Low Franconian Texts

There are four sources for our knowledge of Old Low Franconian, all going back to a single text, the now-lost Wachtendonck Codex. Apparently that original text was a Latin psalter containing, in addition to the Book of Psalms, several hymns and creeds. Written between the Latin lines was a word-for-word translation into a Germanic dialect (an "interlinear" translation).

We know all this because of a letter written by the famous Flemish scholar Justus Lipsius to his friend Henricus Schottius of Antwerp on December 19, 1598. In this letter he informed Schottius that he had obtained such a psalter from Arnoldus Wachtendonck, a minor church official of Liège, and that he had compiled from it a list of words that appeared to him to deviate most from the Netherlandic of his day. He furthermore appended an alphabetical list of 670 of these words, with Latin translations.

Unfortunately, the original letter has not survived either. It was, however, printed in a collection in 1602. There are undoubtedly a great number of errors in this printing, probably mostly due to misinterpretation of Lipsius's exceptionally bad handwriting.

In 1870 a librarian at the University of Leiden discovered among Lipsius's papers a manuscript that contained a longer list of 822 words, including all but two of those found on the shorter list, and generally exhibiting fewer errors. The list is not in Lipsius's handwriting, but was clearly compiled under his direction, since it contains marginal notes written by him. Interesting about this list is that it gives references to the psalm, hymn, or creed from which each word was taken.

In 1612, Abraham van der Myle published a version of Psalm 18 based on a copy made by Lipsius from the same psalter. It is exceptionally unfortunate, given the subsequent loss of that manuscript, that van der Myle saw fit to alter the psalm in the direction of the Netherlandic spelling of his day, apparently to minimize its strangeness.

Finally, we have a manuscript in two different hands (possibly writing at different times), containing Psalms 53.7–73.9. The first copyist was not Lipsius, but undoubtedly a contemporary, perhaps a colleague of his. Comparison of this manuscript (known as the Diez Manuscript) with the glosses leaves no doubt that they derive from the same text.

A fifth manuscript that clearly goes back to the Wachtendonck Codex contains a copy of Psalms 1.1–3.5. But while it represents part of that codex, it is not part of the corpus of Old Low Franconian, the dialect of these psalms being a Central Franconian (thus Old High German) one. Consultation of the glosses makes it clear, in fact, that all of Psalms 1–9 was originally translated into this Central Franconian dialect, while Psalms 10–60, the hymns, and the creeds were all written in Low Franconian.

In addition to this curious circumstance, there are also many words in the Low Franconian parts of the text that betray a Central Franconian origin. As I show in the last section of this chapter, scholars have wrestled with these facts for a long time, seeking clues to the provenience of the original translator of the psalms, and the conditions of the translation.

I also deal below with the question of the precise localization of the psalm translations, and the criteria for this localization. Almost all the scholars studying this language agree at least that the translations repre-

sent an eastern dialect of Low Franconian, spoken near the boundary between present-day Germany and the southern part of the Netherlands.
Most would place it in the southern part of Dutch Limburg or the vicinity
(including, for example, the German city of Aachen, Charlemagne's capi-
tal). The most reasonable dating seems to be at the beginning of the tenth
century.

While I agree with scholars who claim that this language can be
called "Old Dutch," much as, say, Old Alamannic and Old East Franconian (and of course Old Central Franconian) are lumped together in Old
High German, it should be remembered that this is basically the oldest
stage of the Limburgic dialect of Dutch, which differs substantially from
the standard language. The standard language has its roots more to the
west in Flanders and Brabant, and to the north in Holland, than in Limburg. Unfortunately, all that survives from the earliest period of Old West
Low Franconian, beyond a great deal of onomastic material in Latin
texts, is the following remarkable West Flemish sentence of the eleventh
century, found in England in the binding of a Latin manuscript:

hebban olla vogala nestas hagunnan hinase hi(c) (e)nda thu w(at) (u)nbidan
(w)e nu
'all the birds have begun nests except for you and me—what are we
waiting for?'

Readings

The numeration of the psalms, and of the verses in one of them, differs from that
found in most modern translations of the Book of Psalms: Psalm 60 below corresponds to King James 61, and 65 to King James 66.

Psalm 60

2. Gehôri, got, gebet mîn, thenke te
gebede mînin.

hear, God, Gebet, mine, think, to

3. Fan einde erthen te thi riep, so sorgoda herte mîn. An stêine irhôdus-tu mi;

von, end, earth, thee, rief, so, sorgen
heart, on, stone, erhöhen, thou, me

4. Thû lêidos mi, uuanda gedân bist tohopa mîn, turn sterke fan antscêine fiundis.

led, done, bist
hope, Turm, stark, Anschein, fiend

5. UUonon sal ic an selethon thînro an
uueroldi, bescirmot an getheke fetharaco
thînro.

wohnen, shall, ich, thine
world, beschirmt, Decke, feather

6. UUanda thu, got mîn, gehôrdos gebet
mîn, gâui thu erui forhtindon namo thînin.

gave, Erbe, fürchten, name

7. Dag ouir dag cuningis saltu gefuo-   day, over, king, *fügen*
gan, jâr sîna untes an dag cunnis in cunnis.   year, kin

8. Foluuonot an êuuon an geginuuirdi   *ew(ig)*, *Gegenwart*
godis; ginâthi in uuârhêide sîna uue sal thia   *Gnade, Wahrheit, sein*
suocan?   seek

9. Sô sal ic lof quethan namin thînin an   *Lob*, quoth
uuerolt uueroldis, that ik geue gehêita mîna
fan dage an dag.

Psalm 65

2. Singit gode, al ertha, lof quethet na-   sing
mon sînin; geuet guolikhêide loui sînin.   good, -ly, -hood

3. Quethit gode: so eiselika thing sint   thing, *sind*
uuerk thîna, hêrro! An menigi crefti thînro   work, *Herr*, many, *Kraft*
liegon sulun thi fiunda thîna.   lie

4. Al ertha bede thi in singe thi, lof que-   *beten*
the namin thînin.

5. Cumit in gesiet uuerk godis, egislikis   come, see
an râdon ouir kint manno,   *Rat*, over, *Kind*, man

6. Thie kierit sêo an thurrithon; an   *kehren*, sea, *dürr*
fluode ouirlîthon solun mit fuoti. Thâ sulun   flood, *leiden*, foot
uuir blîthan an imo,   *wir*, blithe, *ihm*

7. Thie uualdonde ist an crefte sînro te   wield, is
êuuon. Ôugun sîna ouir thiadi scauuont: eye(s), *schauen*
thia uuitherstrîdunt, ne uuerthint irhauan an   *wider, streiten, werden, heben*
sig seluan.   *sich*, self

8. Geuuîet, thiadi, got unsan, inde ge-   *weihen, uns(er)en*
hôrda duot stemma louis sînis,   heard, do, *Stimme*

9. Thie satta sêla mîna te lîue, in ne gaf   set, soul, life, gave
an giruornussi fuoti mîne.   *rühr(en)*

10. UUanda becorodos uns, got, mit   *uns*
fûire uns irsuohtos, also man irsuokit siluer.   fire, silver

11. Thu lêidos unsig an strike, sattos   *Strick*
aruit an ruggi unsin, gesattos man ouir hôuit   *Arbeit, Rücken*, head
unsa;

12. UUi lithon thuro fûir in thuro uua-   *litten*, water
tir, in brâhtos unsig an cuolithon.   brought, coolth

13. Gân sal ic an hûse thînin an off-   go, house, offering
ringon,

14. Geuan sal ik thi gehêita mîna, thia

undirsciethon lepora mîna, in sprac munt   *unterschieden*, lip(s), *sprach*, mouth
mîn an aruithi mîna.

15. Offringa luttira offran sal ic thi mit   offer
brunni uuithero, offran sal ic thi ohsson mit   burn, *Widder*, ox
buckin.   *Bock*

16. Cumit, gehôrit, in tellon sal ic, alla   tell, all
thia forhtit gode, huo deda sêla mîna.   how, did

17. Te imo mundi mînin riep, in men-
dida undir tungon mînro.   under, tongue

18. Unreht of gisag an hertin mînin,   un-, right, if, saw
ne sal gehôran hêrro. Bethiu gehôrda got in
thâhta stemmon bedon mînro.   thought

19. Geuuîgit got, thie ne faruuarp ge-   *verwarf*
bet mîn in ginâtha sîna fan mi.   *Gnade*

GLOSSARY

In alphabetizing Old Low Franconian, *c* is treated as *k*; *uu* is listed separately
after *u*. Unless specified otherwise, nouns and pronouns are nominative singular,
adjectives are masculine nominative singular, and verbs are infinitives. The parenthetical identification of any form has reference only to the Readings, and is
not necessarily an exhaustive list of all possible identifications of that form in the
language.

al 'all', *al* (fem. nom. sg.), *alla* (masc.
    nom. pl.)
also 'just as'
an 'on, in, to, into, for'
antscêine 'face', *antscêine* (dat. sg.)
aruit 'tribulation', *aruithi* (dat. sg.),
    aruit (acc. pl.)

beda 'prayer', *bedon* (gen. sg.); see
    also *bedon*
bedon 'worship, pray', *bede* (3 sg.
    pres. subj.); see also *beda*
becoron 'prove, test', *becorodos* (2 sg.
    pret. ind.)
bescirman 'protect', *bescirmot* (pret.
    part.)
bethiu 'for that reason, thus'
bist see *uuesan*
blîthan 'rejoice'
bock 'goat', *buckin* (dat. pl.)

brengan 'bring', *brâhtos* (2 sg. pret.
    ind.)
brunni 'incense', *brunni* (dat. sg.)
buckin see *bock*

dag 'day', *dag* (acc. sg.), *dage*
    (dat. sg.)
duon 'do, make', *duot* (2 pl. pres.
    imp.), *deda* (3 sg. pret. ind.), *gedân*
    (pret. part.)

egislik 'terrible (one)', *egislikis* (masc.
    gen. sg.)
einde 'end', *einde* (dat. sg.)
eiselik 'terrible', *eiselika* (neut.
    nom. pl.)
ertha 'earth', *erthen* (gen. sg.)
erui 'inheritance', *erui* (acc. sg.)
êuua 'eternity', *êuuon* (dat. sg.)

fan 'from'
faruuerpen 'turn away, spurn',
   faruuarp (3 sg. pret. ind.)
fetheraco 'of wings' (gen. pl.)
fiunt 'enemy', *fiundis* (gen. sg.),
   fiunda (nom. pl.)
fluot 'flood', *fluode* (dat. sg.)
foluuonon 'abide', *foluuonot* (3 sg.
   pres. ind.)
forhton 'fear', *forhtit* (2 pl. pres.
   ind.), *forhtindon* (pres. part., masc.
   dat. pl.)
fûir 'fire', *fûir* (acc. sg.), *fûire*
   (dat. sg.)
fuot 'foot', *fuoti* (dat. sg. and acc. pl.)

gaf see *geuan*
gân 'go'
gâui see *geuan*
gebet 'prayer', *gebet* (acc. sg.), *gebede*
   (dat. sg.)
gedân see *duon*
gefuogan 'add'
geginuuirdi 'presence', *geginuuirdi*
   (dat. sg.)
gehêita 'vow', *gehêita* (acc. pl.)
gehôran 'hear', *gehôri* (2 sg. pres.
   imp.), *gehôrit* (2 pl. pres. imp.),
   gehôrdos (2 sg. pret. ind.), *gehôrda*
   (3 sg. pret. ind. and pret. part., fem.
   acc. sg.)
gesettan 'impose, set', *gesattos* (2 sg.
   pret. ind.)
gesian 'see', *gesiet* (2 pl. pres. imp.),
   gisag (3 sg. pret. ind.)
getheke 'covering', *getheke* (dat. sg.)
geuan 'give', *geuet* (2 pl. pres. imp.),
   geue (1 sg. pres. subj.), *gâui* (2 sg.
   pret. ind.), *gaf* (3 sg. pret. ind.)
geuuîgen 'bless', *geuuîet* (2 pl. pres.
   imp.), *geuuîgit* (pret. part.)
ginâtha 'mercy, grace', *ginâtha*
   (acc. sg.)

ginâthi 'mercy, grace', *ginâthi*
   (acc. sg.)
giruornussi 'movement', *giruornussi*
   (acc. or dat. sg.)
gisag see *gesian*
got 'God', *got*, *gode* (acc. sg.), *godis*
   (gen. sg.), *gode* (dat. sg.)
guolikhêide 'glory', *guolikhêide*
   (acc. sg.)

he, *hie* 'he', *imo* (dat. sg.)
hêrro 'Lord'
herte 'heart', *hertin* (dat. sg.)
hie see *he*
hôuit 'head', *hôuit* (acc. pl.)
huo 'how, what'
hûs 'house', *hûse* (dat. sg.)

ic, *ik* 'I', *mi* (acc. and dat. sg.), *uui*,
   uuir (nom. pl.), *uns*, *unsig* (acc. pl.)
imo see *he*, *hie*
in, *inde* 'and'
irheuon 'exalt', *irhauan* (pret. part.)
irhôian 'raise, exalt', *irhôdus* (2 sg.
   pret. ind.); *irhôdus-tu* = *irhôdus* +
   -tu (see *thû*)
irsuokan 'test', *irsuokit* (3 sg. pres.
   ind.), *irsuohtos* (2 sg. pret. ind.)
ist see *uuesan*

jâr 'year', *jâr* (acc. pl.)

kêron 'change', *kierit* (3 sg. pres. ind.)
kint 'child', *kint* (acc. pl.)
craft 'power', *crefti* (gen. sg.), *crefte*
   (dat. sg.)
cuman 'come', *cumit* (2 pl. pres. imp.)
cuning 'king', *cuningis* (gen. sg.)
cunni 'generation', *cunnis* (gen. sg.)
cuolitha 'coolness', *cuolithon* (acc. or
   dat. sg.)

lêidon 'lead', *lêidos* (2 sg. pret. ind.)
lepora 'lips' (nom. pl.)
liegon 'lie, dissemble'

lîf 'life', *lîue* (dat. sg.)
lîthon 'go', *lithon* (1 pl. pret. ind.)
lof 'praise', *lof* (acc. sg.), *louis* (gen. sg.), *loui* (dat. sg.)
luttir 'proper' (?: Lat. *medullata* 'filled with marrow'), *luttira* (fem. acc. pl.)

man 'man', *man* (acc. pl.), *manno* (gen. pl.)
man 'one'
manno see *man* 'man'
menden 'praise', *mendida* (1 sg. pret. ind.)
menigi 'multitude, fullness', *menigi* (dat. sg.)
mi see *ic*, *ik*
mîn 'my', *mîna* (fem. nom. and acc. sg.; neut. dat. sg.; masc. nom. pl.; fem. acc. pl.), *mîn* (neut. nom. and acc. sg.), *mînro* (fem. gen. and dat. sg.), *mînin* (masc. and neut. dat. sg.), *mîne* (masc. acc. pl.)
mit 'with, by'
munt 'mouth', *mundi* (dat. sg.)

namo 'name', *namo* (acc. sg.), *namin*, *namon* (dat. sg.)
ne 'not'

of 'if'
offran 'offer'
offringa 'burnt offering', *offringa* (acc. pl.), *offringon* (dat. pl.)
ohsso 'bull', *ohsson* (acc. pl.)
ôuga 'eye', *ôugun* (nom. pl.)
ouir 'over, above, to, upon'
ouirlîthon 'cross over'

quethan 'speak', *quethe* (3 sg. pres. subj.), *quethet*, *quethit* (2 pl. pres. imp.)

rât 'design, plan', *râdon* (dat. pl.)
riep see *ruopen*

ruggi 'back', *ruggi* (dat. sg.)
ruopen 'call out,' *riep* (1 sg. pret. ind.)

sal, *salt*, see *sulun*; *saltu* = *salt* + *-tu*; see *thû*
satta, *sattos*, see *settan*
sêla 'soul', *sêla* (acc. sg.)
selitha 'house', *selethon* (dat. sg.)
selua 'self', *seluan* (dat. pl.)
sêo 'sea', *sêo* (acc. sg.)
settan 'place, set', *sattos* (2 sg. pret. ind.), *satta* (3 sg. pret. ind.)
sig (refl. pro., dat. pl.)
siluer 'silver', *siluer* (acc. sg.)
sîn 'his', *sîna* (fem. acc. sg.), *sînis* (neut. gen. sg.), *sînin* (masc. and neut. dat. sg.), *sînro* (fem. dat. sg.), *sîna* (neut. acc. pl.)
singen 'sing', *singe* (3 sg. pres. subj.), *singit* (2 pl. pres. imp.)
sint see *uuesan*
scauuon 'look upon, gaze', *scauuont* (3 pl. pres. ind.)
so, *sô* 'so, thus, so much, such'
solun see *sulun*
sorgon 'worry, be disturbed', *sorgoda* (3 sg. pret. ind.)
sprecan 'speak', *sprac* (3 sg. pret. ind.)
stêin 'stone', *stêine* (dat. sg.)
stemma 'voice', *stemma* (acc. sg.), *stemmon* (gen. sg.)
sterke 'strength', *sterke* (gen. sg.)
strik 'net', *strike* (dat. sg.)
sulun 'shall', *sal* (1 and 3 sg. pres. ind.), *salt* (2 sg. pres. ind.), *sulun* (1 pl. pres. ind.), *sulun*, *solun* (3 pl. pres. ind.)
suocan 'question'

te 'to, about'
tellon 'tell, relate'
thâ 'then'
thâhta see *thencon*
that 'so that, that'
thencon 'pay attention (to)', *thenke*

(2 sg. pres. imp.), *thâhta* (3 sg. pret. ind.)

thi see *thû, thu, -tu*

thia see *thie*

thiat 'people', *thiadi* (nom. and acc. pl.)

thie 'that one, who, which', *thia* (masc. nom. pl. and fem. acc. pl.)

thîn, thîna 'your, thy', *thînin* (masc. acc. and dat. sg.), *thînro* (fem. gen. and dat. sg. and gen. pl.), *thîna* (neut. nom. pl.)

thing 'thing', *thing* (nom. pl.)

thû, thu, -tu 'you', *thi* (acc. and dat. sg.)

thuro 'through'

thurritha 'dry land', *thurrithon* (acc. sg.)

tohopa 'refuge, hope'

tunga 'tongue', *tungon* (dat. sg.)

turn 'tower'

undir 'under'

undirscêithan 'utter', *undirsciethon* (3 pl. pret. ind.)

unreht 'injustice', *unreht* (acc. sg.)

uns see *ic, ik*

unsa 'our', *unsan* (masc. acc. sg.), *unsin* (masc. dat. sg.), *unsa* (neut. acc. pl.)

unsig see *ic, ik*

untes 'until, up to'

uualdon 'rule', *uualdonde* (pres. part., masc. nom. sg.)

uuanda 'for, because'

uuârhêide 'truth', *uuârhêide* (acc. sg.)

uuatir 'water', *uuatir* (acc. sg.)

uue 'who?'

uuerk 'work', *uuerk* (nom. and acc. pl.)

uuerolt 'age of man, eternity, forever', *uuerolt* (acc. sg.), *uueroldis* (gen. sg.), *uueroldi* (dat. sg.)

uuerthan 'become', 'be' (as pass. auxiliary), *uuerthint* (3 pl. pres. subj.)

uuesan 'be', *bist* (2 sg. pres. ind.), *ist* (3 sg. pres. ind.), *sint* (3 pl. pres. ind.)

uui, uuir, see *ic, ik*

uuither 'ram', *uuithero* (gen. pl.)

uuitherstrîdan 'rebel', *uuitherstrîdunt* (3 pl. pres. ind.)

uuonon 'live, dwell'

Some Aspects of Old Low Franconian Grammar

Spelling and Pronunciation

Consonants

The inventory of Old Low Franconian consonants has few surprises. The letters *p, t, k, b, d* represent the sounds one might expect. The sound [k] is also frequently represented by *c*, but not before *i* and *e*: *ic* or *ik* 'I'.

The letter sequence *sc*, never written *sk*, is replaced very occasionally by *sch*, which would indicate that it was pronounced [sx]. Compare in our text *bescirmot* 'protected' with the word *beschirmedos* 'you protected' found elsewhere in the Psalms.

The letter *g* was probably only pronounced as a stop [g] after a nasal or when geminated. Otherwise it was a fricative, either the voiceless [x] (when syllable-final), or the voiced [g]. Thus:

> *brengan* 'bring' with [g]
> *dag* 'day' with [x]
> *gân* 'go' with [g]

The letter *f* of course stands for [f]. As in several of the other languages, there is a positional alternation with [v], spelled *u*. Note in our texts the alternation of *lof* 'praise' (acc. sg.) with *louis* (gen. sg.). A similar alternation may be assumed for [s] and [z], although both values are symbolized by the same letter, *s*.

The combination *th* no doubt stood for the voiced fricative [ð], tending already in the direction of the stop [d]. Thus *ward* and *warth* are both found as spellings for 'became'.

The letter *h* has pronunciations similar to those in other languages. Syllable-finally and before consonants it was pronounced [x]; otherwise it was [h]:

> *hûs* with [h]   *unreht* with [x]

The letters *m*, *n*, *l*, *r*, *j* all have the expected pronunciation. The sound [w] is written *uu*.

Vowels

Old Low Franconian has the vowels *i*, *e*, *a*, *o*, *u*, both short and long, the latter denoted here with a circumflex. They are normally pronounced as one might expect. As with a number of the other older languages, we may suspect that some of the back vowel symbols (*u*, *o*, etc.) are also used to symbolize front rounded vowels, such as [ü]. This sometimes is confirmed by alternative spellings, as when 'doors' is spelled *duiri* rather than the expected *duri* (the symbol *ui*, sometimes found as *iu*, normally represents the long front rounded vowel [û̃] arising out of the old diphthong [iu]). There is, however, some disagreement as to how extensive umlaut was in Old Low Franconian (see below).

In addition to the simple vowels, Old Low Franconian has the diphthongs *ei*, *ou*, *ie*, *uo*, and *io*, the last sometimes alternating with *ia*. The first two were pronounced as the individual vowel components would indicate, but there is some evidence that the second component of the others was the weakly articulated vowel [ə], or tended in that direction, so that the last four spellings symbolized just two diphthongs, [iə] and [uə].

A number of otherwise unexplained variations in the vowels of endings would seem to indicate that in this position, too, weakening was going on in Old Low Franconian. It is, however, a matter of some debate whether we can totally ignore the actual letters used in such positions and postulate a uniform [ə].

Phonology

1. Unlike Old English and Old Frisian, Old Low Franconian has kept West Germanic [â] (from Proto-Germanic *æ̂*) as *â*:

OLF	Goth.	
gâuon	gêbun	'they gave'
jâr	jêr	'year'

2. Old Low Franconian, not surprisingly, shows the effects of umlaut. As usual, *a*-umlaut is quite obscure. The *i*-umlaut of short *a* is quite apparent, however: *craft* 'power', *crefti* (gen. sg.).

The umlaut of short *u* seems also undisputable, although it is almost never symbolized. (Evidence for its existence comes from later dialects). Thus *irfullit* 'fulfilled' was probably pronounced with [ü].

There is a good deal of disagreement as to whether Old Low Franconian underwent an *i*-umlaut of long vowels. It is certain that the West Low Franconian dialects never did, and this fact is reflected in the modern Dutch standard language. Modern eastern Dutch dialects (for example, Limburgic) do show evidence for the umlaut of long vowels, but this may be an importation from farther east.

The only long-vowel umlaut for which there is any Old Low Franconian evidence is that of *â*. Thus *êhtidon* 'they pursued' is found beside *âhtidon*, and *gewêde* 'clothing' reflects the umlaut of an *â* still symbolized, for example, in Old High German (*giwâti*). Van Helten has argued from this for an umlaut of all long vowels. Cowan, however, has noted that the ratio of actual to expected umlauts of long *â* is 1:3 in Old Low Franconian, and has argued that the umlauted forms either are borrowings from Central Franconian, or are the "residue" of a Central Franconian text from which the Wachtendonck Codex was being copied (see the last section of this chapter).

3. Old Low Franconian shows a twofold development of original *ai* and *au*. The diphthong *ai* becomes the monophthong *ê* before *r* and *w* (and probably also before *h* and in final position, though these are not documented):

OLF	Goth.	
sêo	saiws	'sea'
mêrra	maiza	'more'

Otherwise it is reflected as *ei*: OLF *stein* 'stone' opposite Goth. *stains*.
Similarly, original *au* shows up as *ô* before *h*, *r*, any dental consonant, or in final position, but elsewhere as *ou*:

OLF	Goth.	
gehôran	hausjan	'hear'
ouga	augo	'eye'

4. Older *ê* (*ê₂*) and *ô* diphthongize to *ie* and *uo* in Old Low Franconian:

OLF	Goth.	
hiera	hêr	'here'
fuot	fôtus	'foot'

5. There is no trace of sharpening in Old Low Franconian.

6. The *w* of the original cluster *ngw* has been lost: *singen* 'sing'.

7. Rhotacism has taken place in Old Low Franconian: *gehôran* 'hear' opposite Goth. *hausjan*.

8. Consonant gemination has taken place here as in the other West Germanic languages. The conditioning *j* has frequently been lost:

> *cunni* 'generation', from earlier *kunjam
> *settan* 'set, place', Goth. *satjan*

9. Old Low Franconian shows the initial consonant cluster *fl-* where Gothic shows *þl-*: OLF *flien* 'flee' opposite Goth. *þliuhan*.

10. Unlike Old Saxon, Old English, and Old Frisian, Old Low Franconian does not in general lose nasals before the original fricatives *f*, *s*, and *þ*:

OLF	OE	
uns	ūs	'us'
cundo	cūð	'known'

There are, however, a few forms with nasal loss in Old Low Franconian, which van Helten explains as Saxon borrowings, and Cowan sees as North Sea Germanic (i.e., Frisian) relics in the language. One such word is *sûthon* 'from the south' (cf. OE *suða* 'south', OHG *sundana* 'from the south').

11. Old Low Franconian shows no signs of assibilation: *kint* 'child', *ruggi* 'back'.

12. In the sequence *ft*, *f* has a tendency in Old Low Franconian to

become [x]. This is by no means a straightforward rule, as even variants of the same word will show sometimes *ft*, sometimes *ht*: *eft* or *echt* 'again'.

Nouns and Pronouns

1. In the nominative singular of masculine *a*-stem nouns, Old Low Franconian shows no ending: OLF *dag* 'day' opposite Goth. *dags*. The same holds for the masculine nominative singular of strong adjectives.

2. All undisputed masculine *a*-stem nominative plurals show the ending *-a*: OLF *daga* 'days'; compare Goth. *dagôs*. Cowan has argued that two forms with a final *-as* in the Old Low Franconian corpus may be *a*-stem plurals. The more likely of them (though it is still quite debatable) is *rôwas*, which Cowan suggests may mean 'robberies'. If he is right about this form (or the other), then it, too, would be a North Sea Germanic relic (*rôwas* is normally taken as genitive singular, however).

3. We find no evidence in Old Low Franconian for a dual form of the first and second person personal pronouns. This could, of course, be due to the inadequacy of the corpus.

4. The only personal pronoun in Old Low Franconian that shows an initial *h* is the masculine nominative singular *he*, *hie*.

5. There is no distinction between accusative and dative in the first and second person singular personal pronouns:

	OLF	Goth.	
Acc.	mi	mik	'me'
Dat.	mi	mis	'me'
Acc.	thi	þuk	'thee'
Dat.	thi	þus	'thee'

6. There is a reflexive pronoun *sig* in Old Low Franconian. Its form, with *g* (representing [x]) rather than *k*, betrays its borrowing from a High German dialect.

7. While it seems likely that Old Low Franconian would have had an intensified demonstrative pronoun in addition to the regular one, our limited texts give us no examples.

Verbs

1. The reduplicating verb class of Gothic is represented here by verbs showing vowel alternation in the preterite (thus without reduplication):

OLF	Goth.	
slâpan–slîp	slêpan–saislêp	'sleep–I slept'
farlâtan–farliet	lêtan–lailôt	'leave–he left'

2. There is no class of -na verbs in Old Low Franconian.

3. The ending of the second person singular preterite indicative of strong verbs is -i, as in the other West Germanic languages (except Frisian): OLF gâui 'you gave'; compare Goth. gaft. Note that in Old Low Franconian the root vowel of the second person singular preterite indicative of strong verbs again follows the plural, not the singular: for gâui, compare gaf 'he gave', gâuon 'they gave'.

4. There is no morphological passive or medio-passive in Old Low Franconian, which necessitates the use of periphrastic forms. For example, in Psalm 65:7 note ne werthint irhauan 'be not exalted'.

5. The third person singular present indicative of the verb 'be' is ist, with t.

6. Old Low Franconian has a three-way distinction between the persons in plural verb forms, at least in the present indicative: thus werthun 'we become', *werthit 'you become', werthunt 'they become'.

7. Both long and short forms of the verbs 'go' and 'stand' are found in Old Low Franconian. When short, they contain the vowel â, not ê (as in some dialects of Old High German): OLF gân, stân; compare OHG (Bavarian) gên, stên.

8. Quite distinctively among the older Germanic languages, the regular first person singular present indicative ending in Old Low Franconian is -on: OLF singon 'I sing'; compare OE singe.

The Philological Assessment of the Wachtendonck Codex

At several points in the preceding discussion I have alluded to scholarly disagreements about what we have been calling "Old Low Franconian." In many ways, the issues raised here are representative of the kinds of questions scholars must deal with any time they attempt to analyze a manuscript, or set of manuscripts. For manuscripts rarely come complete with identifying data such as "I, Adso of Melk, set this down in the year of our Lord 1380 at the monastery of Melk in my native dialect of Central Bavarian." (My apologies to Umberto Eco.)

In the first place, it is not always apparent what constitutes a single text, as opposed to a group of texts—recall that we have four sources for Old Low Franconian (or five, counting the copies of Psalms 1–3). On what evidence do we trace them all back to a single codex?

Of course, we are fortunate that Lipsius's letter to Schottius was published. From it we learn that such a thing as the Wachtendonck Codex existed, that Lipsius found it in Liège, that it consisted of a Latin psalter plus hymns and creeds, and that it included an interlinear translation into some Germanic language. We find in the letter itself 670 words taken from the codex, with notations about their Latin meanings plus a classification into nouns and verbs.

The connection between the longer list of glosses found in the Leiden library in 1870 and the shorter list printed in Lipsius's letter is obvious: the long list was found among Lipsius's papers, is annotated in his hand, and contains all but two of the words found in the short list. Though the long list does not identify nouns and verbs, it does give the Latin equivalents of the Germanic words, and, even better, usually specifies the psalm, hymn, or creed from which each was taken.

The van der Myle printing of Psalm 18, though corrupted to conform to contemporary Flemish spelling, is identified clearly as coming from Lipsius, so its assignment to the Wachtendonck Codex is certain. A bit more ingenuity is required to incorporate the Diez Manuscript, however. First, though the manuscript was discovered in Berlin, it is clearly identified as having come from Leiden. Second, the words that the Lipsius glosses identify as coming from those psalms preserved in the Diez Manuscript do indeed occur in those psalms in that manuscript, and a number of obvious errors to be found in the glosses are duplicated there. Finally, the scholar P. Tack was able to show, by comparing watermarks and page sizes, that the first part of the Diez Manuscript was written on paper identical to that used for the last part of the Lipsius glosses found in Leiden.

Although the same physical evidence is not available for our fifth source, the copy of Psalms 1–3, a comparison of them with Lipsius's glosses assures us that they, too, derive from the Wachtendonck Codex.

Besides determining that all these manuscripts derive from the same source, scholars have been concerned with establishing their derivational relationship to each other and to the Wachtendonck Codex. For example, what precisely is the relationship between the two lists of glosses? Does the shorter, published list represent a culling of the longer, handwritten one? And does the fact that the glosses and the psalm fragments contain identical errors mean that the Wachtendonck Codex showed the same errors?

As to the first question, although the published glosses contain more errors than the handwritten ones (which would be consistent with the former's being copied from the latter), the handwritten list contains several errors not repeated in the published one. This, together with the fact that the published list, though shorter, contains two words that the handwritten one does not, suggests that both of them derive independently from an earlier list of glosses, possibly, as Robert Kyes argues, an unalphabetized list taken directly from the Wachtendonck Codex.

There is some dispute about whether, as van Helten appears to feel, both the glosses and the psalm fragments were copied directly from the codex. Emil Steinmeyer, for one, argues that shortly after Lipsius became acquainted with the Wachtendonck Codex he had a copy made, and that all the surviving manuscripts derive from this copy. Thus any common errors may well come not from the original codex, but from this copy.

The likelihood that the various glosses and psalm fragments ultimately come from a single source has never been seriously disputed. But this scholarly unanimity falls apart when we ask precisely what language they are written in, and why this language is not uniform.

It is safe to say that all scholars now agree the principal language of the Wachtendonck Codex is a Netherlandic or Low Franconian dialect. This was not always the case, especially in the nineteenth century: though the notable Dutch scholars L. A. te Winkel and P. J. Cosijn had by 1875 clearly demonstrated the connection between this dialect and later Dutch ones, as late as 1896 the German scholar Franz Jostes quite firmly maintained, with very little evidence, that it was a North Thuringian or Saxon transliteration—not translation—of an original southern (probably East Franconian) translation from the Latin.

Although the Dutch scholar van Helten rejected Jostes's Thuringian or Saxon label for the language, he embraced the notion that the Wachtendonck Codex (except for Psalms 1–9) represented a reworking of a High German (in particular, South Middle Franconian) original into Low Franconian. The original language was, in his view, documented in Psalms 1–9. I will return to the question of precisely how this reworking is supposed to have taken place, but for the moment I will concentrate on some of the evidence van Helten used to support his contentions. As he himself claimed, the introduction to his 1902 edition of the psalms and glosses was the first work to contain a clear presentation of the features that set the dialect off from Old Saxon and Old High German, as well as those that localize it within the Old Low Franconian area.

The major factor that sets most of the psalms and glosses off from Old High German is the overall absence of the *High German Consonant Shift* (see Chapter 9). Thus where our text has forms like *ruopen* 'call, cry out', *betera* 'better', *tunga* 'tongue', and *mikil* 'great', all Old High German dialects show forms like *ruofan, bezzira, zunga,* and *mihhil*.

Yet although the language of the Wachtendonck Codex is clearly a *Low* German dialect like Old Saxon, there are several factors that set it off from Old Saxon. Van Helten cites, among other criteria, the presence of *ei* and *ou* in words like *heilig* 'holy' and *rouc* 'smoke', where Old Saxon has *ê* and *ô*, masculine noun plurals in *-a* (*daga* 'days') where Old Saxon has *-os*, and the three-way differentiation in plural verb endings, where Old Saxon shows a unitary ending.

Van Helten, following other scholars, goes even farther, maintaining that the dialect is an *eastern* dialect of Old Low Franconian. This follows from the presence, in our sources, of language features that in later Dutch dialects show up only in the east, for example the umlaut of long vowels and diphthongs, the ending *-on* in the first person singular present indicative of verbs, and the presence of words like the reflexive pronoun *sig* and the personal pronoun *wir* (frequently used for *wi* 'we'), which can only have been borrowed from Central Franconian (thus High German) dialects to the east and south. Further considerations lead him ultimately to place it in the southeast corner of the Old Low Franconian area, in agreement with Cosijn.

This is the usual placement of the language of the major part of the Wachtendonck Codex. The modern Dutch scholar H. K. J. Cowan has defended this localization with even more data. He compares Old Low Franconian with later, well-localized dialects, using the forms of the words for 'new' and 'and', the reflexes of specific vowels in specific positions, and other criteria, to argue against a northeastern location. Similar arguments lead him ultimately to zero in on a relatively small area around the southern portion of the Dutch province of Limburg, with the cities of Aachen, Maastricht, and Liège as possible places of origin for the texts.

This is the prevailing view, not the only one. The German scholar Willy Sanders, for one, places the origin of our text somewhat farther to the north and east, in present-day Germany, a conclusion that Cowan has attempted to refute.

Less controversy has surrounded the localization of the language found in Psalms 1–9. Van Helten characterizes it as southern Central

Franconian, using among other things evidence of borrowing from Alamannic dialects of the German south (see Chapter 9).

To this day, there is no commonly accepted view of how the Wachtendonck Codex started out in one dialect (Psalms 1–9) and ended up in
another, or why there are so many examples of Central Franconian forms
in the Low Franconian part of the text.

Van Helten holds that the Wachtendonck Codex was copied by a
native speaker of Low Franconian from an original Central Franconian
translation of the psalms, hymns, and creeds. The first nine psalms were
basically copied as they stood, but in the rest of the text the copyist went
over to his own dialect. This he did not do particularly gracefully, since a
number of Central Franconian forms seem to have been left in (the "residue"), while in other cases Old Low Franconian letters have simply, and
inappropriately, been substituted for Central Franconian ones, yielding a
pseudo–Old Low Franconian that never was. A characteristic example is
the rendering of Central Franconian *zz*, in words like *wizzon* 'know',
with the letter sequence *tt*. Although the copyist was correct in noting
that there was a correspondence between Low Franconian *t* and Central
Franconian *z*, his automatic substitution of a *t* for every *z* was wrong. An
analogous case would be one where a modern speaker of English, notic-
ing a correspondence between German *s* and English *t* in cognate words,
wrote "water" as *watter* because of the German word *Wasser*.

Alternatively, Cowan argues that the Wachtendonck Codex was
copied by a native speaker of Central Franconian living in a Low Franconian–speaking area. After simply copying the first nine psalms, this
scribe then attempted a letter-by-letter substitution, or in some cases even
a translation, into the Low Franconian dialect that surrounded him. This,
according to Cowan, gives a better explanation for the many infelicities
found in the Old Low Franconian part. Not being a native speaker, the
scribe was simply not very sensitive to the hash that resulted from his
well-meaning efforts.

As a variant of this, Cowan suggests that there was no copying involved here at all, but rather a translation from the original Latin. Again
the scribe is a Central Franconian, only this time he translates the first
nine psalms into his native dialect, then inadequately translates the rest
into Low Franconian.

A third suggestion is that of Sanders: the entire Wachtendonck Codex represents an attempt by a native speaker of Low Franconian to
render a Central Franconian original in his own dialect. While he was
essentially just copying at the beginning, he gradually became better at his

task, so that after Psalm 9 he was basically writing Low Franconian. There is no sharp division between Psalms 1–9 and the rest of the codex, but rather a fluid transition from the first psalms on. This theory accounts not only for the "residues" in the later psalms, but also for putative Low Franconian forms even in the earliest ones.

It seems highly unlikely that we will ever achieve total clarity in any of these matters, or in any of the other philological disputes I have left untreated here. These include debates over whether a number of the Central Franconian forms in the Low Franconian part of the Wachtendonck Codex represent "residues" from a putative earlier text, or are genuine borrowings from neighboring Central Franconian dialects. Interested readers may consult "Further Reading."

FURTHER READING

Blok, Petrus J. *A History of the People of the Netherlands*. Vol. 1, *From the Earliest Times to the Beginning of the Fifteenth Century*. New York and London: Putnam, 1898.

Cosijn, P. J. "De Oudnederlandse psalmen." *De Taal- en Letterbode* 3 (1872): 25–48, 110–24, 257–70; 4 (1873): 149–76.

Cowan, H. K. J. "Esquisse d'une grammaire fonctionnelle du vieux-néerlandais (vieux bas-francique): D'après le psautier carolingien de Wachtendonck." *Leuvense Bijdragen* 50 (1961): 2–54.

———. "De localisering van het Oudnederfrankisch der psalmenfragmenten." *Leuvense Bijdragen* 48 (1959): 1–47.

———. "Nogmaals de localisering van de Oudnederfrankische psalmenfragmenten." *Leuvense Bijdragen* 58 (1969): 114–32.

———. *De Oudnederlandse (Oudnederfrankische) Psalmenfragmenten*. Leiden: Brill, 1957. [See esp. pp. 5–17.]

Donaldson, Bruce C. *Dutch: A Linguistic History of Holland and Belgium*. Leiden: Nijhoff, 1983.

Fleckenstein, Josef. *Early Medieval Germany*. Amsterdam: North-Holland, 1978.

Gregory of Tours. *The History of the Franks*. Translated and with an introduction by O. M. Dalton. Oxford: Clarendon, 1927.

van Helten, W. L. *Die altostniederfränkischen Psalmenfragmente, die Lipsius'-schen Glossen und die altsüdmittelfränkischen Psalmenfragmente, mit Einleitung, Noten, Indices und Grammatiken*. Groningen: Wolters, 1902.

———. "Een en ander over en naar aanleiding van de Oudnederlandsche psalmvertaling." *Tijdschrift voor Nederlandsche Taal- en Letterkunde* 15 (1896): 146–71, 269.

Jostes, Franz. "Saxonica." *Zeitschrift für deutsches Altertum und deutsche Literatur* 40 (1896): 129–92. [See esp. pp. 190–92.]

Kyes, Robert L. *The Old Low Franconian Psalms and Glosses.* Ann Arbor, Mich.: University of Michigan Press, 1969. [See esp. pp. 1–18.]

Lasko, Peter. *The Kingdom of the Franks: North-West Europe Before Charlemagne.* New York: McGraw-Hill, 1971.

Sanders, Willy. "Zu den altniederfränkischen Psalmen." *Zeitschrift für deutsches Altertum und deutsche Literatur* 97 (1968–69): 81–107.

Schwarz, Ernst. *Germanische Stammeskunde.* Heidelberg: Winter, 1956. [See esp. chs. 26–29.]

Sergeant, Lewis. *The Franks.* New York: Putnam, 1898.

9

OLD HIGH GERMAN

The Tribal Foundations of Old High German

With the discussion of the Saxons in Chapter 5 and the Franks in Chapter 8, we have touched on two of the early tribal groupings important in the formation of German dialects. Thus the Saxons are associated with Old Saxon and the later Low German dialects of northern Germany, and the Franks with Old Low Franconian and the later dialects of Dutch, as well as a number of High German dialects of central Germany, both in Old High German times and later. Most of the High German–speaking area, though, is associated with three further Germanic groups, the Alamanni, the Bavarians, and the Thuringians.

All three of these groups belong to that subdivision of the West Germanic tribes known variously as Elbe Germans, Irminones, and the like (see Map 1, Chapter 1). In the last few centuries B.C., they were grouped around the lower and middle Elbe, with East Germanic tribes to their east and Weser-Rhine tribes, ancestors of the later Franks, to their west. The natural field of expansion for the Elbe Germans was to the south, and specifically those areas that now constitute southern Germany.

The earliest such expansion of which we are aware through historical sources occurred in the first century B.C., when a group known as Suebi, and associated groups including the Marcomanni and Quadi, moved southwest. (The term "Suebi" is frequently used as a superordinate term for all these subgroups, and, as its later reflection in the name of the Swabian subgroup of the Alamanni shows, it could be applied to most of the Elbe Germans.) It was these people who, under the famous leader Ariovistus, challenged the Romans for Gaul in the momentous battle waged in Alsace in 58 B.C. Led by Caesar, the Romans won, thus barring Germanic tribes from any permanent settlement west of the Rhine for several centuries.

Subsequently, Roman domination increased both in the north, on the middle and lower Rhine, and in the south, controlling the territory as far north as the Danube. Faced with this, most of the early Elbe-German invaders beat a strategic retreat between 8 and 3 B.C., abandoning southwest Germany for the comparative safety of Bohemia. There they subsequently became involved in the wars and politics of eastern Europe.

Following this Germanic retreat, the Romans consolidated their hold over southwest Germany. This territory was secured against barbarian attacks by the famous *limes*, a nine-foot palisade incorporating forts and towers, stretching more than three hundred miles from the middle Rhine to the Danube west of Regensburg. For the next two centuries, this boundary was a fairly effective one.

The Elbe Germans were not to be held off indefinitely, however. Around the beginning of the third century, a new confederation of these people, called the Alamanni, began to form along the Main river. From 233 on, their primary goal seems to have been the breaking of the *limes* barrier, which they finally did around 260, when Roman legions were withdrawn from the Rhine because of political instability at home. From 282 on, the Neckar valley and surrounding areas were firmly under Alamannic control.

For a time there was relative peace in the area, but in the middle of the fourth century the Alamanni set their sights across the Rhine to present-day Alsace. They were defeated there in 357 by the emperor Julian. Only temporarily deterred, they renewed their assault in the mid-fifth century, and succeeded in settling most of Alsace. At the same time, they were pushing north and west toward the Moselle river (where they captured Trier after 480) and south into present-day Switzerland.

It was in their northwestward drive that the Alamanni first seriously ran afoul of a newly unified and overwhelming Frankish presence. In 496 there was apparently a decisive battle between the rival forces, which turned out unfavorably for the Alamanni and their continued presence in northern Alsace. This was only the beginning of a long and unhappy relationship between them and the Franks. In the sixth century the Alamanni were already recognized as a part of the Merovingian Frankish kingdom, and in the mid-eighth century the last vestiges of Alamannic independence disappeared.

Characteristic of the Alamanni, especially as compared to the

Franks, was the relative looseness of their confederation. We hear little or nothing about a central kingship; at most we can find reports about war leaders in times of common peril or adventure. This looseness, indeed, is reflected in the relatively great distinctions, even today, among the various subdialects of Alamannic.

Not so with the Bavarians. From their first appearance on the European stage, these people possess a strong central authority (their dukes), and the dialects of Bavarian, at least in the large central area, are correspondingly far less differentiated.

Unfortunately for the historian, their first appearance on the European stage, in the late fifth century, also marks the first appearance of their name. Thus the questions of who these Bavarians were, and where they came from, have taxed scholars for some time. That they represent an original Elbe-German group, rather than, say, an East Germanic one, is generally recognized. Their name is probably derived, via some place designation, from the name of a pre-Germanic (Celtic, or perhaps originally Illyrian) tribe, the Boii. This immediately suggests Bohemia as a staging area for the Bavarians, since that region's name comes from the same linguistic root. The Marcomanni, one of the Suebic groups who fled from the southwest in the beginning of the Christian era, have often been considered the ancestors of the Bavarians. Another view, agreeing that the Bavarians represent a continuation of the Suebi, argues for a Hungarian staging area, perhaps one also bearing the name of the peripatetic Boii.

Be that as it may, the Bavarians appeared in present-day Bavaria and Austria between 488 and 520. They rather quickly submitted to Frankish rule, and it is quite possible that their ruling ducal house from the mid-sixth to the late eighth century was of Frankish origin. Direct Frankish control over Bavaria was necessarily loose, however, especially given the weakness of some of the Merovingian rulers, and the Bavarians remained a thorn in the side of the Franks until their final complete integration in the late eighth century. Later, indeed, Bavaria was to become the effective center of the East Frankish empire.

The name of the Thuringians, too, appears relatively late, first attested about A.D. 400. It seems very likely, however, that the name derives from the same root as *Hermunduri*, the designation of an Elbe-Germanic group documented from the beginning of our era. At that time the Hermunduri apparently lived on both sides of the Elbe, although a little later, under pressure from the Romans, they retreated to the eastern side and mixed with other Elbe Germans. They apparently first cooperated with,

then competed with the Marcomanni for control of Bohemia and surrounding areas when the latter abandoned their southwestern homes.
They also appear to have taken into their confederation a large number of
the smaller Germanic tribes left behind by the Suebi in southern Germany, and their influence reached to the Danube north of Augsburg, to
the Main, and to the Upper Palatinate in present-day Bavaria.

With the formation of the Alamanni around A.D. 200, the strength
of the Hermunduri was severely sapped, since much of the new federation
was formed with fragments of the old. Only with the addition of new
groups from the north in the early fifth century could the Hermunduri
eventually achieve something of their old strength, under the new name of
"Thuringians." Beginning with much of the territory of the old Hermunduri, the Thuringians extended their area of control during the fifth century, especially northward to the Harz mountains. The height of their
power came toward the end of the fifth century, but did not last long. In
alliance with the Saxons, the Franks fought a bitter war with the Thuringians from approximately 529 to 531, crushing Thuringian independence. Northern Thuringia fell to the Saxons, and the rest was integrated
into the Frankish kingdom, at first simply under a Frankish duke, and
later with a full panoply of Frankish counts and institutions.

There is one further Elbe German group to note only briefly here,
the Langobards. They made their way via Hungary to northern Italy,
where they established a kingdom in 568. Like other Germanic groups
(e.g., the Visigoths), they were ultimately assimilated linguistically into
the subject population. Beyond words in Latin texts, they have left us
with no linguistic witnesses, although these words alone are enough to
establish their relationship with the other Upper German dialects. Conquered by Charlemagne in 774, the Langobards essentially dropped out of
history as a separate entity, although they left their name to the present-
day Italian province of Lombardy.

The dialect map of Germany at the end of this chapter shows that
the three major regions of Upper Germany correspond rather well with the
three groups that I have discussed here. The Alamannic dialects lie in the
area originally settled by the Alamanni, the Bavarian dialects in those
areas settled by the Bavarians. When we look at the areas originally occupied by the Thuringians, however, we find that a large part of it, around
Würzburg in the area of the Main river, bears the name East Franconian.
There is some controversy as to whether this is simply the reflex of an
eighth-century political designation, or whether it reflects the actual set-

tlement of a large number of Franks in this area after the overthrow of the Thuringian kingdom. It is certainly true that the dialect found here bears striking resemblances both to the formerly Elbe-Germanic dialects of the south and to the Franconian dialects of central Germany. I will not enter into the dispute here, but I might point out that the intermediate position of East Franconian among the High German dialects may have at least as much to do with its intermediate geographical position as with the ancient tribal provenience of its speakers.

Old High German Texts

The extant Old High German texts are too numerous to list here, although in quantity and in literary value they cannot match Old Norse or Old English. Their dialect differentiation is substantial. I will give only a cursory overview.

Except for a single runic inscription, the name *Idorih* found on a lance shaft in Wurmlingen, all our earliest Old High German linguistic evidence consists until about 765 of names, legal terms, and other words found in Latin texts, and occasional German interlinear glosses written above particular Latin words. The date 765 marks our best guess for what is called the "first German book," the *Abrogans*. This is nothing but an alphabetical Latin–German glossary, named for the first Latin word in its text. The *Abrogans* is Bavarian, but there are many later glossaries, some based on it, in other dialects.

One step up from the individual glosses and glossaries are the many word-for-word interlinear translations of Latin originals. These include liturgical texts such as the Lord's Prayer, confessions, hymns, and the like; other religious texts, such as the Rule of St. Benedict; and biblical texts, such as the Psalms and of course the Gospels (the most famous example being an East Franconian translation, dating to about 825, of a Latin narrative—based on one Tatian's Syriac original—combining all four Gospels in a continuous story).

Some degree of independence (often a great deal) is exhibited by several translations. One example is the early (ca. 800) version of Isidore of Seville's tract *De Fide Catholica*, probably in South Rhenish Franconian. A fine feeling for the German language is certainly exhibited by the late Alamannic work of the monk Notker Labeo (d. 1022), who translated Boethius's writings, among other things.

A number of Old High German works are not translations at all, but native German compositions. These include works with little or no Christian leavening, for example various charms and the much-disputed *Hildebrandslied*, a mixed-dialect work dealing with early Germanic heroes. There are also praise poems such as the late ninth-century West Franconian *Ludwigslied*; a Bavarian eschatological poem from the ninth century, the *Muspilli*, from which a selection is given in the Readings; and a poetic life of Christ, the South Rhenish Franconian *Evangelienbuch* by Otfrid of Weissenburg (ca. 870). On a less literary level, we find also a phrase book for foreign visitors to Germany and the ninth-century Rhenish Franconian *Strassburg Oaths* (including also the oldest example of Old French), in which two of Charlemagne's grandsons undertake a treaty against the third.

Readings

Parable of the Sower and the Seed

(Matt. 13.2–9)

Thô tag uuas giuuortan, gihalôta zi imo sîne iungiron, inti ûzgangenti fon themo hûse, saz nâh themo sêuue, inti gisamanôte uuârun zi imo manago menigi, sô thaz her in skef instîgenti saz, inti al thiu menigi stuont in themo stedu, inti sprah in managu in râtissun sus quedenti: Sênu gieng thô ûz thie thar sâuuit zi sâuuenne. Mit thiu her thô sâta, sumu fielun nâh themo uuege inti vvurdun furtretanu, inti quâmun fugala inti frâzun thiu. Andaru fielun in steinahti lant, thâr ni habêta mihhala erda, inti sliumo giengun ûf, uuanta sie ni habêtun erda tiufi; ûfganganteru sunnun furbrantu vvurdun: bithiu sie ni habêtun vvurzalun, furthorrêtun. Sumiu fielun in thorna; thô uuohsun thie thorna inti furthamftun iz. Andaru fielun in guota erda inti gâbun uuahsmon, andaru zehenzugfalto, andaru sehszugfalto, andaru thrizugfalto. Thisu quedenti riof her: Thie thar habe ôrun zi hôrenne, hôre!

day, *geworden*, hauled, *zu*, him, *seine* younger, *aus*, [Scots] gang, *dem*, house sat, *nahe*, sea, and, *gesammelt*, were many, *Menge*, so, that, *er*, in, ship *einsteigend*, all, *die*, stood (*Ge)stade*, *sprach*, *ihn(en)* quoth, see, now, *ging*, *da* sow(s), *mit*, sowed some, fell, way, *wurden* trodden, came, *Vogel*, *frassen* *andere*, stony, land had, [Scots] mickle, earth, *auf* [Dutch] *want*, *sie*, deep sun, burned *Wurzeln*, *dürr* thorn(s), *wuchsen* *dämpften*, it, good gave, ten, -ty, -fold sixtyfold, thirtyfold these, *rief*, have, ear(s) hear

From the Bavarian Muspilli (End of the World)

Daz hôrtih rahhôn dia uueroltrehtuuîson	heard, *ich*, reckon, world, right, wise
daz sculi der antichristo mit Eliase pâgan.	that, shall, Antichrist, Elias
der uuarch ist kiuuâfanit,	weaponed
denne uuirdit untar in uuîc arhapan.	then, *wird*, under, *erheben*
khenfun sint sô kreftîc,	*Kämpfe*, *sind*, *kräftig*
diu kôsa ist sô mihhil.	cause
Elias strîtit pî den êuuîgon lîp,	*streitet*, by, *ewig*, *Leib*
uuili den rehtkernon daz rîhhi kistarkan:	will, *den*, *gern*, *das*, *Reich*, *stärken*
pidiu scal imo helfan	shall, help
der himiles kiuualtit.	*Himmel*, wield(s)
der antichristo stêt pî demo altfiante,	*steht*, old, fiend
stêt pî demo Satanase	Satan
der inan varsenkan scal:	*ihn*, sink
pidiu scal er in deru uuîcsteti	*der*, *Stätte*
uunt pivallan	wound(ed), fall
enti in demo sinde sigalôs uuerdan.	*Sieg*, less, *werden*
doh uuânit des vilo . . . gotmanno	doch, *wähnen*, viel, god, man
daz Elias in demo uuîge aruuartit uuerde,	*werde*
sô daz Eliases pluot in erda kitriufit,	blood, drip(s)
sô inprinnant die perga, poum ni gistentit	burn, *Berge*, *Baum*, stand(s)
ênîhc in erdu, aha artruknent,	any, [Latin] *aqua*, *trocknen*
muor varsuuilhit sih,	moor, swallow(s), *sich*
suilizôt lougiu der himil,	swelter
mâno vallit, prinnit mittilagart,	moon, fall, middle, yard
stên ni kistentit,	stone
verit denne stûatago in lant,	fare(s), day(s)
verit mit diu vuiru viriho uuîsôn:	fire
dâr ni mac denne mâk andremo	may
helfan vora demo muspille.	(be)fore

GLOSSARY

Owing to Old High German dialect differentiation, words beginning with *ki*- are listed here under *g*; words beginning with *p*-, *th*-, and *v*- are listed under *b*, *d*, and *f*, respectively (for *vv*- see *uu*, listed after *u*). Initial *i* representing [j] is listed after *i*. Unless specified otherwise, nouns and pronouns are nominative singular, adjectives are masculine nominative singular, and verbs are infinitives. The parenthetical identification of any form has reference only to the Readings, and is not necessarily an exhaustive list of all possible identifications of that form in the language.

aha 'water, river', *aha* (nom. pl.)

al 'all' (fem. nom. sg.)

altfiant 'ancient enemy', *altfiante* (dat. sg.)

andar 'other, some, another', *andremo* (masc. dat. sg.), *andaru* (neut. nom. pl.)

antichristo 'Antichrist'

arheffen 'raise, start', *arhapan* (pret. part.)

artrucknen 'dry up', *artruknent* (3 pl. pres. ind.)

aruuarten 'destroy', *aruuartit* (pret. part.)

bâgan, pâgan 'battle'

berg, perg 'mountain', *perga* (nom. pl.)

bî, pî 'for, by'

bifallan, pivallan 'fall'

bithiu, pidiu 'because, wherefore'

bluot, pluot 'blood'

boum, poum 'tree'

brinnan, prinnan 'burn', *prinnit* (3 sg. pres. ind.)

dâr, thâr 'there, where'

daz, thaz 'that' (conj.)

daz, thaz 'that, the' (neut. art. and dem. pro.), *daz* (acc. sg.), *des* (gen. sg.), *themo* (dat. sg.), *diu, thiu* (inst. sg. and acc. pl.)

demo, themo, see *der, ther*; see also *daz, thaz*

den see *der, ther*

denne 'then, when'

der, ther 'the, who, he who' (masc. art. and rel. pro.), *den* (acc. sg. and dat. pl.), *demo, themo* (dat. sg.), *die, dia, thie* (nom. and acc. pl.)

deru see *diu, thiu*

des see *daz, thaz*

dia, die, thie, see *der, ther*

thie thar 'who, he who, whoever' (rel. pro., masc. nom. sg.)

thisu see *thiz*

diu, thiu (fem. art.) 'the', *deru* (dat. sg.); see also *daz, thaz*

thiz (neut. emphatic dem. pro.) 'this, that', *thisu* (acc. pl.)

dô, thô 'when, then'

doh 'but'

dorn, thorn 'thorn', *thorna* (nom. and acc. pl.)

thrizugfalto 'thirtyfold'

Elias 'Elias', *Eliases* (gen. sg.), *Eliase* (dat. sg.)

ênîhc 'any'

enti see *inti, enti*

er, her 'he', *inan* (acc. sg.), *imo* (dat. sg.), *in* (dat. pl.)

erda 'earth, Earth', *erda* (acc. and gen. sg.), *erdu* (dat. sg.)

êuuîg 'eternal', *êuuîgon* (masc. acc. sg.)

fallan, vallan 'fall', *vallit* (3 sg. pres. ind.), *fielun* (3 pl. pret. ind.)

faran, varen 'go, travel', *verit* (3 sg. pres. ind.)

farsenkan, varsenkan 'destroy'

farsuuelhan, varsuuelhan 'swallow', *varsuuilhit* (3 sg. pres. ind.)

verit see *faran, varen*

fielun see *fallan, vallan*

filu, vilo 'a lot, many a'

firiha, viriha 'people', *viriho* (gen. pl.)

fon 'from'

vora 'before'

frezzan 'eat', *frâzun* (3 pl. pret. ind.)

fugal 'bird', *fugala* (nom. pl.)

vuir 'fire', *vuiru* (inst. sg.)

furbrinnan 'burn up', *furbrantu* (pret. part., neut. nom. pl.)

furthemfen 'choke', *furthamftun* (3 pl. pret. ind.)

furthorrên 'dry up', *furthorrêtun* (3 pl. pret. ind.)

furtretan 'step on', *furtretanu* (pret. part., neut. nom. pl.)

gâbun see *geban*
gangan, gân, gên 'go', *gieng* (3 sg. pret. ind.), *giengun* (3 pl. pret. ind.)
geban 'give', *gâbun* (3 pl. pret. ind.)
gieng, giengun, see *gangan, gân, gên*
gihalôn 'gather, get', *gihalôta* (3 sg. pret. ind.)
gisamanôte see *samanôn*
gistantan, -stân, -stên 'stand fast', *gistentit, kistentit* (3 sg. pres. ind.)
gistarkan, kistarkan 'strengthen'
gitriofan, kitriofan 'drip', *kitriufit* (3 sg. pres. ind.)
kiuuâfanit see *uuâffanen*
giuualtan, kiuualtan 'rule', *kiuualtit* (3 sg. pres. ind.)
giuuortan see *uuerdan*
gotman 'servant of God', *gotmanno* (gen. pl.)
guot 'good', *guota* (fem. acc. sg.)

habên 'have', *habe* (3 sg. pres. subj.), *habêta* (3 sg. pret. ind.), *habêtun* (3 pl. pret. ind.)
helfan 'help'
her, see *er, her*
himil 'Heaven, heavens', *himiles* (gen. sg.)
hôren 'hear', *hôre* (3 sg. pres. subj.), *hôrta* (1 sg. pret. ind.), *hôrenne* (gerund, dat. sg.); *hôrtih* = *hôrta* + *ih*
hûs 'house', *hûse* (dat. sg.)

ih 'I'
imo see *er, her*
in 'in, into, on'; see also *er, her*
inan see *er, her*
inbrinnan, inprinnan 'catch fire', *inprinnant* (3 pl. pres. ind.)
instîgan 'get in', *instîgenti* (pres. part., masc. nom. sg.)

inti, enti 'and'
ist see *uuesan, sîn*
iz 'it', *iz* (acc. sg.), *sie* (masc. nom. pl., for neut. *siu*)

iungiro 'disciple', *iungiron* (acc. pl.)

kenfo, khenfo 'champion', *khenfun* (nom. pl.)
kôsa 'matter, cause', *kôsa* (nom. sg.)
kreftîc 'powerful', *kreftîc* (masc. nom. pl.)

lant 'land', *lant* (acc. sg.)
lîb, lîp 'life', *lîp* (acc. sg.)
loug 'flame', *lougiu* (inst. sg.)

mac see *magan*
mâg, mâk 'relative'
magan 'be able, can', *mac* (3 sg. pres. ind.)
mâk see *mâg, mâk*
manag 'many', *manago* (fem. nom. pl.), *managu* (neut. acc. pl.)
mâno 'moon'
menigi 'multitude', *menigi* (nom. pl.)
mihhal, mihhil 'much, a lot, great', *mihhil* (fem. nom. sg.), *mihhala* (fem. acc. sg.)
mit 'with'; *mit thiu* 'while'
mittilagart 'world'
muor 'bog, moor'
muspilli 'end of the world', *muspille* (dat. sg.)

nâh 'next to'
ni 'not'

ôra 'ear', *ôrun* (acc. pl.)

quâmun see *queman*
quedan 'speak', *quedenti* (pres. part., masc. nom. sg.)
queman 'come', *quâmun* (3 pl. pret. ind.)

rahhôn 'tell'

râtissa 'parable', *râtissun* (dat. pl.)

rehtgern, rehtkern 'righteous', *rehtkernon* (dat. pl.)

rîhhi 'realm, kingdom', *rîhhi* (acc. sg.)

ruofan 'cry out, call', *riof* (3 sg. pret. ind.)

samanôn 'gather', *gisamanôte* (pret. part., masc. nom. pl.)

sâta see *sâuuen*

Satanas 'Satan', *Satanase* (dat. sg.)

sâuuen 'sow', *sâuuit* (3 sg. pres. ind.), *sâta* (3 sg. pret. ind.), *sâuuenne* (gerund, dat. sg.)

saz see *sizzen*

sculan 'shall', *scal* (3 sg. pres. ind.), *sculi* (3 sg. pres. subj.)

sê 'sea', *sêuue* (dat. sg.)

sehszugfalto 'sixtyfold'

sênu 'lo'

sêuue see *sê*

sie see *iz*

sigalôs 'without victory'

sih (refl. pro. acc. sg.)

sîn 'his', *sîne* (masc. acc. pl.)

sind 'way', *sinde* (dat. sg.)

sint see *uuesan, sîn*

sizzen 'sit', *saz* (3 sg. pret. ind.)

skef 'ship', *skef* (acc. sg.)

sliumo 'quickly'

sô 'so'

sô daz, sô thaz 'so that'

sprehhan 'speak', *sprah* (3 sg. pret. ind.)

stantan, stân, stên 'stand', *stêt* (3 sg. pres. ind.), *stuont* (3 sg. pret. ind.)

stedi 'shore', *stedu* (inst. sg.)

steinahti 'stony', *steinahti* (neut. acc. sg.)

stên 'stone'

stêt see *stantan, stân, stên*

strîtan 'fight', *strîtit* (3 sg. pres. ind.)

stûatago 'Judgment Day'

stuont see *stantan, stân, stên*

suilizôn 'burn slowly', *suilizôt* (3 sg. pres. ind.)

sum 'one, some', *sumu, sumiu* (neut. nom. pl.)

sunna 'sun', *sunnun* (dat. sg.)

sus 'thus'

tag 'day'

tiufi 'depth', *tiufi* (acc. sg.)

ûf 'up'

ûfgangan 'go up', *ûfganganteru* (pres. part., fem. dat. sg.)

untar 'among, between'

ûz 'out'

ûzgangan, ûzgân, ûzgên, 'go out', *ûzgangenti* (pres. part., masc. nom. sg.)

uuâffanen 'arm', *kiuuâfanit* (pret. part., masc. nom. sg.)

uuahsan 'grow', *uuohsun* (3 pl. pret. ind.)

uuahsmo 'fruit', *uuahsmon* (acc. sg.)

uuânen 'believe', *uuânit* (3 sg. pres. ind.)

uuanta 'for, because'

uuarg, uuarch 'evildoer'

uuârun, uuas, see *uuesan, sîn*

uueg 'way', *uuege* (dat. sg.)

uuellen 'want', *uuili* (3 sg. pres. ind.)

uuerdan 'become' (also pass. auxiliary), *uuirdit* (3 sg. pres. ind.), *uuerde* (3 sg. pres. subj.), *vvurdun* (3 pl. pret. ind.), *giuuortan* (pret. part.)

uueroltrehtuuîs 'pious, just', *uueroltrehtuuîson* (acc. pl.)

uuesan, sîn 'be', *ist* (3 sg. pres. ind.), *sint* (3 pl. pres. ind.), *uuas* (3 sg. pret. ind.), *uuârun* (3 pl. pret. ind.)

uuîcstat 'battleground', *uuîcsteti* (dat. sg.)

uuîg, uuîc 'war, battle', *uuîge* (dat. sg.)

uuili see *uuellen*

uuirdit see *uuerdan*

uuîsôn 'visit'

uunt 'wounded'

uuohsun see *uuahsan*

vvurdun see *uuerdan*

uurzala 'root', *vvurzalun* (acc. pl.)

zehenzugfalto 'hundredfold'

zi 'to'

Some Aspects of Old High German Grammar

Spelling and Pronunciation

A few Old High German texts use rather unusual spelling systems that differ from the norm quite substantially (for example, that found in the OHG Isidore translation). These systems are not treated in the following discussion. In fact my comments below have mainly to do with the normalized orthography found in most editions of Old High German texts, where, for example, vowel length is given even though the manuscript writers usually leave it unsymbolized.

Consonants

On the whole, the sound value of consonant symbols in Old High German comes close to that given in Chapter 2. It should be noted, however, that different dialects may use different symbols for the same consonant in the same word, which must frequently be taken as indicating a difference in pronunciation (see "Dialects in Old High German," below, for many examples of this).

The voiceless stops *p*, *t*, and *k* are pronounced as one might expect. Frequently, however, the symbol *c* is found with the value [k], especially before the vowels *a*, *o*, and *u*, before consonants, and word-finally; note *scal* 'shall' and *wîc* 'war' in the Readings. It also symbolizes the affricate [ts] before *i* and *e*.

The voiced stops *b*, *d*, and *g* are also relatively problem-free, though *g* must sometimes be assigned the value [j] in conjunction with the vowels *e* and *i*: *gehan* 'affirm' is pronounced as if it were *jehan*.

The letters *f* and *v* can in general be read as [f] and [v] respectively. The regular alternation between them in the other Germanic languages has been disturbed, however, by the creation of new intervocalic *f*'s in the High German Consonant Shift (see below). Thus *kiwâfanit* 'armed' has an *f* between vowels (from original *p* via an intermediate geminate stage *ff*), while a word like *zwîval* 'doubt', from original *f*, has a medial *v*.

The situation in the sibilants is far more confusing. By the High

German Consonant Shift, original *t* after vowels resulted in a fricative, symbolized *zz* or *z*. This fricative did not fall together with any preexisting sound, specifically not with the sound spelled *s*. Yet it was the new fricative that was pronounced [s]. The older one, spelled *s*, was most likely pronounced closer to the [š] of English "fish," except between vowels, where it was most likely pronounced with a sound between [z] and the [ž] of English "rouge." Thus:

> *sunna* 'sun' with a sound between [s] and [š]
> *wesan* 'be' with a sound between [z] and [ž]
> *frâzun* 'they ate' with [s]

The letter *h*, too, presents a somewhat confusing picture. On the whole, it follows the rules we have noted in other Germanic languages, with a weak [h] initially and between vowels, a strong [x] before consonants and finally:

> *helfan* 'help' with [h]
> *sehan* 'see' with [h]
> *sah* 'saw' with [x]

But again the High German Consonant Shift has intruded somewhat, creating new intervocalic [x]'s from [k]. In general this is spelled *hh* in older texts and *ch* in later ones, as in *rîhhi* 'realm', also *rîchi*.

The combination *th* should probably be read [ð] (as in English "that").

In addition to stops and fricatives, Old High German also has voiceless affricates (stops released with some friction), as another result of the High German Consonant Shift. The affricate [pf] is in general spelled *pf* or *ph*; [ts] is spelled *z* (note the overlap with the symbolization of [s]), and [kx] is spelled *kh* or *ch* (again note the overlap with the symbolization of [x]):

> *phunt* 'pound' with [pf]
> *wurzala* 'root' with [ts]
> *khenfun* 'battles' with [kx]

The letters *r*, *l*, *m*, *n*, and *w* are all pronounced as one would expect. The sound [j] is usually symbolized with *i*, but sometimes with *g* (as noted above). Standard editions of Old High German texts frequently substitute the symbol *j* for *i* at the beginnings of words, as in *jungiro* 'disciple'.

Vowels

Old High German shows no particular surprises as far as the vowel symbols go. Normalized texts show us five short vowels, *i*, *e*, *a*, *o*, and *u*; five longs, *î, ê, â, ô*, and *û*; and in general six diphthongs, *ie, uo, ei, ou, iu*, and *io* (though other diphthongs can be found in some dialects, e.g., *ia*). Furthermore, most of these symbols can be unambiguously pronounced as the spelling indicates. The following remarks should be made, however.

The symbol *e* stands for both the original Germanic [e] and for the *i*-umlaut of original [a]. Since there is evidence from later dialects that *e*'s from these two sources were in fact pronounced differently, scholars frequently distinguish, in their grammars though not in the normalized texts, between *ë* (from original [e]) and *ę* (from original [a]). The latter is presumed to have been pronounced more in the direction of [i]:

> *ezzan* 'eat' (from Germanic [e]) is spelled *ëzzan*
> *gesti* 'guests' (from Germanic [a]) is spelled *gęsti*

Although the umlaut of short *a* is the only one symbolized in the Old High German manuscripts, all the other non-front vowels and diphthongs must also have had fronted variants (not symbolized because there were no Latin symbols for them) under *i*-umlaut conditions. This follows from the fact that all the descendant dialects have them, whereas the conditions that caused them had disappeared by the end of Old High German times. Thus *hôren* 'hear' (cf. Goth. *hausjan* with *j*) was no doubt pronounced as [hôren], and *fuori* 'if he went' as [füöri].

Phonology

1. As in the other Old Germanic languages besides Gothic, Old High German has changed Proto-Germanic *æ̂* to *â*. Unlike Old English and Old Frisian, it has kept the vowel that way:

OHG	Goth.	
wârun	wêsun	'were'
sâwen	saian (from *ê*)	'sow'

2. Old High German, like many of the other older Germanic languages, shows umlaut. Again *a*-umlaut is quite obscure, being reflected in a few relic alternations (*gold–guldin*). On the other hand, *i*-umlaut is quite apparent, but only for the short vowel *a*, whose umlaut is *e*:

> *verit* 'goes'; cf. *varan* 'go'
> *furthemfen* 'choke' (suffix formerly **-jan*); cf. *furthamftun* 'choked'

Not even all instances of *a* appear to undergo umlaut, however: note *vallit* 'falls' and *kiwaltit* 'rules'. It would appear that umlaut could be prevented by various consonants or consonant clusters intervening between the umlaut factor and the vowel to be umlauted. But the data are misleading. Middle High German texts show us that umlaut frequently took place in these instances, too, but to [ä] rather than [e]. As the Latin alphabet had no really obvious way of symbolizing this vowel, Old High German scribes simply did not capture it.

The same can be said for the *i*-umlaut of all the other back vowels, short and long. We know from Middle High German dialects that Old High German must have umlauted these vowels, even though the scribes did not have distinct symbols for the results.

3. Like Old Low Franconian, Old High German shows twofold reflexes of original *ai* and *au*. Specifically, *ai* went to *ê* before the consonants *h*, *w*, and *r*, and, in some interjections, at the end of the word:

OHG	Goth.	
sê (from *sêw)	saiws	'sea'
mêro	maiza	'more'

Otherwise original *ai* becomes *ei*:

OHG	Goth.	
stein	stains	'stone'
leib	hlaifs	'bread'

The diphthong *au* shows up as *ô* before *h* and dental consonants:

OHG	Goth.	
hôren	hausjan	'hear'
hôh	hauhs	'high'

Otherwise it is reflected as *ou*:

OHG	Goth.	
gilouban	gilaubjan	'believe'
ouga	augo	'eye'

4. As in Old Low Franconian, in Old High German older *ê* (*ê₂*) appears as *ie*, and older *ô* as *uo*:

OHG	OS	
stuont	stôd	'stood'
hiez	hêt	'was called'

5. There is no sharpening in Old High German: *zweiio* 'of two', *triuwa* 'faithfulness'.

6. The cluster *ngw* has lost the *w*: *singan* 'sing'.

7. Rhotacism has taken place: *hôren*.

8. Consonant gemination has taken place fully here, though the conditioning *j* is usually not present any longer. The geminate stops formed in this way play a significant role in the High German Consonant Shift, as I explain in the last section of this chapter. Examples are given there.

9. Old High German shows the initial consonant cluster *fl-* where Gothic shows *þl-*: OHG *fliohan* 'flee' opposite Goth. *þliuhan*.

10. Like Old Low Franconian and other older dialects, Old High German shows no evidence of nasal loss before original *f*, *s*, or *þ*: *fimf* 'five', *uns* 'us', *kund* 'known'.

11. Again like Old Low Franconian, Old High German shows no assibilation of *k* or *g*: *kirihha* 'church', *rukki* or *ruggi* 'back'.

12. One of the most important changes that sets Old High German apart from all the other Germanic languages, indeed for many its defining characteristic, is the High German Consonant Shift, whereby *p*, *t*, and *k* appear as the geminate fricatives [ff], [ss], and [xx] under certain circumstances, and as the affricates [pf], [ts], and [kx] under other circumstances. Additionally, original *b*, *d*, and *g* may show up as *p*, *t*, and *k* under some conditions. As I discuss this change in some detail in the last section of this chapter, I leave the examples until then.

Nouns and Pronouns

1. Like the other West Germanic languages, Old High German shows no trace of the original **-az* ending of the nominative singular in masculine *a*-stem nouns: *tag* 'day'; compare Goth. *dags*.

It has also lost the same ending in the masculine nominative singular of strong adjectives. There a new ending *-êr* is frequently found, which has been added by analogy to the demonstrative pronouns: *blint* or *blintêr* 'blind'.

2. The nominative plural of the masculine *a*-stem nouns in Old High German is regularly *-a*: *berga* 'mountains'; *fugala* 'birds'.

3. Old High German apparently does not distinguish between dual and plural. The Bavarian forms *ös* and *enk*, not documented during Old High German times, while identical with dual forms of the second person in other languages, were used as plurals.

4. In the third person personal pronouns, Old High German in general diverges sharply from the other West Germanic languages by having

no forms in *h-*: *er* 'he', *siu* 'she', *iz* 'it'. The form *her* 'he' found in the Parable of the Sower and the Seed is commonly seen as a "blend" of northern *he* with southern *er*.

5. The accusative and dative of the first and second person singular personal pronouns are sharply distinguished in Old High German:

	OHG	OE	
Acc.	mih	mē	'me'
Dat.	mir	mē	'me'
Acc.	dih	ðē	'thee'
Dat.	dir	ðē	'thee'

6. The reflexive pronoun *sih* is much in evidence in Old High German: *muor varswilhit sih* 'the moor swallows itself up'.

7. Like all the Germanic languages except Gothic, Old High German has an intensified demonstrative pronoun in addition to the regular one: masculine nominative singular *der* and *desêr* opposite Gothic *sa*.

Verbs

1. The reduplicating verb class of Gothic is reflected in Old High German either with a new vowel alternation in the preterite (*vallan* 'fall', *viel* 'fell'), or with the endings of the regular weak verbs (*sâwen* 'sow', *sâta* 'sowed'). In any case, there is no sign of reduplication.

2. The class of *-na* verbs is absent in Old High German.

3. Old High German shows the regular West Germanic ending *-i* in the second person singular preterite indicative of strong verbs, rather than the *-t* of Gothic and Old Norse. In addition, the root vowel of that form is that otherwise characteristic of the preterite plural of strong verbs, not the singular:

		OHG *neman* 'take'	Goth. *niman*
		PRETERITE INDICATIVE	
Sg.	1	nam	nam
	2	nâmi	namt
	3	nam	nam
Pl.	1	nâmum	nêmum
	2	nâmut	nêmuþ
	3	nâmum	nêmun

4. There is no morphological passive or medio-passive in Old High German, which necessitates the use of periphrastic forms.

5. The third person singular present indicative of the verb 'be' is *ist* in Old High German, with *-t*.

6. There is regularly a three-way distinction in the plural endings of the verbs in Old High German, though the precise forms of the endings vary from dialect to dialect:

> *nemumês* 'we take'
> *nemet* 'you take'
> *nemant* 'they take'

7. Although the long forms *gangan* and *stantan* are present for the verbs 'go' and 'stand', the short forms *gân/gên* and *stân/stên* are very frequent (see below for the distribution of *â-* and *ê-*forms).

8. Old High German has an inflected gerund, as shown by the infinitive phrase *zi sâwenne* 'to sow', with a dative ending on the infinitive.

Dialects in Old High German

In Chapter 1 I noted that the notion of a completely unitary language, as implied, for example, by a single point on a family tree, is a definite abstraction from the true state of affairs. There are always dialectal differences between groups of people speaking the "same" language.

In the preceding chapters I have pushed this fact to the side somewhat, speaking of Gothic or Old English as they distinguish themselves from the other Germanic languages, and not so much as they may be internally differentiated by dialect. In some cases this abstraction is abetted by the textual situation: the main witnesses we have to Gothic and Old Low Franconian are single texts, presumably from a single time and place, and even the traditional description of Old Saxon is based mainly on a single text, the *Heliand*.

In other cases, however, one can only speak of a unitary language by choosing one among several dialects to describe, and giving it the name of the language. For example, Old Norse is frequently equated with the Old Icelandic dialect, and, as noted in Chapter 6, Old English is frequently described on the basis of the West Saxon dialect.

It is almost impossible to do this for Old High German. The major abstraction made in descriptions of this "language" has to do with the dictionary: words are usually listed in their East Franconian form (a practice I have followed in the glossary to the Readings). But the major texts of Old High German come from several major sources, and these sometimes differ from one another in significant ways, phonologically and grammatically. This can be seen, indeed, in the two Readings I have used, of which the first comes from East Franconian, the second from Bavarian.

Thus no discussion of Old High German can be considered complete without a discussion of its dialects. In the grammatical section of this chapter I have occasionally made reference to the different dialects, but I have deferred a more complete presentation to this section.

The High German Consonant Shift

I have already mentioned that the High German Consonant Shift is the major factor that distinguishes Old High German from other Germanic languages. In fact, it is also the most important factor that distinguishes the major Old High German dialects from each other. In order to understand this, however, we must understand in a bit more detail what the shift consisted of.

The consonants affected by the change were the voiceless stops *p*, *t*, and *k* and the voiced ones *b*, *d*, and *g*. I will discuss the development of the voiceless stops first, as this is the part of the change that had the most drastic and long-lasting effects.

In the following discussion, one should keep in mind that in all the West Germanic languages almost any consonant could be geminated (doubled) before a following *j*, and before other consonants as well. Thus in addition to the simple consonants we also have to reckon with the doubles *pp*, *tt*, and *kk*. This distinction is important, as the geminates were affected quite differently by the consonant shift than the singles were.

In fact, it is important when talking about the consonant shift to distinguish between two major groups of *p*'s, *t*'s, and *k*'s. Group I consists of those voiceless stops that appear after vowels; Group II comprises those voiceless stops that appear in initial position, those that follow the sonorant consonants *l*, *m*, *n*, and *r*, and those that are geminated.

I list below a number of words from Old Saxon, taking them as representative of the pre–consonant shift situation (and indeed, many of the Modern English translations would serve the same function). When comparing these with the post–consonant shift state exhibited by the Old High German words given further below, the reader should concentrate on the consonants alone, and ignore as irrelevant any possible differences in the vowels:

GROUP I

p	t	k
opan 'open'	etan 'eat'	makôn 'make'
skip 'ship'	hwat 'what'	ik 'I'

GROUP II

p	t	k
plegan 'tend'	tiohan 'pull'	korn 'corn'
helpan 'help'	herta 'heart'	werk 'work'
skeppian 'create'	settian 'set'	wekkian 'wake'

In areas where it applied maximally, the Old High German consonant shift caused the following changes to take place. In words belonging to Group I, p shifted to a geminate ff; t to a geminate [ss], spelled zz and, as noted in "Spelling and Pronunciation" above, pronounced differently from inherited s or ss; and k to a geminate [xx], spelled hh or ch:

p	t	k
offan	ezzan	mahhôn
skif	hwaz	ih

Note that in final position, before consonants, and often after long vowels, these new geminates were simplified to short consonants, as the second row of examples illustrates.

In words belonging to Group II, however, a new set of affricates were created. In a way these can be thought of as consonantal diphthongs: they start out as stops and wind up as fricatives. Thus where English "tin" begins with a stop, and "shin" with a fricative, "chin" shows an affricate. In any case, the effect in Old High German was that p became pf, t became [ts] (usually spelled z), and k became [kx] (frequently spelled ch or kh):

p	t	k
pflegan	ziohan	khorn
helpfan	herza	werch
skepfen	sezzen	wechan

To aid in the presentation of the dialect distribution of these changes, I have reproduced here a map of the major German dialects (Map 8). But it should be noted that the map is based on Middle High German data, not on Old High German, because the texts upon which we base our

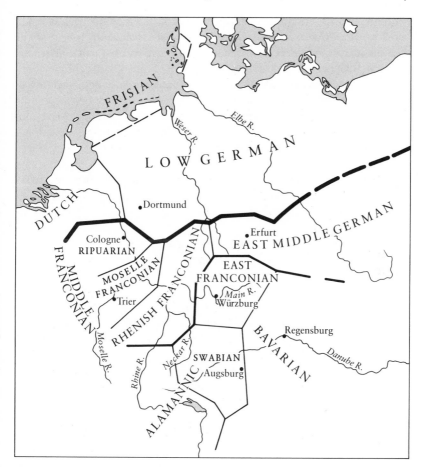

Map 8.   Middle High German literary dialects in the thirteenth century A.D.
(After Paul and Mitzka [1966: Abb. 1], by permission)

knowledge of Old High German come from a small number of scriptoria
in the various dialect areas. Such isolated evidence makes it impossible to
draw even approximate dialect boundaries on a map; for this we must
turn to a later period, when the net of documentation is finer.

When we do this, of course, we risk an inaccurate presentation of
the earlier dialect boundaries, or a differentiation into subdialects not appropriate in the earlier period. Some scholars have argued, for example,
that the heavy line stretching across northern Germany, which separates

Cologne from Dortmund, ran farther south during the Old High German period, somewhere south of Cologne. And it is certainly true that the documents of the Old High German period give us no particular reason to distinguish between Ripuarian and Moselle Franconian; scholars commonly refer to the area simply as Middle Franconian when speaking of this period. Similarly, the subdivision of Alamannic dialects shown on the map cannot be well documented for the Old High German period. Finally, the area labeled "East Middle German" on the map is not documented in Old High German times, since this was primarily a Slavic area in that period.

Given these reservations, this map is probably a fairly accurate reflection of the situation in Old High German times, and indeed is not a bad representation of dialect subdivisions in modern times. But let us now turn to the question of how these dialect divisions correspond with the effects of the Old High German consonant shift.

The heaviest line on the map, the one that runs between Cologne and Dortmund, is called an "isogloss" or "isogloss bundle," and represents a boundary between different pronunciations of the same word or words, in this case between forms showing consonant shift and those not doing so. The equivalent to this line in modern times is frequently called the *maken/machen* line, because the word 'make' is pronounced with [k] to the north of the line, and with [x] to the south. But *machen* is only one of many words that have such a boundary here. In fact, virtually all words belonging to Group I show shifted forms to the south of this line, and non-shifted forms to the north.

In addition to the words found in Group I, some of those in Group II also have an isogloss here, namely those containing original *t*. Thus not only do we find *ezzan* south of this major boundary, we also find *herza*, *sezzen*, and so on. The boundaries for the other Group II consonants, however, are farther south.

This line, then, defines the outermost limits of High German. Any dialect south of the line is a High German dialect, whereas dialects north of the line are now called Low German (in Germany) and Dutch (in the Low Countries). The latter are of course descendants of Old Saxon and Old Low Franconian respectively. It should be noted that the terms "High" and "Low" are not evaluative terms, but geographical ones, the High German dialects being spoken on the higher ground of southern Germany and Switzerland.

If all High German dialects show consonant shift in the words of Group I (with a few exceptions to be noted below), and in those words containing *t* in Group II, obviously these words cannot be used to distinguish between High German dialects. It is to the Group II words containing *p* and *k* that we must look to serve this function.

The second-heaviest line on the map runs between Rhenish Franconian (to the north) and Alamannic or East Franconian (to the south). North of this line, *p* is found unshifted in words like *plegen* and *skeppen*, while to the south it appears as *pf*. This is the boundary between the Middle German dialects of High German and the so-called Upper German dialects (although the latter term is sometimes used to refer just to Alamannic and Bavarian).

In Old High German times, the boundary between East Franconian and the other Upper German dialects was determined by, among other things, the *k* words of Group II. In East Franconian there was no shift of *k* in words like *korn* or *werk*, whereas Alamannic and Bavarian texts show *kh* or *ch*.

Further dialect divisions can be made in Old High German times by looking at subsets of the shiftable consonants. Thus although most words containing *t*, whether in Group I or II, are shifted south of the boundary between High and Low German, a few pronominal forms (*dat* 'that', *wat* 'what', *it* 'it', *allat* 'all, everything') remain unshifted in Middle Franconian, distinguishing it from Rhenish Franconian. And though Rhenish Franconian shares the Middle Franconian unshifted form of words like *plegen* and *skeppen*, it does, unlike them, show a shift of *p* to *pf* after *r* and *l*, thus *helpfan* and *thorpf* 'village' instead of *helpan* and *thorp*. We can even discern a subdialect called South Rhenish Franconian, which alone among Rhenish Franconian dialects shows shifted forms for geminate *pp* (*scephen*) and for *p* after *m* (*limphan* 'be fitting, be necessary').

For further criteria that distinguish Old High German dialects, we turn to the other set of consonants affected by the High German Consonant Shift, the voiced stops *b*, *d*, and *g*. Here the result of the shift is easier to state: If the shift takes place at all, *b* shifts to *p*, *d* to *t*, and *g* to *k*. Examples follow of pre-shift forms from Old Saxon:

b	*d*	*g*
beran 'bear'	dohter 'daughter'	gast 'guest'
geƀan 'give'	biodan 'offer'	stîgan 'climb'
sibbia 'kinship'	biddian 'ask'	liggian 'lie'

As the Old Saxon forms show, we in fact are not in every case dealing with voiced stops at all. This is most obvious in the case of *b/ƀ*, where the second symbol, found between vowels, is a fricative more like English *v*. But the same observation can be made about *g* between vowels, which, though it was written the same as in the other positions, was quite surely a fricative, [g], as the evidence from modern dialects assures us. On the other hand, *d* just as surely was a stop in all positions.

This naturally has implications for this part of the Old High German Consonant Shift. Before a *b* or *g* can possibly go to *p* or *k*, it must first be a stop rather than a fricative. That is, the sequence here is *ƀ* to *b* to *p*, or *g̵* to *g* to *k*. And there are Old High German dialects that show each of the stages along the way.

The only one of these consonants that was a stop in all positions, namely *d*, shows the most widespread change to the voiceless stop. We find *tohter*, *biotan*, and *bitten* in all the Upper German dialects, including East Franconian. South Rhenish Franconian has *biotan* and *bitten* (thus with the shift in geminates and between vowels), but still *dohter*. The rest of Rhenish Franconian changes *d* to *t* only in the geminate, as in *bitten*. Middle Franconian uniformly has *d*.

The next most widespread change is that of the labial consonant *b*. The geminate is found as *pp* (*sippa*) even in the earliest texts in Bavarian and Alamannic, and later in East Franconian and Rhenish Franconian. In non-geminate occurrences, however, both East Franconian and Rhenish Franconian show only *b*, instances of *p* for *b* in these positions being restricted to Alamannic and Bavarian. They are more numerous and last longer in Bavarian, where forms like *peran* and *kepan* predominate from the eighth through the tenth centuries, and initial *p*'s can be found there even later. In Alamannic, *p* can be found for *b* in all positions in the eighth century, but it is far more frequent initially than medially, and in any case the tendency falls off markedly in the ninth century.

Middle Franconian differs from all the other High German dialects by remaining at the stage found in Old Saxon, thus with stops in some positions (initially, after nasals, and in gemination), fricatives in others (after vowels, *l*, and *r*): *beran*, *sibba*, but *gevan*.

The velar *g* shifts the least of all these consonants. The regular spelling in all positions is *g* in Middle Franconian, Rhenish Franconian, and East Franconian, a spelling that no doubt covers both the stop and the fricative. And only the geminate regularly shifts to *kk* in Alamannic and Bavarian (*likkan*). As for the other positions, medial *g* is far more frequent than *k* (*stîgan*), and initial *k* (*kast*), though predominant in the earliest records, is never entirely free from the competition of *g*.

Other Dialect Differences

Besides the varying reflexes of the Old High German Consonant Shift, the Old High German dialects naturally show other differences as well. Below I discuss a few of them.

By the end of the Old High German period, the old Germanic voice-less fricative *þ* (also written *th*) had changed to *d* in all dialects, through an intermediate voiced fricative (as in "then") sometimes spelled *dh*. This change, however, originated in the southeast of the language area, and is documented in different dialects at different times. Thus we find *d* for *þ* in the earliest Bavarian texts, but this change is only completed in the second half of the eighth century in the Alamannic area. East Franconian falls to the change during the ninth century, with Rhenish Franconian a few decades behind it. Only in the tenth and eleventh centuries does Middle Franconian follow suit.

By the Old High German Diphthongization, original *ô* goes to the diphthong *uo*, a change noted earlier in this chapter. Yet this change, too, takes place earlier in some dialects than in others. It appears earliest in Rhenish Franconian, in the eighth century; later in East Franconian, South Rhenish Franconian, and Alamannic, in the late eighth and early ninth centuries; and latest of all in Bavarian, in the late ninth century. In the ninth century, Alamannic and South Rhenish Franconian show the characteristic intermediate form *ua*, which sets them off both from the northern forms (Rhenish Franconian *uo*) and from the eastern ones (Bavarian *ô* and, later, *uo*).

By a combination of *a*-umlaut and *i*-umlaut, the original Germanic diphthong *eu* shows a twofold reflex in the Franconian dialects: *io* (earlier *eo*) when *a*, *e*, or *o* follows in the next syllable (*biotan* 'offer', *liogan* 'tell a lie', *klioban* 'cleave'); *iu* otherwise *biutu* 'I offer', *liugis* 'you lie', *kliubit* 'he cleaves'). This rule is disrupted in Alamannic and Bavarian, where *iu* is found before labial or velar consonants regardless of the following vowel. Thus before the labial consonant *b* we find *kliuban* as well as *kliubit*, and before the velar *g* we find *liugan* as well as *liugis*. Only before *h* and dental consonants like *d* do Alamannic and Bavarian follow the Franconian alternation rule.

Though all the Old High German dialects show short forms of the verbs for 'go' and 'stand', all the Franconian dialects show a marked preference for *gên* and *stên*. Alamannic, on the other hand, shows only *gân* and *stân*. Bavarian appears to be happy with either pronunciation.

The above by no means exhausts the catalogue of differences between the various Old High German dialects, but exhaustiveness was not the intention. Rather, I have tried in this section, using Old High German as an example, merely to illustrate the degree of variation that can be found in what is sometimes characterized as a single language or language stage.

FURTHER READING

Bostock, J. Knight. *A Handbook on Old High German Literature.* Rev. K. C. King and D. R. McLintock. Oxford: Clarendon, 1976.

Braune, Wilhelm, and Hans Eggers. *Althochdeutsche Grammatik.* 13th ed. Tübingen: Niemeyer, 1975.

Eggers, Hans. *Deutsche Sprachgeschichte.* Vol. 1, *Das Althochdeutsche.* Reinbek bei Hamburg: Rowohlt, 1963.

Keller, R. E. *The German Language.* Atlantic Highlands, N.J.: Humanities Press, 1978.

Lockwood, W. B. *An Informal History of the German Language.* Cambridge: Heffer, 1965.

Penzl, Herbert. *Geschichtliche deutsche Lautlehre.* Munich: Hüber, 1969. [See esp. chs. 2, 3.]

Schwarz, Ernst. *Germanische Stammeskunde.* Heidelberg: Winter, 1956. [See esp. chs. 30–37.]

Sonderegger, Stefan. "Althochdeutsche Sprache." In L. E. Schmitt, ed., *Kurzer Grundriss der germanischen Philologie bis 1500,* vol. 1, *Sprachgeschichte,* pp. 288–346. Berlin: de Gruyter, 1970.

Thompson, E. A. *The Early Germans.* Oxford: Clarendon, 1965.

Waterman, J. T. *A History of the German Language.* 2d ed. Seattle: University of Washington Press, 1976.

10

THE GROUPING OF THE GERMANIC LANGUAGES

In Chapter 1, I presented a family tree for the Germanic languages, indicating, however, that many problems attach to it. Below I repeat that tree, somewhat modified, as Figure 4. This particular tree has a long history, going back to 1860, when it was first proposed by the German linguist August Schleicher, and it is still found in many handbooks. Remarkably, it has enjoyed this longevity in the face of massive objections almost from the very beginning. The actual existence of a proto-language one could call "West Germanic" has always been doubtful, and the existence of troubling correspondences between, for example, the West Germanic languages and Old Norse on the one hand, and Old Norse and Gothic on the other, has called the initial tripartite split of Proto-Germanic into question. Furthermore, the implications of using any family-tree model (*Stammbaum*) at all have made some scholars seek a new way of representing the relationship.

In this chapter I would like to present some of the theories that have been advanced concerning the interrelationships of the Germanic languages, along with the data upon which they have been based. Thus to begin with, in the chart below I have brought together many of the observations I have already made in discussing the individual Old Germanic languages. Not all the language phenomena treated in the individual chapters will be found here, however. Specifically, many phenomena that are peculiar to a given language have been omitted, since what I am interested in at this point are those features that may shed some light on the connections between the various languages, and thus enable us to order them in some systematic way.

There are several notable exceptions to this principle. That is, I note several cases where a single language shows a development that none of the other languages does, or fails to show a development that all the

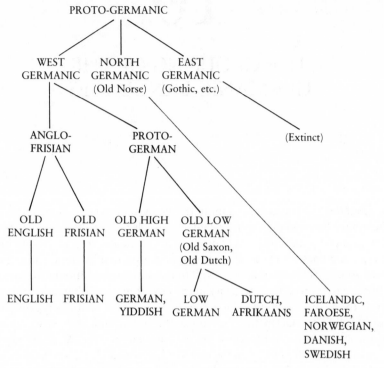

Fig. 4.   The traditional Germanic family tree.

others undergo. In such cases I have presented the data because one scholar or another has considered them significant for the grouping of the Germanic languages.

Before I go on to study the various language groupings that have been suggested, and the linguistic evidence for them, I should point out that an individual linguistic feature may be found in two or more languages for a number of different reasons:

1. The languages in question may have retained an archaic feature already found in the proto-language, whereas other languages have replaced that feature with a new one.

2. The languages in question may have chosen one feature from among options already available in the proto-language (sometimes called *doublets*, though the number is not necessarily restricted to two), while other languages chose a different one.

3. The languages in question may have developed the feature independently and coincidentally.

4. The languages in question may have developed the feature semi-independently, but in line with structural similarities between them (sometimes called *drift*).

5. The languages in question may have developed the feature when the people speaking them formed a single speech community, albeit with some dialectal variation.

As one might expect, scholars disagree about the probative value of shared features derived from several of these sources (should one count at all shared features of type 1?), and about which sources account for particular features (does a given similarity belong to type 3, 4, or 5?). They also disagree on the weight one should give to phonological, grammatical, or lexical similarities, on the time period during which a given change took place, and even on issues such as whether intervening seas help or hinder common development of language.

Virtually all twentieth-century scholars recognize that the traditional family tree (*Stammbaum*) seriously distorts the ways that languages and dialects relate to each other. Thus with no geographical component to the model, such a diagram essentially denies the possibility of a common development in two dialects after they have been relegated to separate branches by some change found in one but not the other. The situation found in the Germanic languages will scarcely allow one to hold on to this view of language relationship. Nevertheless, I agree with Hans Kuhn (1952–53, 1955–56) when he accuses some of the scholars in this field of allowing the old *Stammbaum* way of thinking to influence their evaluation of the data.

Another thorny point in the discussion of how to group the Germanic languages is the weighting one should give to archeological evidence. Some scholars give it great weight, to the extent that it influences their evaluation of the linguistic data. Others feel that the linguistic data should be evaluated in their own right, then correlated if possible with findings from archeology and ethnography. In view of my impression that there exists no more consensus in the latter fields than among Germanic linguists, this attitude strikes me as wise. Nonetheless, the findings of archeology and ethnography are indispensable to the arguments of a number of scholars, and we will thus have some occasion to discuss them below.

Before I point out the linguistic connections existing between the various older Germanic languages, I should perhaps outline how the chart is to be interpreted. On the left I have listed a number of features (though by no means all of them) that have played a role in the determination of Germanic dialect grouping. In some cases I need simply note (with a plus or a minus sign) whether a given language shows that fea-

Comparative Features in the Older Germanic Languages

	Goth.	ON
PHONOLOGY		
Vowels:		
1. PGmc. $\mathit{\ae}$ $(\hat{e}_1)$	$\hat{e}$	$\hat{a}$
2. *i–e, u–o* regulated before C*	+	−
3. Umlaut	−	+
4. PGmc. *a, â* → *o, ô* before nasal	−	−
5. PGmc. *ai*	*ai*	*ei*
6. PGmc. *au*	*au*	*au*
7. PGmc. $\hat{e}_2$ → *ie, ô* → *uo*	−	−
Consonants:		
8. Sharpening	+	+
9. Rhotacism	−	+
10. PGmc. *ngw* → *ng*	−	−
11. PGmc. *fl-* → *þl-*	+	−
12. Gemination	−	*k, g* only
13. PGmc. nasal lost before fricative	−	with *s*
14. Assibilation	−	−
15. PGmc. *CrV* → *CVr*	−	−
16. PGmc. *-n* lost	−	+
17. Consonant shift	−	−
MORPHOLOGY		
Nouns, pronouns:		
18. PGmc. masc. nom. sg. *-az*	*-s*	*-r*
19. Masc. *a*-stem nom. pl.	*-ôs*	*-ar*
20. Masc. 3 pers. pro., nom. sg.	*is*	*hann*
21. Intensified demonstrative	−	+
22. Dual pronouns	+	+
23. Distinct dat. & acc. in 1 & 2 pers. pro.	+	+
24. Reflexive pro.	+	+
Verbs:		
25. Reduplication	+	−
26. *-nan* class	+	+
27. 2 sg. pret. ind.	*-t*	*-t*
28. 3 sg. pres. ind., 'be'	*ist*	*er*
29. Pres. ind. pl.	*-am, -iþ, -and*	*-om, -eþ, -a*
30. Short forms of 'stand', 'go'	−	−
31. Gerund	−	−

* See Chapter 3, pp. 58–59.

OS	OE	OF	OLF	OHG
		PHONOLOGY		
â	(*â* →) *ǣ*	(*â* →) *ê*	*â*	*â*
–	–	–	–	–
+	+	+	+	+
(–)	+	+	–	–
ê	*ā*	*â, ê*	*ei, ê*	*ei, ê*
ô	*ēa*	*â*	*ou, ô*	*ou, ô*
(–)	–	–	+	+
–	–	–	–	–
+	+	+	+	+
+	+	+	+	+
–	–	–	–	–
+	+	+	+	+
f, s, þ	*f, s, þ*	*f, s, þ*	–	–
–	+	+	–	–
–	+	+	–	–
–	–	+	–	–
–	–	–	–	+
		MORPHOLOGY		
0	0	0	0	0
-os	*-as*	*-ar, -a*	*-a*	*-a*
hê	*hē*	*hi*	*he*	*er*
+	+	+	(+)	+
+	+	–	–	–
–	–	–	–	+
–	–	–	(+)	+
–	–	–	–	–
–	–	–	–	–
-i	*-i*	(*-st*)	*-i*	*-i*
is, ist	*is*	*is*	*ist*	*ist*
-ad	*-að*	*-ath*	*-un, -it, -unt*	*-emês, -et, -ant*
+	+	+	+	+
+	+	+	+	+

ture. In other cases, I have found it useful or necessary to list language features. These may be simply the reflexes in each language of a Proto-Germanic sound given on the left (as in rows 5 and 6), or they may be the conditions for the change given on the left (as in rows 12 and 13). In many instances I exemplify the word, grammatical category, or grammatical distinction listed on the left (as in rows 19 and 20).

The items in parentheses are in the nature of interpretations rather than direct observations, although none of these interpretations is very controversial. In row 1, I simply reiterate the argument, given in the individual language chapters, that Proto-Germanic *ǣ* (*ê₁*) originally went to *â* in Old English and Old Frisian, with *ǣ* and *ê* being later developments. In row 4, I mean to note the fact that Old Saxon in general does not show the phenomenon, though there are some examples in the texts. A similar interpretation should be given to the parentheses in row 7, although it may be that some Old Saxon dialects organically showed this development.

The parentheses in row 21 are meant to indicate that Old Low Franconian probably had an intensified demonstrative pronoun, though the texts do not show us one. Those in row 24 emphasize the fact that the reflexive pronoun found in Old Low Franconian is a clear borrowing. Finally, the parentheses in row 27 enclose the form of the second person singular preterite indicative actually found in Old Frisian, but are meant to remind the reader that this is probably a late development.

Similarities Between Gothic and Old Norse

Of the features that I have listed in the chart above, a number stand out by virtue of their being shared by Gothic and Old Norse but not by any of the West Germanic languages. These include rows 8, 10, 12 (insofar as gemination does not happen in Old Norse), 18, 26, 27, 30, and 31. In addition to these common features, some scholars have claimed significance for the presence of a different inflection of the feminine present participle in Gothic and Old Norse (*-în*) as opposed to West Germanic (*-jô*), and for a number of other features I have not discussed in the individual chapters.

Ernst Schwarz (1951) lists 25 such points of similarity between Gothic and Old Norse, including most of the ones cited above. On the basis of this linguistic evidence, and in line with the archeological probability that the Goths originally came from Sweden, Schwarz proposes that the first basic split in the Germanic languages was one between North and South Germanic, with Gothic and the other East Germanic languages belonging to North Germanic. The languages labeled "West Germanic" in Figure 4 constitute the South Germanic branch in this view. The elements that Gothic and Old Norse share, according to Schwarz, were jointly developed at least before the Goths departed for the south coast of the Baltic in the first century B.C., and probably significantly earlier. Those elements shared by North and West Germanic, on the other hand, are much later, and are mainly due to southern influence on the north into the sixth century A.D.

The existence of an early connection between Gothic and Old Norse has been accepted by other scholars (e.g., Lehmann, Schirmunski). In general, however, they assign the weight of evidence to fewer features, and also seem more flexible than Schwarz about the likelihood of significant realignment over time.

On the other hand, Schwarz's theory has been sharply attacked, especially by Kuhn. The latter scholar basically rejects any early affinity between Gothic and Old Norse, especially one established as early as Schwarz would have it, and grants at most that Gothic and those dialects of pre–Old Norse clustered around the Baltic Sea might, at a relatively late date, have shown the superficial beginnings of a common language community.

A corollary of Kuhn's view is that the ancestors of Old Norse and the West Germanic languages remained relatively undifferentiated until a rather late date (Kuhn suggests the fifth century). This corollary is on the whole supported by runic inscriptions in the older futhark, which show remarkably archaic and uniform language forms through that century. We will discuss this proposed relationship between Old Norse and the West Germanic languages further below.

Kuhn completely rejects nineteen of the twenty-five features listed by Schwarz, eighteen because they are simply cases of common retention of an older situation, and one because it involves the common loss of a single lexical item (though the item in question is 'do'). Of the features I have listed above, rows 10, 12, 18, 26, 27, 30, and 31 may all be seen as common retentions (or a common choice from doublets), as may the common feminine present participial ending. Thus of the features I have cited in this section precisely one represents a common innovation, namely row 8, the sharpening of original *jj* and *ww*. This shared feature is indeed the centerpiece of the so-called Gothonordic hypothesis.

Kuhn maintains that most, if not all, of the few true innovations shared by Gothic and Old Norse are in fact not found in the entire Old

Norse area, but only in the east (Sweden, and perhaps Denmark). And though the manuscripts of Old Norse do show instances of sharpening even in the west, we find no evidence of sharpening in the runic inscriptions until the age of the vikings, long after any possible contact with the Goths. Thus here, too, we are probably confronted with an innovation originally shared only by Gothic and some eastern Norse dialects.

Kuhn is clearly reluctant to concede even these limited common innovations, and places them quite late, at a point after the Goths' emigration from Sweden (first century B.C.), but before their departure for the southeast (second century A.D.). The phenomena in question, then, would reflect a nascent speech community, linked by trade, on the shores of the Baltic Sea, a community sundered by the departure of the Goths.

Kuhn may have been a bit hasty in simply dismissing shared features as shared retentions, however. And in any case, not all scholars would agree that shared retentions are worthless as evidence. Lehmann, for example, gives weight not only to sharpening (row 8), but also to the retention of -t as marker of the second person singular preterite indicative (which Schirmunski would see as a common choice from doublets) and the failure to develop short forms for 'go' and 'stand'. In addition, although he concedes that the -nan verbs make use of inherited material, he points out that Gothic and Old Norse stand apart from the other Germanic languages in utilizing this material to form a productive class of inchoative verbs. A similar argument may be made for the -în inflection on feminine present participles.

It seems obvious that there is no last word in this argument. T. L. Markey, for example, in general shares Kuhn's skepticism about a Gothic–Old Norse speech community. Regarding the five points Lehmann finds persuasive, given in the last paragraph, Markey suggests (1) that sharpening is a late development, with disturbing divergences between Gothic and Old Norse (ddj vs. ggj), runic counterexamples for Old Norse, exceptions in Gothic, and possible parallels in West Germanic; (2) that the -nan class has some parallels in West Germanic (note that Lehmann would not deny this, but for him it is the productivity of this class that sets Gothic and Old Norse apart); (3) that -t as the marker of the second person singular preterite indicative was a parallel but independent choice between doublets for Gothic and Old Norse (no real evidence is given, though possible reasons for the particular choice in each language are adduced); (4) that even the earliest texts in Old Swedish show instances of stâ for 'stand' and gâ for 'go'; (5) that the choice of -în over -jô for the feminine present participle is another parallel but independent choice for Gothic and Old Norse (Markey advances some reasons for West Germanic's not choosing -*in*).

The current consensus, I believe, is that there are a few significant points of similarity between Gothic and Old Norse, indicating close contact at some point. They are hardly numerous enough to argue for the existence of a distinctly separate Gothonordic group in early Germanic. Indeed, they may not be older than some of the features that Old Norse and West Germanic share in opposition to Gothic, and the latter are clearly more extensive (see below). It seems to me only the specter of the old *Stammbaum* that causes scholars to take such strong positions pro or con on the value of the features linking Gothic and Old Norse.

Similarities Between Old Norse and West Germanic

If we now look at the features on our chart that are shared by Old Norse and the West Germanic languages, but not by Gothic, we note the following rows: 1, 2, 3, 9, 11, 12 (insofar as there is gemination in Old Norse), 21, and 25. I omit here characteristics shared by Old Norse and *some* of the West Germanic languages; these will be discussed further below. We might also add to those features found on the chart the loss in all languages but Gothic of the original passive inflection on verbs, the selection of new abstract noun suffixes (-*dôm* and -*skapi*) found only as root nouns in Gothic, and numerous other innovations it is unnecessary to list here.

On the whole, scholars do not deny the existence of these shared characteristics. They do disagree somewhat about their age, and, as I showed in the last section, about their relative importance in setting up the Germanic family tree. Still, it is clear that the characteristics shared by North and West Germanic range widely in both phonology and grammar, affect a very large part of the lexicon, and attest to a long period of contact between speakers of the languages involved.

Kuhn, for one, believes that the period of common development, and of relative linguistic uniformity, lasted through the fifth century, and that the break between North and West Germanic occurred only with the great migrations of that century, especially that of the Angles and Saxons to Britain. Thereafter the North Germanic group underwent a rather rapid series of changes, which differentiated it greatly from the southern groups. Within the northern group, developments were remarkably uniform for several centuries, though eventually it diverged into two subgroups, western and eastern.

Perhaps the linchpin of Kuhn's argument, as indicated above, is the remarkable uniformity, and, as far as the later northern and western languages are concerned, dialect neutrality of the runic inscriptions through the fifth century. Other scholars have maintained that runic writing was inherently conservative, and that it served as a kind of dialect-neutral koiné long after the spoken language had undergone differentiation. Markey, on the evidence of the (admittedly vague) dating of various phonetic and grammatical changes, sees the split between North and West gradually occurring between about 300 and 450, a dating that seems reasonable.

Similarities Within West Germanic

Up to this point, I have used the term "West Germanic" as if it were on a par somehow with "North Germanic" and "East Germanic," that is, as if the subgroup had the kind of uniformity and consistency that are found in the various dialects of Old Norse, and that are assumed, given the limited data from a single language (Gothic), for East Germanic. Some such uniformity is indeed presupposed by any attempt to make West Germanic a node on a family tree, as is frequently done.

Yet any such assumption of a unitary West Germanic encounters major problems. There are enormous differences between the various languages assigned to this subgroup, differences that in some cases surely go back to a point preceding the split between North and West mentioned in the last section.

Nonetheless, there are a few significant features that the West Germanic languages share with each other, but not with either North Germanic or East Germanic. In our chart, these include rows 10, 12 (though remember the more restricted gemination in Old Norse), 18, 26, 27, 30, and 31. We may also list the feminine present participle ending -jô, already mentioned above.

Kuhn would place many of these developments quite late, in the fourth century or later. Others would claim that they occurred centuries earlier. It seems clear, however, that, whenever they occurred, there were already some fairly significant differences among the dialects called West Germanic. In fact, most modern scholars are quite chary of postulating anything like a unitary West Germanic language at all: they see almost from the beginning of the split between North and West a threefold division of West Germanic into Ingvaeonic, Istvaeonic, and Irminonic (sometimes under other names, such as North Sea Germanic, Weser–Rhine Germanic, and Elbe Germanic respectively). At best, then, we can speak of an extended West Germanic language community, through which common innovations could spread more or less quickly, despite other differences.

A number of innovations that appear to have spread less quickly, rather than more, will be discussed in the next section.

Features of the Ingvaeonic Languages

I should begin by noting that "Ingvaeonic," though sometimes taken as referring to a subgroup of West Germanic containing Old English and Old Frisian, commonly has a wider application. A number of languages besides Old English and Old Frisian (though not equally strongly, and not always the same languages) show what are called Ingvaeonic features mixed in with non-Ingvaeonic ones, and sometimes Old English or Old Frisian may fail to show a feature commonly called Ingvaeonic. Worse, perhaps, a number of Ingvaeonic features appear to be present in Old Norse, not a West Germanic language at all.

I mention below several features from the chart that are taken to be Ingvaeonisms, but that are shared by different groups of languages. These by no means exhaust the linguistic features that have been identified as Ingvaeonic, but they do give a reasonable overview of the most important ones.

Old English and Old Frisian alone, with a few reflections in the lesser Old Saxon texts, share items 1, 4, 5 (though Frisian has $\hat{e}$ in addition to $\hat{a}$ for older ai), 14, and 15. Frisian alone shows a development of au to $\hat{a}$ (row 6), which is considered to be the "genuine" Ingvaeonic development. Arguments deriving Old English $\bar{e}a$ from $\hat{a}$ must be considered unlikely. English probably followed its own unique route.

Old English, Old Frisian, and Old Saxon share items 13 (also found, in a more restricted way, in Old Norse), 24 (though recall that the reflexive pronoun is clearly borrowed in Old Low Franconian), 28 (with some backsliding in Old Saxon; note also the t-less form found in Old Norse), and 29. Old English and Old Saxon, but not Old Frisian, share feature 19 (plural in -Vs). Markey feels that both documented Old Frisian plurals are secondary, the original ending having been -as. The ending -ar, so like Old Norse, is probably a later borrowing from Scandinavian.

Old English, Old Frisian, Old Saxon, and Old Low Franconian, finally, share features 20 (where note that Old Norse also shows initial h-, but otherwise goes its own route) and 23.

There is a great deal of disagreement about the age of some of these features. Theodor Frings (see "Further Reading"), for example, sees especially features like items 13, 20, and 23 as representing early Ingvaeonic and Istvaeonic innovations in opposition to Irminonic at a time when tribes speaking the latter dialect were still around the middle Elbe. But Markey clearly finds the h-pronouns (or at least their extension to other than masc. nom. sg. forms) to be a relatively late innovation, as the h-less form can frequently be found in enclitic position (after the verb and attached to it; see the Readings for Chap. 7). He agrees on the age of the nasal loss before spirants, and also on the age of the r-less (originally dative) forms mi/me and di/de, but believes with Kuhn that the actual coalescence of accusative and dative is late.

Schwarz believes that all Ingvaeonic innovations must have taken place before about 450, when the Angles and the Saxons decamped for England. Kuhn (and, less aggressively, Markey) would place a good number of them, including a large group of features peculiar to Old English and Old Frisian, at a point after the Anglo-Saxons were already settled in their new home. These include such famous Ingvaeonisms as the reflection of Proto-Germanic $\hat{æ}$ ($\hat{e}_1$) as $\hat{e}$ and $\bar{æ}$ (row 1 on the chart above), assibilation (row 14), and, as noted above, the coalescence of accusative and dative in first and second person personal pronouns. Schwarz is again clearly influenced by the idea that the North Sea was a barrier to further common development, whereas Kuhn sees it as a binding element.

These differences in the dating assigned to many Ingvaeonisms are reflected in the way that scholars approach Old Saxon. Everyone agrees that some Ingvaeonisms are well attested in Old Saxon texts, and others less well attested or absent. The question is whether they were present earlier, as, for example, Frings and Lehmann would maintain. In this case, we must assume that the earlier Saxon language, very Ingvaeonic in nature, was first changed and overlaid by the Istvaeonic characteristics of the tribes the Saxons had conquered, then subjected to even more de-Ingvaeonization by the increasing Frankish influence in Saxony.

Kuhn and Markey explain most of the absence of Ingvaeonic features in Old Saxon by maintaining that the language never had them. These particular innovations, in their view, are centered not in Schleswig-

Holstein, but on the more westerly North Sea coasts, both mainland and insular.

What, then, can we say about Ingvaeonisms and about Ingvaeonic? That Ingvaeonic was ever a unified linguistic subgroup of Germanic seems very doubtful. Even English and Frisian, clearly the central languages of the Ingvaeonic cluster, seem to have carried out independently (though in a mutually reinforcing way) a number of the innovations that supposedly characterize this group, while going different ways in other respects.

Obviously the North Sea area was a hotbed of innovations, even from the early period when North Germanic and West Germanic formed a reasonably unified dialect complex. A number of Ingvaeonisms, especially those shared at least in part by North Germanic, are probably from this period, such as item 13 on the chart above (nasal loss before fricative). Others, shared by Old Saxon and Old Low Franconian, can hardly have come much later, such as item 20. Even the merging of the accusative and dative in first and second personal pronouns, despite Kuhn's and Markey's well-argued objections, has such a wide distribution that it must have at least started taking place before 450. There is no question that the loss of *r* shown by *mi/me* and *di/de* antedates this period. It should be noted that it is inaccurate to designate many of these features as "Ingvaeonic," since they are shared by Istvaeonic dialects like Old Low Franconian.

Other Ingvaeonisms, including items 1, 4, and 15 on our chart, affecting essentially only Old English and Old Frisian, are arguably later than those mentioned above, and probably postdate the Anglo-Saxon move out of northern Germany. Some may have taken place while the bulk of the invaders of Britain were on the mainland, others after the invasion was complete, and still others (e.g., item 14, assibilation) centuries after the invasion of Britain. (Note that the assibilation itself may have been independent, but the preconditions, heavily palatalized [k^j] and [g^j], are unlikely to have been.)

Similarities Between Old High German and Old Low Franconian

In the last section we noted several similarities between Old Low Franconian and the "Ingvaeonic" languages proper. But of course in a great many ways Old Low Franconian is closer to Old High German, as is shown by rows 1, 4, 5, 6, 7, 13, 14, 15, 19, 28, and 29 on the chart above. To a great extent it is this middle position between Ingvaeonic and Irminonic dialects that characterizes Istvaeonic dialects, though they have a few distinctive characteristics of their own. Note, for example, the change of [ft] to [xt] found already in Old Low Franconian, and characteristic also of Modern Dutch. In addition, some of the innovations found in Old High German clearly spread out of the Franconian (hence Istvaeonic) area, for example the diphthongization of $\hat{e}$ ($\hat{e}_2$) and $\hat{o}$ to *ie* and *uo* (item 7).

Similarities Between Old High German and Gothic

In 1924, the famous German dialectologist Ferdinand Wrede published an article that shook the world of Germanic scholarship (see "Further Reading"). In his dialect work, Wrede had noted that a general loss of nasal before voiceless fricative in words like 'five' was not confined to northern Germany; it also occurred in a large part of southwestern Germany, in the Alamannic dialects. Furthermore, where the north had a unitary plural verb ending (thus without distinguishing the three persons), so did the southwest. The areas without nasal loss and without a unitary plural formed a sort of wedge between these two dialect regions, which was widest to the southeast, in the Bavarian area.

Wrede was already familiar with such wedges from his previous work in German dialectology. In general, they were the visible path left behind by language phenomena spreading from the southeast to the northwest and north, leaving untouched the relatively out-of-the-way southwest, and not making it all the way to the more northerly dialects. Undisputed examples of such phenomena are the expansion of Bavarian *gên* 'go', leaving relic *gân* areas to the southwest and the north, and the spread of the so-called Early New High German Diphthongization, which is responsible for changing (among other things) *hûs* 'house' to *haus*.

But in the case Wrede was looking at here, the characteristics found in the unaffected "relic" areas were Ingvaeonic! This observation led Wrede to the astonishing hypothesis that almost all of West Germanic had at one time had these and other Ingvaeonic characteristics, such as the pronoun *he* 'he', no reflexive pronoun, no distinction between accusative and dative in first and second personal pronouns, and so on, and that these characteristics had been overrun by a flood of non-Ingvaeonic characteristics from the southeast. And from whom were these characteristics supposed to have spread? From the Goths, of course, who at the appropriate time period were interacting with the Germans of the southeast. Note in this regard especially the correspondences between Gothic and Old High German in rows 13, 20, 23, 24, 28, and 29 on the chart above.

It should be noted that, except in the first two cases he examined, (nasal loss and unitary plural, items 13 and 29 on our chart), Wrede could not point to relic areas in the southwest that had escaped this "Gothicization." Thus even there we find *er* 'he', distinctions between accusative and dative in first and second personal pronouns, and the like. But far worse, scholars were soon able to show that even Wrede's central pieces of evidence, nasal loss and unitary plural endings, were relatively recent developments in Alamannic dialects, thus many centuries newer than Wrede would need them to be. They must be seen as parallel, totally independent developments of a not altogether unusual kind.

This is not to deny that Gothic and Old High German had opportunities to interact and even share language characteristics. Historically, they had at least two different opportunities: before the second century, when the Irminones and the Goths were settled in more or less adjacent areas in northern Germany; and in the fifth and sixth centuries, when both peoples were in and around the southeastern part of the Irminonic expansion area (Bavaria and Austria).

Frings has attributed at least a few shared characteristics to the earlier period, such as the nominative singular form of the masculine third personal pronoun *er = is*, and the etymologically identical word for 'how' (Goth. *hvaiwa*, OHG *hweo*). I see no way his attribution can be proved, since such examples clearly represent the continuation of older material, or at best a parallel choice between doublets.

From the later period, we have a number of Gothic loan words in Bavarian that clearly have to do with Gothic participation in the Christianization of Bavaria. Nobody disputes these rather superficial examples of language contact.

A Late-Breaking Theory

In a recent linguistically sophisticated and well-argued article, the German scholar Theo Vennemann advances a hypothesis whose implications go far beyond the issues discussed here, but that clearly have a bearing on the grouping of the Germanic languages. Against the standard view that the consonants of Old High German are secondary to those of the rest of the Germanic languages (since they are considered to be derived from the latter), Vennemann argues that these two systems are co-equal descendants of a Proto-Germanic consonant system different from either. He draws evidence not only from Germanic, but from Indo-European as well, and his conclusions, if accepted, will force a revision of large parts of Germanic and Indo-European scholarship.

The implications for the grouping of the Germanic languages are of course profound. As Vennemann notes, his theory could be seen as grouping High German dialects together as one major branch of Germanic, with all the other dialects (including Gothic, Norse, and the residue of West Germanic) forming the other. Vennemann himself seems to consider this conclusion unnecessary.

If Vennemann's hypothesis is correct, it would serve to indicate with even greater force how inadequate the family-tree method is for representing language relationships. For regardless of precisely when those innovations occurred that Vennemann calls the High Germanic and Low Germanic Sound Shifts (for High German and all the other Germanic dialects respectively), we run into major problems. If these shifts occurred early—say while Gothic was still being spoken in the north (an unlikely assumption, given most scholars' placing of the High German Consonant Shift in the sixth century)—then Old High German, now on a completely different branch from the other languages, nonetheless underwent a great number of changes in common with all of them except Gothic, then with a subset of them excluding Norse. On the other hand, if Vennemann's shifts occurred a bit later, say after the Goths' departure from northern Germany, another major common shift between languages on different branches would be involved (Gothic and the northwest languages besides pre–High German undergoing the Low Germanic Shift). Moreover, if the High Germanic part of the shift occurred as late as the sixth century, as most scholars would have it, then it really cannot be counted as the primary Germanic split at all, since both Old Norse and the soon-to-be-defunct Gothic had by then established their clear separation through other innovations. Given the traditional interpretation of a tree diagram, their common participation in the Low Germanic shift must then be seen as independent.

Conclusions

It seems clear, as Kuhn has noted, that one of the major issues in the grouping of the Germanic languages is whether one should give so much weight to archeological or ethnological evidence that it dominates the discussion, or even replaces linguistic argument entirely. His objections to the work of Schwarz and Frings highlight this issue well. They project much later linguistic distinctions, sometimes based on strikingly few examples, back into a period when only nonlinguistic distinctions can be observed—and not always very reliably, either. Yet even Kuhn will occasionally appeal to archeological data, as he does when arguing for a rather late linguistic contact between the Anglo-Saxons and the Frisians.

Vennemann's article represents the opposite end of the spectrum (though the task of grouping the Germanic languages is clearly far from his mind). Here we have no idea about when the significant split is supposed to have taken place, and we can only speculate about the possible geographic collocations of tribes that would give flesh to the proposed common developments.

I hope that the preceding discussion has given the reader some insight into the possible, and even likely, course of events. Once one abandons the rigid dichotomies of the *Stammbaum*, one is dealing with a fluid, changeable situation in which dialect communities may alternately diverge, diverge only in part, converge, converge only in part, and otherwise behave like human groupings rather than biological species trees. It seems unlikely that we will ever be able to impose more order on the relationships between the Germanic languages than has already been established.

FURTHER READING

van Coetsem, Frans. "Zur Entwicklung der germanischen Grundsprache." In L. E. Schmitt, ed., *Kurzer Grundriss der germanischen Philologie bis 1500*, pp. 1–93. Berlin: de Gruyter, 1970.

Frings, Theodor. *Grundlegung einer Geschichte der deutschen Sprache*. 3d ed. Halle (Saale): Niemeyer, 1957.

Kufner, Herbert L. "The Grouping and Separation of the Germanic Languages." In Frans van Coetsem and Herbert L. Kufner, eds., *Toward a Grammar of Proto-Germanic*, pp. 71–97. Tübingen: Niemeyer, 1972.

Kuhn, Hans. Review of Ernst Schwarz, *Goten, Nordgermanen, Angelsachsen* [q.v.]. *Anzeiger für deutsches Altertum und deutsche Literatur* 66 (1952–53): 45–52.

———. "Zur Gliederung der germanischen Sprachen." *Zeitschrift für deutsches Altertum und deutsche Literatur* 86 (1955–56): 1–47.

Lehmann, Winfred P. "The Grouping of the Germanic Languages." In Henrik Birnbaum and Jaan Puhvel, eds., *Ancient Indo-European Dialects*, pp. 13–27. Berkeley and Los Angeles: University of California Press, 1966.

Markey, Thomas L. *Germanic Dialect Grouping and the Position of Ingvaeonic.* Innsbrucker Beiträge zur Sprachwissenschaft, 15. Innsbruck: Institut für Sprachwissenschaft der Universität, 1976.

Schirmunski, V. "Über die altgermanischen Stammesdialekte." *Acta Linguistica Academiae Scientiarum Hungaricae* 15 (1965): 1–36.

Schwarz, Ernst. *Goten, Nordgermanen, Angelsachsen: Studien zur Ausgliederung der germanischen Sprachen.* Bern: Francke, 1951.

Vennemann, Theo. "Hochgermanisch und Niedergermanisch: Die Verzweigungstheorie der germanisch-deutschen Lautverschiebungen." *Beiträge zur Geschichte der deutschen Sprache und Literatur* 106 (1984): 1–45.

Voyles, Joseph B. "Gothic and Germanic." *Language* 44 (1968): 720–46.

Wrede, F. "Ingwäonisch und Westgermanisch." *Zeitschrift für deutsche Mundarten* 19 (1924): 270–83.

APPENDIX

APPENDIX: TRANSLATIONS
OF READINGS

Chapter 3: Gothic

Parable of the Sower and the Seed

And again Jesus began to teach at (the) sea, and gathered themselves to him of multitude much, so that him going into a ship to sit on (the) sea; and all that multitude next to (the) sea on (the) shore was. And he taught them in parables much, and said to them in teaching his: "Listen! Lo, went out the sower to sow with his seed. And it happened, while he sowed, one (lot) then fell beside (the) way, and came birds and ate that. Another then fell on (a) stony (place), where it did not have much earth, and soon went up, because it did not have of deep earth; at (the) sun then going up it burned up, and because it did not have roots, it dried up. And some fell in thorns; and rose up over the thorns and strangled that, and fruit it did not give. And some fell in earth good, and gave fruit going up and growing and bore one thirty and one sixty and one a hundred. And he said: the (one who) may have ears hearing, let him hear."

Gabriel and Mary

Thereupon then in month sixth sent was angel Gabriel from God into (the) city of Galilee that is called Nazareth, to (a) virgin in engagement to (a) man, of whom (the) name (was) Joseph, from (the) house of David, and the name of the virgin (was) Mary. And going inside the angel to her said: "Rejoice, blessed with grace, (the) Lord (is) with you; blessed (are) you among women. . . ." And said (the) angel to her: "Do not fear ye, Mary, for you have received grace from God. And lo, you (will) conceive into (your) womb and (will) bear (a) son, and you should call his name Jesus. And he (will) become great, and (the) son of the Highest (will) be called, and (will) give to him (the) Lord God (the) seat of David his father. And that (one will) rule over (the) house of Jacob into eternity, and of kingdom his (will) not become (an) end." Said then Mary to the angel: "How could be that, since (a) man I do not know?" And answering the angel said to her: "(The) Spirit Holy (will) come to you, and (the) power of the Highest (will) come upon you, so that he who is born, holy (will) be called, the son of God. . . ." Said then Mary: "Lo, (I am the) maiden of (the) Lord, let it happen to me according to word your." And went away from her the angel.

Chapter 4: Old Norse

Parable of the Sower and the Seed

That one who to sow wants with seed his, then goes he out. And while he is on the way, then falls some down on next to the way, and come birds to (there) and eat it. And some falls on dry earth and stony, and because there was shallow soil and no moisture, then ran quickly up, and dried up then immediately from (the) sun's over-heat. Some ran up in the middle of thorn bushes and hawthorns, and from their sharpness then falls that soon down to the earth and perishes. But some came in good earth and turned out to yield with a hundred parts more than he sowed.

Thor and the Giant Skrymir

Then spoke Skrymir to Thor that he wants to lie down to sleep, "but you* take the supplies bag, and prepare for dinner for you." Next goes to sleep Skrymir and snored hard, and Thor took the supplies bag and shall untie (it). But such is to say, as unbelievable (as it) may appear, that no knot got he untied, and no strap-end (got he) moved so that then it were looser than before. And when he sees that that work cannot be of use, then became he angry, gripped then the hammer Mjollnir with two hands and walked forward with the other foot [*i.e.*, 'step by step'] to there (where) Skrymir lay, and strikes on head to him; and Skrymir wakes up and asks whether leaf any fell on head to him, or whether they had then eaten, and are ready for beds. Thor says that they will then to sleep go. Go they† then under another oak. Is it to you true to say, that not was

---

* In this episode, Thor is traveling with several other people of both sexes: hence the plural (in the third person occasionally neuter plural).
† See preceding note.

then fearless to sleep. But at mid night, then hears Thor that Skrymir snores so that it resounds in the woods. Then stands he up and goes to him, swings the hammer quickly and hard and strikes from above into the middle of crown to him; he sees that the end of (the) hammerhead sinks deep in the head. But in that moment wakes up Skrymir and spoke: "What is it now? Fell acorn some on head to me? Or what is going on concerning you, Thor?" But Thor went back quickly and answers that he was then newly woken, said that then was mid night and still was time to sleep. Then considered Thor that, if he were to come thus on (the) opportunity to hit him the third blow, that never should he see himself afterwards; lies now and watches if Skrymir went to sleep fast. And a little before dawn then hears he that Skrymir must gone to sleep have; stands then up and runs at him, swings then the hammer with all (his) strength and strikes at the temple that was turned up; sinks then the hammer up to the handle. But Skrymir sat up and stroked over (his) cheek and spoke: "May birds some sit in the tree over me? Me suspected [*i.e.,* 'I suspected'], when I woke up, that droppings some from the branches were falling on head to me. Awake are you, Thor? Time it must be up to stand and get dressed. And not have you now long journey forward to the fortress that called is Utgard."

Chapter 5: Old Saxon

Parable of the Sower and the Seed

He stood* then by a water's shore,
not wanted (he) then with that crowd   over that of men folk
on the land above   the teaching to make known,
but went him then the good (one)   and his disciples with him,
peacechild of God,   to the flood nearer
onto a ship in,   and it to push off ordered
from (the) land farther,   that him the people so many,
people might not crowd.   Stood man many,
people by the water,   where mighty Christ
over that of people folk   (the) teaching said:
"Well, I to you say can," said he,   "companions my,
how him a man began   on earth to sow

---

* Here, as elsewhere in this Reading, apparently reflexive pronouns are used with no clear contribution to the meaning; the translation reflects this by leaving such pronouns untranslated.

wheat with his hands.   Some it on hard stone
from above fell,   of earth did not have,
that it there could grow   or of roots get,
sprout or hold fast,   but became that seed lost,
that there on the rock lay.   Some it afterwards on land fell,
on earth of noble sort: it began after that
to grow prosperously   and of roots to get,
grew to joys: was the land so good,
splendidly equipped.   Some afterwards fallen was
on a hard street,   where steps went,
of horses (the) hoofbeats   and of men (the) steps;
it became there on the earth   and afterwards went up,
it began on the way to grow;   then it afterwards of the people
    destroyed,
of the folk (the) traffic great   and birds gleaned (it),
that of it to the owner anything   afterwards was not able
to become according to wish,   of that (which) there on the way fell.
Some was it then fallen,   where so many stood
of thick thorns   in the day;
it became there on (the) earth   and afterwards went up,
sprouted there and held fast.   There struck there afterwards weeds in
    and among,
prevented for it the growth: had it of the forest (the) covering
from the beginning covered over,   so that it not could to any good
    thing become,
if it the thorns so   crowd could."

The Lord's Prayer

Father our   of people's children,
you are in the high   of (the) heavens kingdom,
hallowed be your name   with every word.
Come your   powerful kingdom.
Let become your will   over this world all,
as same on earth   as there above is
in the high   of (the) heavens kingdom.
Give us of days every aid,   lord the good,
your holy help,   and absolve us, heaven's protector,
of many offenses,   just as we for other men do.
Not let us lead astray   evil demons

so forth according to their will,   if we worthy are,
but help us against all   evil deeds.

Chapter 6: Old English

Parable of the Sower and the Seed

And again he began them at the sea to teach. And him was (a) great multitude to gathered, so that he on ship went, and on the sea was; and all that multitude around the sea was on land. And he them much in parables taught, and them to said in his teaching, "Listen: out went the sower his seed to sow. And when he sowed, some fell next to the way, and birds came and it ate. Some fell onto (a) stony (place), where it did not have much earth, and soon up went; and because it did not have of earth thickness, when it up went, the sun it scorched, and it withered, because it root did not have. And some fell in thorns; then rose the thorns and choked that, and it fruit did not bear. And some fell on good land, and it gave climbing up and growing fruit; and one brought thirtyfold, one sixtyfold, one (a) hundredfold." And he said, "Listen, that one who ears may have to hear."

Cynewulf and Cyneheard

Here [*i.e.*, 'at this time'] Cynewulf deprived Sigebryht of his kingdom, and of (the) West Saxons (the) counselors (did too), for unjust deeds, except for Hampshire. And he kept that until he slew the nobleman who him longest stayed by, and him then Cynewulf to Andred expelled and he there remained until him a swineherd stabbed to death at Privet's Flood; and he avenged the aldorman Cumbra.

And that Cynewulf often in great battles fought against (the) Britons. And after 31 winters after he (the) kingdom had, he wanted to expel a prince who was Cyneheard called; and that Cyneheard was that Sigebryht's brother. And then discovered he [*i.e.*, Cyneheard] the king with (a) small band of men in (the) company of a woman at Merantown and him there overtook and the bower from without surrounded before him the men discovered who with the king were. And then perceived the king that, and he to the door went and then nobly him(self) defended until he on the prince looked, and then out (he) rushed at him and him greatly wounded; and they all at the king were fighting until they him slain had.

And then at the woman's cries discovered the king's thanes the disturbance, and then thither ran whoever then ready became, and most quickly. And of them the prince to each cattle and life offered, and of them none it to take wanted:* but they always fighting were until they all lay dead except for one British hostage, and he very wounded was.

Then in (the) morning heard that the king's thanes who him behind were, that the king slain was. Then rode they thither, and his nobleman Osric and Wiferth his thane and the men who he behind him left earlier, and the prince at the fort met where the king slain lay. And the gates (the king's men) them against locked up had [*i.e.*, 'and they had the gates locked against them'], and then to there went. And then offered he [the prince] them their own judgment of cattle and land, if they him of the kingdom granted, and to them made known that their kinsmen him with were, those who him from did not want (to go). And then said they [the king's men] that to them no kinsman dearer was than their lord, and they never his killer follow would, and then offered they [the king's men] to their kinsmen [with the prince] that they safe away might come. And they [the prince's men] said that the same to their companions offered was who earlier with the king were; then said they that they that would not care for "any more than your companions who with the king slain were." And they then around the gates fighting were until they [the king's men] into there penetrated and the prince slew and the men who him with were, all except for one: that one was the nobleman's godson and he his life saved, and nevertheless he was often wounded.

And that Cynewulf reigned 31 winters and his body lies at Winchester, and the prince's at Axminster; and their paternal lineage goes (back) to Cerdic.

Chapter 7: Old Frisian

The Ten Commandments

This law wrote God (him)self, our Lord, when it was that Moses led the Israelite folk through the Red Sea, and from the wild desert, and they came to the mountain, which is called Sinai. Then fasted Moses twice forty days and nights; after that gave God to him two stone tablets, where He on written had the Ten Commandments, which should he teach to the Israelite folk.

---

* Constructions with multiple negatives commonly have a simple negative interpretation, as in this sentence and a number of others in the Readings. They are all translated accordingly.

That was the First Commandment: Thy God that is the One (God), Who Creator is of Heaven and Earth, that (One) shalt thou serve.

That was the Second Commandment: Thou not shalt thy God's name idly take; with that are thee forbidden all false oaths.

That was the Third Commandment: Thou shalt observe the holy Sabbath. . . .

That was the Fourth Commandment: Thou shalt honor thy father and thy mother, that you all the longer may live.

That was the Fifth Commandment: Thou not shalt any murder do.

That was the Sixth Commandment: Thou not shalt any fornication or any adultery do, rather with thy legal wife shalt thou in accord with God live.

That was the Seventh Commandment: Thou not shalt any theft do, and not shalt covet concerning thy fellow Christian's possessions, which to you by law be coming not can.

That was the Eighth Commandment: Thou not shalt any false witness do.

That was the Ninth and the Tenth Commandment: Thou shalt love God thy Creator with (a) pure heart and thy fellow Christian like thyself. These two Commandments encompass all the other Commandments.

Those are the Ten Commandments that God presented to Moses, and he further taught the Israelite folk (these Commandments kept they the forty years when they in the desert were) and freed them from much suffering and led them to the land that flowed with milks and with honey— that was the holy land at Jerusalem. Just so leads our Lord God all those to the Kingdom of Heaven, who the law follow, and all those who that law or any law break (it not be [*i.e.*, 'unless'] that one it through grace do, because grace is more than that law), so closes up them God in Hell, just as He closed up the Egyptian people in the Red Sea, when they His people to harm wanted, the Israelite folk.

On the Man Who Flees into a Church

If here a man flees into (a) church, and the enemy him there in hunt, all that he then in the defense does, that should lie uncompensated. Kills one him there in, so should pay one (for) him with four and a half death price, and to the people a hundred marks, and the house (of the offender becomes the property) of the people. (If) not wants he [*i.e.*, the fugitive] then out to go, when the enemy out goes by holy men's and by judges' command, so should pay he just as much, as the (one) who the church occupies (with weapons). And whoever a man strikes in the church, so should pay he a hundred marks to the people and sixty to the church; (if) not want they from the church nought to come, who there then in are, so should go the judge, who over the church sworn has [*i.e.*, is responsible for it], and should order them out. (If) not want they out to come, so should burn he the first beacon fire at (a penalty of) eight marks on the same day. And (if) not come they then out, so should burn all his (judicial) colleagues the beacons on the next day and should assemble the people, each of them at (a penalty of) eight marks; and whichever of them so the beacons not burns and his people not brings, so should lead [*i.e.*, 'go'] one against him of all first, and fights he against the colleagues, so should be fined it double.

Chapter 8: Old Low Franconian

Psalm 60

2. Hear, God, prayer my, pay attention to prayer my.

3. From (the) end of (the) earth to you I called out, so disturbed was heart my. Onto (a) stone elevated you me;

4. You led me, for made you are refuge my, (a) tower of strength from (the) face of (the) enemy.

5. Live shall I in house your to eternity, protected in (the) covering of wings your.

6. For you, God my, heard prayer my, gave you inheritance to (those) fearing name your.

7. Day upon day of (the) king shall you add, years his until to (the) day of generation and of generation.

8. He abides to eternity in (the) presence of God; grace and truth his, who shall those question?

9. So shall I praise speak to name your to eternity of eternity, that I should give vows my from day to day.

Psalm 65

2. Sing to God, all (the) earth, praise speak to name his; give glory to praise his.

3. Say to God: such terrible things are works your, Lord! In (the) fullness of power your lie shall to you enemies your.

4. Let all (the) earth pray to you and should sing to you, praise should speak to name your.

5. Come and see (the) works of God, of (the) terrible (one) in designs over (the) children of men.

6. That one changes (the) sea to dry land; on (the) flood cross over we shall by foot. Then shall we rejoice in him,

7. Who ruling is in power his to eternity. Eyes his over (the) people gaze: (those) who rebel, not may be exalted in themselves.

8. Bless, people, God our, and heard make (the) voice of praise his,

9. Who set soul my to life, and not gave to movement feet my.

10. For you proved us, God, with fire us you tested, just as one tests silver.

11. You led us into (a) net, you set tribulation on back our, you set men over heads our;

12. We went through fire and through water, and you brought us to coolness.

13. Go shall I to house your for burnt offerings,

14. Give shall I to you vows my, which uttered lips my, and spoke mouth my in tribulation my.

15. Burnt offerings proper[?] offer shall I to you with incense of rams, offer shall I to you bulls with goats.

16. Come, hear, and tell shall I, all (you) who fear God, how he made soul my.

17. To him with mouth my I called, and I praised under tongue my.

18. Injustice if he saw in heart my, not shall hear (the) Lord. Thus heard God and paid attention to (the) voice of prayer my.

19. Blessed God, who not turned away prayer my and grace his from me.

Chapter 9: Old High German

Parable of the Sower and the Seed

When day was become, he gathered to him his disciples, and going out from the house, sat next to the sea, and gathered were to him many multitudes, so that he in ship getting in sat, and all the multitudes stood on the shore, and he spoke to them many (things) in parables thus speaking: "Lo, went then out he who sows to sow. While he then sowed, some fell next to the way and were stepped on, and came birds and ate those. Others fell on stony land, where not it had much earth, and quickly went up, for they not had earth's depth; with upgoing sun burned became: because they not had roots, they dried up. Some fell in thorns; then grew the thorns and choked it. Others fell on good earth and gave fruit, some (a) hundredfold, some sixtyfold, some thirtyfold." These (things) speaking called he: "He who may have ears to hear, let him hear!"

From the Bavarian Muspilli (End of the World)

That heard I tell   the pious (people)
that would the Antichrist   with Elias battle.
The evildoer is armed,   then becomes between them war started.
(The) champions are so powerful,   the cause is so great.
Elias fights   for the eternal life,
wants for the righteous   the kingdom to strengthen:
therefore shall him help   He who Heaven rules.
the Antichrist   stands by the ancient enemy,
stands by the Satan   who him destroy shall:
therefore shall he on that battleground   wounded fall
and on the way   without victory become.
But believes that many a (one) . . . of servants of God
that Elias in the battle   destroyed will become,
so that Elias's blood   on (the) earth drips,
so catch fire the mountains,   tree not stands fast
any on (the) earth,   waters dry up,
(the) moor swallows itself,   burn slowly with flame the heavens,
(the) moon falls,   burns (the) world,
stone not stands fast,   goes then Judgment Day in (the) land,
goes with the fire   people to afflict:
there not can then (a) relative another   help before the end of
    the world.

REFERENCE MATTER

BIBLIOGRAPHY

Alberts, W. Jappe. "Friesland und die Friesen im ersten Jahrtausend." In V. H. Elbern, ed., *Das erste Jahrtausend: Kultur und Kunst im werdenden Abendland an Rhein und Ruhr*, Textband 2, pp. 634–52. Düsseldorf: Schwann, 1964.

Almgren, Bertil, et al. *The Viking*. Gothenburg: Tre Tryckare, 1966.

Bennett, William H. *An Introduction to the Gothic Language*. Ann Arbor: Ullrich's, 1972.

Blair, Peter Hunter. *An Introduction to Anglo-Saxon England*. 2d ed. Cambridge: Cambridge University Press, 1977.

Blok, Petrus J. *A History of the People of the Netherlands*. Vol. 1, *From the Earliest Times to the Beginning of the Fifteenth Century*. New York and London: Putnam, 1898.

Bostock, J. Knight. *A Handbook on Old High German Literature*. Rev. K. C. King and D. R. McLintock. Oxford: Clarendon, 1976.

Braune, Wilhelm, and E. A. Ebbinghaus. *Gotische Grammatik*. 18th ed. Tübingen: Niemeyer, 1981.

Braune, Wilhelm, and Hans Eggers. *Althochdeutsche Grammatik*. 13th ed. Tübingen: Niemeyer, 1975.

Buma, W. J. *Die Brokmer Rechtshandschriften*. The Hague: Nijhoff, 1949.

Cassidy, Frederic G., and Richard N. Ringler. *Bright's Old English Grammar and Reader*. 3d ed. New York: Holt, Rinehart & Winston, 1971.

van Coetsem, Frans. "Zur Entwicklung der germanischen Grundsprache." In Schmitt, ed. [q.v.], pp. 1–93.

van Coetsem, Frans, and Herbert L. Kufner, eds. *Toward a Grammar of Proto-Germanic*. Tübingen: Niemeyer, 1972.

Cosijn, P. J. "De Oudnederlandse psalmen." *De Taal- en Letterbode* 3 (1872): 25–48, 110–24, 257–70; 4 (1873): 149–76.

Cowan, H. K. J. "Esquisse d'une grammaire fonctionnelle du vieux-néerlandais (vieux bas-francique): D'après le psautier carolingien de Wachtendonck." *Leuvense Bijdragen* 50 (1961): 2–54.

―――. "De localisering van het Oudnederfrankisch der psalmenfragmenten." *Leuvense Bijdragen* 48 (1959): 1–47.

―――. "Nogmaals de localisering van de Oudnederfrankische psalmenfragmenten." *Leuvense Bijdragen* 58 (1969): 114–32.

―――. *De Oudnederlandse (Oudnederfrankische) Psalmenfragmenten*. Leiden: Brill, 1957.

Cummins, Adley H. *A Grammar of the Old Friesic Language*. London: Trübner, 1887.

Donaldson, Bruce C. *Dutch: A Linguistic History of Holland and Belgium*. Leiden: Nijhoff, 1983.

Düwel, Klaus. *Runenkunde*. Stuttgart: Metzler, 1968.

Ebert, Robert Peter. *Historische Syntax des Deutschen*. Stuttgart: Metzler, 1978.

Eggers, Hans. *Deutsche Sprachgeschichte*. Vol. 1, *Das Althochdeutsche*. Reinbek bei Hamburg: Rowohlt, 1963.

Eichhoff, Jürgen, and Irmengard Rauch, eds. *Der Heliand*. Wege der Forschung, 321. Darmstadt: Wissenschaftliche Buchgesellschaft, 1973.

Feist, Sigmund. *Kultur, Ausbreitung und Herkunft der Indogermanen*. Berlin: Weidmann, 1913.

Fisher, D. J. V. *The Anglo-Saxon Age: C. 400–1042*. London: Longman, 1973.

Fleckenstein, Josef. *Early Medieval Germany*. Amsterdam: North-Holland, 1978.

Frank, Roberta. *Old Norse Court Poetry: The Dróttkvætt Stanza*. Ithaca, N.Y.: Cornell University Press, 1978.

Frings, Theodor. *Grundlegung einer Geschichte der deutschen Sprache*. 3d ed. Halle (Saale): Niemeyer, 1957.

Gallée, Johan Hendrik. *Altsächsische Grammatik*. 2d ed. Halle: Niemeyer, 1910.

Gimbutas, Marija. "Proto-Indo-European Culture." In G. Cardona, H. M. Hoenigswald, and A. Senn, eds., *Indo-European and Indo-Europeans: Papers Presented at the Third Indo-European Conference at the University of Pennsylvania*, pp. 155–97. Philadelphia: University of Pennsylvania Press, 1970.

Gordon, E. V. *An Introduction to Old Norse*. 2d ed. Rev. A. R. Taylor. Oxford: Clarendon, 1957.

Greenberg, Joseph H. "Some Universals of Grammar, with Particular Reference to the Order of Meaningful Elements." In J. H. Greenberg, ed., *Universals of Language*, 2d ed., pp. 73–113. Cambridge, Mass.: M.I.T. Press, 1966.

Greenfield, Stanley B. *A Critical History of Old English Literature*. New York: N.Y.U. Press, 1965.

Gregory of Tours. *The History of the Franks*. Translated and with an introduction by O. M. Dalton. Oxford: Clarendon, 1927.

Haugen, Einar. *The First Grammatical Treatise: The Earliest Germanic Phonology. An Edition, Translation and Commentary*. 2d ed. London: Longman, 1972.

―――. *The Scandinavian Languages*. Cambridge, Mass.: Harvard University Press, 1976.

van Helten, W. L. *Altostfriesische Grammatik*. Leeuwarden: Meijer, 1890.

————. *Die altostniederfränkischen Psalmenfragmente, die Lipsius'schen Glossen und die altsüdmittelfränkischen Psalmenfragmente, mit Einleitung, Noten, Indices und Grammatiken*. Groningen: Wolters, 1902.

————. "Een en ander over en naar anleiding van de Oudnederlandsche psalmvertaling." *Tijdschrift voor Nederlandsche Taal- en Letterkunde* 15 (1896): 146–71, 269.

Holthausen, F. *Altsächsisches Elementarbuch*. 2d ed. Heidelberg: Winter, 1921.

Hopper, Paul J. *The Syntax of the Simple Sentence in Proto-Germanic*. The Hague: Mouton, 1975.

Hutterer, Claus Jürgen. *Die germanischen Sprachen: Ihre Geschichte in Grundzügen*. Budapest: Akadémiai Kiadó, 1975.

Jespersen, Otto. *Growth and Structure of the English Language*. 9th ed. New York: Doubleday, 1955. [Reprint of the 1948 ed.]

Jostes, Franz. "Saxonica." *Zeitschrift für deutsches Altertum und deutsche Literatur* 40 (1896): 129–92.

Keller, R. E. *The German Language*. Atlantic Highlands, N.J.: Humanities Press, 1978.

Krahe, H., and W. Meid. *Germanische Sprachwissenschaft*. 7th ed. Vol. 1, *Einleitung und Lautlehre*; vol. 2, *Formenlehre*; vol. 3, *Wortbildungslehre*. Berlin: de Gruyter, 1967 [vol. 3], 1969 [vols. 1, 2].

Krause, Wolfgang, with Herbert Jankuhn. *Die Runeninschriften im älteren Futhark*. Vol. 1, *Text*. Abhandlungen der Akademie der Wissenschaften in Göttingen, Phil.-Hist. Klasse, Ser. 3, 65. Göttingen: Vandenhoeck and Ruprecht, 1966.

Krogmann, Willy. "Altsächsisch und Mittelniederdeutsch." In Schmitt, ed. [q.v.], pp. 211–52.

Kufner, Herbert L. "The Grouping and Separation of the Germanic Languages." In van Coetsem and Kufner, eds. [q.v.], pp. 71–97.

Kuhn, Hans. Review of Ernst Schwarz, *Goten, Nordgermanen, Angelsachsen* [q.v.]. *Anzeiger für deutsches Altertum und deutsche Literatur* 66 (1952–53): 45–52.

————. "Zur Gliederung der germanischen Sprachen." *Zeitschrift für deutsches Altertum und deutsche Literatur* 86 (1955–56): 1–47.

Kyes, Robert L. *The Old Low Franconian Psalms and Glosses*. Ann Arbor, Mich.: University of Michigan Press, 1969.

Lasko, Peter. *The Kingdom of the Franks: North-West Europe Before Charlemagne*. New York: McGraw-Hill, 1971.

Lehmann, Winfred P. *The Alliteration of Old Saxon Poetry*. Norsk Tidsskrift for Sprogvidenskap, Supplement 3. Oslo: Universitetsforlaget, 1953. [Reprint in Eichhoff and Rauch, eds. (q.v.), 144–76.]

————. *The Development of Germanic Verse Form*. Austin, Tex.: University of Texas Press, 1956.

————. "The Grouping of the Germanic Languages." In Henrik Birnbaum and

Jaan Puhvel, eds., *Ancient Indo-European Dialects*, pp. 13–27. Berkeley and Los Angeles: University of California Press, 1966.

———. *Historical Linguistics: An Introduction.* 2d ed. New York: Holt, Rinehart, & Winston, 1973.

———. "Proto-Germanic Syntax." In van Coetsem and Kufner, eds. [q.v.], pp. 239–68.

Lintzel, Martin. *Der sächsische Stammesstaat und seine Eroberung durch die Franken.* Historische Studien, 227. Berlin: Ebering, 1933. [Reprint, Vaduz: Kraus, 1965.]

———. *Zur altsächsischen Stammesgeschichte.* Berlin: Akademie-Verlag, 1961.

Lockwood, W. B. *Historical German Syntax.* Oxford: Clarendon, 1968.

———. *Indo-European Philology.* London: Hutchinson University Library, 1969.

———. *An Informal History of the German Language.* Cambridge: Heffer, 1965.

Marchand, James W. "Gotisch." In Schmitt, ed. [q.v.], vol. 1, pp. 94–122.

Markey, T. L. *Frisian.* The Hague: Mouton, 1981.

———. *Germanic Dialect Grouping and the Position of Ingvaeonic.* Innsbrucker Beiträge zur Sprachwissenschaft, 15. Innsbruck: Institut für Sprachwissenschaft der Universität, 1976.

Markey, T. L., R. L. Kyes, and P. T. Roberge. *Germanic and Its Dialects: A Grammar of Proto-Germanic.* Vol. 3, *Bibliography and Indices.* Amsterdam: Benjamin, 1977.

Meillet, A. *Caractères généraux des langues germaniques.* Paris: Hachette, 1917.

Mierow, Charles Christopher. *The Gothic History of Jordanes.* Princeton, N.J.: Princeton University Press, 1915.

Mitchell, Bruce. *Old English Syntax.* 2 vols. Oxford: Clarendon, 1985.

Mitchell, Bruce, and Fred C. Robinson. *A Guide to Old English.* Rev. ed., with texts and glossary. Oxford: Blackwell, 1982.

Mühlbacher, Engelbert. *Deutsche Geschichte unter den Karolingern.* Darmstadt: Wissenschaftliche Buchgesellschaft, 1959. [Reprint of the 1896 ed.]

Musset, Lucien. *The Germanic Invasions: The Making of Europe, A.D. 400–600.* Trans. Edward James and Columba James. University Park, Pa.: Pennsylvania State University Press, 1975.

Noreen, Adolf. *Altisländische und altnorwegische Grammatik: Laut- und Flexionslehre.* 4th ed. Halle (Saale): Niemeyer, 1923.

Owen, Francis. *The Germanic People.* New York: Bookman, 1960.

Paul, H., and W. Mitzka. *Mittelhochdeutsche Grammatik.* 19th ed. Tübingen: Niemeyer, 1966.

Pedersen, Holger. *The Discovery of Language: Linguistic Science in the Nineteenth Century.* Bloomington, Ind.: Indiana University Press, 1962. [Reprint of the 1931 ed.]

Penzl, Herbert. *Geschichtliche deutsche Lautlehre.* Munich: Hüber, 1969.

———. *Methoden der germanischen Linguistik.* Tübingen: Niemeyer, 1972.

Prokosch, Eduard. *A Comparative Germanic Grammar.* Philadelphia: Linguistic Society of America, 1938.

Ramat, Paolo. *Das Friesische*. Innsbrucker Beiträge zur Sprachwissenschaft, 14. Innsbruck: Institut für Sprachwissenschaft der Universität, 1976.

Renfrew, Colin. *Archaeology and Language: The Puzzle of Indo-European Origins*. London: Cape, 1987.

Sanders, Willy. "Zu den altniederfränkischen Psalmen." *Zeitschrift für deutsches Altertum und deutsche Literatur* 97 (1968–69): 81–107.

Sawyer, P. H. *The Age of the Vikings*. 2d ed. New York: St. Martin's, 1971.

Schirmunski, V. "Über die altgermanischen Stammesdialekte." *Acta Linguistica Academiae Scientiarum Hungaricae* 15 (1965): 1–36.

Schmidt, Ludwig. *Geschichte der deutschen Stämme bis zum Ausgang der Völkerwanderung*. Vol. 1, *Die Westgermanen*. Munich: Beck, 1938.

Schmitt, L. E., ed. *Kurzer Grundriss der germanischen Philologie bis 1500*. Vol. 1, *Sprachgeschichte*. Berlin: de Gruyter, 1970.

Schwarz, Ernst. *Germanische Stammeskunde*. Heidelberg: Winter, 1956.

———. *Goten, Nordgermanen, Angelsachsen: Studien zur Ausgliederung der germanischen Sprachen*. Bern: Francke, 1951.

Sergeant, Lewis. *The Franks*. New York: Putnam, 1898.

Sievers, Eduard. *Altgermanische Metrik*. Sammlung kurzer Grammatiken germanischer Dialekte, Ergänzungsreihe 2. Halle: Niemeyer, 1893.

———. *An Old English Grammar*. 3d ed. Trans. Albert S. Cook. New York: Greenwood, 1968. [Reprint of the original translation of 1903.]

Sjölin, B. *Einführung in das Friesische*. Stuttgart: Metzler, 1969.

Skomal, Susan Nacev, and Edgar C. Polomé, eds. *Proto-Indo-European: The Archaeology of a Linguistic Problem. Studies in Honor of Marija Gimbutas*. Washington: Institute for the Study of Man, 1987.

Sonderegger, Stefan. "Althochdeutsche Sprache." In Schmitt, ed. [q.v.], pp. 288–346.

Stearns, MacDonald, Jr. *Crimean Gothic: Analysis and Etymology of the Corpus*. Saratoga, Calif.: Anma Libri, 1978.

von Steinmeyer, E. E. Review of W. L. van Helten, *Die altostniederfränkischen Psalmenfragmente* [q.v.]. *Anzeiger für deutsches Altertum und deutsche Literaturkunde* 29 (1903): 53–62.

Stenton, Frank M. *Anglo-Saxon England*. 3d ed. Rev. Doris M. Stenton. Oxford: Clarendon, 1971.

Tack, P. "Het handschrift der Wachtendoncksche psalmen en dat der Lipsiaansche glossen." *Tijdschrift voor Nederlandsche Taal- en Letterkunde* 15 (1896): 137–44.

Thompson, E. A. *The Early Germans*. Oxford: Clarendon, 1965.

———. *The Visigoths in the Time of Ulfila*. Oxford: Clarendon Press, 1966.

Thompson, James Westfall. *Feudal Germany*. Chicago: University of Chicago Press, 1928.

Traugott, Elizabeth C. *A History of English Syntax*. New York: Holt, Rinehart & Winston, 1972.

Tschirch, Fritz. *Geschichte der deutschen Sprache.* 2d ed. Vol. 1, *Die Entfaltung der deutschen Sprachgestalt in der Vor- und Frühzeit.* Grundlagen der Germanistik, 5. Berlin: Schmidt, 1971.

Turville-Petre, E. O. G. *Myth and Religion of the North: The Religion of Ancient Scandinavia.* London: Weidenfeld and Nicolson, 1964.

———. *Origins of Icelandic Literature.* Oxford: Clarendon, 1967. [Reprint of the 1953 ed.]

Valfells, Sigrid, and James E. Cathey. *Old Icelandic: An Introductory Course.* Oxford: Oxford University Press, 1981.

Vennemann, Theo. "Hochgermanisch und Niedergermanisch: Die Verzweigungstheorie der germanisch-deutschen Lautverschiebungen." *Beiträge zur Geschichte der deutschen Sprache und Literatur* 106 (1984): 1–45.

———. "Topics, Subjects, and Word Order: From SXV to SVX via TVX." In J. M. Anderson and C. Jones, eds., *Historical Linguistics,* vol. 1, pp. 339–76. Amsterdam: North-Holland, 1974.

Voyles, Joseph B. "Gothic and Germanic." *Language* 44 (1968): 720–46.

de Vries, Jan. *Altnordische Literaturgeschichte.* 2 vols. Berlin: de Gruyter, 1964–67.

Waterman, J. T. *A History of the German Language.* 2d ed. Seattle: University of Washington Press, 1976.

te Winkel, L. A. "Over de psalmen van Wachtendonck en de glossen van Lipsius." *Verslagen en Mededelingen der Koninklijke Akademie van Wetenschappen, Afdeeling Letterkunde* 10 (1866): 315–33.

Wrede, F. "Ingwäonisch und Westgermanisch." *Zeitschrift für deutsche Mundarten* 19 (1924): 270–83.

INDEX

In this index, "f" after a number indicates a separate reference on the next page, and "ff" indicates separate references on the next two pages. A continuous discussion over two or more pages is indicated by a span of page numbers, e.g., "57–59." *Passim* is used for a cluster of references in close but not necessarily consecutive sequence.

Abrogans, 226
Accent, 10–11
Accusative case, 31
Acrophonic principle, 93, 97
Active voice, 39
Acute accent, 26
Adjectives, 37–39, 41, 166–67
Aelfric, 147
Affricates, 233, 240
Age and comparison of languages, 195–98
Age of Migrations, 69, 74
Alamanni, 17, 201, 222–24, 225
Alamannic dialects, 260f
Alfred the Great, 71, 141–42, 145, 146–47
Alliteration, 126, 128, 133, 135
Alliterative verse, 125–35
Alphabet: Gothic, 47f, 65; Old Norse, 91–94
Anacrusis, 126
Analogy, 87, 198
Angles, 136f, 177, 255, 258
Anglo-Saxon Chronicle, 144, 147
Anglo-Saxons, 71f, 101, 136–43, 177, 255, 258f
Archeology, and linguistics, 13–15
Ari Þorgilsson, 75
Article, 34
Aspectual distinctions, 167–68
Assibilation, 159, 193, 197–98, 258f
Assimilation, 8, 88
Attributive adjectives, 37
Auxiliaries, *see* Modal auxiliaries

Battle-ax Culture, 16
Bavarians, 222, 224f
Bede, 136, 137, 139, 145–46, 147
Beowulf, 132f, 143–44
Bible: Gothic, 48, 65; poetic texts, 109–11, 144; Wachtendonck Codex, 203–4, 215–20; Old High German texts, 226
Borrowing, 2–4, 65–66, 198
Breaking, 158, 192
British, 136–37, 139f
Busbecq, Oghier Ghislain de, 50
Byrhtferth, 147

Case, 29–32, 35–39 *passim*, 196
Celts, 17, 71f, 136–37, 139f
Charlemagne, 106ff, 140, 179, 202–3, 225
Christianity, 45, 48, 50, 73, 106ff, 110, 144f, 179, 201, 261
Circumflex, 26
Clause subordination, 171–74
Cognates, 6, 20–21
Comparative adjectives, 38–39
Comparative method, 5–13
Complementary distribution, 58
Consonants: Germanic, 25–26; Gothic, 55–56; Old Norse, 82–84; Old Saxon, 116–18; gemination, 121–22, 159, 192, 213, 236, 239f, 244; alliterative verse, 128; Old English, 154–56; Old Frisian, 189–90; High German Consonant Shift, 203, 218, 232–33, 236,